Wise Church

WISE CHURCH

Forming a Wisdom Culture in Your Local Church

EDITED BY

Scot McKnight

AND

Daniel J. Hanlon

CASCADE *Books* · Eugene, Oregon

WISE CHURCH
Forming a Wisdom Culture in Your Local Church

Cascade Books
An Imprint of Wipf and Stock Publishers
199 W. 8th Ave., Suite 3
Eugene, OR 97401

www.wipfandstock.com

PAPERBACK ISBN: 978-1-7252-9406-6
HARDCOVER ISBN: 978-1-7252-9407-3
EBOOK ISBN: 978-1-7252-9408-0

Cataloguing-in-Publication data:

Names: McKnight, Scot, editor. | Hanlon, Daniel J., editor.

Title: Wise church : forming a wisdom culture in your local church / edited by Scot McKnight and Daniel J. Hanlon.

Description: Eugene, OR: Cascade Books, 2021 | Includes bibliographical references.

Identifiers: ISBN 978-1-7252-9406-6 (paperback) | ISBN 978-1-7252-9407-3 (hardcover) | ISBN 978-1-7252-9408-0 (ebook)

Subjects: LCSH: Wisdom—Biblical teaching. | Well-being—Religious aspects—Christianity. | Christian life. | Church.

Classification: BV600.2 W57 2021 (print) | BV600.2 (ebook)

03/31/21

CONTENTS

CONTRIBUTORS

Daniel J. Hanlon and his wife, Kari, have lived and served in Kigali, Rwanda for ten years as missionaries from Church of the Redeemer, Highwood, Illinois. Dan is the lead pastor of the English service at St. Etienne Cathedral in Kigali. He is an Anglican Priest in the Kigali Diocese, and a graduate of Northern Seminary (DMin) and Trinity Evangelical Divinity School (MANT). Dan and Kari have three children: Josiah, Norah, and Abigail.

Scot McKnight is Julius R. Mantey Professor of New Testament, Northern Seminary, and is an author of more than eighty books, including commentaries on Colossians, Philemon, and Galatians.

Jeff Banman is lead pastor of Cornerstone Ministries Church in Crystal City, Manitoba. He is married to Nicole and together they have two teenaged daughters, Calli and Erica. Jeff's heart as a preacher is to unlock the world of the first century, exploring how the gospel of King Jesus impacted the early church and how it can impact us today.

Jeremy Berg is founding and lead pastor of MainStreet Covenant Church where he has served since 2010, and professor of Bible and Theology at Solid Rock Discipleship. He is a graduate of Northern Seminary (DMin), Bethel Seminary (MATS) and Bethel University (BA). He and his wife, Kjerstin, have three children—Peter, Isaak, and Abigail—and make their home near the Twin Cities, Minnesota. Jeremy writes at Daily Illumination (www.jeremyberg.org).

Brandon Evans pastors at Reno Christian Fellowship in Reno, Nevada. He has an MA in biblical studies from Multnomah Biblical Seminary and a DMin in New Testament context from Northern Seminary. He is married to Caitlin and they have three children—Zephyr, Gwen, and Quentin.

Pete Goodman is the executive pastor of Rise City Church in Lakeside, California and an adjunct professor at San Diego Christian College. A graduate of Asbury Theological Seminary (MTS) and Northern Seminary (DMin), he and his wife Julie have four children.

David S. Johnston is husband to Brandi and father to Tallulah and Phineas. Dave earned his bachelor of arts from Ouachita Baptist University and his master of divinity from George W. Truett Theological Seminary at Baylor University. He then continued his studies at Northern Seminary where he earned his doctorate of ministry in New Testament context focusing on slavery and the New Testament. Dave is on staff at Little Rock Church giving leadership to house-church based discipleship.

Ernest F. Ledbetter III served as the lead pastor of the Mt. Pisgah Missionary Baptist Church in Chicago's historic Bronzeville community for seven years. He received his MDiv in Christian community development and his doctorate in New Testament context from Northern Seminary. He is married to his lovely wife, LaToyia M. Ledbetter.

Joshua Little holds an MDiv from Emmanuel Christian Seminary in eastern Tennessee and is pursuing a DMin from Northern Seminary in Lisle, Illinois. He serves as the executive pastor of the RiverTree Network and preaching pastor of RiverTree Lake. Josh's wife, Becky, serves as an administrator with Stadia, a church-planting organization. Josh and Becky have two children: Elsie and Avery.

Julie Murdock graduated from Ashland Theological Seminary in 2015 with an MA in biblical studies. After working part-time for ATS for a few years, she enrolled at Northern Seminary and graduated with a DMin in 2021. She is currently pursuing ministry in North Central Ohio. Julie and her Husband Matthew have been married for 25 years and have 2 children.

John M. Phelps is the academic director for the Awakening School of Theology with Celebration Church in Jacksonville, Florida, adjunct professor at Southeastern University in Jacksonville. Graduate of Dallas Theological Seminary. Married to Baby Luv for 37 years.

Ivan Ramirez came to Christ in a county jail after being falsely accused of a crime. While incarcerated, God developed a passion for his Word and his people within Ivan. That passion then led to pastoring a church in the Chicagoland area where he and his wife, Amy, have served for the last 16 years. They have three children: Grace, Wesley, and Elliot.

William D. Shiell is the president and professor of pastoral theology and preaching at Northern Seminary. Bill holds degrees from Samford University (BA) and Baylor University (MDiv, PhD) and has published six books. Bill and his wife Kelly have two sons, Parker and Drake.

PREFACE

I n the heart of this book is a study by Ernest Ledbetter III that, like the sermon of a Black preacher, starts a bit slow and keeps that pace for perhaps just a little longer than you'd prefer when all of a sudden you are caught up in the swirl of a gospel experience that needed all the build-up. What strikes me about Pastor Ledbetter's chapter is that it emerges from a wisdom culture. When this cohort of doctor of ministry students first discussed our final project, a project about forming a wisdom culture and I explained a little bit of what I thought we could focus on, Ernest said aloud, "That's the Black church. We are a wisdom culture." His chapter embodies in words and stories what this book is about: rethinking church cultures so they become more of a wisdom culture.

What will that take? John Phelps in his chapter says it takes "experts." He's right, and one can call such persons "sages." A sage is not someone old, though age is a great teacher of wisdom, but someone experienced. Pastor-sages are people who have walked with the Lord long enough and deeply enough to know from experience how one is to walk with the Lord. Our churches need to form a wisdom culture, one in which sages formed in experience with Christ mentor parishioners in the way of Christ-likeness. But wisdom has to be defined and examined, too, and Daniel J. Hanlon, an Anglican missionary pastor in Rwanda, opens this book with an exceptional study of what wisdom is—sapiential, ethical, and theological—and each of the authors kept Hanlon's study in mind as each worked out something dis- tinct about an area in church life where we need wisdom.

The students chose their topics, and they vary as widely as church life: letter writing as pastoral care, the work life of congregants, evangelism, music, church economics, spiritual formation as the pursuit of wisdom, racial justice, marriage, learning how to teach like Jesus, gospeling like the apostles, and I added a study on the wise use of social media. These studies are pastors pondering wisdom but more than that, they are pondering the life we all live in a wise way that we pray will be an opening of wisdom for you and your church. You and your church need wisdom, not simply because we live in an ever-changing world, but because the God we worship is himself wise. Wise church cultures reflect the wisdom of God back into the world, a world looking for wisdom.

There is a tendency for people of my ilk—professor—to operate as if we professors have the goods and we pass them on to our students, the pastors, who will then pass them on to congregations. That's part of the story. The other side is that congregants are forming pastors who come into classes like ours and teach professors what's happening in the churches. I learned from these pastors immensely, both hearing them present these chapters in class and in reading them for *Wise Church*.

WHAT IS WISDOM?

The Foundation of a Wisdom Culture

By Daniel J. Hanlon

As readers of the Bible likely know, the wisdom books of the Old Testament (OT) are Proverbs, Job, Ecclesiastes, sometimes Song of Songs, and a few psalms, with the letter of James as the New Testament (NT) contribution. To those are added Ben Sira's Sirach and Wisdom of Solomon from the Apocrypha, as well as a smattering of texts from Qumran. These writings comprise what is known as the wisdom genre, a modern approach to the placement of these books in the Bible, which some find helpful and others prefer to abandon. The place of wisdom in the Bible impacts the way we address the primary question this chapter seeks to answer, namely, What is wisdom? So, we begin with another.

Where is Wisdom?

Long ago Job asked a question that aptly describes the modern scholarly debate of the place of wisdom in the Bible: "Where shall wisdom be found?"[1] Two Old Testament experts open our discussion. Tremper Longman suggests "there are significant similarities between the books that are typically identified as the core of the genre (Proverbs, Job, Ecclesiastes)."[2] According to Longman, "The main identifier of the wisdom genre is simply that these texts are interested in the concept of wisdom."[3] More specifically, "These books we call 'wisdom' are also specifically concerned with the unique intersection of

---

1. Job 28:12. Bible quotations are from the NRSV, unless otherwise indicated. On scholarly discussion, see Sneed, *Was There a Wisdom Tradition?*

2. Longman, *Fear of the Lord*, 280.

3. Longman, *Fear of the Lord*, 281.

ways of knowing—epistemology and education; ways of living—ethics; and human nature—anthropology."[4] Thus, it is reasonable to suppose that biblical wisdom is found in the wisdom books of the Bible.

Will Kynes, however, argues that wisdom is an unhelpful genre category. Why? Starting with a wisdom genre produces a definition based on a questionable assumption: that the Wisdom books define what wisdom is. He calls this "a restrictive hermeneutical hegemony," and says, "This discourages comparisons outside the category, unless those other texts conform to the characteristics of Wisdom, demonstrating their 'Wisdom influence.' This echo-chamber effect undermines the interpretive help Wisdom could provide, making it a hindrance."[5] So, Kynes proposes an alternative, an intertextual approach, in which texts exist together in "constellations." He explains, "This would encourage the texts to be interpreted from varied 'points of view,' each of which considers different affinities 'relevant' as they inspire different textual groupings. This would appreciate how each text demonstrates its particularity by 'participating' in multiple genres without 'belonging' to any one of them."[6] In this way, the wisdom of Proverbs could be brought into dialogue with other Solomonic traditions, or other paraenetic literature, such as Deuteronomy.[7]

The difference between Longman and Kynes is not as substantial as sometimes claimed. While maintaining the wisdom genre category, Longman is sympathetic to the concerns of Kynes, and believes his genre based approach achieves the same results as Kynes's intertextual approach.[8] In fact, both treatments may be categorized under a canonical approach to wisdom in biblical theology: "commitment to the Scripture as canon warrants reading any part within the context of the whole."[9] Accordingly, the canon is the primary context for biblical interpretation, so that the meaning of wisdom is found in the Bible. The Bible is a book that helps us find wisdom (2 Tim 3:15–17; Josephus, *Antiquities*, 20.265). So, what is wisdom according to the Bible? The intertextual/canonical approach of Kynes and Longman will help with an answer as we explore not only terminology, or genre, but the concept of Wisdom in the Bible.[10]

---

4. O'Dowd, *Proverbs*, 28.

5. Kynes, "'Wisdom Literature' Category," 23.

6. Kynes, "'Wisdom Literature' Category," 18.

7. Kynes, "'Wisdom Literature' Category," 21–22.

8. Longman, *Fear of the Lord*, 282.

9. Longman, *Fear of the Lord*, 181; cf. Kynes, "'Wisdom Literature' Category," 24.

10. The relevance of intertestamental wisdom literature for this endeavor is threefold (cf. Longman, *Fear of the Lord*, 220). It shows 1) the appropriation and 2) the development of OT wisdom (cf. Bennema, "Strands of Wisdom Tradition in Intertestamental Judaism," 61–82). Furthermore, 3) intertestamental wisdom is a bridge from

What is Wisdom?

There are many biblical words for wisdom, but the first word is *hokmah*. There are two levels of meaning for *hokmah*.[11] The first level of meaning is "skill" or "ability," and those who are thus skilled are wise, *hakam*.[12] Wisdom is the skill to do something well. Wisdom is the skill of artists, craftsmen, and weavers (Exod 35:10, 26, 35). Wisdom is the skill to lead and govern (Deut 34:9; 1 Kgs 3:28; 2 Chr 1:10). Wisdom is the skill for war and conquest (Isa 10:13). Wisdom is the ability to make wealth through trade (Ezek 28:4–5), and the vocal abilities of professional mourners (Jer 9:17). Wisdom is expertise in sailing (Ezek 27:8–9). Wisdom is seen in the skill of ants, badgers, locusts, and lizards (Prov 30:25–28), and in a wife and mother's abilities as a homemaker and provider (Prov 31:10–31).

The second level meaning of *hokmah* builds on the first level. If wisdom is skill, then wisdom is also the skill to do *life* well. Skill at life is exactly what the book of Proverbs is about, the only book in the Bible explicitly to claim to make its adherents wise. We turn to Proverbs in order to further understand the second level meaning of *hokmah*.

Wisdom According to Proverbs

The prologue or preamble to Proverbs (1:2–7) provides a purpose statement and a hermeneutical lens through which to understand the wisdom the book offers. It also expands our understanding of wisdom by placing a further six wisdom words alongside *hokmah*.

> For learning about wisdom and instruction,
>> for understanding words of insight,
> for gaining instruction in wise dealing,
>> righteousness, justice, and equity;
> to teach shrewdness to the simple, knowledge and prudence to the young—
> Let the wise also hear and gain in learning,
>> and the discerning acquire skill,
> to understand a proverb and a figure,
>> the words of the wise and their riddles.
> The fear of the LORD is the beginning of knowledge;
>> fools despise wisdom and instruction.

OT to NT wisdom. For example, there is clearly an influence by Ben Sira on Jesus and James (see deSilva, "In the School of Ben Sira of Jerusalem," 58–85).

11. Pemberton, *Life That Is Good*, 9–12.

12. Waltke, *Book of Proverbs*, 76.

Wisdom, instruction, shrewdness, knowledge, prudence, learning and skill; these wisdom words fill out the meaning of *hokmah*. Michael Fox attempts to delineate the nuances of meanings for wisdom terms by separating them into the categories of faculty, activity, and knowledge. He explains, "A *faculty* is a power to undertake various types of mental actions; it exists prior to them and is present even when not being used. A *mental activity* is the thinking itself, the exercise of the mind during a definite period of time. *Knowledge*—the communicable content of thoughts and ideas—is the product of mental activity."[13] We can take "instruction" (*musar*), a form of knowledge, as an example. Clearly a significant wisdom term (cf. 8:33), *musar* appears three times in the preamble, two of these occurrences place it directly alongside *hokmah* (vv. 1:2, 7). *Musar* may also be rendered as discipline or correction, "whether verbal or physical," implying a threat of punishment for failure to follow instruction.[14] Waltke observes, "*Wisdom* cannot be possessed without *instruction* to correct a moral fault."[15] This is similar to the "reproof" and "correction" Paul talks about in 2 Tim 3:16. Regardless of individual nuances, the piling up of near synonymous terms for wisdom has a rhetorical effect: "By the cumulation of many terms the text seems to aim at something larger, something more comprehensive which could not be expressed satisfactorily by means of any one of the terms used."[16] Thus the preamble is dealing with wisdom as a concept bigger than *hokmah* itself.

The meaning of wisdom in Proverbs is not exhausted by the preamble's opening sketch, rather the preamble invites the audience to hear two distinct voices, those of the father and Lady Wisdom. Proverbs 1–9 "presents two ideas of wisdom" offered by the persona of the father in discourses, and the persona of personified Wisdom in interludes.[17] The father says:

> Hear, my child, your father's instruction,
>   and do not reject your mother's teaching (1:8).

The father's words (4:4–5, 10) are wisdom:

> My child, be attentive to my wisdom;
>   incline your ear to my understanding (5:1).

Yet, according to Fox, the wisdom the father seeks to impart "is not reducible to his own precepts . . . the father is aiming at a higher goal, wisdom

13. Fox, "Words for Wisdom," 151, emphasis original.
14. Fox, *Proverbs 1–9*, 59; Longman, *Proverbs*, 95.
15. Waltke, *Proverbs*, 175, emphasis original.
16. Von Rad, *Wisdom in Israel*, 13.
17. Fox, "Ideas of Wisdom in Proverbs 1–9," 618.

of a different sort . . . . Wisdom must mean something more than simply *knowing* [precepts]."[18] So, the father also says:

> For the LORD gives wisdom;
> from his mouth come knowledge and understanding (2:6).

Thus, wisdom "is a power" activated by God to produce the "faculty of wisdom . . . that guides a person through life."[19] For the father, "Wisdom is a configuration of soul; it is *moral character* . . . which comes down to desiring the right things."[20]

The other voice is that of Lady Wisdom, who is the personification of the mental power, or faculty needed to live life well.[21] From her we hear:

> Wisdom has built her house,
> she has hewn her seven pillars.
> She has slaughtered her animals, she has mixed her wine,
> she has also set her table.
> She has sent out her servant girls, she calls
> from the highest places in the town,
> "You that are simple, turn in here!"
> To those without sense she says,
> "Come, eat of my bread
> and drink of the wine I have mixed.
> Lay aside immaturity, and live,
> and walk in the way of insight" (9:1–6).

Her antitype, the foolish woman also calls and invites the simple to enter and to eat and drink with her, but her way leads to death (9:13–18).

Wisdom comes down to a life or death choice, a decision between two ways, expressed in an implied question: whose house will you enter, with whom will you dine?[22] Entering the house of Lady Wisdom leads to life: "She is a tree of life to those who lay hold of her" (3:18). The house-building imagery is a metaphor for living wisely.[23] Just as God has built and ordered the world with wisdom and skill (3:19–20), and as Lady Wisdom has built and provisioned her house (9:1–2), so also "By wisdom a house [i.e. life] is built, and by understanding it is established; by knowledge the rooms are filled" (24:3–4a). We find here an emphasis on listening and

18. Fox, "Ideas of Wisdom in Proverbs 1–9," 619.
19. Fox, "Ideas of Wisdom in Proverbs 1–9," 619.
20. Fox, "Ideas of Wisdom in Proverbs 1–9," 620.
21. Fox, "Ideas of Wisdom in Proverbs 1–9," 624.
22. Longman, *Fear of the Lord*, 23.
23. Cf. Van Leeuwen, "Cosmos, Temple, House," 67–90.

accepting wisdom.[24] Through the figure of Lady Wisdom Proverbs culti-
vates desire, and a sense of the importance of life within the limits of the
world God made.[25]

The poems of Lady Wisdom in Proverbs, as well as Job 28, lay a foundation on which other similar poems are developed.[26] The greatest development is probably in the association of Law and Wisdom in Sirach 24. Ben
Sira identifies Lady Wisdom, saying:

> All this is the book of the covenant of the Most High God,
>   the law that Moses commanded us
>   as an inheritance for the congregations of Jacob (24:23; cf.
> Bar 4:1).

This association was probably influenced by the Hellenistic context of Second
Temple Judaism. A comparison of Prov 9:10 LXX with the HB text ("The fear
of the LORD is the beginning of wisdom, and the knowledge of the Holy One
is insight") reveals this addition: "for to know the law is a good mind."[27] The
result of this association is to make the Law a source of wisdom, and to more
closely associate universal wisdom with the Law of Israel.[28]

Returning to Proverbs' preamble, we may discern three dimensions of
biblical wisdom, and these three dimensions will become formative for this
chapter and our book in general: sapiential, ethical, and theological. Richard
Clifford explains, "Wisdom in Proverbs has a threefold dimension: sapiential
(a way of knowing reality), ethical (a way of conducting oneself), and religious (a way of relating to the divinely designed order or to God)."[29] We can
shape our investigation of wisdom by tracing these three dimensions. We will
conclude with the way they intersect in practical living.

Sapiential Wisdom

O'Dowd explores the epistemology of wisdom, noting, "Proverbs guides us
to a particular way of getting knowledge and being assured that our knowledge is valid."[30] Wisdom is the fruit of observation and experience. Observa-

---

24. See Pemberton, *Life*, 18–19.

25. Cf. Van Leeuwen, "Liminality and Worldview in Proverbs 1–9," 111–44.

26. See the helpful overview in Murphy, "Lady Wisdom," 133–49.

27. See Cook, *Septuagint of Proverbs*, 261–65.

28. Cf. Collins, *Jewish Wisdom in the Hellenistic Age*, 58.

29. Clifford, *Proverbs*, 19–20; cf. O'Dowd, *Proverbs*, 56–57; Longman, *Fear of the Lord*, 6.

30. O'Dowd, *Proverbs*, 56.

tion of an insect (6:6–8) and the experience of a foolish youth (7:6–13) lead
to wisdom. Wisdom is obtained by study of language and literature (1:6).
The parent and child relationship in which wisdom is both given and received (1:2–3), implies that wisdom is also found in tradition. The speeches
of the father throughout Prov 1–9 are designed to lead the son to wisdom
and cultivate receptivity. The father is of course analogous to the sage, who,
like Ben Sira, is a source of wisdom (Sir 24:30–35). Like the father in Proverbs, Ben Sira encourages the "son" to receptivity and discipleship:

> Listen, my child, and accept my judgment; do not reject my
> counsel. If you love to listen you will gain knowledge, and if you
> pay attention you will become wise. Stand in the company of the
> elders. Who is wise? Attach yourself to such a one. Be ready to
> listen to every godly discourse, and let no wise proverbs escape
> you" (Sir 6:23, 33–35).

It has been suggested that wisdom offers a path to knowledge other
than revelation. Yet, in apocalyptic literature we find that revelation requires
wisdom.[31] The book of Daniel connects wisdom and apocalyptic thinking:
"To these four young men God gave knowledge and skill in every aspect of
literature and wisdom; Daniel also had insight into all visions and dreams"
(1:17, cf. Prov 1:2). N. T. Wright explains:

> Daniel's apocalyptic visions are not an example of wisdom, as
> though the book were simply commending wisdom and using
> Daniel's ability to interpret dreams as a striking instance of this
> great quality. It is the other way round. Daniel's wisdom is the
> thing that enables him to grasp the secrets of *what Israel's god is
> doing with Israel and the world.*[32]

A similar point is made in Wisdom of Solomon.[33] In a prayer for wisdom
we find:

> We can hardly guess at what is on earth,
> and what is at hand we find with labor;
> but who has traced out what is in the heavens?
> Who has learned your counsel,
> unless you have given wisdom
> and sent your holy spirit from on high?
> And thus the paths of those on earth were set right,

---

31. See Gregory, "Wisdom and Apocalyptic," 848–50.

32. Wright, *Jesus and the Victory of God*, 313, emphasis original.

33. According to Gregory, "Wisdom and Apocalyptic," 852, Wisdom of Solomon
blurs the categories of wisdom and apocalyptic.

and people were taught what pleases you,
and were saved by wisdom (9:16–18).

Again, revelatory wisdom is needed to grasp what God is doing in the world. (Pseudo-) Solomon, who offered the prayer, also announces, "I learned both what is secret and what is manifest, for wisdom, the fashioner of all things, taught me" (7:21–22). Knowledge of secret things in the present is offered by personified Wisdom who was involved in creation.

One cannot miss the correlation of the gift of wisdom with the sending of the Holy Spirit, a "spirit of wisdom" (*pneuma sophias*) given by God (7:7) for which (Pseudo-) Solomon prayed. We find similar language in Paul's prayer report: "I pray that the God of our Lord Jesus Christ, the Father of glory, may give you a spirit of wisdom [*pneuma sophias*] and revelation [*apokalupseōs*] as you come to know him" (Eph 1:17).[34] The believers in Ephesus need the Holy Spirit who is wisdom and revelation, so that they can have insight into God and what God is doing (vv. 18–23). In this way Spirit-centered and apocalyptic strands of Second Temple Jewish wisdom merge.[35]

This spiritual wisdom and revelation are available through the work of the Holy Spirit, who renews minds. Paul exhorts the Ephesians not to "live as the Gentiles live, in the futility of their minds" (4:17), instead, "be renewed in the spirit of your minds" (4:23).[36] Similarly, in Romans Paul says, "be transformed by the renewing of your minds, so that you may discern what is the will of God" (12:2).[37] Conceptually, discernment is connected with wisdom in the OT (Gen 41:33, 39; Deut 1:13; 4:6; 32:29; Prov 1:5; Isa 29:14), and relates to knowledge of the Lord's will, which is pleasing (Rom 12:2; cf. Eph 5:10). Knowledge of what pleases God comes through wisdom (Wis 9:10), and the Holy Spirit (Wis 9:17). Thus, renewed minds result in wise ways of thinking (Rom 12:3).[38]

Spiritual wisdom and revelation stand in contrast to the world's wisdom. James juxtaposes wisdom from above with earthly wisdom (Jas 3:15, 17), and Paul deconstructs the wisdom of the world in light of God's wisdom in 1 Corinthians. God's wisdom is foolishness to the world, and yet God's

---

34. Against the NRSV's "a spirit," (i.e., a human disposition), Paul is likely referring to "the Spirit" (i.e., the Holy Spirit). The preceding use of spirit in Ephesians is the Holy Spirit (1:13), and in 3:5 the Spirit is the agent of revelation. See Fee, *God's Empowering Presence*, 674–76.

35. See Bennema, "Strands."

36. See Fee, *Presence*, 710–12.

37. Fee, *Presence*, 602–4.

38. Paul's wisdom term in 12:3 is *phronein*, "to think," the noun of which is used synonymously with the spirit of wisdom in Wis: "Therefore I prayed, and understanding [*phronesis*] was given me; I called on God, and the spirit of wisdom came to me" (7:7).

foolishness is wiser than human wisdom, this is because God is not knowable through human wisdom, nor does human wisdom have the power to save (1:20–25). Only the Spirit knows the things of God (2:11). In his preaching Paul offers secret and hidden wisdom, revealed (*apekalupsen*) through the Spirit (2:6–10), namely Christ, who is wisdom from God (1:30): "we proclaim Christ crucified . . . Christ the power of God and the wisdom of God" (1:23–24). The sapiential dimension of wisdom is ultimately Spirit-centered, and it is also Christ-centered: "we have the mind of Christ" (2:16).

Ethical Wisdom

Proverbs' prologue also highlights the ethical dimension of wisdom: "Wisdom is knowing how to *act* rightly."[39] Wisdom is ethical since it has to do with "instruction in wise dealing," which is spelled out as "righteousness, justice, and equity" (1:3).[40] Fox notes that the three terms have "distinguishable, if overlapping, meanings, though here they combine to convey a single concept that embraces the entire range of honest and equitable behavior in personal and social relations."[41]

Wisdom and righteousness are especially linked in Proverbs. Longman observes, "Throughout the book of Proverbs, righteousness and wisdom are interchangeable terms."[42] Bruce Waltke adds that wisdom *needs* righteousness since wisdom is a neutral concept; indeed, *hokmah* can be used negatively: God says of his people, "they are *skilled* in doing evil" (Jer 4:22).[43] The correlation with righteousness makes wisdom ethical. Conversely, "folly and wickedness are inextricably intertwined. Foolish behavior is evil."[44] Thus, wisdom deals with the formation of character, and we will consider three modes of ethical wisdom (law, Spirit, and Christ).

---

39. Clifford, *Proverbs*, 35.

40. The nouns of v. 3b are in apposition to "wise dealing." Cf. Fox, *Proverbs 1–9*, 60. The significance of v. 3b in to the prologue is seen by observing the chiastic arrangement of vv. 2–7: a b c (vv. 2a, 2b, 3a), c′ b′ a′ (vv. 4–5, 5, 7), with d (v. 3b) in the center; see Murphy, *Proverbs*, 4. This arrangement may be signaled by the repetition of "wisdom" and "instruction" in v. 2a and v. 7. By structuring these verses in "concentric circles" the central place of the ethics is highlighted and all the wisdom terminology is invested with ethical significance.

41. Fox, *Proverbs 1–9*, 60.

42. Longman, *Fear of the Lord*, 11.

43. Waltke, "Righteousness in Proverbs," 233.

44. Longman, *Fear of the Lord*, 11.

Wisdom and the Law

An important feature of wisdom in Second Temple Judaism is the association of law and wisdom, as we saw above. This correlation is inherently ethical. Eckhard Schnabel comments, "The ethical dimension constitutes the
main and fundamental focus of the identification of law and wisdom: law
and wisdom contain and promulgate the norms and the criteria of moral
conduct and lead to a pious, holistic way of life."[45]

This relationship is inherent in the Law itself. John Walton and Harvey Walton state the point bluntly: "The Torah (like the legal lists in the
ANE) embodies wisdom; it does not establish legislation."[46] Ancient legal
collections like the Torah are legal lists, which "are not intended to be comprehensive; rather, they are 'aspective.' That is, they offer a wide variety
of aspects pertaining to the topic of the list. This accumulation of aspects
serves to produce a sense of understanding of the field as a whole. In a
word, the accumulated aspects provide wisdom."[47] These aspects would be
used by the king or other rulers to render judgments based on intuition,
not legislation. For example, the commands in Lev 19 circumscribe, rather
than legislate, holiness (19:2). Thus, the command to love your neighbor
(19:18b) is an aspect of holy living.[48] In his ethical vision of the kingdom
Jesus distilled wisdom from the law into the two commands to love God
and love your neighbor (Mark 12:28–34).[49] In this way Jesus circumscribed
behavior using the double love command.[50]

The law as wisdom leads to ethical conduct. Although Paul rejects the
law as law-covenant, he re-appropriates the law as wisdom for the ethical
conduct of his churches.[51] Paul sometimes quotes an OT command as ethical wisdom. Like Jesus, Paul states that the fulfillment of the command to
love your neighbor fulfills the Law (Rom 13:8, 10). He then lists several of
the Decalogue commands, including the command against murder (13:9;
cf. Exod 20:13; Deut 5:17). In Romans both gentile and Jewish sin includes
murder or is depicted as murderous. Gentiles are "full of . . . murder" (1:29).
Both are in view in 3:13–16, humanity under sin is murderous in speech
("Their throats are opened graves," "The venom of vipers is under their

45. Schnabel, *Law and Wisdom from Ben Sira to Paul*, 344.

46. Walton and Walton, *Lost World of the Torah*, 39.

47. Walton and Walton, *Lost World of the Torah*, 32.

48. See Akiyama, "How Can Love Be Commanded?," 1–9.

49. Early Christians seem to have understood this to be the case according to the
Didache, which connects Wisdom's "two ways" with the love command (1:1–2).

50. See McKnight, "Ethics of Jesus," 248.

51. Rosner, *Paul and the Law*, 160.

lips"), and in deeds ("Their feet are swift to shed blood; ruin and misery are in their paths"). Paul offers wisdom from the Law to inculcate an ethic of peace (14:19) among the Roman Christians.

Spirit-led Ethical Wisdom

Paul's ethical vision is of course bigger than the re-appropriation of the law as wisdom. The Holy Spirit is needed for wise living in the church. We saw already that the church needs the Spirit to know God's will, what is pleasing to him. This spiritual knowledge will result in ethical conduct: "bear fruit in every good work" (Col 1:9–10). The fruit is the ethical behavior in the life of the believer who is guided by the Spirit (Gal 5:22, 25).

We see Spirit-led ethical wisdom in the NT household instructions, especially in the context of Paul's argument in Ephesians.[52] In 5:18 Paul says, "Do not get drunk with wine, for that is debauchery; but be filled with the Spirit." On the surface, the reason for this antithesis is not obvious. Yet, Paul is arguing for ethical wisdom in the church, and he does so with three contrastive exhortations. The contrastive exhortations parallel one another synonymously, so that the negative and positive ideas are repeated three times in different terms:

	Negative Exhortation	Positive Exhortation
v. 15	"not as unwise . . . "	"but as wise"
v. 17	"do not be foolish . . . "	"but understand what the will of the Lord is"
v. 18	"do not get drunk with wine . . . "	"but be filled with the Spirit"

Thus, drunkenness is synonymous with foolishness and unwise living, while being filled with the Spirit is synonymous with wise living and the wisdom concept of knowing the Lord's will. This is reinforced by references to drunkenness in Proverbs, where it is linked to lack of wisdom (20:1), especially 23:29–35. In fact, Paul nearly quotes Prov 23:31 LXX when he says "do not get drunk with wine." Thus, the antithesis between drunkenness and the Spirit is possibly another reference to the Spirit of wisdom. Being filled with the Spirit is then explained by four participles: "speaking," "singing," "giving thanks," and "submitting" (5:19–21). Each of these expresses the ethical wisdom of the Spirit, but Paul spends the most

52. Schnabel, "Wisdom," 689.

time with the concept of submission which begins the household instructions (5:22—6:9). Thus, the household instructions are ethical wisdom for
mutual relationships in the church.

Christ-shaped Ethical Wisdom

Ethical wisdom is not only Spirit-led, it is also Christ-shaped. Whereas the
sage Ben Sira found motivation for wisdom ethics in the needs of honor
and shame,[53] NT ethical wisdom is motivated by the example of Christ. We
find ethical motivations in Phil 2:5 and 1 Pet 4:1, where reference is made
to Christ-shaped ways of thinking. Paul says, "Let the same mind be in you
that was in Christ Jesus," which is literally a command to think (*phroneite*).
Paul wants them to cultivate a way of thinking that is exemplified by Jesus.
Jesus's way of thinking is then laid out in the Christ-hymn, which details
the humility of his incarnation and crucifixion (2:6–8). Paul offers this as
a motivation for the ethic of humility he wants to see in Philippi, which
includes references to a way of thinking that puts others first (2:2–4). The
example of Jesus is "intentionally paradigmatic."[54] Similarly, Peter exhorts
suffering Christians to holy living, which begins with prepared minds
(1:13–16), by offering motivation from the example of Christ: "Since therefore Christ suffered in the flesh, arm yourselves also with the same intention . . . ." That intention (*ennoia*) is "the content of mental processing,"[55]
which "issues in right moral action."[56] By sharing Christ's intention believers will be equipped to live for the will of God (4:2), because "whoever has
suffered in the flesh has finished with sin." For Peter and Paul, the example
of Christ offers ethical wisdom for the church to live as God's holy and
humble people. Thus, ethical wisdom is Christ-shaped.

Theological Wisdom

Wisdom is theological because of the relationship of God and wisdom.
This relationship comes to expression in the poems Lady Wisdom, especially Proverbs 8.[57] Wisdom's origins are divine, she was the first of God's

53. See Collins, *Jewish Wisdom*, 64, 77.

54. Fee, *Paul's Letter to the Philippians*, 199.

55. BDAG s.v. ἔννοια.

56. Jobes, *1 Peter*, 262; cf. Prov 2:11; 3:21; 16:22; 23:19 LXX.

57. The nature of the relationship between God and the personification of wisdom is
debated. Fox ("Ideas of Wisdom," 630) believes she symbolizes a transcendent universal,
but not God's wisdom. According to Waltke (*Proverbs*, 86) she personifies Solomon's

creations (vv. 22–26), and she was present with him when he created and ordered the world (vv. 27–31). Those who listen to her receive wisdom and instruction (v. 33), those who find her find life, and favor from the Lord (v. 35). The summons to find Lady Wisdom raises the question articulated by Job: "Where shall wisdom be found?" (28:12). While Proverbs maintains the essential accessibility of wisdom, for Job wisdom is hidden from mankind (vv. 20–21).[58] Yet, as in Proverbs, wisdom is closely associated with God: "God understands the way to it, and he knows its place" (v. 23). Wisdom is accessible, but only to God, only God sees everything (v. 24), so only he has found it (v. 27). Thus, "he said to humankind, 'Truly, the fear of the Lord, that is wisdom'" (v. 28).

The Fear of the Lord

Proverbs 1:7 is the climax of the preamble: "The fear of the LORD is the beginning of knowledge; fools despise wisdom and instruction." The significance of fear of the Lord for Proverbs and for biblical wisdom (Job 1:1; 28:28; Eccl 12:13) cannot be overstressed. Fear of the Lord forms an inclusion around the first major section of Proverbs (1:7; 9:10), and around the whole book (1:7; 31:31). Moreover, the wisdom offered by Proverbs leads to fear of the Lord (2:5). Clearly this is the lens through which Proverbs needs to be read, and the foundation on which wisdom is gained.

The meaning of fear of the Lord is established in Deuteronomy:

> So now, O Israel, what does the LORD your God require of you?
> Only to fear the LORD your God, to walk in all his ways, to love
> him, to serve the LORD your God with all your heart and with
> all your soul, and to keep the commandments of the LORD your
> God and his decrees that I am commanding you today, for your
> own well-being (10:12–13).

What it means to fear the Lord is explained in the parallelism of the following words: to walk in his ways, to love and serve him, and to keep his

---

wisdom, agreeing with the voice of the father in Proverbs. Others more closely associate her with God, identifying her as an attribute of God, or as God himself. According to Longman (*Fear of the Lord*, 24), this is indicated by the location of her house on the heights of the city (9:3). Thus, Murphy (*Tree of Life*, 138–39) says, "The call of Lady Wisdom is the voice of the Lord . . . [she] speaks in the accents of God." The personification of Wisdom in Ben Sira (24:23) and Baruch (4:1) is identified as the Law, God's commandments, which indicates a close association, but not identification with God or an attribute of God. A close relationship is also indicated in Wisdom of Solomon, which has wisdom sit by the throne of God (9:4), from whence she is sent forth (9:10).

58. Bartholomew and O'Dowd, *Old Testament Wisdom Literature*, 181.

commandments.[59] Duane Christensen notes, "the command 'to love him' stands in the structural center . . . of the unit."[60] Both love and fear of God are covenant concepts (Deut 5:10, 29; 6:2, 5).[61] The command to love God (Deut 6:5) is similar to Ancient Near Eastern suzerainty treaties which included an appeal for love to the king.[62] Love and fear have in mind fulfillment of covenantal obligations, keeping God's commands (Deut 6:2; 8:6; 13:4; 17:19; 28:58; 31:12). Thus, fear of the Lord grounds wisdom in a covenant relationship with God (cf. Deut 4:6).[63]

Covenantal fear of the Lord is the "beginning of knowledge." Knowledge, according to the categories proposed by Fox, is an intellectual faculty. Here it is nearly synonymous with wisdom, as seen in the antithetical parallelism ("fools despise wisdom and instruction"), and because elsewhere fear of the Lord is also the beginning of wisdom (9:10; Ps 111:10). That fear of the Lord is the beginning of knowledge and wisdom means it is the prerequisite.[64] It is the foundation on which the house is built, and the starting place from which the journey is made. As the alphabet is to reading, so fear of the Lord is to wisdom. Proverbs gives its own summary of the fear of the Lord (3:5–7):

> Trust in the LORD with all your heart,
>   and do not rely on your own insight.
> In all your ways acknowledge him,
>   and he will make straight your paths.
> Do not be wise in your own eyes;
>   fear the LORD, and turn away from evil.

The fear of the Lord is central for Ben Sira.[65] The fear of the Lord is a commitment to God requiring faithfulness (*pistis*), humility, and obedience (1:27–28a). It cannot be achieved with a divided heart (v. 28b); it is antithetical to self-exaltation (v. 30). Fear of the Lord is worked out in patience,

59. Christensen, *Deuteronomy 1–21:9*, 204; Grant, "Wisdom and Covenant," 861.

60. Christensen, *Deuteronomy 1–21:9*, 204.

61. See Waltke, *Proverbs*, 101.

62. See Moran, "Ancient Near Eastern Background of the Love of God in Deuteronomy," 77–87.

63. Grant, "Wisdom and Covenant," 859.

64. Fox, *Proverbs 1–9*, 68. Fox thinks "beginning" ("first in time") is the best rendering of the Hebrew term, rejecting other options, i.e., best part, essence. Henri Blocher, "Fear of the Lord as the 'Principle' of Wisdom," 14–15, agrees, but thinks "beginning" lacks the necessary value connotation; "When wisdom is in question, priority is likely to be logical as much as chronological," so he opts for "principle." Waltke, *Proverbs*, 181, holds both together.

65. See Skehan and Di Lella, *Wisdom of Ben Sira*, 76.

trust, and hope (2:7–9). But he also goes further, fear of the Lord is wisdom's beginning, fulness, crown, and root (1:14, 16, 18, 20); thus it is "the very essence of wisdom."[66] Like Deuteronomy, Ben Sira connects fear of the Lord with love of the Lord, which are linked to obedience and humility:

> Those who fear the Lord do not disobey his words,
>   and those who love him keep his ways.
> Those who fear the Lord seek to please him,
>   and those who love him are filled with his law.
> Those who fear the Lord prepare their hearts,
>   and humble themselves before him (2:15–17).

Patrick Skehan and Alexander Di Lella summarize, "In Ben Sira's theology, the one who fears God must have a deep and abiding relationship of trust and love with God."[67]

Life within Limits

At this point it is necessary to grapple with the opposite side of the coin. Another aspect of theological wisdom implied in Prov 3:5–7 is the reality of human limitation. God's "incalculability" "expresses a sense of dependence and finitude that is common to all religious experience."[68] Further, "The experience of limit is also central to the various contradictions that put the meaning of life in question and give rise to religious doubt . . . ."[69] So, while Proverbs relies on the accessibility of wisdom, Job wrestles with its inaccessibility (28:12–27). Thus for Job, fear of the Lord is what is needed to face life's uncertainties, and to make a way in a world that does not always make sense (28:28). Similarly, Qoheleth's search for meaning in the contradictions of life leads back to the stability of the fear of God (Eccl 12:13).[70] In these cases, fear of the Lord/God is humility that appreciates human limitation before the Creator. Thus, wisdom is life within limits.

The recognition of human limitation is based on the order built into creation. Returning to the personification of Wisdom, it needs to be observed that those limits are woven into the fabric of the cosmos, making wisdom the key to life in God's world. It is hard to tell whether or not Wisdom was

---

66. Skehan and Di Lella, *Wisdom of Ben Sira*, 76–77.

67. Skehan and Di Lella, *Wisdom of Ben Sira*, 79.

68. Collins, "Biblical Precedent for Natural Theology," 98.

69. Collins, "Natural Theology," 98.

70. See Grant, "Wisdom and Covenant," 860.

an agent of God in creation.[71] Either way, her presence with God at creation gives her special insight into the order with which God has built the world (Prov 8:29; Job 28:25–27; Wis 8–9).[72] Thus wisdom is needed to live wisely, and to live wisely is to live along the grain of created order; according to God's design. The person who finds wisdom and gets understanding (Prov 3:13) is pursuing a life in keeping with the way God built the world (3:19).

One aspect of the created order is the act-consequence relationship, or the principle of retribution. The Creator has ordered his world to work according to certain principles, including retribution. John Walton explains this as "the conviction that the righteous will prosper and the wicked will suffer, both in proportion to their respective righteousness and wickedness."[73] Choices and actions have consequences. These consequences are woven into the fabric of creation. Ben Sira seems to suggest that God's justice in upholding the principle of retribution is grounded in the order of creation and giving the Law, so that all humans are responsible for their choices (Sir 17:1–24). Paul says generally, "Do not be deceived; God is not mocked, for you reap whatever you sow" (Gal 6:7), while more specifically, Baruch thinks Israel's exile is a just consequence of their failure to live wisely (3:9–4:1). The principle is related to a sense of good and evil: "good means staying within prescribed [moral] boundaries and evil means the trespassing of these limits."[74] The humility that comes with appreciating human limits requires that one accept that this principle does not work mechanistically, sometimes good people suffer, and evil people prosper. Ecclesiastes and Job deal head on with this reality.[75]

Reference to the fear of the Lord is rare in the NT, though it does occur. Paul exhorts, "work out your own salvation with fear and trembling" (Phil 2:12), and he connects a sincere heart with fearing the Lord (Col 3:22). The concept of fear of the Lord maps onto NT concepts of love and obedience.

---

71. There is debate over the meaning of the unique Hebrew term, *amōn* in Proverbs 8:30, translated as "master worker" by the NRSV, a rendering preferred by Longman (*Proverbs*, 207) and Murphy (*Proverbs*, 48). Waltke (*Proverbs*, 417–20) lays out the possibilities deciding on "constantly," due to the parallelism in the verse ("and I was daily his delight, rejoicing before him always"). Fox ("Ideas of Wisdom," 628), argues for the rendering of the term as "nursling," "she played while God worked." The first rendering seems to be behind the LXX translation (*harmozousa*) and is supported by Wisdom of Solomon: "I learned . . . for wisdom, the fashioner [*technitis*] of all things, taught me" (7:21–22). *Technitis* is the feminine form of *technitēs*, meaning "craftswoman."

72. Her presence is reinforced by an inclusion: "I was there" (v. 27), "I was beside him" (v. 30); see Waltke, *Proverbs*, 417.

73. Walton, "Retribution," 647.

74. Van Leeuwen, "Liminality," 116.

75. See Longman, *Proverbs*, 61–63.

Jesus said, "If you love me, you will keep my commandments" (John 14:15). Also, in light of the covenantal connections, fear of the Lord relates to NT concepts of faith in Christ, or more appropriately faithfulness to Christ; allegiance and loyalty to him. The commitment must be total, as James reminds, saying, those who ask wisdom from God must "ask in faith, never doubting . . . for the doubter, being double-minded and unstable in every way, must not expect to receive anything from the Lord" (Jas 1:6–7). Furthermore, the kind of humility that trusts in the Lord with all one's heart is expressed in Peter's words, "Humble yourselves therefore under the mighty hand of God, so that he may exalt you in due time. Cast all your anxiety on him, because he cares for you" (1 Pet 5:6–7). Peter's God is the "faithful Creator" who can be trusted with the lives of his people in the midst of suffering (4:19).

Jesus and Wisdom

The persona of Lady Wisdom is also thought to lay in the background of NT Wisdom Christology. On one hand, wisdom is identified with the *teaching* of Christ: Jesus the sage. Josephus called him a "wise man" (*Antiquities* 18.3.3), and some of Jesus's audience saw him in this light (Matt 13:54). The Sermon on the Mount can be described as a wisdom discourse, which begins with beatitudes, centers on aspects of the law and righteousness, and concludes by saying (in a parable) that those who hear and do his words will be wise (7:24). Several of the sayings of Jesus indicate that Jesus saw himself as a messenger sent by personified Wisdom. For example, in Matt 11:16–19 and Luke 11:49–51 Jesus casts himself as the culmination of a long line of Wisdom's rejected messengers to "this generation."[76]

On the other hand, wisdom is identified with the *person* of Christ: Wisdom incarnate. The personification of Wisdom addressed the place or dwelling of wisdom (Prov 8:20; Job 28:12; Sir 24:7–8; Bar 3:14; Wis 6:22), which the NT identifies with Christ. Paul says, "in [Christ] are hidden all the treasures of wisdom and knowledge" (Col 2:3), and "[Christ] became for us wisdom from God" (1 Cor 1:30).[77] Similarly, John wrote, "the [Logos] became flesh and lived among us" (1:14). Craig Keener observes, "everything John says about the Logos—apart from its incarnation as a particular historical person—Jewish literature said about divine Wisdom."[78] Keener detects the following resemblances: preexistence, unique relationship to God, role

76. See Burnet and Bennema, "Wisdom," 996–97.

77. Cf. Fee, "Wisdom Christology in Paul," 251–79; Dunne, "Regal Status of Christ in the Colossian 'Christ-Hymn,'" 3–18.

78. Keener, *Gospel of John*, 352.

in creation, eternality, related to life, light and salvation, appearance in the world among people, and associated with truth and glory.[79]

Matthew also presents Jesus as Wisdom incarnate. A key passage is 11:29–31: "Come to me, all you that are weary and are carrying heavy burdens, and I will give you rest. Take my yoke upon you, and learn from me; for I am gentle and humble in heart, and you will find rest for your souls. For my yoke is easy, and my burden is light." In these words, Jesus echoes Wisdom's invitation (Prov 8), and the yoke he offers to the weary is the yoke of Wisdom. We find a close parallel in Sirach:

> Come to her like one who plows and sows,
>   and wait for her good harvest.
> For when you cultivate her you will toil but little,
>   and soon you will eat of her produce . . .
> Put your feet into her fetters,
>   and your neck into her collar.
> Bend your shoulders and carry her,
>   and do not fret under her bonds.
> Come to her with all your soul,
>   and keep her ways with all your might.
> Search out and seek, and she will become known to you;
>   and when you get hold of her, do not let her go.
> For at last you will find the rest she gives,
>   and she will be changed into joy for you.
> Then her fetters will become for you a strong defense,
>   and her collar a glorious robe.
> Her yoke is a golden ornament,
>   and her bonds a purple cord (6:19, 24–30).

Ben Sira invites his student to come to Wisdom and find rest by taking her yoke, which he later identifies with his own teaching (51:23–27). Similarly, Jesus invites those who are weary (literally, "toiling") to take a yoke that is easy and find rest. Observe, however, that Jesus says, "come to *me*" and "take *my* yoke," so that his invitation is to come to him as to Wisdom. Jesus speaks here not as a representative of Wisdom, but as Wisdom in person.[80] True wisdom is found in Christ, who is the fulfillment of Wisdom.[81]

---

79. Keener, *Gospel of John*, 355.

80. See Suggs, "Wisdom and Law in the Gospel of Matthew," 99–127.

81. Witherington, *Jesus the Sage*.

Three-Dimensional Wisdom in Colossians

We can conclude our discussion of wisdom's three dimensions by looking at the way they converge in Colossians. In Colossians Paul brings together sapiential, ethical, and theological wisdom for the church. Colossians is framed as a wisdom discourse with a polemical core focused on achieving wisdom. The frame is found in 1:9–10 and 4:5 with the first and last uses of "wisdom" (*sophia*) in the letter.[82] Richard Demaris argues that the polemical core of Colossians is the pursuit of wisdom: "The conflict over knowledge at Colossae appears to revolve around this question: how is wisdom achieved?"[83] He explains, "Central to the Colossian philosophy's outlook was the pursuit of divine knowledge or wisdom through (1) the order of the cosmic elements (2.8, 20), (2) a bodily asceticism that sets free the investigative mind (2.18, 23), and (3) intermediaries between heaven and earth (angels or demons; 2.18)."[84] Paul exposes this philosophy as having "an appearance of wisdom," but ultimately of no value (2:23), since it is "not according to Christ" (2:8). The Colossian philosophy offered inadequate foundations for wisdom, "a philosophy not according to Christ (2.8) is one devoid of an epistemological base . . . . apart from Christ no source of wisdom exists."[85]

Paul seeks to establish the Colossians on the true foundation for wisdom. This gets to the heart of Paul's ministry, which includes teaching "in all wisdom" (1:28; 3:16). Paul struggled for the Colossians to know Christ (2:2), so that they would not be deceived (2:4). Indeed, his desire for them is first expressed in a prayer for sapiential wisdom, "asking that you may be filled with the knowledge of God's will in all spiritual wisdom and understanding" (1:9). As in Eph 1:17, "spiritual wisdom" is given by the Holy Spirit.[86] Sapiential wisdom from the Spirit has an ethical result: "so that you may lead lives worthy of the Lord, fully pleasing to him, as you bear fruit in every good work and as you grow in the knowledge of God" (1:10). The phrase, "lead lives worthy," is literally, "walk worthy." The language of walk denotes conduct in the way of life and is similar to imagery found in wisdom literature. By combining knowledge of God's will with conduct pleasing to him, Paul gives the believers' walk a distinct wisdom shape (cf. Bar 4:4; Wis 9:9–10, 13, 18). This is echoed in the framing passage: Walk in

82. See Heil, *Colossians*, 33–34.

83. Demaris, *Colossian Controversy*, 73.

84. Demaris, *Colossian Controversy*, 16–17. Demaris identifies the philosophy at work in Colossae as "a distinctive blend of popular Middle Platonic, Jewish, and Christian elements that cohere around the pursuit of wisdom."

85. Demaris, *Colossian Controversy*, 142.

86. Fee, *Presence*, 641–43.

wisdom (4:5). The use of walk terminology points to the theological nature
of wisdom in Colossians. Paul exhorts the church to walk in Christ (2:6),
"in whom are hidden all the treasures of wisdom and knowledge" (2:3).[87]
Demaris suggests that the high Christology of the letter (1:15–20; 2:9–15)
is a response to the philosophy: "The rich christological language is not the
product of unfocused or unmotivated reflection; much of it coheres around
a Christocentric theology of knowledge, the obvious stimulus of which was
the Colossian philosophy's wisdom claim."[88] Paul's exhortation moves from
theological wisdom to ethical wisdom: Paul exhorts, "Set your minds on
things that are above" (3:2), "where Christ is" (3:1), and then continues into
practical ethical exhortations from 3:5 on. Ultimately the wisdom Paul offers in Colossians is practical, and that is where we need to conclude our
investigation into the meaning of wisdom.

Practical Wisdom and the Life of the Church

Wisdom is fundamentally concerned with the present, exhibiting a kind of
realized eschatology.[89] Thus, we will round out our discussion of biblical
wisdom with a look at the practical nature of wisdom. It is important to see
that the practical and the theological dimension of wisdom are tied together.
Theological wisdom is the context for practical wisdom. This is clear in
Prov 1–9 with the interplay of parental admonitions and cosmic speeches of
personified Wisdom explored above.[90] O'Dowd notes, "these two sources of
wisdom are interwoven, giving the son two witnesses or testimonies, the one
practical and momentary and the other theological and trans-temporal."[91]
He explains, "The very point of knitting parental wisdom together with the
cosmic speeches in Proverbs 1–9 is to situate the particular knowledge of
human experience within the cosmic order of God's creation."[92] Further,
"The cosmic imagery reminds us that what appears to us to be the mundane activity of our daily life has, in reality, been structured by God to fit

---

87. See Prov 2:3–6; Sir 1:24–25; Wis 6:22; 7:13–14; Bar 3:15.

88. Demaris, *Colossian Controversy*, 145.

89. Miller, "Wisdom in the Canon," 100–103.

90. O'Dowd, *Proverbs*, 29.

91. O'Dowd, *Proverbs*, 34.

92. O'Dowd, *Proverbs*, 35. Importantly, Van Leeuwen ("Cosmos" 81) makes a distinction between metaphor formation and concepts communicated by the metaphor.
On the level of metaphor formation, the cosmic imagery is modeled on reality, while
conceptually the cosmic imagery becomes the basis of reality.

the architectural plans he made for our world . . . "[93] This is why the father's instruction is so urgent; it is a matter of life and death.

Wisdom is practical because it has to do with life. Practical wisdom is offered throughout Proverbs in the form of advice for the skill of living well in different areas of life: relationships, parenting, money, work, and the like.[94] In fact, life was the primary interest of Israel's sages, "Their concern was the present, and how to cope with the challenges provoked by one's immediate experience."[95] In the NT, wisdom is given for the life of the church. We conclude by looking at two examples of practical wisdom in the life of the church.

We find the first example in James. James writes, "If any of you is lacking in wisdom, ask God, who gives to all generously and ungrudgingly, and it will be given you" (1:5). The wisdom needed by the diaspora church relates to the trials they are facing (1:2). Scot McKnight explains that the trial is both what the church is forced to endure, *and* how they would choose to respond.[96] Specifically, the trial is both socio-economic suffering, and the temptation to resort to violence.[97] It seems violence was a real temptation: "You must understand this, my beloved: let everyone be quick to listen, slow to speak, slow to anger; for your anger does not produce God's righteousness" (1:19–20). Wisdom is needed for both dimensions of the trial. McKnight explains, "'wisdom' is more than intellectual sagaciousness . . . it is a kind of life that pursues 'justice' (1:20), 'love' (2:8–11), and 'peace' (3:18) along proper moral lines—that is, without resorting to violence or volatile language."[98] James's church needs wisdom for this real life, practical situation.

A second example is Paul's attempt to help the Roman Christians overcome divisions related to ethnic identity markers, especially food (14:1–4), probably during gathered fellowship. The Jewish (weak) and gentile (strong) believers have separated along kosher (weak) and non-kosher (strong) keeping lines.[99] Each group believed that they were living according to the Lord's will. The weak judged the strong for what they ate, while the strong would not put up with the foibles of the weak. Ultimately, Paul's aim in Romans is that the weak and strong welcome one another (15:7;

---

93. Bartholomew and O'Dowd, *Wisdom Literature*, 86.

94. See Longman's very helpful topical studies (*Proverbs*, 549–78).

95. Murphy, *Tree of Life*, ix.

96. McKnight, *Letter of James*, 76.

97. McKnight, *Letter of James*, 76.

98. McKnight, *Letter of James*, 86.

99. See McKnight, *Reading Romans Backwards*, 21.

14:1).[100] For this they need wisdom with regard to good and evil (16:19b), which requires discernment (2 Sam 14:17; 1 Kgs 3:9, 11). Wisdom needs the mental activity of discernment when there is a difference of opinion about the right course of action. The Spirit renews the mind of the community (12:2), allowing the believers to discern different positions with regard to food: "The faith that you have, have as your own conviction before God. Blessed are those who have no reason to condemn themselves because of what they approve" (14:22; cf. 14:5). Paul doesn't lay down legislation. Whatever they choose, the guiding principle for discernment is love: "Love does no wrong to a neighbor" (13:10), therefore, "If your brother or sister is being injured by what you eat, you are no longer walking in love" (14:15). In love the weak and strong will discern ways to please their neighbor, and in so doing fulfill God's will for them.

Bibliography

Akiyama, Kengo. "How Can Love Be Commanded?: On Not Reading Lev 19,17–18 as Law." *Biblica* 98 (2017) 1–9.

Bartholomew, Craig G., and Ryan P. O'Dowd. *Old Testament Wisdom Literature: A Theological Introduction*. Downers Grove, IL: InterVarsity, 2011.

Bennema, Cornelis. "The Strands of Wisdom Tradition in Intertestamental Judaism: Origins, Developments and Characteristics." *Tyndale Bulletin* 52 (2001) 61–82.

Blocher, Henri. "The Fear of the Lord as the 'Principle' of Wisdom." *Tyndale Bulletin* (1977) 14–15.

Burnet, Fred W., and Cornelis Bennema. "Wisdom." In *Dictionary of Jesus and the Gospels*, edited by Joel B. Green et al. Downers Grove, IL: InterVarsity, 2013.

Christensen, Duane L. *Deuteronomy 1–21:9*. 2nd ed. Waco: Thomas Nelson, 2001.

Clifford, Richard J. *Proverbs: A Commentary*. Louisville: John Knox, 1999.

Collins, John J. "The Biblical Precedent for Natural Theology." In *Encounters with Biblical Theology*. Minneapolis: Fortress, 2005.

———. *Jewish Wisdom in the Hellenistic Age*. Louisville: John Knox, 1997.

Cook, Johann. *The Septuagint of Proverbs: Jewish And/or Hellenistic Proverbs?: Concerning the Hellenistic Colouring of LXX Proverbs*. Leiden: Brill, 1997.

Demaris, Richard E. *Colossian Controversy: Wisdom in Dispute at Colossae*. Sheffield: Sheffield Academic Press, 1994.

DeSilva, David A. "In the School of Ben Sira of Jerusalem." In *The Jewish Teachers of Jesus, James, and Jude: What Earliest Christianity Learned from the Apocrypha and Pseudepigrapha*, 58–85. New York: Oxford University Press, 2012.

Dunne, John Anthony. "The Regal Status of Christ in the Colossian 'Christ-Hymn': A Re-Evaluation of the Influence of Wisdom Traditions." *TrinJ* 32 (2011) 3–18.

Fee, Gordon. *God's Empowering Presence: The Holy Spirit in the Letters of Paul*. Peabody, MA: Hendrickson, 1994.

———. *Paul's Letter to the Philippians*. Grand Rapids, Eerdmans: 1995.

---

100. McKnight, *Reading Romans Backwards*, 41.

————. "Wisdom Christology in Paul: A Dissenting View." In *The Way of Wisdom: Essays in Honor of Bruce K. Waltke*. Grand Rapids: Zondervan, 2000.

Fox, Michael V. "Ideas of Wisdom in Proverbs 1–9." *JBL* 116 (1997) 613–33.

————. *Proverbs 1–9*. New Haven, CT: Yale University Press, 2000.

————. "Words for Wisdom." *ZAH* 6 (1993) 149–69.

Grant, Jamie. "Wisdom and Covenant." In *Dictionary of the Old Testament: Wisdom, Poetry and Writings*, edited by Tremper Longman III et al. Downers Grove, IL: InterVarsity, 2011.

Gregory, Bradley. "Wisdom and Apocalyptic." In *Dictionary of the Old Testament: Wisdom, Poetry and Writings*, edited by Tremper Longman III et al., 847–53. Downers Grove, IL: InterVarsity, 2011.

Heil, John Paul. *Colossians: Encouragement to Walk in All Wisdom as Holy Ones in Christ*. Atlanta: SBL, 2010.

Jobes, Karen H. *1 Peter*. Grand Rapids, Baker: 2005.

Keener, Craig S. *The Gospel of John*. 2 vols. Grand Rapids: Baker, 2010.

Kynes, Will. "The 'Wisdom Literature' Category: An Obituary." *JTS* 69 (2018) 1–24.

Longman, Tremper, III. *The Fear of the Lord Is Wisdom: A Theological Introduction to Wisdom in Israel*. Grand Rapids: Baker, 2017.

————. *Proverbs*. Grand Rapids: Baker, 2006.

McKnight, Scot. "Ethics of Jesus." In *Dictionary of Jesus and The Gospels*, edited by Joel B. Green et al., 242–51. Downers Grove, IL: InterVarsity, 2012.

————. *The Letter of James*. Grand Rapids: Eerdmans, 2011.

————. *Reading Romans Backwards: A Gospel of Peace in the Midst of Empire*. Waco, TX: Baylor University Press, 2019.

Miller, Douglas. "Wisdom in the Canon: Discerning the Early Intuition." In *Was There a Wisdom Tradition? New Prospects in Israelite Wisdom Studies*, edited by Mark R. Sneed, 87–113. Atlanta: SBL, 2015.

Moran, William L. "Ancient Near Eastern Background of the Love of God in Deuteronomy." *CBQ* 25 (1963) 77–87.

Murphy, Roland. "Lady Wisdom." In *The Tree of Life: An Exploration of Biblical Wisdom Literature*. 3rd ed. Grand Rapids: Eerdmans, 2002.

————. *Proverbs*. Grand Rapids: Zondervan, 2015.

O'Dowd, Ryan P. *Proverbs*. Grand Rapids: Zondervan, 2017.

Pemberton, Glenn. *A Life That Is Good: The Message of Proverbs in a World Wanting Wisdom*. Grand Rapids: Eerdmans, 2018.

Rosner, Brian S. *Paul and the Law: Keeping the Commandments of God*. Downers Grove, IL: InterVarsity, 2013.

Schnabel, Eckhard J. *Law and Wisdom from Ben Sira to Paul*. Tübingen: Mohr Siebeck, 1985.

————. "Wisdom." In *Dictionary of Paul and His Letters*, edited by Gerald F. Hawthorne et al., 689. Downers Grove, IL: InterVarsity, 1993.

Skehan, Patrick, and Alexander Di Lella. *The Wisdom of Ben Sira*. New York: Anchor Bible, 1987.

Sneed, Mark R. *Was There a Wisdom Tradition? New Prospects in Israelite Wisdom Studies*. Atlanta: SBL, 2015.

Suggs, M. Jack. "Wisdom and Law in the Gospel of Matthew." In *Wisdom, Christology, and Law in Matthew's Gospel*. Cambridge: Harvard University Press, 1970.

Van Leeuwen, Raymond. "Cosmos, Temple, House: Building and Wisdom in Mesopotamia and Israel," in *Wisdom Literature in Mesopotamia and Israel*, ed. Richard J. Clifford (Atlanta: SBL, 2007), 67–90.

———. "Liminality and Worldview in Proverbs 1–9." *Semeia* 50 (1990) 111–44.

Von Rad, Gerhard. *Wisdom in Israel*. Nashville: Abingdon, 1972.

Waltke, Bruce K. *The Book of Proverbs: Chapters 1–15*. Grand Rapids: Eerdmans, 2004.

———. "Righteousness in Proverbs." *WTJ* 70 (2008) 233.

Walton, John. "Retribution." In *Dictionary of the Old Testament: Wisdom, Poetry and Writings*, edited by Tremper Longman III et al. Downers Grove, IL: InterVarsity, 2011.

Walton, John, and J. Harvey Walton. *The Lost World of the Torah: Law as Covenant and Wisdom in Ancient Context*. Downers Grove, IL: InterVarsity, 2019.

Witherington, Ben, III. *Jesus the Sage: The Pilgrimage of Wisdom*. Minneapolis: Augsberg Fortress, 1994.

Wright, N. T. *Jesus and the Victory of God*. Minneapolis: Fortress, 1997.

WISE LETTER WRITING

By Jeremy Berg

P astors know all too well the unbearable silence of Monday that can pre-
cipitate a torrent of internal voices—some accusing, some doubting,
but all of them ultimately asking, "Did yesterday's sermon make any difference?" Another sermon has been tossed like seed across a field of varied
soils. Was it the right word at the right moment for the right person? Will
it take root? Will it be choked out? Will it be blown away like chaff in the
summer breeze? The unbearable silence of Monday is a weekly reminder
to pastors that shepherding souls requires something more relational and
intimate than just the weekly sermon.

Eugene Peterson's question was not "What should I preach on this Sunday?" but rather, "Who are these particular people, and *how can I be with
them* in such a way that they can become what God is making them?"[1]
An increasing number of people find themselves living in digital isolation,
settling for pseudo-connection, pursuing online relationships and distance
education. In our digital age, many (if not most) of the messages we receive
throughout the week come stark naked—that is, *disembodied*. We get sprin-
kled with text messages throughout the day, but what we really long for is a
hug. We read someone's Facebook rant and make false assumptions about
the mood and emotions behind it. We shoot off a rushed email that leaves
the recipient questioning our heart and motives. We make phone calls on
our drive home from work each day to catch up with friends, but we haven't
seen them face to face for far too long.

For many Christians today, spiritual growth and nourishment are often
sought in the disembodied voices of celebrity pastors speaking into our ear-
buds through online sermons and podcasts. Many of our own revered "teachers" we've never even met face to face. Their sermons and books have changed

1. Peterson, *Contemplative Pastor*, 4, emphasis mine.

our lives, and they mean the world to us. Yet, in reality, they have no clue
we even exist. We have forgotten the significance of "embodied words" and
have settled for raw information, naked facts and stripped-down soundbites
that, like cracked cisterns, cannot hold the living water we need and will not
adequately feed our souls. In the words of N. T. Wright:

> The word became flesh, said St. John, and the Church has
> turned the flesh back into words: words of good advice, words
> of comfort, words of wisdom and encouragement, yes, but
> what changes the world is flesh, words with skin on them,
> words that hug you and cry with you and play with you and
> love you and rebuke you and build houses with you and teach
> your children in school.[2]

I am convinced people today are hungry for personal spiritual guidance and
wise mentors in-the-flesh. In an age of personal life coaches and focused
fitness programs, the church still gathers in rows and hopes three songs and
a sermon is the one-size-fits-all spiritual workout regimen that will lead to
spiritual growth. The facts reveal otherwise. I suspect the future impact of
Christianity will depend less on which organizational models it adopts, and
more on whether or not pastors recover their true and ancient calling to
be personal spiritual guides and wise sages in a modern church that has
been more enamored with spiritual short-cuts and religious consumerism.
The true spiritual seekers of the next generations are looking for holy men
and women steeped in ancient wisdom offering practical pathways to inner
growth; not slick visionary leaders with impressive business portfolios who
can draw a crowd and balance the budget.

This chapter explores the need for pastors to adopt more personal
and "embodied" modes of spiritual teaching and guidance in their ministry today. In particular, I will recommend pastors recover the ancient art
of letter writing as a time-tested mode of passing on embodied spiritual
wisdom from pastor to disciple. Let us first highlight the current trend
in church ministry of increasingly disembodied teaching and impersonal
communication.

A Hunger for Embodied Wisdom and Wise Spiritual Guides

I was fortunate to find wise guides with open office doors during my formative years in college when I was wandering confused and helpless, beginning

2. Wright, "New Creation," 64.

to ask big questions and make significant life decisions. No matter the time of day, I could usually find a door open with a professor inside ready and willing to listen. I gained *knowledge* from my professors' lectures, but it was only from those whose doors I walked through between lectures that I gained *wisdom*. More than just talking heads filled with knowledge, these modern-day sages became embodied examples of lived-out truth. Eventually, I no longer just wanted to know what they knew; I wanted to become like they were: wise and godly men and women. I know I was not alone.

During those same college years, I attended a megachurch where the Sunday sermons were awakening my soul to a new life of faith and devotion to Christ. Unfortunately, the beloved pastor to whom I owed my newfound faith had no idea I even existed. I was just one in a crowd of a couple thousand anonymous faces in a dim-lit auditorium he preached to each week. If he had an office, I didn't know where to find it. If I had gone looking for it, would I have found it open? I don't know. Nor do I blame him. It is just part of the culture of a megachurch. The sad fact is I attended that church for nearly a decade without ever having met or had a personal face-to-face conversation with the pastor. I was lost and confused like a sheep without a shepherd, a disciple without a teacher, a Christian without a true pastor. (In hindsight, maybe this is why I wanted to become a professor back then, and never aspired to be a pastor.)

Walking through the open door of an available professor, or hearing the right words spoken by the right person at the right time with just the right personal touch: this is the promising potential for pastors who recognize the need for more *embodied* approaches to ministry in an age of increasingly disembodied communication. We are back to Eugene Peterson's question: "Who are these particular people, and *how can I be with them*" as a spiritual guide and soul companion between Sundays?

For much of history, letter correspondence was the way to nurture long-distance relationships in the days before the dawn of modern transportation and other technologies designed to help us stay connected. Ironically, despite all our technological advances and additional ways of "being with" others—automobiles, airplanes, phones, Facebook, video chat, email, etc.—we seem to be more relationally detached and isolated today than our ancient letter-writing ancestors. We will explore this irony later on, especially as it relates to the growing distance between pastors and their congregation, caused in part by our increased use of modern technology. But first we must explore the rich and enduring practice of letter writing in the ancient world.

First, we will examine ancient epistolary practice in the Greco-Roman world, in the ministry of Paul in the New Testament, and among the early

Church Fathers. Then we will explore our current cultural moment and how
written correspondence can be a powerful and effective way for pastors to
pass on embodied wisdom to folks adrift in a world of increasingly disembodied ministry and communication.

Letter Writing and Moral Formation in the Greco-Roman World

Letters were used in many areas of life and for many purposes in the ancient Hellenistic world, but nurturing and maintaining friendship was chief
among them.[3] "The ideals of Greek male friendship greatly influenced
ancient epistolography," notes Stanley Stowers. "The sharing of two selves,
which was a classical definition of friendship, was also used to character-
ize the function of the letter."[4] That is, "the letter permitted absent friends
to share in one another."[5] Seneca, the Roman Stoic and contemporary of
Paul, writes to his friend and protege Lucilius:

> I thank you for writing to me so often; for you are revealing your
> real self to me in the only way you can. I never receive a letter
> from you without being in your company forthwith. If the pic-
> tures of our absent friends are pleasing to us, though they only
> refresh the memory and lighten our longing by a solace that is
> unreal and unsubstantial, how much more pleasant is a letter,
> which brings us real traces, real evidences, of an absent friend!
> For that which is sweetest when we meet face to face is afforded
> by the impress of a friend's hand upon his letter,—recognition.[6]

The most famous and prolific letter writer of Roman antiquity was Cicero.
His letters drip with the emotive intimacy of friendship and demonstrate
the power of letters to bring two people together in a mutually enriching
way: "What could give me greater pleasure, failing a tete-a-tete talk with
you, than either to write to you, or to read a letter of yours? What often
annoys me still more is my being tied up with such pressing engagements

---

3. For a list of "things people could do with letters," see Stowers, *Letter Writing in Greco-Roman Antiquity*, 15–16.

4. Stowers, *Letter Writing in Greco-Roman Antiquity*, 29; see also 58–70. On "the friendly letter" (*philikos typos*) see Malherbe, *Paul and the Thessalonians*, 68ff. On classical Greek friendship, see Konstan, *Friendship in the Classical World*. On friendship
and pastoral ministry, see McKnight, *Pastor Paul*, 32–53.

5. Stowers, *Letter Writing*, 29.

6. Seneca, *Moral Letters to Lucilius* 40.1.

that I find it impossible to write to you when the spirit moves me."[7] In his friendly correspondence with Atticus he confides, "I rest only so long as I am writing to you or reading your letters"[8] and "when I seem to talk with you, I have some little relief from sorrow, and, when I read a letter from you, far greater relief."[9]

More than just conveying ideas or communicating facts, ancient letters *mediated one's personal presence.* So Cicero writes, "Though I have nothing to say to you, I write all the same, because I feel as though I were talking to you."[10] A far cry from today's two-dimensional emails or quickly shot off one-phrase text messages, Cicero could write, "*All of you* was revealed to me in your letter."[11]

Such letter-based friendships also shaped the letter-based moral formation tradition of Greco-Roman philosophers and their students. As early as the fourth century BC, Epicurus used letters to instruct his community of learners who held him in high esteem as their master.[12] Moral exhortation through letters became a preeminent form of philosophical pedagogy within the major philosophical schools—Platonists, Peripatetics, Epicureans, Stoics, Cynics, and Pythagoreans.[13] Joining one of these philosophical schools was very much a "conversion" experience.[14] "Usually the initial conversion, whether a quiet commitment or a dramatic transformation, was not considered enough," writes Stowers. "The aspiring student needed a philosophical guide or a doctor of the soul."[15] A great example is found in the third Cynic letter of Pseudo-Diogenes where Diogenes offers himself as a philosophical guide to Hipparchia, a relationship to be carried on by means of letters:

> I admire you for your eagerness in that, although you are a woman, you yearned for philosophy and have become one of our school, which has struck even men with awe for its austerity. But be earnest to bring to a finish what you have begun. And you will cap it off, I am sure, if you should not be outstripped by Crates, your husband, and if you frequently write to me, your

7. Cicero, *To Friends,* 12, 30, 1, cited in Malherbe, *Ancient Epistolary Theorists,* 27.

8. Cicero, *To Atticus,* 9, 4, 1.

9. Cicero, *To Atticus,* 8, 14, 1.

10. Cicero, *To Atticus,* 12, 53.

11. Cicero, *To Friends,* 16, 16, 2.

12. Malherbe, *Paul and the Thessalonians,* 68–69, esp. n. 18.

13. See Malherbe, *Moral Exhortation;* Meeks, *Moral World of the First Christians,* 40–64.

14. On comparing "conversion" in philosophy with Christianity, see Malherbe, *Paul and the Thessalonians,* 36–52.

15. Stowers, *Letter Writing,* 37.

benefactor in philosophy. For letters are worth a great deal and are not inferior to conversation with people actually present.[16]

Such "hortatory literature" traces its origins back to Isocrates's *Antidosis* and *To Nicolcles,* as well as Aristotle's *Protepticus* in the fourth century BC, and played a part in popular moral pedagogy, philosophy, and rhetoric throughout antiquity.[17] Eventually, handbooks were written to offer practical instruction and to describe the various types of letters one could employ.[18] The letter type of most interest for our purposes is *parenesis,* defined as "a type of exhortation in which one sought to influence someone's conduct (paraineo) rather than teach something new."[19] *Parenesis* is found in Paul's pastoral letter writing as well as the early fathers of the church in the task of nurturing communities and individuals in faith.

For now, we conclude that letters were a primary—*even preeminent*—means by which a wise friend exhorted a less mature friend in the process of moral formation. Such letters were an "embodied pedagogy" that mediated one's personal presence and deepened relational bonds between the teacher and pupil. That is, letters have the power to bring two people virtually into the same room and enjoy each other's company. In Seneca's words: "I prefer that my letters should be just what my conversation would be if you and I were sitting in one another's company or taking walks together—spontaneous and easy; for my letters have nothing strained or artificial about them."[20]

Letter Writing in Paul's Pastoral Ministry

Paul's ministry was an attempt to re-embody Christ's love, wisdom and power—his very presence—in his interactions with those under his care. A primary way Paul accomplished this embodied ministry was through letter writing.[21] Thirteen books of the New Testament are letters bearing Paul's

16. Pseudo-Diogenes quoted by Stowers, *Letter Writing,* 37–38.

17. Stowers, *Letter Writing,* 91–152.

18. See e.g., Julius Victor, *The Art of Rhetoric 27 (On Letter Writing)* in Malherbe, *Ancient Epistolary Theorists,* 62ff; Pseudo Demetrius (second century BC to third century AD) lists twenty-one types of letters and Pseudo Libanius (fourth to sixth centuries AD) later expanded it to forty-one types. See Pseudo Libanius, *Epistolary Styles* in Malherbe, *Ancient Epistolary Theorists,* 67ff. See also deSilva, *Introduction to the New Testament,* 531–34, for a nice summary of epistolary types.

19. Malherbe, *Paul and the Thessalonians,* 70.

20. Seneca, *Epistle,* 75.

21. On Paul the letter writer, see Richards, *Paul and First-Century Letter Writing*; Weima, *Paul the Ancient Letter Writer*; Stirewalt, *Paul the Letter Writer*; Roetzel, *Letters of Paul*; Murphy-O'Connor, *Paul the Letter Writer*; O'Brien, "Letters, Letter Forms";

name. They don't quite fit the category of "literary letters" popular at the time (e.g., Seneca's *Epistle Morales*) which were designed for a general readership. Nor do they fit the category of "private letters" intended only for those individuals it was addressed to (e.g., papyrus letters of Egypt).[22] A. D. Nock has suggested that Paul's letters were a new type of epistle, that of the "encyclical," which became the pattern for later bishops and popes in addressing their churches.[23] For our purposes, we are not so much concerned with Paul's *letterform* as we are with his *epistolary relationships* for the purposes of pastoral care and passing on spiritual wisdom. My basic claim is that *letter writing was an invaluable pedagogical tool in Paul's pastoral toolkit,* and his letters were a powerful and personal *embodied approach* that strengthened the bond between Paul and those under his spiritual tutelage.

Do Paul's letters share the characteristics of the Greco-Roman philosophical tradition of moral exhortation examined above? Abraham J. Malherbe makes a strong argument that "Paul adopted some of the techniques of the moral philosophers when he founded the church in Thessalonica" and adapted "the convention of writing letters to continue the nurture of his converts."[24] Stowers is quick to note that Paul's "hortatory letters differed widely from that of the Epicureans and other philosophical groups" in that "Paul's focus is not on individual character but on building communities. Individuals are exhorted to have virtues and dispositions that contribute to the life of the community."[25] Likewise, while some aspects of the Greek-styled "friendly letter" do appear in Paul's writings, Paul is more focused on how to govern the church as a new kind of household.

We nevertheless find Paul doing the pastoral work of *paraenesis*—admonishing, instructing, encouraging, rebuking and nurturing individuals within a community—by way of a very active pastoral pen.[26] Stowers notes that similar to the paraenetic letters of the moral philosophers, "In the pastoral epistles . . . Paul becomes a model of the bold but gentle teacher

---

Richards, *Secretaries in the Letters of Paul.*

22. For a helpful introduction, see Polhill, *Paul and His Letters,* 120–33.

23. Nock, *St. Paul,* 146.

24. Malherbe, *Paul and the Thessalonians,* 69, is the clearest argument for Paul and a "The Philosophical Tradition of Pastoral Care" shaped, in part, by Paul's Greco-Roman milieu. For Paul's use of letters in this task, see 68–78.

25. Stowers, *Letter Writing,* 42.

26. Malherbe says this of 1 Thessalonians: "The style in which Paul writes his friendly letter is that of paraenesis, which assumed a friendly relationship. The Paul who writes this letter is not an apostle who makes demands of his converts (2:6), but a nursing mother (2:7), father (2:11), and orphan (2:17), who always has the well-being of the Thessalonians at heart" (*Paul and the Thessalonians,* 73).

and community builder, as he exhorts Timothy and Titus to the same behavior."[27] And again, one cannot read his letters without experiencing Paul's personality, his temperament, the deep passions of his shepherd's heart and his unrelenting desire for his spiritual children to grow in Christoform wisdom in order to "become mature, attaining to the whole measure of the fullness of Christ" (Eph 4:13).

A matter of particular interest for our study is the common view that Paul's letters were a *substitute for his personal presence*,[28] and were "to be accorded weight equal to [his] physical presence."[29] This "substitute" view often insinuates that one's physical presence was much to be preferred, and a letter was an inferior next-best option.[30] More recently, however, Margaret Mitchell has argued from Paul's own comments that on certain occasions he actually preferred letters over a personal visit.[31] "The letter (and envoys, in some cases) was not an inadequate substitute for the more desirable Pauline physical presence," she asserts, "but was in fact deemed by him a superior way to deal with a given situation."[32] Likewise, Richards states, "While Paul may have initially turned to letters to meet the practical needs of his situation, the extensive length and development of themes indicate that Paul saw enormous benefit in sending letters."[33]

I suggest that Paul's letter-writing ministry from a distance should be seen as working symbiotically with his ministry up-close in the flesh. Paul often writes in order to set the stage for a forthcoming personal visit. For example, in the case of his strained relationship with the Corinthians, he opts for an emotionally sensitive pastoral letter instead of a personal visit—apparently to let things simmer and give the Corinthians a chance to reassess their relationship with Paul:

27. Stowers, *Letter Writing*, 43.

28. Malherbe, *Paul and the Thessalonians*, 69: "A substitute for one's presence, a letter was expected to contain what one would have said had one been present and to say it in a style appropriate to the occasion."

29. W. G. Doty quoted by P. T. O'Brien in *Dictionary of Paul and His Letters*, 552; cf. Doty, *Letters in Primitive Christianity*. See the classic study by Funk, "Apostolic *Parousia*: Form and Significance," 249–68.

30. Cf. Richards, *Paul and First-Century Letter Writing*, 16: "It was thought the Paul's first choice was to visit personally, failing that he sent a representative, such as Timothy, and only as a last resort did he send a letter."

31. See e.g. 2 Cor 2:1–4, 9; 10:8–11.

32. Mitchell, "New Testament Envoys in the Context of Greco-Roman Diplomatic and Epistolary Conventions," 641–62.

33. Richards, *Paul and First-Century Letter Writing*, 16.

So I made up my mind that *I would not make another painful visit to you.* For if I grieve you, who is left to make me glad but you whom I have grieved? *I wrote as I did, so that when I came I would not be distressed by those who should have made me rejoice.* I had confidence in all of you, that you would all share my joy. For I wrote you out of great distress and anguish of heart and with many tears, not to grieve you but to let you know the depth of my love for you . . . Another reason I wrote you was to see if you would stand the test and be obedient in everything (2 Cor 2:1–4, 9, emphasis added).

This is just one instance of many where we see a loving and, in this case, grieving pastor wisely shepherding his community through a thoughtful and pastorally sensitive letter. His "epistolary presence" is not the least bit inferior to his "apostolic presence" in terms of both relational and emotional potency. Paul himself says this much: "For some say, 'His letters are weighty and force-ful, but in person he is unimpressive and his speaking amounts to nothing.' Such people should realize that what we are in our letters when we are absent, we will be in our actions when we are present" (2 Cor 10:10–11).

This passage is illuminative in a couple ways. On the one hand, Paul is reasserting the divine origin of his apostolic authority regardless how impressive his writing or speaking may be in the eyes of the Corinthians.[34] On the other hand, this passage seems to suggest that *Paul's letter-writing ministry was, at times, even more powerful and effective than his face-to-face ministry.* If this was true of the Spirit-filled apostle and pastor *par excellence,* might it also be true of certain pastors today? Do we have pastors in churches today who, while "unimpressive" in the pulpit, might be uniquely gifted at shepherding their flocks by way of a wise and loving pen? And, if so, will our churches learn to appreciate and learn from "Writing Pastors" as much as they appreciate and learn from "Preaching Pastors"? We will come back to this shortly.

Let us now examine how the early church fathers carried forward both the apostolic letters of Paul and the Greco-Roman "Friendly Letters" of the philosophers in their work of nurturing wisdom and forming souls in the early centuries of the church.

Letter writing and the church fathers

The so-called Apostolic Fathers such as the letters of Ignatius, Polycarp, and the first letter of Clement, are primarily letters of exhortation written

34. Cf. 1 Cor 2:1–5; Gal 1:11–12.

very much after the style of Paul. They have the tone of apostolic authority and read more like "encyclicals" from a bishop than a Friendly Letter
from Cicero, Pliny, or Seneca. However, this changes dramatically with the
rise of great teachers such as Justin Martyr, Clement of Alexandria, Tatian,
Valentinus, Pantaenus, and Origen who emerge out of the Greco-Roman
philosophical schools and traditions.[35]

After Constantine we enter what Stowers calls the "golden age of
Christian letter writing" in the fourth and fifth centuries. The writers of this
age include Athanasius, Ambrose, Gregory of Nazianzus, Basil the Great,
Gregory of Nyssa, John Chrysostom, Jerome, and Augustine. To Isidore of
Pelusium alone are attributed 2,000 letters! Here we find the emergence of
a new Christian educated class whose wise leadership and ministry—writing activity chief among them—draws heavily from the classical style of the
Greco-Roman aristocracy. For writers such as Basil or Augustine, letters
once again became "a means of aesthetic expression" which "belonged to
an extremely small group of writers, who lived in a rarefied world of elite
sensitivities."[36] Stowers describes this key transition from the letter style of
the New Testament to the those of the early church fathers:

> It was the study of rhetoric which developed these sensitivi-
> ties, and it was the cultivation of these classical aesthetic in-
> terests which most distinguishes the letter writing of certain
> later Christian authors like Gregory of Nazianzus or Jerome
> from Paul or Ignatius. Beginning in the second century, the
> great models of artistic letter writing were produced by Greek
> sophists such as Dio Chrysostom, Philostratus, and Libanius.
> In style, Christian writers like Gregory and Jerome resemble
> these pagan sophists.[37]

So, in the Nicene and Post-Nicene Fathers, we witness the epistolary marriage of the styles of Seneca's *Epistulae Morales* and Paul's letters to his
churches. We see the intimacy and charm of a Seneca-Lucilius relationship
now baptized in ecclesiastical conversations about Christian doctrine and
catechesis. We see the flowering of pastoral epistolary activity as the great
sages of the early church send their teachings far and wide on the wings of
a thousand personal letters.

The many types and vast number of letters we possess from this age
is overwhelming.[38] We offer here just a small sampling of letters of a more

35. In this historical survey, I am following Stowers, *Letter Writing*, 43–47.

36. Stowers, *Letter Writing*, 34.

37. Stowers, *Letter Writing*, 34–35.

38. A nice overview is found in Stowers, *Letter Writing*, 42–47.

"pastoral nature." Eusebius describes the ministry of Dionysius, bishop of Corinth in the late second century, as one who "gave inspired service not only to those under him, but also those distant, especially through the general epistles he wrote for the churches."[39] Chrysostom possessed a golden pen as well as a golden mouth[40]—leaving us 242 letters, nearly all written during his three-year exile. Seventeen letters are addressed to Olympias, a young widow of noble birth to whom "he revealed his inner life, upon her virtues he lavished extravagant praise, which offends modern taste as fulsome flattery."[41] Among Jerome's extant letters we find descriptions of the clerical life (Letter 52) and of the monastic life (Letters 125 and 147); as well as a letter of spiritual counsel to a mother and daughter (Letter 117). Augustine has left us some 272 letters, many of which we would consider ecclesiastical treatises and theological lectures. Nebridius expresses appreciation for Augustine's pastoral letters:

> Your letters I have great pleasure in keeping as carefully as my own eyes. For they are great, not indeed in length, but in the greatness of the subjects discussed in them, and in the great ability with which the truth in regard to these subjects is demonstrated. They shall bring to my ear the voice of Christ, and the teaching of Plato and of Plotinus. To me, therefore, they shall ever be pleasant to hear, because of their eloquent style; easy to read, because of their brevity; and profitable to understand, because of the wisdom which they contain. Be at pains, therefore, to teach me everything which, to your judgment, commends itself as holy or good.[42]

In all of these letters, we see on display not only the pastoral wisdom but the personality of each writer. As Philip Schaff rightly observes:

> In a man's published writings we see the general character of his mind, and we ascertain his opinions in so far as he deemed it safe or advisable to lay these before a perhaps unsympathizing public; in his letters he reveals his whole character . . . In his familiar

39. Eusebius, *Church History* 4.23, in Maier, *Eusebius: The Church History*, 140–42, who mentions a letter to the Spartans offering "instruction in peace and unity"; to the Athenians calling them "to faith and to life in accord with the Gospel"; a letter to the Nicomedians that "contests Marcion's heresy"; to a church in Pontus on "marriage and celibacy"; and to the Romans urging them to "send contributions . . . relieving the distress of those in need."

40. The epithet Χρυσόστομος (*Chrysostomos*, anglicized as Chrysostom) means "golden-mouthed" in Greek and denotes his celebrated eloquence.

41. Schaff, *Nicene and Post-Nicene Fathers Vol. 9: Saint Chrysostom*, 15.

42. Augustine, *Letter*, 6, in Schaff, *Nicene and Post-Nicene Fathers Vol. 1*, 223.

correspondence we see the man as he is known to his intimate friends, in his times of relaxation and unstudied utterance.[43]

Perhaps the best example of the classical "Friendly Letter" being adopted and repurposed for Christian ministry is Basil of Caesarea (AD 330–379). Among his 366 extent letters, we find a wide variety that include, for example, a friendly apologetic letter to a heathen philosopher (Letter 1); a consolatory letter to the church of Neocaesarea on the death of their bishop (Letter 28); disciplinary letters rebuking lapsed monks (Letters 44 and 45) and a fallen virgin (Letter 46) with calls to repentance. But it is his heartfelt friendship letters to Gregory of Nazianzus (e.g., Letters 2, 7, 19, 47) and his correspondence with other bishops that evoke the spirit of Seneca's letters to Lucilius or Paul's letters to Timothy.

A few excerpts from Basil's letters reinforce the power of the written word to mediate one's pastoral presence to another and are a worthy model for pastoral letter writing today. He writes to Origenes celebrating their mutually enriching correspondence: "It is delightful to listen to you, and delightful to read you; and I think you give me the greater pleasure by your writings."[44] In a letter to a widow, he expresses his desire to "visit your incomparable Nobility not only in bodily presence, but also when you are absent not to fail you, but by letter to supply the want."[45] In a letter to Constantine, Basil expresses his desire to visit and enjoy a fireside conversation in person. Until then he finds satisfaction in their letters:

> But to me it is no slight thing to be permitted, if only by letter, to communicate with your reverence, and to rest tranquil in the hope of your reply. However, should the season permit, and further length of life be allowed me, and should the dearth not prevent me from undertaking the journey. . . . I may be able to fulfill my earnest wish, may find you at your own fireside, and, with abundant leisure, may take my fill of your vast treasures of wisdom.[46]

To Leontius the Sophist, he writes:

> I too do not write often to you, but not more seldom than you do to me, though many have travelled hitherward from your part of the world. If you had sent a letter by every one of them, one after

43. Philip Schaff's preface to The Letters of St. Augustine, *The Nicene and Post-Nicene Fathers Vol. 1*, 211.

44. Basil, *Letter*, 17.

45. Basil, *Letter*, 297.

46. Basil, *Letter*, 27.

the other, there would have been nothing to prevent my *seeming to be actually in your company*, and enjoying it as though we had been together, so uninterrupted has been the stream of arrivals. But why do you not write?[47]

In his letter to Bishop Meletius of Antioch, Basil testifies to the power of being ministered to through letters—even a short one—from other bishops:

> If your holiness only knew the greatness of the happiness you cause me whenever you write to me, I know that you would never have let slip any opportunity of sending me a letter; nay, you would have written me many letters on each occasion . . . Everything here is still in a very painful condition, and the thought of your holiness is the only thing that recalls me from my own troubles; a thought made more distinct to me by my communication with you through that letter of yours which is so full of wisdom and grace. When, therefore, I take your letter into my hand, first of all, I look at its size, and I love it all the more for being so big; then, as I read it, I rejoice over every word I find in it; as I draw near the end I begin to feel sad; so good is every word that I read, in what you write.[48]

Likewise, he praises Bishop Innocentius for his ability to wrap his fatherly arms around a church in need and refresh their souls by way of a letter:

> Whom, indeed, could it better befit to encourage the timid, and rouse the slumbering, than you, my godly lord . . . For you have condescended to minister to us your spiritual gladness, to refresh our souls by your honored letter, and, as it were, *to fling the arms of your greatness round the infancy of children.*[49]

These excerpts wonderfully capture the ministry potential of pastoral letters. With some prayerful strokes of the pen or heart-felt clicks on a keyboard, a pastor can encourage the timid, rouse the slumbering, share one's spiritual joy, and refresh weary souls. Instead of flinging an impersonal sermon out over a nameless crowd each Sunday, a personal letter to the right person at the right time can fling a shepherd's arms around a wounded or wandering sheep, refreshing their soul. A sermon speaks a general word to the masses, while a pastoral letter becomes a personalized sermon directed at a single soul in need.

47. Basil, *Letter*, 20.

48. Basil, *Letter*, 57.

49. Basil, *Letter*, 50.

Having surveyed the ancient epistolary practice of the Greco-Roman world, the New Testament world of Paul, and the early Church Fathers, we conclude that pastoral letter writing has been a longstanding effective *embodied pedagogy*, a means by which wise spiritual guides have engaged others in personal conversations for the purpose of spiritual nurture, moral exhortation, church catechesis, and fostering a deeper teacher-learner relationship. We now turn to application and implementation today.

Pastoral Letter Writing for Ministry Today

The question lingering in the patient reader's mind up until now is: How can an archaic practice of a bygone era be useful for pastoral ministry in our rapidly changing Digital Age? Should pastors ditch their Twitter accounts, shut down their blogs, log off of Facebook and start using fountain pens and licking stamps instead of sending emails? Moreover, if the primary aim of this study is to foster more *relational* approaches to ministry, hasn't the Digital Age provided us with more ways to connect with people than ever before?

David Bourgeois is one of many who thinks social media and increased digital connectivity provides church leaders with "unprecedented opportunities to connect with people yearning for community with others and God."[50] His book gives pastors a step-by-step guide for how to "make the most of every opportunity to extend your ministry's electronic reach and impact."[51] Other churches now have full time Social Media Pastors who are leveraging every possible online platform to expand their ministry reach.[52]

While few would argue against the importance of engaging with and utilizing technology and social media in ways that advance the gospel and enhance human relationships, others are more concerned about what is being lost in this Digital Age and the challenges that accompany it.[53] Studies are just beginning to pour in on the effects of social media on

50. From the book summary to Bourgeois, *Ministry in the Digital Age*, https://www.ivpress.com/ministry-in-the-digital-age. He states his modus operandi simply: "The Internet is the greatest communication technology ever invented by man, and it is imperative that those who follow Christ understand how to use it well."

51. Bourgeois, *Ministry in the Digital Age*.

52. See, e.g., Smith, *Social Media Guide for Ministry*, who is the Social Media Pastor at Community Bible Church in San Antonio, TX, where he helped to launch the CBC Online community that has grown to over 10,000 in weekly online worship attendance. CBC Online has also launched Online LifeGroups and boasts of an active Facebook community of over 190,000 people from all over the world.

53. See, e.g., Crouch, *Tech-Wise Family*.

the first generation to "grow up online."[54] My claim for the purposes of this study is that *while digital media has allowed us to be connected with more people more often, the quality and depth of our interactions is steadily diminishing.* The most connected people in the history of the human race are also proving to be some of the most lonely and isolated.[55] Our days are filled with a continuous stream of emoji-laden text messages and hurried "Just-give-me-the-facts" emails that sound tinny compared with the time-consuming, heart-throbbing, wisdom-dispensing correspondences of bygone eras.[56] Do we realize what we are losing with the diminishment of personal letters?[57] Simon Garfield does:

> The world once used to run upon their transmission—the lubricant of human interaction and the freefall of ideas, the silent conduit of the worthy and the incidental, the time we were coming for dinner, the account of our marvelous day, the weightiest joys and sorrows of love. It must have seemed impossible that their worth would ever be taken for granted or swept aside. A world without letters would surely be a world without oxygen . . . .The recent decline in letter writing marks a cultural shift so vast that in the future historians may divide time not between

54. For two recent studies, see Reinke, *12 Ways Your Phone Is Changing You*; Koch, *Screens And Teens*.

55. See Rhitu Chatterjee, "Americans Are A Lonely Lot, And Young People Bear The Heaviest Burden," *NPR*, May 1, 2018, www.npr.org/sections/health-shots/2018/05/01/606588504/americans-are-a-lonely-lot-and-young-people-bear-the-heaviest-burdeno; Barna Study, "U.S. Adults Have Few Friends—and They're Mostly Alike," *Barna*, October 23, 2018, https://www.barna.com/research/friends-loneliness/.

56. While our focus has been ancient letters, some other famous letter correspondences through the ages include Abelard and Heloise, Ernest Hemingway, Virginia Woolf, William Cowper, Georgia O 'Keeffe and Alfred Stieglitz, C. S. Lewis, F. Scott Fitzgerald. For two recent great collections, see Peterson and Peterson, *Letters to a Young Pastor*; Nouwen, *Love, Henri*. For an endearing novel built on fictional letters from an elderly pastor to his son, see Robinson, *Gilead*. Lewis fans must read Lewis, *Letters to an American Lady*; see also Joel S. Woodruff, "C.S. Lewis's Humble and Thoughtful Gift of Letter Writing," *C. S. Lewis Institute: Knowing and Doing*, August 27, 2013, https://www.cslewisinstitute.org/CS_Lewis_Humble_and_Thoughtful_Gift_of_Letter_Writing_page1.

57. This technological shift and decline in letter writing began long ago as attested by Thomas Handford's lament in 1890: "Letter writing is fast becoming one of the lost arts. The means of rapid communication, and more frequent personal intercourse, have increased almost miraculously during the present century. The railway, the steamship, the telegraph and the telephone, the science of photography and that most wonderful instrument the type-writer, are all helping to crowd letter writing out of the ordinary occupations of life" (Handford, *Complete Letter Writer*, 17).

BC and AD but between the eras when people wrote letters and when they did not.[58]

Garfield's book, *To the Letter: A Journey Through A Vanishing World*, attempts to recover the lost art of letter writing today in order to "create a form of expression, emotion, and tactile delight we may clasp to our heart."[59] I suggest pastors do the same by supplementing their preaching, blogging, tweeting, and the daily ministry routine with the practice of thoughtful pastoral letter writing. Whether it be handwritten letters or a more thoughtful emails, this one relatively simple way for shepherds to bless their people with a tangible "expression, emotion and tactile delight"—something they can "clasp to [their] heart" and carry with them longer than the memory of the latest sermon.

Pastors are equally at risk of letting more efficient forms of connectivity diminish the personal nature and quality of our ministry. Pastors can now broadcast their thoughts all week long through a sermon podcast, blog, and Twitter; but are they *personally* engaging individuals in wise and meaningful ways? Consider the pastoral implications of podcasting "disembodied" sermons to a nameless, faceless mass of people "out there" who lack any relationship with a pastor.[60] A megachurch pastor may have 50,000+ people downloading their sermons each week, but has he even met more than a handful of these faceless and nameless congregants? Many of these people, to echo Jesus, are "lost and confused"—like podcast subscribers without a pastor. They are being "fed" content but are they truly known? They are being informed, but are they being transformed? Letters hold powerful potential to bridge this relational and formational gap.[61]

58. From the introduction to Simon Garfield, *To the Letter: A Journey Through A Vanishing World* (New York: Gotham, 2013), available online: https://www.simongarfield.com/books/to-the-letter/.

59. From the book summary "To the Letter: A Celebration of the Lost Art of Letter Writing," https://www.goodreads.com/book/show/17415171-to-the-letter. On recovering the art today, see e.g., Benke, *Write Back Soon! Adventures in Letter Writing*; O'Shea, *For the Love of Letters*.

60. Mercer Schuchardt asserts that "Disembodying the message and the congregation keeps pastors from plausibly promoting the embodied message of our embodied Lord and Savior Jesus Christ. By podcasting the content of the sermon, churches unwittingly promote the same cultural gnosticism of digital media's disembodied form that is itself a primary driver of declining church attendance." See Mercer Schuchardt, "How Podcasting Hurts Preaching," https://www.christianitytoday.com/ct/2018/january-web-only/podcasting-hurts-preaching-sermon-podcasts-pastors.html.

61. British novelist and literary critic E. M. Forster says, "Letters have to pass two tests before they can be classified as good: they must express the personality both of the writer and the recipient." Quoted in Benke, *Write Back Soon!*, 6.

In one of his last interviews, Eugene Peterson offered this sage advice to young pastors: "I don't think you can help anyone live a congruent life without knowing their name. How can you be personally involved in someone's life and not know who their children are, who their spouses are, or the trials they go through every day? It just doesn't work." Before we protest that this is only possible for small town-and-country congregations, Peterson says, "If you're content to stay with one congregation for a while, you could have a congregation of four, five, six hundred, and still know everyone. I had a congregation of 600, and I knew everybody's name."[62] Whether pastoring a church of 50 or 5,000, one way to begin engaging more of your people by name is through the wisdom of pastoral letter writing.

The Benefits and Suitability of Letter Writing for Pastors

As we move toward implementing this method for today, let me offer some practical benefits of pastoral letter writing. For many reasons, pastoral letter writing is a natural extension of already existing ministry and most pastors already developed the necessary skills to thrive in it. First, pastors are already trained in the "word business," as Eugene Peterson calls it. Like poets, pastors are "caretakers of language, the shepherds of words, keeping them from harm, exploitation, misuse."[63] What better way to ply the art of "word work"[64] than through personal letters?

Second, letters have an enduring quality that sermons and face-to-face conversations lack. I may put 20 or 30 hours into a sermon that most of my people won't recall two days later. On the other hand, a congregant recently told me she came across an email I sent her 6 years ago, and how much the words ministered to her again a second time. (And I spent less than an hour on it.) Likewise, while face-to-face spiritual conversations over coffee are ideal, they can lack the permanent quality of a written exchange that one can print out, tuck into their Bible, and return to again and again.

Third, like many pastors I am not always the most articulate and insightful when offering pastoral wisdom in passing or in off-the-cuff conversations in the fellowship hall after the service. My counsel is typically more thoughtful

---

62. Drew Dyck, "Eugene Peterson Wanted to Know Your Name," https://www.christianitytoday.com/ct/2018/december/eugene-peterson-wanted-know-your-name.html.

63. Peterson, *Contemplative Pastor*, 155.

64. I don't recall where I heard the pastor's trade described as "word work," but it sounds like Eugene Peterson to me.

and precise if I have time to reflect, pray, and search the Scriptures for my response to a person's situation. Likewise, my pastoral *writing* tends to include more scriptural quotations than my face-to-face conversations, as citing chapter and verse is more difficult on the spot from memory.

Fourth, and very significantly, pastoral letter writing allows us to "be with" and minister to people whose busy schedules often make it difficult to meet with face to face. Like many pastors, I have spent years decrying our culture's excessive "busyness" and trying to get people to slow down and prioritize showing up for worship, small group, and other ministry gatherings. While I am not ready to give up this fight for face-to-face discipleship, why not avail ourselves of this other means of getting into another's heart and home through writing? While it often takes two or three weeks to meet up with a parishioner, I have found that even the busiest people in my church usually find time to read an email from me and will respond within a day or two (and often within the hour!). If letters have the power to bring two people together while physically apart, and if the people in our churches are run ragged from hectic schedules and too emotionally drained to "show up" (but also feeling increasingly lonely and isolated as they lie at home binging Netflix), why not sneak our way into their living room by way of an encouraging email they can ponder as their head hits the pillow?

Fifth, letter writing can be a life-giving and emotionally sustainable practice for many pastors relationally exhausted and emotionally overextended from too many meetings and long hours of ministry. Pastors often find weeknight ministry meetings competing with their own family time. Do I miss a third night in a row of tucking my kids into bed in order to meet Bill for coffee to discuss his career woes? Perhaps, this time my pastoral presence and care can be extended through an encouraging email I can send on my own schedule *after* I read my children to sleep.

Sixth, and related to the previous, pastoral letter-writing can be a muchneeded refuge and invigorating playground for introverted pastors trying to survive an extroverted church world. Adam McHugh's book *Introverts in the Church,* is itself a love letter to introverted pastors who continually wonder if there is a place in pastoral ministry for their "monastic" personality and temperament.[65] Our extroverted church age favors warm and gregarious pastoral personalities and has excelled at drawing crowds, launching ministries, and mobilizing people into action. Yet, we continually bemoan the shallow faith of many church attenders today. Perhaps the church is waiting for contemplatives and mystics, intellectuals and poets, to harness the power of the pastoral pen and get busy doing the "word work" that can foster deeper

65. McHugh, *Introverts in the Church.*

spiritual conversations with our parishioners. For this to happen, churches need to embrace the pastoral gift of "spiritual writing" as enthusiastically as it celebrates the gift of public speaking.[66] A church might even consider staffing a "Writing Pastor" who can teach and exhort people all week long through writing, with an impact equal to (or greater than) the preaching pastor through the weekly sermon that many will never hear.[67]

Finally, the burnout rate among pastors continue to be very high and one key factor is a sense of loneliness and isolation. Peter Drucker once said that the four hardest jobs in America (and not necessarily in order) are the president of the United States, a university president, a CEO of a hospital, and a pastor. Pastors as full-time professional encouragers are often starving for some encouragement themselves. The vast majority of the letters of Augustine, Basil, and others were collegial letters written from one bishop to another filled with affirmation and mutual encouragement in their shared calling and mutual burden. Pastors who struggle to get together often enough with peers would be wise to imitate their letter-writing forefathers to spur one another on in this spiritually intense and emotionally exhausting vocation.

These are just a few reasons pastoral letter writing should be recovered for more personal and embodied ministry in an age of increasingly impersonal and disembodied ministry.

---

66. Imagine for a moment that the great spiritual classics such as Augustine's *Confessions*, Bunyan's *Pilgrim's Progress*, or Thomas A' Kempis's *Imitation of Christ* never came to be because these great minds were too preoccupied with staff meetings, prepping sermons and the business of "running the church"? How many current-day would-be mystics will never pen their would-be classic for the same reason?

67. According to Dave Olson, only about 17.7 percent of Americans attend church "regularly" which is defined as 3 out of 8 Sundays. Another study discovered that 78 million Protestants who still identify with their church roots nevertheless attend less than 12 times a year. See Outreach Magazine, "7 Startling Facts: An Up Close Look at Church Attendance in America," https://churchleaders.com/pastors/pastor-articles/139575-7-startling-facts-an-up-close-look-at-church-attendance-in-america.html. See also Olson, *American Church in Crisis*. According to the Nielsen Total Audience Report, the average American adult consumes over 11 hours of media *per day* listening, watching, reading and generally engaging on social media. The average church-goer who attends and hears two 30-minute sermons a month will get just 12 hours of Christian teaching the *entire year!* See "Time Flies: U. S. Adults Now Spend Nearly Half A Day Interacting With Media," https://www.nielsen.com/us/en/insights/article/2018/time-flies-us-adults-now-spend-nearly-half-a-day-interacting-with-media/.

Conclusion: Mister Rogers Among the Sages

Awhile back I spent a couple nights of personal retreat at a nearby monastery. My walks in the woods, quiet study in the library, and other monk-like activities (or non-activity) were lovely and renewing. However, the real epiphany came when I snuck away to a movie theater one night (lest anybody mistake me for a real monk). For two hours I sat in a theater, wiping tears as I watched the Fred Rogers documentary *Won't You Be My Neighbor* (2018). Mr. Rogers wasn't revered for his ivory-tower wisdom or outspoken social critiques. Mr. Rogers wasn't known for bestselling books peddling the latest trends in child psychology. He certainly wasn't known for a loud and bombastic personality. What then explains the peerless appeal and impact of this soft-spoken and gentle educational giant?

I suggest his greatest pedagogical advantage wasn't a teaching strategy, or the content of his message (which was really quite basic), or even his groundbreaking use of the medium of television for teaching children. Rather, we were brought to tears when we heard his reassuring voice and looked into his friendly eyes, because we fell in love with *the teacher himself*. His legacy lives on in our hearts because his teaching and wisdom were so beautifully and consistently *embodied* in his life and character. He didn't just teach us; he befriended us. He didn't just give us good advice; he gave us himself. He didn't just speak words of wisdom at a screen; he spoke personal words *through* the screen that made their way deep into our shy and fragile souls. Each recorded episode had the same effect on the viewer that a warm pastoral letter can have on its intended reader.

For 31 years, Fred Rogers embodied and broadcasted the heart of Jesus' most well-known wisdom, and we never even realized he was doing it! When asked to sum up the entire faith, Jesus said, "Love God and Love your neighbor as yourself." Another man then asked Jesus, "And who is my neighbor?" Mr. Rogers answered this million-dollar question every day for children looking for a place to belong and a loving teacher they could trust. And it isn't hard to imagine these simple words on Jesus's lips as well (and the careful ear might detect subtle echoes of John's Gospel hidden throughout):

> I have always wanted to have a neighbor just like you,
> I've always wanted to live in a neighborhood with you.
> So let's make the most of this beautiful day,
> Since we're together, we might as well say,
> Would you be mine? Could you be mine?
> Won't you be my neighbor?
> Won't you please, won't you please,
> Please won't you be my neighbor?

What Mister Rogers did through the medium of television, pastors can do through heartfelt pastoral letters to souls in need of a wise and loving word from their neighborhood pastor.

It was said of John the Baptist that he "was a lamp that burned and gave light, and [others] chose for a time to enjoy his light" (John 5:35). All the red eyes walking out of theater after *Won't You Be My Neighbor* were expressing their gratitude for all the years Fred Rogers "was a lamp that burned brightly and gave light" to our world through public television. In our day of shallow connection and increasingly disembodied ministry, I urge pastors to harness the power of embodied wisdom, to put pen to paper (or fingers to keys) and, in the words of John Donne, start mingling souls through the lost art of pastoral letter writing.

> Sir, more than kisses, letters mingle souls.
> For, thus friends absent speak.
>
> —John Donne[68]

Bibliography

Benke, Karen. *Write Back Soon! Adventures in Letter Writing.* Boston: Roost, 2015.

Bourgeois, David T. *Ministry in the Digital Age: Strategies and Best Practices for a Post-Website World.* Downers Grove, IL: InterVarsity, 2013.

Crouch, Andy. *The Tech-Wise Family: Everyday Steps for Putting Technology in Its Proper Place.* Grand Rapids: Baker, 2017.

DeSilva, David A. *An Introduction to the New Testament.* Downers Grove, IL: InterVarsity, 2004.

Donne, John. *Poems of John Donne.* Vol 2. Edited by E. K. Chambers. London: Lawrence & Bullen, 1896.

Doty, W. G. *Letters in Primitive Christianity.* Philadelphia: Fortress, 1973.

Funk, R. W. "The Apostolic *Parousia*: Form and Significance." In *Christian History and Interpretation: Studies Presented to John Knox,* edited by W. R. Farmer et al. Cambridge: University Press, 1967.

Garfield, Simon. *To the Letter: A Journey Through A Vanishing World.* New York: Gotham, 2013.

Handford, Thomas W. *The Complete Letter Writer: A Comprehensive and Practical Guide and Assistant to Letter Writing.* Chicago: Donohue & Henneberry, 1890.

Koch, Kathy. *Screens And Teens: Connecting With Our Kids in a Wireless World.* Chicago: Moody, 2015.

Konstan, David. *Friendship in the Classical World.* New York: Cambridge University Press, 1997.

Lewis, C. S. *Letters to an American Lady.* Edited by Clyde Kilby. Grand Rapids: Eerdmans, 1967.

Maier, Paul L. *Eusebius: The Church History.* Grand Rapids: Kregel, 2007.

Malherbe, Abraham J. *Ancient Epistolary Theorists.* Atlanta: Scholars, 1988.

---

68. Donne, *Poems of John Donne,* 7–9.

———. *Moral Exhortation, A Greco-Roman Sourcebook*. Philadelphia: Westminster, 1986).

———. *Paul and the Thessalonians: The Philosophic Tradition of Pastoral Care*. Eugene, OR: Wipf & Stock, 1987.

McHugh, Adam. *Introverts in the Church: Finding Our Place in an Extroverted Culture*. Rev. ed. Grand Rapids: InterVarsity, 2017.

McKnight, Scot. *Pastor Paul: Nurturing a Culture of Christoformity in the Church*. Grand Rapids: Brazos, 2019.

Meeks, Wayne A. *The Moral World of the First Christians*. Philadelphia: Westminster, 1986.

Mitchell, Margaret. "New Testament Envoys in the Context of Greco-Roman Diplomatic and Epistolary Conventions: the Example of Timothy and Titus." *JBL* 111 (1992) 641–62.

Murphy-O'Connor, Jerome. *Paul the Letter Writer*. Collegeville, MN: Liturgical, 1995.

Nock, A. D. *St. Paul*. New York: Harper & Brothers, 1937.

Nouwen, Henri J. M. *Love, Henri: Letters on the Spiritual Life*. New York: Convergent, 2016.

O'Brien, P. T. "Letters, Letter Forms." In *Dictionary of Paul and His Letters*, edited by Gerald Hawthorne et al., 550–53. Downers Grove, IL: InterVarsity, 1993.

Olson, David T. *The American Church in Crisis: Groundbreaking Research Based on a National Database of over 200,000 Churches*. Grand Rapids: Zondervan, 2008.

O'Shea, Samara. *For the Love of Letters: A 21st Century Guide to The Art of Letter Writing*. New York: HarperCollins, 2007.

Peterson, Eugene. *The Contemplative Pastor: Returning to the Art of Spiritual Direction*. Grand Rapids: Eerdmans,1989.

Peterson, Eugene H., and Eric E. Peterson. *Letters to a Young Pastor: Timothy Conversations Between Father and Son*. Colorado Springs: NavPress, 2020.

Polhill, John B. *Paul and His Letters*. Nashville: Broadman & Holman, 1999.

Reinke, Tony. *12 Ways Your Phone Is Changing You*. Wheaton: Crossway, 2017.

Richards, E. Randolph. *Paul and First-Century Letter Writing*. Downers Grove, IL: InterVarsity, 2004.

———. *The Secretaries in the Letters of Paul*. Tubingen: Mohr, 1991.

Robinson, Marilynne. *Gilead: A Novel*. New York: Farrar, Straus and Giroux, 2004.

Roetzel, Calvin J. *The Letters of Paul: Conversations in Context*. 6th ed. Louisville: Westminster John Knox, 2015.

Schaff, Philip, ed. The Letters of Basil, Gregory Nazianzus, Augustine, and Chrysostom. In *The Nicene and Post-Nicene Fathers*. Peabody, MA: Hendrickson, 2012.

———. *The Nicene and Post-Nicene Fathers Vol. 1*. Grand Rapids: Eerdmans, 1956.

———. *The Nicene and Post-Nicene Fathers Vol. 9*. Grand Rapids: Eerdmans, 1956.

Seneca. *Epistles*, Volumes 1–3. Translated by Richard M. Gummere. Loeb Classical Library. Cambridge, MA: Harvard University Press, 1917–1925.

Smith, Nils. *Social Media Guide for Ministry*. Loveland: Group, 2013.

Stirewalt, M. Luther, Jr. *Paul the Letter Writer*. Grand Rapids: Eerdmans, 2003.

Stowers, Stanley K. *Letter Writing in Greco-Roman Antiquity*. Philadelphia: Westminster Press, 1986.

Weima, Jeffrey A. D. *Paul the Ancient Letter Writer*. Grand Rapids: Baker, 2016.

Wright, N. T. "The New Creation." In *The Crown and the Fire: Meditations on the Cross and the Life of the Spirit*. Rev. ed. Grand Rapids: Eerdmans, 2014.

WISDOM IN THE WORKPLACE

By William D. Shiell

C hristians work, worship, and train from home now more than ever. Before COVID-19, most workers commuted to offices. During the pandemic, however, most workplaces have begun to resemble the dynamics of a first-century home: an integrated family, work, and worship space. Without Facebook live, Zoom, and YouTube, ancient households shared religion, the marketplace, and family relationships.[1] Depending on their social status, an ancient household was an extended network of biological relatives, renters, and household slaves.[2] What better place, then, to learn wisdom for the workplace than from them?

An ancient household, however, was not an exemplary institution by any means. Despite their integrated lives, women, children, and slaves were often subject to abuse and scorn from others. With a few rare exceptions, most slaves were considered evil and treated unfairly.

The book of Colossians, however, provides a counter-cultural example to first-century norms and the earliest evidence of a "code of conduct" in a household of Christ-followers. In Colossae, slaves trained others to work and live wisely together under a new Master—Jesus Christ. Two slaves, Tychicus and Onesimus, delivered a message about wisdom from Paul to early believers.[3] After they read the epistle to the audience, they delivered Colossians throughout the Lycus Valley, including to a house church led by a woman named Nympha.

The content and function of Colossians remain a matter of debate even today. Especially in an era where racism, injustice, and women's abuse

---

1. Talbert, "Are There Biblical Norms for Christian Marriage?," 24.

2. Oakes, *Reading Romans in Pompeii*, 80–88.

3. For an overview of authorship, see McKnight, *Letter to the Colossians*, 5–6. In this chapter, I'm less concerned about who "wrote" Colossians and more interested in who delivered and listened to the epistle.

are at the forefront of our minds, Colossians' household code provides a provocative example of workplace culture. The purpose of this chapter is not to condone or advocate for ancient family structures or slavery.[4] We can no easier use Colossians in the human resource department any more than we could use Lewis and Clark's first maps of Colorado to find Denver. We can, however, engage the epistle in its context and listen to these instructions as a working household where Christ dwells. These early Christians live into the tension of workplace relationships, knowing that Christ had liberated slaves. Colossians provides wisdom for Christians working in a society that perpetuates injustice, even those who work for Christians who own businesses, work in churches, or serve in Christian institutions. Christians who are especially engaged in the faith at work movement will find Colossians to be a timely resource today.[5]

To immerse ourselves in their world, we will study Col 3:16—4:6 as an oral performance to household believers. For this chapter, a "performance" is an event that includes oral reading, listening, feedback, response, and extemporaneous communication. The "household" is often called the *oikonomia* in the New Testament, from which we get our word "economy." It is the network of family and business relationships that lived and worked together in an ancient villa, farm, or estate gathering to hear Colossians read to them. The first listeners in the Lycus Valley heard this epistle read by slaves to people who followed Jesus as Lord and lived and worked with each other.

When I was a pastor I generally avoided this section. The language of submission and slavery, similar to a parallel passage in Eph 5:22—6:9, can be mistreated by pastor and listener alike. This chapter reframes this passage in light of workplace culture as a small ancient family business, not from the perspective of an American nuclear family that rarely sees each other and spends most of their time together in a mini-van. By listening to Col 3:16—4:6, we can discover how early Christians worked within even worse conditions than our own to spread a wise message. They lived in a society that did not worship Jesus Christ as Lord and worked within households and businesses that did not yet fulfill Paul's vision in Gal 3:27–28 or Col 3:11. Instead of overthrowing or subverting the dominant system of ancient households, we will discover that Colossae's Christ-followers leveraged the system to live differently, address injustices, and buy time for Christ to address evil and wrongdoing. As slaves communicated the message, the household became a platform to bind the church, encourage the

---

4. Martin, "Haustafeln (Household Codes) in African American Biblical Interpretation," 213.

5. Joyce and Forster, *Economic Wisdom for Churches* as well as the resources at https://oikonomianetwork.org/.

group, teach a wise lifestyle in the Lycus Valley, and train earthly masters to follow a risen Master.

Performing Wisdom in Ancient Households

Before we address Colossians, we will look at the conventional mindset about a wise household in the Colossian world. Then we will turn to the perception and role of slaves in this environment. We turn now to some details for historical context, given here without much discussion.

Household Teaching and Performances

In Greco-Roman, Hellenistic Jewish, and Qumran communities, the household transmitted and preserved societal wisdom. Society regarded the master of the house based on his management of the household (Quintilian, *Inst.* 10.2.18–20; Cicero, *Brut.* 22.87; Nepos, *Atticus* 25.13–14; Seneca, *Ep.* 15.6).[6] If a household behaved wisely, the state and religion could be stable, and the household would benefit (Artistotle, *Rhet.* 2.12–17; Dionysisus, *Ant. Rom.,* 2.8–9; Cicero, *De Or.* 1.11.48–49; Josephus, *Apion* 2.31, 2.215; *Life* 8–12; *Let. Arist.* 287).

People passed wisdom along from one generation to the next through a combination of formal education, oral performances, religious rituals, and on-the-job training while working. Formal teaching and instruction in wisdom fell to parents and private instructors, who were often slaves in the household (Pseudo Plutarch, *De Lib. Educ.* 10). Slaves could be educated, and they were also educators; but ironically, society rarely sought slaves for advice or wisdom. A slave was a *paidagōgos,* overseeing upper-class boys as they went to rhetorical schools. Children regarded their pedagogue affectionately, but most people were suspicious of their character.[7]

Formal training in oral reading followed the conventions of ancient rhetorical schools. For instance, one convention of oral delivery students practiced, which we will see in Colossians, is inflection. Orators learned to read and speak by changing the case of nouns and verbs in a story. In performance, the technique entertained an audience and drew attention to a story's theme or main character (Theon, *Progymnasmata* 101–103; *Rhet. Her.* 4.21.29–4.23.32).[8]

---

6. Shiell, *Reading Acts,* 31.

7. Young, "Figure of the *Paidagogos* in Art and Literature," 65.

8. Reich, *Figuring Jesus,* 35–66.

Families cultivated wisdom and harmony by singing, dancing, and performing poetry for religious and entertainment purposes (Prov 10:18—11:31 LXX; Plato, *Leg.* 7.816C–7.817E; Cicero, *De Off.* 3.15.63). The performer helped hold the group accountable to a philosopher or religious figure's message. In religious settings the audience mutually agreed to follow the instructions like a covenant. Audiences participated through listening, response, feedback, and extemporaneous comments. In the case of wise instruction, these performances carried additional weight because they were often associated with religious devotion and connection to order in society. A performance on the theme of wisdom gave someone contact with the gods (Wis. 6:17–20; Philo, *Contempl.* 3.25; Cicero, *Tusc.* 1.27.66). The soul retained memories, and the performances "sprang to birth" what was already inside the person (Cicero, *De Or.* 2.87–356).

Households hosted events that validated the reader's status and demonstrated their allegiance to the reader or the topic that the reader addressed (Pliny, *Ep.* 1.3.4; 2.10.4; 5.5; 5.8.7). If the author was absent, ironically, slaves read the text aloud to the audience. The performance closed the gap between the sender and the recipient, creating a virtual connection between them. By listening to sacred texts together, they created a love of learning, engendered a love for the other persons in the group, and inspired them to transform their character (Arian, *Epict. diss.* 3.23.3.23.1–32; 4 Macc 5:22–30; 7:31–34; 13:22–26 LXX).

Household Conduct

In addition to formal training from a slave or school, the household business provided "on the job training" for a wise life. Ancient household codes of conduct that date back to Aristotle were well known in the first century AD. These codes described and prescribed. They named what was typical for society and provided an "employee handbook" for farms and business management. The Greeks and Romans perpetuated the Aristotelian view that each person submitted to another person's authority in pairs: husband to state, wife to husband, children to parents, slave to master. For Romans, the husband's authority in a household maintained state stability (Aristotle, *Pol.* 1.1253a–1.1253b).[9] Wives, and presumably everyone else in the household, worshiped the same gods as their husbands (Dionysius of Halicarnassus, *Rom. Ant.* 2.25.2). Persons cultivated wisdom through harmony in household work and family responsibilities. They formed strong marital bonds, cared

9. Balch, *Let Wives Be Submissive.*

for their children, and behaved morally, fearing the gods (Xenophon, *Mem.* 4.4.18–24; Plato *Leg.* 3.689C–690D; 6.771E–7.824C).

Stoic philosophy and Hellenistic Judaism, both prevalent in Colossae, shared these views and adapted them for their households.[10] Stoics tied wise and virtuous living to status and rank. The lower one's place, the more foolish, weak-minded, and prone to misbehavior the person was (Diogenes Laertius, *Lives* 122–123; Dio Chrysostom, *Discourse* 4.80; 69.2). For the privileged males, the study of philosophy played an important role in developing wisdom culture. One specific sign of wisdom was how a child related to his father or a worker related to his work. Each person knew one's role in society and related to others in light of their family bonds. In other words, no one ever broke the bonds of family or work relationships. Once a son, always a son; once a carpenter, always a carpenter. Each person had a duty to remain responsible and stay in their social place (Epictetus, *Diss.* 2.14.6–10; 2.10.1–23; 2.17.31).

A wise person exhibited several virtues: courage, practical wisdom, good counsel, temperance, justice, order, constancy, equality, and fair-mindedness. They performed religious duties and sacrificed to the gods. They suppressed public displays of grief because grief was evidence of a divided soul (Diogenes Laertius, *Lives* 119).

Hellenistic Jews shared the structure of the household codes but adapted them for their purposes. The foundation of the household code was built on the fifth commandment from Exodus. Parents were co-creators and mediators between children and God, and the order of the household revolved around honoring one's parents. Adherence to the law was evidence of wise living (Josephus, *Ap.* 2.31, 215). Except for the Qumran community, Jews in the first century widely viewed the temple as the primary source of wisdom (Sir 24:7–11; 51:13–14).[11] This sentiment caused concern among Romans that the Jews were sending money to Jerusalem instead of Rome and "despised the gods." (Tacitus, *Hist.* 4.1–5.5).

The Qumran community, which dismissed the temple, turned to their ascetic lifestyle for wisdom.[12] Their ascetic views echoed similar sentiments that the Colossians faced.[13] They taught gratitude toward God's provisions and respect for those within the household. Although relatively few women were present at Qumran, evidence from Cave 4 suggested that Qumran's men bonded with their wives who were disciples as an example to others,

10. Crouch, *Origin and Intention of the Colossian Haustafel*, 102–19.

11. Hayward, "Sirach and Wisdom's Dwelling Place," 33.

12. Wold, "Family Ethics in 4QInstruction and the New Testament," 292–93.

13. Yamauchi, "Qumran and Colosse," 143–44.

and they honored their parents with their poverty. The same carried over in the marketplace. A wise man was honorable in his commerce and wise and discerning in the marketplace so he was not cheated (4Q418 Frags. 167 a–b).[14] Unlike Cicero, they did not see the accumulation of wealth as an essential part of the household; instead, they intentionally remained poor to demonstrate wisdom.

Slaves as Devious Messengers

Despite their service as educators, the culture mistreated slaves. As we have noted, because rank and status determine one's nature and sagacity, most people dismissed a slave's advice and viewed them suspiciously. A household slave either lived above the shop entrance facing the street and its well-known night time noise, or in the back of the house in cramped quarters.[15] For instance, Cicero's speech *Against Piso* is an example of the physiognomic prejudice against slaves. In this speech, he railed against someone who was elected consul by critiquing his face, voice, and mouth because he looked and acted like a slave (Cicero, *Against Piso* 1.1–10).[16] Jews wanted to treat slaves fairly, but they left slaves on the bottom of the hierarchy, and like Diogenes Laertius, they did not regard slaves as wise people (Philo, *Spec. Leg.* 2.13.48; 2.39.226–227; *Hyp.* 7.1–9; *Dec.* 165–167; and *Spec. Leg.* 2.13.48).

There were a few notable exceptions in the ancient world, especially among Stoics and Hellenistic Jews. Seneca mentioned the treatment of slaves and the role philosophy played in teaching appropriate conduct toward them (*Epistle* 94.1). He advised treating slaves well and even urged masters to plan with their slaves, help them attain honors, and pronounce judgment (*Epistle* 47; Ps. Plutarch, *De Lib. Educ.* 10). Pseudo-Phocylides advised households to treat slaves fairly and to "accept advice from a judicious slave" (227; Prov. 30:10 LXX). This scant evidence from Stoicism and Hellenistic Judaism were the exceptions that proved the rule. Slaves were useful to an extent but foolish because of their status. The only motivation to treat slaves fairly would be to appear wise in the community and to leave a legacy of wisdom to their households.

14. Wise et al., *Dead Sea Scrolls*, 488–89.

15. Oakes, *Reading Romans in Pompeii*, 12, 39.

16. Suggested by Harrill, *Slaves in the New Testament*, 46–47.

Library as Expression of Wisdom

To get a sense of the perception of wisdom, simply walk down the road from Colossae approximately 100 miles to the remains of Celsus's library and funerary monument in Ephesus. Completed no later than AD 150, Celsus's library remains a testament to wisdom's importance in one's life and legacy. Built by his son, Tiberius Iulius "Aquila" Polmaeanus in memory of his father's life, and later completed after Aquila's death by Tiberius Claudius "Aristion," the library rises 17 meters high and extends 21 meters wide above seven steps. On the façade are four life-size marble statues on marble pedestals depicting the virtues Celsus aspired to *sophia*/wisdom, *arête*/diligence, *ennoia*/understanding, and *episteme*/erudition. Each one would have originally been cast in bronze and depicted the main character in costume. In this case, likely, Sophia would have featured Celsus dressed as a philosopher. In the sixth century, locals replaced them with marble statues of women (see Fig. 1). Wisdom/*sophia* is depicted as a woman with a toga similar to a philosopher's attire but without the iconographic beard of the male wise sage. Three of the statues were for Celsus, and one was for Aquila, the son and benefactor. The Sophia statue is on the south side and just to the left of the main entrance. Above is an inscription dedicating the library to Celsus as a gift from his son Aquila. The statue's prominence illustrates the significance of wisdom in Asia Minor. People would have traveled to see the library in Ephesus, and remembered Celsus as an example of wise living for his generation.[17]

17. Strocka, "Celsus Library in Ephesus," 41–42.

Figure 1. Statue of Sophia. Library of Celsus. From http://www.my-favourite
-planet.de/english/middle-east/turkey/ephesus/ephesus-gallery-1-031.html.

To summarize, in a world where households valued wisdom, slaves
delivered the message but were not trusted with the message. They were
part of a natural hierarchy that preserved their status as slaves and kept the
state stable. The household connected family, work, and worship. In this
place, families taught and transmitted wisdom as part of their civic duty to
preserve society's order. People viewed the master-father as the primary ex-
emplar and breadwinner for their work, family, and religious duties. Upon
death, people honored persons who lived wisely.

Wisdom at Work in a Colossian Household

With this background, we can better understand the mindset of wisdom
in an average Colossian household. The people that figure prominently in
communicating Christ's wisdom in a household are the slaves Tychicus, addressed as a "slave in the Lord," and Onesimus, likely the same one from
the book of Philemon, who is now called "faithful and beloved brother."
These messengers likely read the letter to the Colossians and delivered the

SHIELL—WISDOM IN THE WORKPLACE

epistle to others in the Lycus Valley.[18] But unlike their Greco-Roman and Hellenistic Jewish counterparts, these slaves exemplify the kind of wisdom that persons should aspire to. They function with the same authority as the sender and substitute for Paul's presence. To begin our study, we should listen to the text with these performers in mind as if we were overhearing their delivery in a Colossian household. We start at the end of Colossians to learn some important interpretative clues.[19]

Slaves as Encouragers and Models (4:8–9)

Tychicus and Onesimus join with their fellow "slave in the Lord" Epaphras (1:7; 4:12). They inform the household about Paul's condition, "encourage their hearts," and report everything (4:8, 9). They likely deliver the epistle to the Laodiceans (4:16). Tychicus and Onesimus play important roles. They represent Paul's presence and authority, closing the gap between the sender and the recipient. They possibly read the letter to the recipients but certainly provide additional details, answer questions, and extemporaneously address the audience.

As slaves, the rhetorical effect of their presence and the language they use would likely have had a profound impact on a household where Christ dwells. Their example is a stark contrast to a society that scorned slaves. They are living examples of how the early church lived into the tension between slaves freed in Christ and slaves still subject to earthly masters. They treat them as honorable messengers of apostles. Tychicus and Onesimus arrive to encourage, model, and entertain. They do not come to defend or evangelize. For most who largely dismiss slaves as property or "bad men" (Diogenes Laertius) and associate them with evil, Paul treats Tychicus and Onesimus as coworkers. They fit the expectations of someone familiar with Seneca or Pseudo-Phocylides and so treat slaves fairly and seek their counsel and advice. They are also the "slave teachers" familiar to children who grew up in Greco-Roman households or had a *paidagogos* at home (1 Cor 4:14–21).[20] From this perspective, then, we can hear the words of Colossians with the Colossians. Those on the bottom of the social strata in the ancient world are now admonishing, advising, training, and helping

18. Oestreich, *Performance Criticism of the Pauline*, 77–79.

19. Suggested by McKnight, *Reading Romans Backwards*, 10–11. Just as Phoebe delivered Romans, so Tychicus and Onesimus's delivery can affect interpretation of Colossians.

20. Garland, *Colossians and Philemon*, 247.

the church discern how to live, work, worship, and engage the community. They have Paul's "apostolic presence."[21]

Household Wisdom (1:1—3:15)

Wisdom (*sophia* in Greek) figures prominently in their delivery of Colossians to the household. In performance, Tychicus and Onesimus are part of the "we" who pray for the Colossians with all wisdom (1:9) and proclaim Christ, teaching others with all wisdom (1:28). If Paul and Timothy are examples, so are also Tychicus and Onesimus visual and verbal expressions of Christ's wisdom in their midst. They likely sing or chant the Christ hymn as part of the performance (1:15–20).

The risen Christ is the source of all wisdom (2:3), and they urge the Colossians to continue to live and build up their lives in him. Tychicus and Onesimus deliver instructions for households who have "received Christ Jesus the Lord/Master," to "continue to live your lives in him, rooted and built up in and established in the faith, just as you were taught, abounding in thanksgiving" (2:6–7). For those caught up in worshiping the creation more than the creator and fearful of the "elements," Christ provides life, forgiveness, and victory (2:13–15).[22] The same Christ, who is the image of the invisible God, creates the world, reigns over the world, reconciles all things to himself, and is now dwelling in Tychicus, Onesimus, and the Colossians. His death, resurrection, and conquest erase the status and rank of barbarian, slave, Scythian, Jew, and Greek (3:11). "Christ is all and in all."

How then does this Christ-dwelling wisdom become a part of the lives of the Colossians? They use the platform of the work, worship, and interactions inside and outside the household. The Colossians need to listen to wise teaching and train for a new mindset (1:9–10). They learn about their orientation to Christ and each other in order to root their lives in Christ (2:6–7). When heard this way, the household code is part of the *probatio* or "how to" section (3:1—4:6). A household's worship, work, and family relationships strengthen their faith and encourage each other. The listeners would have likely heard this text as encouragement and instructions. They would not have used Colossians evangelistically or apologetically as a defense of their faith to outsiders. Rather, Colossians helps them work with each other and prepare to encounter outsiders in the marketplace.

---

21. Botha, "Verbal Art of the Pauline Letters," 21.
22. Talbert, *Ephesians and Colossians*, 223.

Household Worship (3:16–17)

The context of the household code includes instructions on worship (3:16; 4:2–4) work (3:17—4:1, 5–6), and family (3:18—4:1). The people of Colossae do not compartmentalize like Americans. Their lives are integrated. Since slaves deliver the message, we can imagine then the impact of the household code in this venue.

This section is bracketed by the inclusion to "teach and admonish one another in all wisdom" as they worship together (3:16) and "conduct themselves wisely toward outsiders" (4:5). Tychicus and Onesimus speak and represent the "word of Christ" in house church worship (3:15), a setting where Christ's oral Word is spoken, read by them, and dwells in them. This message "takes up residence" as a "verbal communication" among Christ, reader, courier, and audience.[23] In response, the audience hears their words, extemporaneous messages, and words about Christ and Paul as wise instruction. They offer sage direction and lead the psalms, hymns, and spiritual songs (3:16–17). Their gifts of teaching and their status as messengers validate their work. Their performance allows them to teach, admonish, and help discern God's will (1:9).[24] Because the whole church can serve as teachers, Tychicus and Onesimus demonstrate that slaves (and anyone else including women) are teachers and admonishers.[25] The setting of worship is a place where the slave-performers train people and sing to people in the wisdom that reigns through the peace of Christ. Both the words of Christ and the response to the instruction arise from the Word.

In the text's performance, Christ is regarded as the "Lord/Master" of the household. The creator Christ triumphing and dwelling in them is now the one who is viewed as the Master of the household—not the earthly master/lord figure (3:17). Whatever you *do* then is done in the name of a new Master—whether in word or deed. In other words, their actions extend from worship and into the work and family life of the household.

Household Work (3:18—4:6)

Because Christ is Master of the household in worship, the household code focuses on the earthly master-slave relationship. The instructions about wisdom from slaves in worship informs then how they address the issues. This section asks a question unusual in our context today: "Now that we

23. McKnight, *Colossians*, 215.

24. Lohse, *Colossians and Philemon*, 151.

25. Garland, *Colossians and Philemon*, 212.

have worshiped together, how does wisdom culture take shape as we work together and relate to one another?"

The text addresses working pairs similar to what we find in ancient household codes. These pairs would be present to watch and listen to a new working pair slave and slave-brother—Tychcicus and Onesimus—deliver the epistle.[26] Each person has a coworker: husband and wife, master and slave, parent and child. They work two by two together to learn peace, concord, and encouragement with each other in an emerging *oikonomia*. Their work together embodies what it means to teach and admonish one another with all wisdom.

The code contains a significant lexical nuance in the pairing of master-slave. Because Colossians identifies Christ as Master, then the household's commercial relationships play just as vital of a role as the familial ones. The household code can be heard as a first-century accountability chart for a business seeking to maintain peace operating with the resurrected Christ as their Master.[27] The play on the word "Lord/Master" and the pairing of the household work relationships suggests a new submission to the Master and an ethic of equal treatment for all. Colossians uses the rhetorical figure of the *polyptoton* to identify the main subject: the role of Christ as Master and to delight the audience (*Rhet. Her.* 4.21.29—4.23.32). A performance of this section emphasizes these nuances, and performers use gestures to emphasize the point. Colossians inflects the case of the Greek words for Lord/Master to heighten the audience's response to wise conduct toward Christ as Master. To hear this passage as if Tychicus and Onesimus were delivering, we should render *kurios* as "master" instead of "Lord" and *doulos* as "slave(s) instead of "servant."[28]

I have translated these verses as literally as possible to capture the sound of the Greek text.

> 3:18: "Wives submit to your husbands as fitting in the **Master**."

> 3:20: "Children obey your parents in everything, for this is well pleasing in the **Master**."

> 3:22: "**Slaves**, obey all of the flesh **masters**, not in eye-service as men-pleasers but with genuineness of heart, fearing the **Master**."

> 3:23 "Whatever you do, work from the soul as to the **Master** and not men.

26. McKnight, *Colossians*, 217.

27. Talbert, "Biblical Norms," 23.

28. Walsh and Keesmaat, *Colossians Remixed*, 207.

3:24 "Knowing that from the **Master** you will receive the reward of an inheritance—the **Master** Christ you are **slaves** [to].

4:1 "**Masters** offer justice and equality to your **slaves**, knowing that you also have a **Master** in heaven.

In these verses, the listener is drawn into the working relationships with masters in all arenas of life. Tychicus and Onesimus are not defending slavery or the church against opposition. Nor are they attempting to convert outsiders into the community. They are announcing a new hierarchy under Christ. The Lycus Valley households will be the first ones to adopt the pattern. Tychicus and Onesimus are wise examples of two persons living under a new Master (3:10–11). They teach extemporaneously and personally how this wisdom works (4:7–8).

For wives, Christ as Master changes "what is fitting" (3:18). Stoicism is not the norm. A spouse willingly submits by her own choice because Christ is Master.[29] Christ's wisdom permeates the place and helps them maintain harmony and unity for each other. The purpose is not to defend the Christians against accusations of sedition but to unite the church toward each other. The idea of submission as performed by a wife, child, or a slave reinforces the notion that submission is "something expected of all Christians regardless of rank or gender."[30] The phrase "what is fitting" anticipates that Nympha will apply this code to her situation as a likely household leader in the Lycus Valley (4:15).[31] In turn, husbands love their wives and are not harsh with them because Christ is their Master. Children obey their parents because of their relationship to the Master (not their parents) (3:19–20).

The Master-Christ expression also changes the way a slave works (3:21–22). The slave obeys their literal "flesh" master, the one they can see (2:1), but they are no longer concerned with pleasing him. They work genuinely ("single-minded" or "sincere" in most versions), fearing the true Master (3:22). They also do everything in the household—"from the soul." This word is usually interpreted as "wholeheartedly," referring to the emotional motivation of work. From the perspective of a slave now under a new Master, the soul takes on a different meaning. "Soul" in this context suggests putting one's true Christ-dwelling self into the work (3:22–23). Status in Christ now changes the way the slaves serve, allowing his Christ-formed nature to come through. They put their "true self" as the image of Christ into their work.[32]

29. Gupta, *Colossians*, 166.
30. Garland, *Colossians and Philemon*, 243.
31. Gupta, *Colossians*, 167.
32. Rohr, *Immortal Diamond*, 23.

To reinforce the point, and to draw attention to their true self, Colossians says, "The Master Christ you are slaves to" (3:24). It's hard to capture the force of this statement in English as "The Master Christ" is alliterated in Greek, and slave is used as a verb. The sense in English is, "You are enslaved to Jesus. Christ has already destroyed the artificial human-made categories of status and race. Slaves are called to be obedient to their master because they are really obeying the Master" (Did. 4:11; Barn. 19:7). Both masters and slaves will one day stand before the judge, and they must hold one another accountable to serve Christ (3:25).[33] Unlike some other slaves in the ancient world, these Christ-serving slaves receive an inheritance from their Master.[34]

In 4:1, Tychicus and Onesimus turn their attention from other slaves in the room to the earthly master (4:1–6). The master is now under a new Master.[35] In delivery, they address the master and instruct him, who is likely a father and husband, to treat slaves justly and equally (2 Cor 8:13–14). As Schweizer notes, Christ's lordship protects slaves from masters. The stronger party's rights are limited because Christ dwells with them. The standard is now the same for everyone, and everyone must benefit equally.[36] Tychicus and Onesimus, representing Paul, limit the master's dominance over slaves.[37] As slaves addressing other slaves in the room, the household holds the master accountable to the new conduct.

There is no formal transition between 4:1 and 4:2, and a reader would not have observed a break here. The section from 4:2–6 would have fit naturally within the instructions for family businesses and the marketplace, addressed to the master of the household. Because they serve the Master, they are to demonstrate that service through prayer for Paul's fellow workers and service in the marketplace. Slaves are models for them as they set an example. Prayer to open a door for Paul is an integral part of their service.

The theme continues in 4:5. To "buy up or buy backtime" is a commercial term, suggesting a delay while evil looms. (See a similar expression in Daniel 2:8 LXX.) By living this way, the household can delay evil through work, worship, and family harmony. Instead of thinking of a particular point in time (*chronos*) when this will be resolved, the performance of wisdom thickens time into *kairos* time that anticipates Christ's reign. The household works as a witness to demonstrate their fidelity to the Master. What they do as

33. Schweizer, *Letter to the Colossians*, 227.
34. Gupta, *Colossians*, 173.
35. Lincoln, "Household Code and Wisdom Mode of Colossians," 105.
36. Schweizer, *Colossians*, 227.
37. Garland, *Colossians and Philemon*, 251.

a worshiping and working family translates into the marketplace. They learn together from Tychicus and Onesimus how to "conduct themselves wisely toward outsiders." The words they have learned from the risen Christ and shared through Tychicus and Onesimus now affect the words that they speak to outsiders (4:6–7). They bond and hold one another accountable to Christ's wisdom, and together they learn the right conduct to those who are not a part of the community but presumably with whom they conduct business.

Performing Wisdom to Others

Tychicus and Onesimus presumably share this message with others, including those in Nympha's household (4:7–17). We cannot be certain how the Colossian code influenced others. Evidence from other early Christian writings suggests that Christian households maintained the structure while adapting household code to fit their identity in Christ and contexts where Christ-followers are slaves and spouses to a master who is not a believer (1 Clem 1:3; 21:6–9; Shepherd of Hermas 2:4.1; Eph 5; Matt 19:1–15; 1 Pet 2:12, 15; 3:2–3). The father/master figure in the household takes on the role of a "type" for God, reflecting Christ as Master, and the bishop plays a similar role in the church (Ignatius, *Polycarp* 2.1; 4.1—6.1; Polycarp, *Phil.* 4.2—6.3; Did. 4:9–11; Barn. 4:2—6:3). Slaves regrettably continue to remain present in the structure.

Wisdom is applied to conduct as a church with each other (Polycarp, *Philippians* 2.1, 4.1–6.2) and toward spouses who are caught in adultery (Shepherd of Hermas 2:4.1). Slaves are cautioned to be respectful toward believing masters (1 Tim 5:2).[38]

To summarize, we might prefer to see a revolution of society's systems or resistance to cultural norms. Instead, an oral reading of Colossians reveals a case study. One household discerns wisely what to do at home, work, and worship, and hold one another accountable to carry out these instructions. They in turn deliver this message to others. By submitting to Christ as Master, they could change their mindset about how society was ordered and live under a new hierarchy. Masters treat slaves and everyone else justly and equally. Status does not shape character, Christ's wisdom does. Following a cultural code does not mean condoning the wrongs conducted in that system. Instead, those oppressed find their voice by literally working in the system for Christ's purposes. Their wise living buys time for gospel doors to open and the vision of Col 3:21 to become a reality.

---

38. Talbert, "Biblical Norms," 21.

Pastoral Wisdom

If slaves are the messengers, and Christ is Master, then the church has several lessons to learn and the concept of "faith at work" has even greater implications. First, let me share a word about what not to do with this household code. We should not treat the household code as an organizational chart for the modern business. We live in a different, highly regulated world where there is constant interaction with government and business. We have protections against mistreatment of employees and rightly so. Instead, we can learn to interpret Colossians as an ongoing performance. Tychicus and Onesimus's delivery was not a static event. Paul's admonition to "have this [epistle] read" continues through those who read the text aloud today (4:16). We join a living conversation begun by Tychicus and Onesimus that requires feedback, listening, extemporaneous interpretation, and engagement with our culture.[39] Like the early Christians, as Eduard Lohse suggests, we do not "renounce the world and flee it, but face it head-on and try to learn from the rules of life" that are part of society.[40] Colossians gives us an audition (auditory-vision) to imagine how the indwelling Christ is Master of households today. We use their experiences as a mirror to reflect on our own conditions and be transformed by the indwelling Word of wisdom they deliver. Because Jesus is Master, we can approach our households, primarily where we work and learn together, with new ears and new motivations. Pastors and teachers have a wealth of content to lead a discussion about conduct as Christ-followers at work. Colossians is especially relevant to family businesses, farms, and firms owned by Christians, Christians who work from home independently, and for house church planters in the marketplace who use their businesses as a platform for new church plants.

"Christ as Master" Eliminates Titles and Status

We are all slaves with newfound equality under Christ. We learn from this position and work "from the soul" not from the job description. Under Christ we bring our true self to work as Christ sees us. We view our rank, title, and authority (or lack thereof) through the eyes of Christ who dwells in our work, works through us, and we work through him. We approach our work with the mindset that Christ will hold wrongdoers accountable for their evil. No matter our status or salary, we work wholeheartedly, not because someone is

39. Shiell, *Delivering from Memory*, 105.
40. Lohse, *Colossians*, 154.

watching us, or for a raise or bonus from a performance review. We work to please Christ because Christ is already pleased with us.

Supervisors Take the Lead

Supervisors have the most significant responsibility to lead sacrificially and submissively to the Master Christ. As Col 4:1 suggests, supervisors are to treat subordinates "justly and equally" (*dikaion kai ten isoteta*). Anyone in a position of authority, especially the head of the household and/or business, takes the lead by inviting accountability in the new organizational chart. This role of supervisors was uniquely Christian in the ancient world.[41]

To implement the system at work, Colossians suggests a pairing system. Everyone needs an accountability partner in the workplace to hold them to the commitments of treating persons justly and equally. They should review their work, help them learn from mistakes, and help supervisors learn to listen to those who have a lower societal rank. Coworkers hold them accountable for their treatment of a spouse, child, and the under-resourced. They have a responsibility to care for their subordinates and persons that society marginalizes.[42]

Christian business owners and their companies provide for families through employment and benefits. The model of the Colossian household goes a step further to help Christian-owned businesses flourish. They begin to see Christ as owner and their role as a steward of the company. They are entrusted with workers who are equally valued as "coworkers" in the ministry of "doing everything in the name of the Lord. They flourish because they are providing a job, assisting families, and creating an environment where persons are valued because of their identity in Christ.

Change Systems that Perpetuate Injustice

Christians in the workplace should routinely listen to and empower persons lower on the organizational chart to speak wisely and clearly about issues they see and improvements that can be made. Just as Tychicus and Onesimus deliver the message, businesses can listen to their workers share their experiences. Paul urges Philemon to treat Onesimus no longer as a slave but as a sibling (Phlm 16). At work, they treat persons as current or potential siblings in Christ. They can empower their hourly and contract employees to

41. Witherington and Wessels, "Do Everything in the Name of the Lord," 329.

42. Schweizer, *Colossians*, 229.

be responsible for outcomes and give them autonomy over their work. Invite lower-ranking persons to help address the injustices of white privilege and systemic racism. Listen carefully to persons of color, and restructure systems to provide equal access to opportunities and benefits. Remunerate victims of abuse and those who have been wrongfully convicted and imprisoned. By viewing Christ as Master, Christian workers can redeem unjust conditions. Women like Nympha can lead the way toward systems that improve everyone's lives and promote the common good.

At work, Christians courageously call out instances of injustice, raise awareness about workplace behavior, and speak up for those who do not have power. Taking our faith to work means that Christians learn how to advocate for women and persons of color who have been passed over for promotions or who are marginalized by their companies. At the risk of their own positions, Christians create workplace cultures that treat people fairly and equally and advocate for just policies and protections. In so doing, a person exercises faith at work by creating a virtuous, just system for the common good where everyone can flourish.

Church Models Community

Church is a community for listening and learning from those with lower rank and authority. Because most persons in church today approach or avoid these passages through the language of "submission," they miss the opportunity to discuss these issues through the filter of work relationships. Pastors should certainly seek advice from business persons. Pastors should also be careful not to look solely to CEOs and VPs as examples. Invite churches to hear the text read aloud from a blue-collar worker or someone on society's margins. The "master-slave" nuance is significant. Church systems are designed to defer to persons with longevity in the church, wealth, and connections. Churches can become more intentional about training persons with lower rank in society to become leaders. Leadership in psalms, hymns, and spiritual songs can provide a platform for spiritual accountability and wise leadership in other areas. The prayers that are offered as a worshiping community affect the prayer life of the marketplace. Churches can engage in prayer for businesses and workers as much as they are praying for missionaries. Churches can treat business owners and frontline workers as those who are opening doors for the gospel. Consider the power of the prayers for health care workers, grocery clerks, and teachers amid a pandemic.

Churches can also train persons for a new mindset around the workplace. Colossians demonstrates the importance of education in the training of workplace disciples. Issues of racism, injustice, poverty, and abuse should be front and center as churches acknowledge their complicity as workers and seek to be Christ's agents of reconciliation and healing. In this arena, business is not treated as "the real world," and discussing these issues is not considered "politics." They are considered workplace conduct for disciples under Christ as Master.

Churches should see business as "on the job training" for spiritual gift-edness and leadership in the church. Women especially who are promoted in the workplace are often marginalized in church structures that defer to men. Congregations can seek out women leaders in the workplace and invite them to use their gifts as leaders in churches.[43]

Build Networks and Ecosystems

Churches can network and build friendships through households. Colossians demonstrates the value of coworkers in the marketplace and in the church. Just as Tychicus, Onesimus, Timothy, Epaphras worked together at church and in the marketplace, so the Colossians formed a network throughout the Lycus Valley. Their work together with Nympha formed inseparable courageous bonds that helped the households thrive. The friendships provide the bonds we need as we "buy time," foster peace, and build unity for Christ's work to continue.[44] Working from home does not mean working alone.

As an example, in Alton, Illinois, Hugh Halter and his team have created a model of business, church, and networking in a struggling area of Illinois. They have renovated a post office and converted it into a roaster, coffee bar, co-working space, and reception hall for the community. They operate "The Post Commons" as a business and use the space as a hub to form missional communities in the Alton area. This network is treating the business as mission, and the church deploys in the neighborhoods to serve and worship.

In conclusion, let me share just one example of how transformation can happen in a small family-owned company when a Christian decides to advocate for victims of injustice. One of my former church members worked in his family's coffee business. They owned several franchises in the area and operated them efficiently. They never went into debt and were widely regarded as a respected local brand where people shopped frequently. They primarily catered to a blue-collar crowd. Customers liked the personal treatment.

43. Martin, "Household Codes in African American Interpretation," 228.

44. Gupta, *Colossians*, 191.

The father inherited the business from his father, and he worked himself to death. He attended a large Presbyterian church in town on the weekends and worked every other day of the week. His work was his life.

When his son moved back to town to join the company, he and his family joined my church. It soon became very apparent to the son that he would be running into conflict with his dad. The son worked hard, beginning as a cashier in the store, learning the business. His dad promoted him to head of human resources. Soon the son discovered a secret in the industry. Over sixty years, the company never hired a person of color to be a store manager. They intentionally and systematically prevented anyone other than a white person to be promoted. He decided to speak to his dad about the situation and expected a warm reception. Instead, he received a rebuke. His father told him that if he hired a black person to be a store manager, "The Bubbas would not like it."

At the time, our church was openly addressing racism and injustice from the pulpit and small groups. The son decided to pray about a response and seek Christ's wisdom to address the injustice. He reached out to me, and together we prayed about the right thing to do, doing the right thing, and trusting in Christ's wisdom for the long haul, no matter the cost. He responded to his dad by hiring the most qualified person he could find, and the person he hired was an African-American man. As head of H.R. he had the authority to make the hire and risked his job to do so. When he reported the decision to his dad, he was able to keep his career, and the man is still working in the store even today. The son certainly would have every right to report the company to the EEOC and quit his job. Instead, he chose to "buy time," take a risk, and change a system. By doing so, he changed workplace culture as a Christian.

Each situation requires similar discernment. A supervisor can take the lead to address injustices and open doors for the gospel. Tychicus and Onesimus are still delivering a message today.

Bibliography

Balch, David L. *Let Wives Be Submissive: The Domestic Code in 1 Peter*. Chico, CA: Scholars, 1981.

Botha, Pieter J. J. "The Verbal Art of the Pauline Letters: Rhetoric, Performance and Presence." In *Rhetoric and the New Testament: Essays from the 1992 Heidelberg Conference*, 409–28. JSNTSup 90. Sheffield: Sheffield Academic Press, 1993.

Crouch, James E. *The Origin and Intention of the Colossian Haustafel*. Forschungenzur Religion und Literaturdes Altenund Neuen Testaments 109. Gottingen: Vandenhoeck & Ruprecht, 1972.

Garland, David E. *Colossians and Philemon*. NIV Application Commentary. Grand Rapids: Zondervan, 1998.

Gupta, Nijay F. *Colossians*. Smyth and Helwys Commentary. Macon, GA: Smyth and Helwys, 2013.

Harrill, Albert. *Slaves in the New Testament: Literary, Social, and Moral Dimensions* Minneapolis: Augsburg Fortress, 2006.

Hayward, C. R. T. "Sirach and Wisdom's Dwelling Place." In *Where Shall Wisdom Be Found? Wisdom in the Bible, The Church and the Contemporary World*, edited by Stephen C. Barton, 31–46. Edinburgh: T. & T. Clark, 1999.

Joyce, Adam, and Greg Forster, eds., *Economic Wisdom for Churches: A Primer on Stewardship, Poverty and Flourishing*. Deerfield, IL: Trinity International University, 2017.

Lincoln, Andrew T. "The Household Code and Wisdom Mode of Colossians." *Journal for the Study of the New Testament* 74 (1999) 9–112.

Lohse, Eduard *Colossians and Philemon*. Hermeneia. Philadelphia: Fortress, 1988.

Martin, Clarice J. "The Haustafeln (Household Codes) in African American Biblical Interpretation: 'Free Slaves' and 'Subordinate Women.'" In *Stony the Road We Trod: African American Biblical Interpretation*, 206–31. Minneapolis: Fortress, 1991.

McKnight, Scot. *The Letter to the Colossians*. Grand Rapids: Eerdmans, 2018.

———. *Reading Romans Backwards*. Waco, TX: Baylor University Press.

Oakes, Peter. *Reading Romans in Pompeii: Paul's Letter at Ground Level*. Minneapolis: Fortress, 2009.

Oestreich, Bernhard. *Performance Criticism of the Pauline Letters*. Translated by Lindsay Elias and Brent Blum. Biblical Performance Criticism Series 14. Eugene, OR: Cascade, 2016.

Reich, Keith A. *Figuring Jesus: The Power of Rhetorical Figures of Speech in the Gospel of Luke*. Biblical Interpretation Series 107. Leiden: Brill, 2011.

Rohr, Richard. *Immortal Diamond: the Search for our True Self*. San Francisco: Josey-Bass, 2006.

Schweizer, Eduard. *The Letter to the Colossians*. London: SPCK, 1982.

Shiell, William D. *Delivering from Memory: The Effect of Performance on the Early Christian Audience*. Eugene, OR: Pickwick, 2011.

———. *Reading Acts: The Lector and the Early Christian Audience*. Biblical Interpretation Series 70. Leiden: Brill Academic, 2004.

Strocka, Volker Michael. "The Celsus Library in Ephesus." In *Ancient Libraries in Anatolia: Libraries of Hattusha, Pergamon, Ephesus, Nysa*, 41–42. Ankara: Middle East Technical University Library, 2003.

Talbert, Charles. "Are There Biblical Norms for Christian Marriage?" *Journal of Family Ministry* 15 (2001) 16–27.

———. *Ephesians and Colossians*. Paideia. Grand Rapids: Baker Academic, 2007.

Walsh, Brian, and Sylvia C. Keesmaat. *Colossians Remixed: Subverting the Empire* Downers Grove, IL: InterVarsity, 2004.

Wise, Michael et al., trans. *The Dead Sea Scrolls: A New Translation*. New York: HarperSanFrancisco, 2005.

Witherington, Ben, III, and G. Francois Wessels. "Do Everything in the Name of the Lord: Ethics and Ethocs in Colossians." In *Identity, Ethics, and Ethos in the New Testament*, 303–34. Beiheftezur Zeitschriftfürdie neutestamentliche Wissenschaftund die Kunde der altereneKirche 141. Berlin: De Gruyter, 2006.

Wold, Benjamin G. "Family Ethics in 4QInstruction and the New Testament." *Novum Testamentum* 50 (2008) 292–93.

Yamauchi, Edwin. "Qumran and Colosse." *Bibliotheca Sacra* 121 (1964) 143–44.

Young, N. H. "The Figure of the *Paidagogos* in Art and Literature." *The Biblical Archaeologist* 53 (1990) 65.

WISE EVANGELISM

By Jeff Banman

W isdom does not always reveal herself at first glance. In fact, what is wise can sometimes initially be perceived as unwise, perhaps even foolish. Consider the paradigmatic wisdom story in the Bible, that of Solomon and the disputing prostitutes found in 1 Kgs 3. The two women each claim one baby as their own, prompting King Solomon to suggest cutting the child in two and giving half to each woman. If we pause the story here, before the true mother intervenes, thus revealing Solomon's wisdom, the words of the king seem downright foolish. Who but a fool would suggest cutting a baby in two as the best way forward? If a modern judge decided to settle a maternity dispute this way, we would hardly use the word "wise" to describe them. Yet, Solomon's verdict was in fact very wise and it undeniably produced the desired results. At first glance it seemed foolish, but upon reflection it was truly the wise path. What if our approach to evangelism requires a "Solomon-esque" solution? This chapter outlines a path that, at first glance, may seem less evangelical and even counter-intuitive to the aims of evangelicalism, but in the end, it points us down a biblical path of wisdom that, if followed, has the potential to bear significantly more evangelistic fruit.

We know that God is a missional God and that He desires ultimately for all nations to come to Him, so as evangelicals we naturally promote any and every method that, in our view, accomplishes this goal. For our evangelical tribe, this has often meant promoting more and more evangelistic efforts, training believers to share their faith, inspiring them with success stories and motivating them to join in proclaiming the gospel to the world. Many evangelical pastors and leaders aim to have all believers regularly sharing their faith with people they meet, yet research shows that we continually fall short of this goal.[1] The fact remains that the majority of evangelical Chris-

---

1. "Is Evangelism Going Out of Style?," https://www.barna.com/research/is-

tians do not regularly evangelize. So, if we are to reach our communities and our country for Christ, we must either redouble our efforts in this same path and simply try harder or we must pursue a new path. It should be noted that the path this chapter promotes is actually not "new" at all—it is the old path of the first-century that has so long been neglected that it appears new to us who have long been walking a different path.

Before we embark down this so-called new path, a few words about the old path. Evangelism in North American churches is often unfortunately reduced to a narrow definition of verbally sharing the gospel with friends, family and coworkers. The aim of these evangelistic endeavors is usually to be obedient to the Great Commission and to grow the church. For many evangelicals this is all that evangelism entails—verbally sharing the gospel with unbelievers. Sadly, this misses the point of what the New Testament has to say about mission, which *encompasses* evangelism, but also envisions a much grander form of witness that centers on the embodied gospel living of the local church. This is the path that as evangelicals we will be wise to explore.

This path may look at first like we are cutting the baby in two, because it acknowledges the uncomfortable truth that the New Testament has far less to say about evangelism than we might have imagined—at least in terms of the traditional, narrow definition of evangelism. When we examine the Gospels and the Epistles, we find that there are few, if any, clear instructions for *all* believers to evangelize. Undoubtedly the twelve apostles, Paul, and his coworkers are called to verbally proclaim the gospel, but the ordinary believers, which comprise most Christians, do not share the same calling—at least it looks quite different than we might imagine. Of course, there is the Great Commission in Matt 28, which nearly all evangelistic teaching is built upon and we will address this passage in the following pages, but the New Testament does not generally aim to turn all believers into evangelists, as many modern evangelicals presume. Rather, it places a distinct emphasis on producing communities of believers who *embody* the gospel, living kingdom lives. The New Testament writers believe that participation in these new communities is the primary way that ordinary believers announce the good news to the world—that is, the primary way they evangelize.

While suggesting that ordinary believers do not have a clear responsibility to verbally evangelize may seem very "un-evangelical," it is only a shift in emphasis that, when realized, produces the very results that the evangelism push hopes to attain. The emphasis throughout the New Testament is on

---

evangelism-going-out-of-style/. Many other sources could be cited here that suggest we are not doing enough to evangelize and that we are trending in the wrong direction. The evangelism problem is common knowledge in most evangelical circles.

participating in the gospel rather than *proclaiming* it. Perhaps a better way of putting it is that participating in the gospel is *how* we proclaim it. This is what Jesus taught, how the Pauline churches were intended to operate, and the way that the early church grew to six million believers by the end of the third century. As we turn to these sources, we consistently see that the emphasis for ordinary believers is not on proclaiming the gospel, but on living it out. This is wisdom. This is the way the first Christian communities won over vast numbers of converts and the way we would be wise to follow if we hope for a similar harvest. In order to fully grasp this wisdom we need to dig deeper into the Gospels, Paul's letters, and the witness of the early church.

Evangelism in the Gospels

My seminary library has an extensive collection of books on mission and evangelism; shelf after shelf give testimony to our evangelical heritage. One book, pulled almost at random, entitled *Christian Discipleship*, communicates clearly the prevalent evangelical interpretation of proclamation in the Gospels:

> First, the Great commission—"Go . . . make disciples"—is a command, not merely a suggestion or option. Not only is it a command, it's also directed to all believers. It isn't reserved for pastors or evangelists or professional ministers or "super-saints." It's directed at you, personally, no matter who you are. If you are a true believer in Christ, you have as your responsibility the fulfillment of this imperative. There are no exceptions.[2]

While this assessment of the Great Commission may seem a bit heavy-handed and even dated, it is nonetheless indicative of the way many evangelicals continue to understand the Great Commission. Little, if any, distinction is made regarding evangelists, apostles, or others called to ministries of proclamation compared with ordinary Christians who have no particular evangelistic calling. The Great Commission is for every Christian, therefore we all have a responsibility to evangelize. The debate is settled.

Cru (formerly Campus Crusade for Christ), one of the largest mission agencies in the world states that "The Lord Jesus Christ commanded *all believers* to proclaim the Gospel throughout the world and to disciple people from every nation."[3] Or consider the doctrinal statements of Youth

---

2. Collins, *Christian Discipleship*, 237.

3. "Statement of Faith," https://www.cru.org/us/en/about/statement-of-faith.html. Emphasis added.

With A Mission, the world's largest network of discipleship training centers: "We [Christians] are called to share the gospel of Jesus Christ with
those who do not know Him."[4] Furthermore, endless books on evangelism
could be surveyed and almost all would begin with the assumption that all
Christians are called to evangelize, appealing to the Great Commission. To
question this fundamental evangelical doctrine is tantamount to challenging Evangelicalism itself.

Yet, we must ask if this is how the early Christian communities understood the Great Commission. Was this, in their minds an instruction
for all believers to fulfill or was it for the eleven who heard it firsthand? The
evidence from Acts suggests that the twelve apostles understood it to be
their commission. At Pentecost, the apostles immediately began carrying
out the Great Commission in preaching to all nations. Furthermore, in
Acts 6:2 the apostles did not think it right that they should give up preaching to serve tables; they had a strong sense of their particular calling to
proclaim the gospel. The belief that the Great Commission applied strictly
to the apostles was, in fact, how all early Christians read Matt 28.[5] In the
early church the commission was used as a Trinitarian text, a historical
text to explain the work of the twelve, but it was never used to apply to
all believers. It was not until the modern missionary movement, perhaps
commencing with William Carey in the eighteenth century, that Christians
began to use this text to apply to all believers.[6] The standard evangelical
belief that the Great Commission is for all believers is a relatively new idea
in Christian history and its roots only go back to the post-Reformation
period, not to the early church.

I realize that the Great Commission is a "sacred cow" in evangelicalism and to suggest that it might not be normative for all believers is
heretical to some. My aim is only to demonstrate that 1) our current use
of the text is a relatively recent interpretation and, more importantly, 2) to
show that the mission of the church reaching the nations is actually not
dependent on the Great Commission. The Gospels and Epistles paint a full

---

4. "Youth With A Mission—Purpose, Beliefs, Values," https://www.ywam.org/
about-us/values/.

5. Many early Christian writers could be cited here to make this point, including
Justin Martyr, Irenaeus, and Tertullian, but Origen will speak for all: "And the Apostles
on this account left Israel and did that which had been enjoined on them by the Saviour,
'Make disciples of all the nations,' and, 'You shall be my witnesses both in Jerusalem and
in all Judea and Samaria, and unto the uttermost part of the earth'" (*Commentary on
Matthew*, Book 10, XVIII).

6. Hunsberger, "Is There Biblical Warrant for Evangelism?," 62.

and complete picture of our participation in God's mission, even without appealing to Matt 28:19–20.

However, even though the twelve saw the calling as unique to them, by the second half of Acts 6, the task of proclamation was already extending beyond the twelve as Stephen boldly proclaimed the word, becoming the first Christian martyr. Likewise, in the Gospels we had already seen that proclamation ministry extended beyond the twelve when Jesus commissioned and sent out the seventy-two (Luke 10). Clearly twelve men were not enough workers for the harvest—not in the Gospels and not in Acts. So, if the call to evangelize extends beyond the Twelve, does it then extend to all believers? The Gospels demonstrate scant evidence that all believers are to evangelize. In fact, when the Great Commission is removed from the equation, as we understand it in its historical context, we find very little in the Gospels suggesting that all believers are to verbally proclaim the gospel.

In the Gospels there are only two occurrences where Jesus commands someone other than the twelve (or seventy-two) to proclaim the good news. In the first instance Jesus tells the man freed of the legion of demons to go home and tell his friends what has happened (Mark 5:19–20; Luke 8:38–39). The purpose of Jesus's command is not to turn this man into an evangelist, though in some sense his story would have been evangelistic, but to remove the curse of isolation and to reunite him with his friends and family. Morna Hooker likens Jesus's command here to the one given to the healed leper who was to report to the priest in Mark 1:44—both are instructed to rejoin society, the leper by visiting the priest and being declared clean and the demoniac by reporting to his family who will see the obvious change.[7] The second story involves the man who wishes to bury his father before following Jesus to whom Jesus says, "Leave the dead to bury their own dead. But as for you, go and proclaim the kingdom of God" (Luke 9:60). Jesus is not suggesting that this untrained man leave and engage in a ministry of evangelism on his own, rather that he would join Jesus and first become a disciple and then become one of the proclaimers like the other apostles. Beyond these two examples, Jesus never instructs ordinary believers to verbally present the gospel.

From the Gospel evidence it seems that Jesus did not have widespread evangelistic goals for all of his followers. This is not to say that the ordinary believer was normally prevented by Jesus from sharing the good news, though there are a few instances where Jesus issues a temporal command not to report miracles to others (Mark 1:44; 5:43; 7:36). Obviously, ordinary people did, in fact, share the good news of Jesus—how else would

---

7. Hooker, *Gospel According to Saint Mark*, 145.

one explain the large crowds that gathered to hear Jesus teach? There were certainly many non-commissioned individuals who reported the good news of Jesus to others. We see this in the Samaritan woman (John 4:39), the witnesses to Lazarus's resurrection (John 12:17), and a myriad of other events not recorded in the Gospels, but that surely occurred in the natural course. These mostly spontaneous reports of Jesus's works are natural and seem to happen whether Jesus instructs them to do so, prohibits them, or says nothing at all. The gospelers may have intended these as paradigms for us to follow, but either way this would be the natural response even to-day. If God does a miraculous work in our life, we report it, not because we are instructed to do so, but because we naturally want to tell our friends and family the good news. Certainly, the news spread organically from one person to the next, but this is not the same as a divine command for all people to evangelize.

At this point it seems like we are cutting the baby in two. How can this be the right way forward, suggesting that it was not a priority for Jesus that all of his followers verbally proclaimed the gospel? And if it was not Jesus's desire to turn every believer into at least some sort of evangelist, how did Jesus envisage the good news spreading and what role did ordinary believers play in this endeavor? Make room for the wisdom of Jesus. There is, in fact, a significant evangelistic role that each and every believer gets to play in the gospel going forward and, if we are attentive to it, we will see a beautiful vision laid out that involves *all* believers working alongside the commissioned proclaimers to create a powerful witness to the world. Ordinary believers create new communities that in and of themselves become a loud proclamation to the world, as well as an attractive landing spot for new converts brought in by the workers in the harvest.

When Jesus addressed the crowds of ordinary people, his primary concern was not to create evangelists, but to teach a new kingdom ethic—a vision of how he expected his followers to live under his rule and reign. Jesus revealed through parables and discourse the kind of kingdom he was establishing and the requirements for people to live under his rule. While most of the people who followed him would not be commissioned and sent out as apostles or evangelists, all were expected to "repent for the kingdom is near" and to live lives of faithful obedience to the Father and his Messiah. The emphasis for the crowds is always on participating in the gospel rather than proclaiming it.[8] This participation can be reduced in its simplest form

---

8. While working primarily with Pauline literature, Michael Gorman is leading the way in discussing how we are called to participate in the gospel. See *Becoming the Gospel, Participating in Christ,* and *Abide and Go.*

to the Jesus Creed—love God and love others (Mark 12:29–31), but it is also fleshed out throughout the Gospels in various contexts.

It is widely agreed that the finest example we have of Jesus's kingdom lifestyle is contained in Matthew's Sermon on the Mount. This block of teaching, probably delivered on many occasions in many locales, best exemplifies the kingdom ethic Jesus expected of ordinary followers. Beyond the profound christological and eschatological aspects of the sermon, Jesus is painting a picture of what life with him as King looks like. This is not the place for a full treatment of Jesus's ethics, but rather an opportunity to highlight the fact that Jesus *had* an ethic for his followers, a moral expectation in the light of his inaugurated kingdom. And while Jesus technically delivers the message to the Twelve, it is clearly with the crowds in mind. The sermon begins with Jesus "seeing the crowds" in 5:1 and concludes with the crowds being amazed at his teaching in 7:28. The sermon is for everyone equally. There is no sense that the kingdom living Jesus is promoting is in any way only for the Twelve, or for specially anointed followers; it is for the masses. If ever we want to know what Jesus's expectations were for ordinary believers, we need look no further than the Sermon on the Mount.

Embedded in the sermon's introduction is a small but profound reference to the role of these moral behaviors in the life of the believer: "Let your light shine so that they may see your good works and give glory to your Father who is in heaven" (Matt 5:16). The entire sermon is largely a compendium of good works and attitudes exemplified by faithful disciples and Jesus points to a specific function of living this way—the world will take notice and be drawn to the Father. So, even though the Gospels lack exhortations for ordinary believers to proclaim the gospel, it is not as though these disciples do not play an important role in advancing the kingdom of God through faithful obedience. Letting one's light shine is to implement Jesus's kingdom ethic and to thereby manifest the presence of the kingdom for everyone to see. This is largely how Second Temple Jews saw themselves anyway, carrying on a way of life that did not conform to the surrounding culture, thus bearing witness to that culture by their very existence. Jesus's goal for his everyday followers is no different. Though his ethical demands are different, the good works they produce function much the same as keeping the law did for the Jews—it becomes in and of itself a powerful proclamation that the world is forced to acknowledge and respond to.

Unfortunately, some cannot see wisdom in this approach. They do not see any value in good works on their own, only as an addition, perhaps not even a necessary one, to our verbal proclamation. DeYoung and Gilbert exemplify this: "But when you do those things [good works], you also need to know and admit that you are *not* fulfilling part of the church's mission, you are not 'expanding the borders of the kingdom,' and you are *not* 'sharing the gospel without words.'"[9] In this view, good works do not have any witness in and of themselves, a view that contradicts Jesus, later New Testament writings such as 1 Pet 2:12, and the practice of the early church. It is not uncommon in evangelicalism and post-Reformation traditions to view good works through this negative lens, an overreaction to works-based righteousness that the Reformation stood against. Yet, Jesus, who had not lived through the Reformation, still sees value in good works and even ascribes to them a certain evangelistic quality in and of themselves. We would be wise to listen to Jesus.

Based on the evidence we have in the Gospels, it seems that Jesus envisaged a church that embodied the gospel in their daily life, living as beatitude people with one another and with the world. When Jesus speaks to the masses, to the ordinary believers he preaches a new ethic, an upside-down kingdom that, when truly inhabited, becomes an unmistakable proclamation to the world.[10] Out of this church certain disciples would be commissioned as apostles (lit., "ones who are sent") and sent out to proclaim the kingdom to those who had not heard. This began with the twelve, expanded to the seventy-two, and then would be reproduced continuously until the task was accomplished. This combination of the verbal proclamation of the apostles and the living, breathing example of the church would create a powerful witness to the world. The preaching of the apostles and evangelists would be confirmed by the church, which practices what the proclaimers preach. The consistency between message and lifestyle would attract unbelievers to give allegiance to the King and to embrace a way of living that is truly good news.

Evangelism in the Letters

Several years ago I embarked on a personal project to read through the New Testament from Romans to Revelation and to record every imperative. I was simply curious and my aim was to compile a list of every single thing that the New Testament writers told their churches to do. After reading and compiling

9. DeYoung and Gilbert, *What Is the Mission of the Church?*, 229, emphasis original.

10. Pete Goodman's chapter in this volume is in view here as Goodman describes spiritual formation as "the primary end goal of ministry." Jesus's goal for his followers was indeed spiritual formation, living out his kingdom ethics. I am taking Goodman's thesis one step further to see that the goal of spiritual formation is to ultimately play the key role in drawing the nations to the kingdom.

a list of several hundred commands I arranged them into categories. I found that the largest category, by a wide margin, was the category on how Christians ought to treat one another (well over one hundred commands). Other discoveries were made as well, but the most striking discovery was that the evangelism category was non-existent. Not once in those twenty-two letters did I find a command to evangelize. I read and reread, but soon became convinced that the New Testament letters did not talk about evangelism the way that I or my evangelical tribe did. This sent me on a long path to discover what the New Testament actually says about evangelism, eventually resulting in a doctor of ministry thesis project and this current chapter. It is not that Paul and the other writers are not interested in mission or the gospel being proclaimed, only that the way ordinary believers contribute to this is not how modern evangelicals might imagine.

When we come to Paul's letters and the rest of the New Testament, we must ask how these apostles expected the ordinary believer to engage in furthering the gospel. Did Paul expect his churches to engage in evangelism the same way he did? How did Paul see the gospel progressing to the ends of the earth and what role would ordinary believers play in carrying this out? We are looking for the wisdom of Paul when it comes to evangelism. While some scholars see evidence of pervasive evangelistic efforts on the part of Paul's churches,[11] many do not. Those who do are often seeing Paul through modern evangelical eyes, assuming that Paul's evangelism strategy was the same as ours when, in fact, it was not. When surveying the Pauline literature, we discover that there is not a single, undisputed command for his churches to evangelize. This seems strange coming from a man whose entire life was dedicated to proclaiming the gospel. If Paul expected all the believers in his churches to evangelize their cities, why does he fail to ever mention it? One would expect that he would congratulate some churches for their evangelistic efforts and rebuke others for their lack of evangelistic zeal. Why is it that Paul, whose life was consumed with preaching the gospel (Gal 1:15–16; 1 Cor 9:16, etc.), did not pass on the mantle of evangelism to his churches as a whole?[12]

---

11. Michael Green, John Piper, Eckhard Schnabel, Peter O'Brien, and many other accomplished scholars and leaders hold this view to varying degrees.

12. Many fine scholars and missionaries have recognized this apparent inconsistency in Paul. They include Paul Bowers, John Dickson, and Leslie Newbigin, a premiere missiologist of the twentieth century who writes: "It is, is it not, a striking fact that in all his letters to the churches Paul never urges on them the duty of evangelism. He can rebuke, remind, exhort his readers about faithfulness to Christ in many matters. But he is never found exhorting them to be active in evangelism." Newbigin, *Mission in Christ's Way*, 21.

To be fair there are some Pauline passages that may point in this direction, though each one is debatable. For example, Eph 6:15 describes the armor of God and the Christian as being fitted with shoes, "having put on the readiness given by the gospel of peace." Some see in this picture a call for all believers to be ready to proclaim the gospel, while others see a call for believers to stand firm in the face of opposition, preserving the gospel of peace against those who battle against it. The interpretation hinges on whether one reads "readiness of the gospel of peace" as a subjective genitive or an objective genitive and it can be taken either way.

In Phil 1:5 Paul praises the Philippians for their "partnership (*koinonia*) in the gospel from the first day until now." Again, some see this partnership pertaining to their mutual effort in evangelism, but most likely Paul is referring to their financial partnership and support which began on his first visit to Philippi in Acts 16.[13] This is the usual interpretation of *kononia* in Paul and he uses it again later in the letter when he explicitly refers to their financial partnership (4:15).

Paul also praises the Thessalonians for the way "the word of the Lord has sounded forth from you" (1 Thess 1:8). For some this is a clear indication of the missionary efforts of the church at Thessalonica and thus paradigmatic for all believers. If, in fact, Paul was referencing the evangelistic efforts of the Thessalonian church, he could have found a clearer way to say it. Instead, it is likely that Paul's intent here is similar to what he writes to the Romans, "your faith is proclaimed in all the world" (Rom 1:8), and to the Corinthians, "you are our letter . . . known and read by all" (2 Cor 3:2). It is to say that the faithful experience of these communities is communicative to the whole world. The reports of faithful Christian communities are spreading quickly and people everywhere are hearing what God is doing. This is the simplest reading of these texts.

Space does not permit an examination of each debated text, nor of Paul's imitation commands, which always refer to imitating his character and not his evangelistic efforts, but it is sufficient to say that there are no clear, undisputable commands in Paul's letters, nor the rest of the New Testament, for all believers to engage in evangelism. Paul always saw evangelism as his task, as well as his co-laborers, of whom there are several. It is apparent from the simplest reading of the Pauline literature that Paul did not see evangelism the way modern evangelicals do. He did not see the Great Commission as a command for all believers, but one that was meant for the apostles, which included himself.

13. When Paul uses *koinonia* alongside the preposition *eis,* as he does in Phil 1:5, he is usually talking about financial partnership. See Rom 12:13 and 15:26; 2 Cor 8:4 and 9:13; as well as Phil 4:15 for examples of this usage.

So, we are compelled to ask again, what is the role of the ordinary believer when it comes to spreading the good news to all nations? First of all, there *is* a verbal responsibility for all believers and it has an evangelistic quality. In Col 4:5–6, Paul instructs all believers to "walk in wisdom toward outsiders, making the best use of the time. Let your speech always be gracious, seasoned with salt, so that you may know how you ought to answer each person." The picture here is of Christians living public lives that do not conform with the surrounding culture, sparking questions from outsiders as to why they live the way they do. Paul wants all believers to be ready to give a wise and gracious answer. Similarly, 1 Pet 3:15 says, "always be prepared to make a defense to anyone who asks you for a reason for the hope that is in you; yet do it with gentleness and respect." Again, the expectation is that pagans would inevitably inquire or even bring accusations and Christians should be prepared with a gentle and respectful response. This is an important call for all believers, but also one that ought not to be confused with a call for all believers to regularly engage in evangelism. Lesslie Newbigin says it well: "If the Church which preaches [the gospel] is not living corporately a life which corresponds with it . . . then by its life it closes the doors which its preaching would open."[14]

Michael Gorman's *Becoming the Gospel* is paramount in understanding Paul's missional strategy for these communities. The central thesis of Gorman's work is that "Paul wanted the communities he addressed not merely to *believe* the gospel but to *become* the gospel, and in doing so to participate in the very life and mission of God."[15] We understand mission too narrowly when we only think of evangelism as trying to have a spiritual conversation with your neighbor or coworker—as something we *do* as opposed to something we *are*. When Christians *become* the gospel, their entire lives become immersed in, and contribute to the mission of God. This echoes the words long ago attributed to Francis of Assisi, "Preach the gospel at all time; when necessary, use words." Attributed or mis-attributed, the words continue to speak truth.

The focus on *being* rather than *doing* is not to suggest that ordinary Christians are not mission-minded. On the contrary, every Christian should desire to inhabit a lifestyle that is not only exemplary, but winsome—that is attractive to outsiders. David Bosch describes this missionary lifestyle as implicit rather than explicit; it is *missionary* rather than *missionizing*. Bosch describes the role of ordinary Christians to be missional even if they are not overtly evangelistic:

14. Newbigin, *Gospel in a Pluralist Society*, 140.
15. Gorman, *Becoming the Gospel*, 2. Italics original.

Paul's whole argument is that the attractive lifestyle of the small Christian communities gives credibility to the missionary outreach in which he and his fellow-workers are involved. The primary responsibility of the "ordinary" Christians is not to go out and preach, but to support the mission project through their appealing conduct and my making "outsiders" feel welcome in their midst.[16]

Consider Paul's words to Titus on the island of Crete. Paul issues a long list of moral behaviors for men, women and slaves with the goal that in living this way "they will make the teaching about God our Savior attractive" (Titus 2:10). The role of the ordinary believers here is to live the gospel in such a way that it becomes beautiful to outsiders.

Returning to Gorman, an important aspect of his argument is that this embodied participation in the *missio Dei* is not primarily an individual endeavour; rather it is a corporate act carried out by the entire church community. An individual Christian can certainly embody the gospel in such a way that their singular life becomes a proclamation to others, but the primary witness is in the living and breathing church. Gorman opens his work by quoting theologian John Colwell: "The world has no access to the gospel story other than as it is narrated in the life, worship, and proclamation of the Church."[17] God is a missional God who has chosen to use the church as his primary strategy to make Himself known to the nations. Gorman maintains that "one of the primary intentions of this book is the inseparability of the church's life together and its activity, or witness, in the world . . . the inseparability of being and act."[18] This is to say that how we live with one another cannot be compartmentalized from mission or evangelism; they are one and the same. To be true to Paul and to the New Testament, we can no longer think of evangelism or mission as an aspect of the church or something the church does. Rather, mission is what the church is. We, as a community of believers are a living, breathing witness of God in our particular communities.

Another way to say this is that the primary manner is which the church bears witness is through its faithful presence in this world. One of the theses of James Davison Hunter's book, *To Change the World,* is that the church needs to rethink its strategies about how to influence the world, moving away from grabbing power and instead focusing on establishing faithful communities of Christians. The apostle Paul, I believe, would give a

16. Bosch, *Transforming Mission*, 138.

17. Colwell, *Living the Christian Story*, 85. Quoted in Gorman, *Becoming the Gospel*, 1.

18. Gorman, *Becoming the Gospel*, 18.

hearty "Amen!" to Hunter's work. Hunter says, "A theology of faithful presence means a recognition that the vocation of the church is to bear witness
to and to be the embodiment of the coming Kingdom of God."[19] David Fitch
echoes this in his work entitled *Faithful Presence*:

> Faithful presence names the reality that God is present in the
> world and that he uses a people faithful to his presence to make
> himself concrete and real amid the world's struggle and pain.
> When the church is this faithful presence, God's kingdom be-
> comes visible, and the world is invited to join with God.[20]

This theology of faithful presence, articulated by Hunter and Fitch, finds
corollaries in many other theologians and missiologists. John Yoder, Stanley
Hauerwas, and Lesslie Newbigin were some of the most prominent voices
of the last century promoting a radical embodiment of the gospel that will
in turn proclaim a message to the world.[21]

This is the wisdom of Paul and the rest of the New Testament writers.
Given the evidence before us—Paul's paucity of commands to evangelize
coupled with a plethora of commands to live as faithful communities—the
best way to imagine Paul's missional strategy can be summed up as "faithful
presence." So, when we return to the initial question of whether or not Paul
expected his congregations to evangelize, we are compelled to look in a different direction. Gorman argues that this is not the question we should be asking, but rather the question should be, "How did Paul expect his communities
to participate in the *missio Dei*?"[22] God has a mission and our joining with
Christ makes us complicit in that mission. So, we must ask ourselves, when
reading Paul's letters, how it is that God desires us to live so that his mission
may be advanced through our lives and through our churches?

This is by no means to suggest that evangelism is off the table for everyone but "professionals." Scripture is clear that all believers are to be ready to
engage gently and respectfully with the world and we ought to be led by the
Holy Spirit at all times. It is unthinkable to imagine that a Christian would
never explain to an unbeliever why they live as they do, or even that they might
initiate an evangelistic conversation when prompted by the Spirit. There *is* a
verbal responsibility for all believers. However, to suggest that all Christians

---

19. Hunter, *To Change the World*, 95.

20. Fitch, *Faithful Presence*, 10.

21. Yoder and Koontz, *Theology of Mission*; Hauerwas and Willimon, *Resident
Aliens*; Newbigin, *Mission in Christ's Way*. Consider also other more recent works such
as Dickson, *Best Kept Secret of Mission*; Kreider, *Patient Ferment of the Early Church*;
Stone, *Evangelism after Christendom*.

22. Gorman, *Becoming the Gospel*, 58.

should be actively seeking out opportunities to proclaim the gospel, that we are all expected to be evangelists as Paul and others were, is to go beyond the biblical text and to miss the point. The primary concern for Christians, according to Paul's letters, should be to embody the gospel, to radically live out the kingdom Jesus proclaimed, and in doing so we will be doing the most evangelistic thing we can do. As Bryan Stone writes, "The most evangelistic thing the church can do today is to be the church."[23]

The Early Church

When we look briefly at the church after the writing of the New Testament and up until Constantine in AD 313, we see that the blueprint laid in the Gospels and Epistles was followed in the first Christian communities. In the first three centuries the church grew at a steady and rapid rate, as much as 40 percent per decade.[24] We do not know exactly how the gospel spread so widely and prodigiously, but we can make some inferences from the early Christian writings. From the earliest Christian texts like The Didache, The Shepherd of Hermas, and 1 Clement up through the theologians and apologists of the second and third centuries like Justin Martyr, Tertullian, and Origen, we see a fairly consistent picture. Some missionaries saw themselves carrying on the tradition of the apostles by teaching and preaching in schools and itinerantly throughout the Roman empire, but most believers engaged the world by living in faithful communities that spurned worship of the emperor and the pagan gods and instead lived in allegiance to their true King, Jesus of Nazareth.

The earliest Christian texts mentioned above focus almost entirely on how to live as a Christian in a pagan world. These texts make no mention of the evangelistic responsibilities of individual believers, rather they focus their energy on instructing Christians how to live as Christ's followers. Ignatius, the bishop of Antioch, who at the turn of the first century, was on his way to his martyrdom in Rome, writes to the Magnesians "It is right, therefore, that we not just be *called* Christians, but that we actually *be* Christians."[25] The writings of Ignatius's time, like The Shepherd of Hermas and The Didache, are full of moral instruction for Christians so

23. Stone, *Evangelism after Christendom*, 15.

24. Stark, *Rise of Christianity*, 7.

25. Ignatius, *Letter to the Magnesians*, IV. He writes to the Romans in a similar fashion, showing the importance for Ignatius of living the true Christian life: "pray that I . . . might not merely be *called* a Christian, but actually prove to *be* one." *Letter to the Romans*, III.

that believers might know how they ought to live. 1 Clement, perhaps the earliest Christian document not in the canon, paints a clear picture of the Christian call to live a morally upright life: "Put an end to your evil deeds; learn to do good; pursue justice, rescue those who are treated unjustly, render a decision for the orphan and do what is right for the widow."[26] The degree to which Christians met these moral standards differed in time and place, but the overall impression is that the early Christians were largely successful at creating communities built on the teachings of Jesus and Paul. Christians were known by church historians, and even their opponents, as inhabiting a lifestyle that was marked by charity, kindness, and even love of enemies, the ultimate mark of Christoformity.

This Christoform living was the primary way that ordinary Christians promoted the gospel. They may have verbally shared the good news with friends and family in natural settings, but we do not know for certain how that looked. We are, however, confident that they aspired to live lives worthy of the gospel, that in many times and places they succeeded in doing so, and that this radical new kingdom ethic resulted in millions of people coming to faith in Jesus Christ. All of this was in spite of the fact that these believers had few church buildings, no political power and faced regular opposition and even persecution. Yet, what the early church did "worked" and what they did was focus their efforts on living like Jesus. They were not nearly as concerned with missions and evangelism as we are today and yet their message was proclaimed so effectively through their embodying the gospel that the church would soon become the dominant religion of the empire. Athenagoras, a somewhat unknown second-century apologist from Athens perfectly encapsulates the role of the ordinary Christian in the early church and the powerful effect of Christoform living:

> But among us you will find uneducated persons, and artisans, and old women, who, if they are unable in words to prove the benefit of our doctrine, yet by their deeds exhibit the benefit arising from their persuasion of its truth: they do not rehearse speeches, but exhibit good works; when struck, they do not strike again; when robbed, they do not go to law; they give to those that ask of them, and love their neighbours as themselves.[27]

This was the wisdom of the early church. They faithfully inhabited the gospel, sought to live Christoform lives and in doing so they loudly proclaimed to the Roman empire that a new King was on the throne.

26. 1 Clement 7. On the dating of 1 Clement see Ehrman, *Apostolic Fathers, Volume I*, 25.

27. Athenagoras, *Plea for Christians*, XI.

Conclusions for Wise Evangelism

So, what is wisdom when it comes to evangelism? With the Gospels and the New Testament letters in hand, what would be the wise way forward if we desire to reach our cities and our country for Christ? Daniel Hanlon's opening chapter describes wisdom as a skill for doing life well. When it comes to evangelism, we are sorely in need of divine skill to do this well—a great deal is at stake. So, as we look at the New Testament churches and the life of the early church and reflecton how Christianity grew at an alarming rate with no recorded instruction on personal evangelism, we would be wise to consider this phenomenon. Again, suggesting that we focus *less* on verbally proclaiming the gospel may seem unwise at first. It is natural to question how this approach could yield greater results. We also ask how the idea of cutting a child in two could reveal the true mother, yet it did. In actuality, the path laid out in this chapter is no less evangelistic than any other path—it simply promotes a different strategy for reaching the same goal.

As a pastor I have found this to be a conversation my church needs to have. I have met many faithful Christians who are burdened by guilt over the fact that they are not evangelizing regularly, or even at all. They know from decades of swimming in evangelical waters that all Christians need to verbally share the gospel and they feel guilty for not doing so. At the same time, I see that our churches have underemphasized Christoform living and have simply been content with not committing the big sins and trying to be somewhat charitable with one another and with the world. These two problems find a single solution when we realize that ordinary believers evangelize primarily by the way they form Christoform communities. In this sense all believers have an evangelistic responsibility and it looks nothing like trying to engage a coworker in an awkward conversation about the gospel. Rather, each believer, in the particular ways that God has called and equipped them, contributes to the life of a church in such a way that this living, breathing church becomes a light that shines before the world, causing people to give glory to the Father in heaven (Matt 5:16).

This is an evangelistic call that ordinary believers can grab hold of, because it removes the yoke of trying to verbally share the gospel in unnatural settings and replaces it with the yoke of contributing boldly to your church community to promote God's kingdom in your city or town. It is no less of a call to embody the gospel than it is to evangelize on the street corner—in fact, it is arguably a more difficult call. However, it is a yoke that fits better, and one that leads people to give more of themselves to Christoform living, with the hopes that it will have a greater impact on reaching their community, which they deeply care about. The witness of a faithful community of believers, living radical lives of generosity and love, speaks volumes to a world that every day experiences less of these qualities. Hauerwas and Willimon say it best: "This church knows that its most credible form of witness (and the most 'effective' thing it can do for the world) is the actual creation of a living, breathing, visible community of faith."[28] As a church we are most influential, not when we try to evangelize more, but when we take seriously Jesus's command to love our enemies, to forgive freely, and to give generously. This kind of living becomes the most effective form of evangelism we can find.

Evangelists, pastors, and those with similar proclamation ministries should and must continue to verbally proclaim the good news of Jesus as they are called. Ordinary Christians likewise, ought to be ready to answer when asked by an unbeliever about their faith or even to initiate an evangelistic conversation if the Spirit leads them to do so. The gospel must continue to be verbally shared in a variety of settings and by many Christians. It would be unwise to suggest that ordinary Christians never have a responsibility to verbally share the gospel. It would be wise, however, to follow the lead of the New Testament and the early church in realizing that traditional evangelism is not the primary prerogative of every believer. Rather, Christians are called to focus their efforts on Christoform living, inhabiting a lifestyle of the gospel that becomes a much louder proclamation to the world than any soap-box preacher or gospel tract handed out on a street corner. When Christian communities commit themselves to living truly Christoform lifestyles of self-sacrifice and humility we shout to the world that a new King has come and that living under his rule and reign is truly good news. Choosing to put less emphasis on proclamation and more emphasis on participation may be the most evangelical thing we could ever do, perhaps even the wisest thing we could ever do.

Bibliography

Bosch, David J. *Transforming Mission: Paradigm Shifts in Theology of Mission*. American Society of Missiology Series 16. Maryknoll, NY: Orbis, 1991.

Collins, Steven *Christian Discipleship: Fulfilling the Great Commission in the 21st Century*. Rev. ed. Albuquerque, NM: Trinity Southwest Christian Press, 2013.

Colwell, John. *Living the Christian Story*. New York: T. & T. Clark, 2001.

DeYoung, Kevin, and Greg Gilbert. *What Is the Mission of the Church?: Making Sense of Social Justice, Shalom, and the Great Commission*. Wheaton, IL: Crossway, 2011.

Dickson, John. *The Best Kept Secret of Mission: Promoting the Gospel with More Than Our Lips*. Grand Rapids: Zondervan, 2013.

28. Hauerwas and Willimon, *Resident Aliens*, 47.

Ehrman, Bart D., trans. *The Apostolic Fathers, Volume I*. Loeb Classical Library 24 Cambridge: Harvard University Press, 2003.

Fitch, David E. *Faithful Presence: Seven Disciplines That Shape the Church for Mission*. Downers Grove, IL: InterVarsity Academic, 2016.

Gorman, Michael J. *Abide and Go: Missional Theosis in the Gospel of John*. Eugene, OR: Cascade, 2018.

———. *Becoming the Gospel: Paul, Participation, and Mission*. Grand Rapids: Eerdmans, 2015.

———. *Participating in Christ: Explorations in Paul's Theology and Spirituality*. Grand Rapids: Eerdmans, 2019.

Hauerwas, Stanley, and William H. Willimon.*Resident Aliens: Life in the Chritian Colony*. Nashville: Abigdon, 1989.

Hooker, Morna. *The Gospel According to Saint Mark*. London: Hendrickson, 1991.

Hunsberger, George. "Is There Biblical Warrant for Evangelism?" In *The Study of Evangelism: Exploring a Missional Practice of the Church*, edited by Paul Wesley Chilcote et al., 59–72. Grand Rapids: Eerdmans, 2008.

Hunter, James Davison. *To Change the World: The Irony, Tragedy, and Possibility of Christianity in the Late Modern World*. New York: Oxford University Press, 2010.

Kreider, Alan.*The Patient Ferment of the Early Church: The Improbable Rise of Christianity in the Roman Empire*. Grand Rapids: Baker Academic, 2016.

Newbigin, Lesslie. *Gospel in a Pluralist Society*. Grand Rapids: Eerdmans, 1989.

———. *Mission in Christ's Way: A Gift, a Command, an Assurance*. New York: Friendship, 1988.

Stark, Rodney. *The Rise of Christianity: How the Obscure, Marginal Jesus Movement Became the Dominant Religious Force in the Western World in a Few Centuries*. San Francisco: HarperOne, 1997.

Stone, Bryan P. *Evangelism after Christendom: The Theology and Practice of Christian Witness*. Grand Rapids: Brazos, 2007.

Yoder, John Howard, and G. Gerber Koontz. *Theology of Mission: A Believers Church Perspective*. Downers Grove, IL: InterVarsity Academic, 2014.

WISE MUSIC

By Julie Spahr Murdock

There are almost as many differing uses of music in church services as there are denominations and traditions. In some traditions the sermon and service are established and then three hymns are chosen (almost as an afterthought) to fit the sermon or the season. In some churches, music takes center stage (literally) with lights and cameras to pump up the crowd and prepare them for the speaker. And, of course, one finds every possible variation in between. But music rarely drives the service; it does not deliver the sermon or preside over sacraments. Its role is secondary, one of support. Why, then, do we see so much division and strife in our congregations focusing on the type and tenor of music? Is it good that a tool used for praise, adoration, and edification can become the source of so much division?

I will go out on a limb, a strong one I believe, and say that we are all familiar with "hymn wars" from at least one time in our church lives. Traditional hymns versus contemporary ones. Organ music versus guitar (or rock band). Inclusive language versus traditional wording. However, you name the battle, it is often a heated and emotional one because music appeals to the emotions. It is also heated as it is often seen as pitting the older generations against the younger or vice versa. I have witnessed families leave churches over the choice of music. I once attended a church that used three hymnals simply to accommodate everyone's views. Hymn wars, and the proposed solutions, can drain time and resources, as well as community good will, robbing the church of its intended *koinonia*. This is foolishness. Worship begins with God; it does not begin with us. Worship is a response to God and his redemptive works in our lives through Jesus Christ, through whom we now offer praise as our sacrifice (Heb 13:15). "Gratitude, joy, praise, repentance, love, and service—all of these are responses to the God who calls us to know him and obey him," writes H. Wayne Johnson in his discussion of worship as spiritual formation.[1] The singing of hymns is not for our comfort nor our entertainment, but to glorify God.

Music is a time-honored way of lifting our voices together in praise and thanksgiving to God our Father as well as introducing and reinforcing important lessons of our faith. It can also, when employed wisely, be used to build a culture of wisdom within our congregations. As church leaders, we must ask ourselves the following questions: Where and how do wisdom and music intersect? How might church leaders best avail themselves of the powerful reflections and conceptualizations that derive from song in order to create or encourage a culture of wisdom in our congregations?

This chapter will offer a survey of the history of music within the church and its changing roles. It will also briefly examine the impact music has on the conscious and sub-conscious participation in and learning from music. By examining how music has developed within the church and the role it plays today and combining that with an understanding of how music impacts and molds the understanding of the congregant, we can hopefully achieve a clearer focus on our use of music in worship and employ it as a building-block for wisdom in the church.

Historical Survey

"The Christian liturgy was born singing, and it has never ceased to sing," states J. Gelineau in his study of music and singing in the history of church liturgical practices.[2] Music and praise accompanied the announcement of the birth of Jesus to the shepherds as the a heavenly host appeared praising God, although the text itself does not mention singing (Luke 2:13).[3] Jesus and the disciples, before leaving the upper room for the Mount of Olives, sung a hymn after eating the meal we now celebrate as the Lord's Supper (Matt 26:30; Mark 14:26). Paul and Silas, imprisoned in Philippi, prayed and sang hymns of praise to God (Acts 16:25) and Paul encouraged the nascent church in Ephesus to renounce the ways of the pagan world in which they lived and instead "be filled with the Spirit as you sing psalms and hymns and spiritual songs among yourselves" (Eph 5:19). From these few examples we can see that music and singing were present at the open and close of Jesus's earthly life and that song was part of praise and spiritual conduct in the earliest life of the church. Throughout the history of the church music and singing have

1. Johnson, "Practicing Theology on a Sunday Morning," 5–6.

2. Gelineau, "Music and Singing in the Liturgy," 440.

3. Gordley, *New Testament Christological Hymns*, 205. Matthew Gordley identifies the *Gloria In Excelsis* as the third song and hymn in Luke's narrative of the nativity.

been constants, whether as part of the liturgy or worship. At times its role has
been contested, at others, celebrated, but rarely absent.

The earliest accounts of the church using song are the biblical accounts and are found in the letters from Paul to the churches. In his letter to
the church at Ephesus Paul contrasts their old ways of life as pagans, calling
them to shun those ways, to live wisely, and to "be filled with the Spirit, as
you sing psalms and hymns and spiritual songs among yourselves, singing
and making melody to the Lord in your hearts" (Eph 5:19). In a similar
vein, teaching on the new life in Christ, Paul encourages the Colossians
among other things, "with gratitude in your hearts sing psalms, hymns,
and spiritual songs to God" (Col 3:16). In his first letter to the church in
Corinth, in response to the competing cacophony of spiritual gifts and the
competitive and prideful nature arising from it, Paul urges not only love
but mindfulness in order to build up the body: "What should I do then? I
will pray with the Spirit, but I will pray with the mind also; I will sing praise
with the Spirit, but I will sing praise with the mind also" (1 Cor 14:15). Paul
goes on to discuss orderly worship urging, "When you come together, each
one has a hymn, a revelation, a tongue, or an interpretation. Let all things
be done for building up" (1 Cor 14:25). One can glean from just these few
directives that singing was a part of established worship, something done
together in fellowship, and something extemporaneously composed and
shared by the influence of the Spirit.

Much of the hymnody of the New Testament is strongly rooted in Old
Testament traditions of confessional statements.[4] As Martin explains, "the origin of the church in the womb of the Jewish faith made it inevitable that the
first followers of the risen Lord Jesus, themselves Jews by birth and tradition,
who formed the nucleus of the Jerusalem community, would wish to express
their religious devotion in a way to which they were accustomed."[5] Following closely upon the birth of the church in Palestine, the church spreads to
gentile areas dominated by pagan worship and interfaces with a world that
sang hymns to the deities of the Greco-Roman pantheon and the emperor.
One can see similarities in the form odes to pagan gods, praising their divine
origins, superhuman accomplishments, and cosmic honors, to many of the
christological hymns identified in Paul's letters.[6] Yet, for all the similarities between its Jewish roots and gentile adaptations, Christian hymnody developed

4. Martin, "Hymns, Hymn Fragments, Songs, Spiritual Songs," 420.

5. Martin, "Hymns, Hymn Fragments, Songs, Spiritual Songs," 420.

6. Gordley, *Christological Hymns*, 48. Gordley writes extensively on the comparison
between various forms of praise known in the Roman empire and christological hymns
and if this is a topic of interest, as it was for me, I highly recommend further reading for
a true appreciation of their similarities and differences.

into a path of its own for the early church. Gordley lists several characteristics unique to the hymnody of the early church:

- Centered around the life, death, and resurrection of Jesus

- Deeply rooted in the Jewish conception of the divine while appropriating aspects of Greek and Roman culture

- Conscious of its imperial aspect

- "It was much more than doctrinal or cognitive; it also had an affective dimension and an allusive quality. Accordingly, early Christian worship offered imagery and language that had an allusive power capable of engaging the emotions of its participants."[7]

While we do not have evidence as to the role the New Testament hymns played in the actual worship of the early church, we know that the text of the hymns found in Paul's letters, as well as those found in other New Testament texts, served a clear didactic function as well as one of praise. Others note the functions of NT hymns as used for sacramental purposes (baptism) and making confessions.[8]

As with many topics, the exact practices of the early church concerning music and singing are difficult to discern due to the lack of solid extrabiblical evidence and the existence of contradictory accounts from different areas of the world. As noted above, however, most experts do believe that praising God and Christ through song was practiced by the earliest churches in some form or another and for one purpose or another throughout the Christian world.[9] In a letter to the emperor Trajan (ca. 111–113 AD), Pliny the Younger detailed that among what he had learned from interrogating Christians they were, "accustomed to meet on a fixed day before dawn and sing responsively a hymn to Christ as to a god."[10] It is possible that Justin Martyr, in his *First Apology* dated between 150 and 160 AD, notes the singing of hymns by Christians to give God glory and thanks, "for our creation, and for all the means of health, and for the various qualities of the different kinds of things."[11] Clement of Alexandria (ca. 150–220 AD), in his many writings, urges his flock to sing hymns of praise throughout the day, "Holding festival, then, in our whole life, persuaded that God is

---

7. Gordley, *Christological Hymns*, 36–37. This is an abbreviated list.

8. Martin, "Hymns, Hymn Fragments, Songs, Spiritual Songs," 421–22.

9. Lohr, "Christian Hymnody," 166, 167.

10. Pliny the Younger, *Letters*, 10.96–97. Tertullian and Eusebius, in later study on this letter, also concur that he was referring to the singing of hymns. Lohr, "Christian Hymnody," 167.

11. Justin Martyr, *First Apology*, 13.2.

altogether on every side present, we cultivate our fields, praising; we sail the
sea, hymning."[12] He also instructs those newly baptized to communicate,
"to God at night as well as by day; for let not much sleep prevail to keep you
from your prayers and hymns to God."[13] While these two previous examples
seem to exhort Christians to sing praise and hymns individually, making
no mention of corporate worship, there is a hymn, "Hymn to Christ the
Savior" attributed to Clement in his work, *Paedagogus*, that may have been.
Gordley notes that this hymn was most likely used in a communal setting,
and within the strophes themselves is an exhortation for the children to be
gathered together to sing hymns of praise.[14]

Not all were in favor of music and singing in the early church for there
was some resistance to instrumentation. Some instruments, such as the flute,
were seen as too closely related to pagan worship practices.[15] Basil the Great
saw the cithara, an instrument similar to the guitar, as a threat and those who
played the instrument as worthy of excommunication.[16] Other instruments
were lauded as "virtuous" on the basis of their scriptural use, such as the "psal-
tery" or "harp and lyre" as used by David in praising God.[17]

The third century saw a major movement of hymns being composed for
the purpose of establishing orthodoxy in the face of heresies.[18] It was believed
that music was an effective and particularly attractive tool for conveying ideology as well as a tool for propaganda and manipulation of its listeners. Thus,
the church used hymnody to teach and convince hearers of the true gospel
and apostolic teaching. Though, because of the unease at the relation between music/singing and pagan practices, the singing of hymns during services was reserved only for certain parts of the liturgy.[19] Songs of praise and
hymns were sung, but they were not yet considered an important part of the
liturgy and their use was not standardized across the young church. Entering
into the fourth century AD, the number of hymns increased significantly.[20]
Leonhard notes that the increase of hymns used in the liturgy coincided with
the decline of the Eucharist as a small, communal meal. He posits that as
the Eucharist was offered in larger, more public forums (post Constantine),

---

12. Clement of Alexandria, *Stromata*, Book 7, ch. 7.

13. Clement of Alexandria, *To the Newly Baptized*, par. 3.

14. Gordley, "Clement of Alexandria's Hymn to Christ the Savior."

15. Leonhard, "Which Hymns Were Sung in Ancient Liturgies?," 179.

16. Basil the Great, *Commentary on Isaiah* 5, cited in Paul James-Griffiths, "The
Church Fathers on Musical Instruments": https://www.christianheritageedinburgh.org.
uk/2016/08/20/the-church-fathers-on-musical-instruments/.

17. Clement of Alexandria, *Instructor*, Book 2.4.

18. Leonhard, "Which Hymns Were Sung in Ancient Liturgies?," 181.

19. Leonhard, "Which Hymns Were Sung in Ancient Liturgies?," 191.

20. Leonhard, "Which Hymns Were Sung in Ancient Liturgies?," 177.

artful chanting and hymnic involvement of the congregation gave rise to an increase in composition.[21] However, the Council of Laodicea (363–364 AD) decreed that no psalms composed by private individuals should be used in liturgical services, only those found in scripture. This was not necessarily the view of all of the church fathers and leaders moving forward. St. Basil the Great stated that the Holy Spirit "added the grace of music to the truth of doctrine" so that those who hear and sing the music would "pluck the fruit of the words without realizing it." In the next century, St. Augustine of Hippo writes in his *Epistles* (ca. 411 AD):

> But when brethren are assembled in the church, why should not the time be devoted to singing of sacred songs, excepting of course while reading or preaching is going on, or while the presiding minister prays aloud, or the united prayer of the congregation is led by the deacon's voice? At the other intervals not thus occupied, I do not see what could be a more excellent, useful, and holy exercise for a Christian congregation.[22]

This was a part of his discussion of the varying practices between different churches, noting that many of the African churches at that time were indifferent to singing.

Music continued to flourish as part of the church's liturgy and as a source of devotion and education for the laity. The Ars Nova era, which blossomed in the fourteenth century, gifted the human race with masterpieces of sacred music. But this artistic movement which filtered into the church was more concerned with music to be performed and listened to than music for use in liturgy or in transmitting scripture.[23] Enter the sixteenth century and the Reformation, and music again would again see a wide variety of opinion and usage throughout the church. Luther and those of his following used hymnody within the church, Luther having penned many hymns of his own. Calvinists, on the other hand, rejected much of inherited traditional religion including a good deal of traditional church music, preferring psalmody and strict paraphrases of Scripture.[24] Nonetheless, the Reformers in large part saw a new purpose for hymnody within the church, that of actively involving the congregation in the service, and it is at this point that hymn-singing begins to take on the role that we associate with it today.[25]

21. Leonhard, "Which Hymns Were Sung in Ancient Liturgies?,"178.

22. St. Augustine of Hippo, "Letter 55": https://www.newadvent.org/fathers/1102055.htm.

23. Gelineau, "Music and Singing," 441.

24. Dunstan, "Hymnody in Christian Worship," 457.

25. Dunstan, "Hymnody in Christian Worship," 456.

The next two centuries saw hymnography flourish in Germany and take root in other countries to which Protestantism spread.

In England, metrical Psalms were still the most common form of music and singing up to the eighteenth century. Within the Presbyterian and Puritan traditions psalms and paraphrased Scripture were the only forms of singing permitted.[26] However, in the eighteenth century, hymnody in England grew significantly. "The 18th century flowering of English hymnody did not immediately affect the worship of the [Church of England]. But it represented new enthusiasm for hymns, and a new concept of the purpose which they were to serve," explains Dunstan.[27] This new purpose was to create hymns, both from Scripture and from poetic reflection, that would guide a Christian through scriptural understanding of Christian living, warn against common error, teach all to strive for perfection in holiness, and always maintain a holy fear of God.[28] Isaac Watts concentrated his hymnography on reorienting the Psalms through the lens of the New Testament to achieve these ends. For example, phrases concerning the sacrifices of goats or bulls were changed to the sacrifice of Christ, the Lamb of God, and verses dealing with the fear of God become fear with faith and love. Notice below the evolution of Psalm 90 into a well-known hymn:

Psalm 90	Tate & Brody adaptation[29]	Isaac Watts Hymn
Lord, you have been our dwelling place	O Lord the Savior and Defense	Our God, our help in ages past,
In all generations.	Of us thy chosen race	Our hope for years to come.
Before the mountains were brought forth,	From age to age thou still hast been,	Our shelter from the stormy blast,
Or ever you had formed the earth and the world,	Our sure abiding place	And our eternal home.
From everlasting to everlasting you are God.		

26. Dunstan, "Hymnody in Christian Worship," 458.

27. Dunstan, "Hymnody in Christian Worship," 458.

28. The classic of John Wesley, "Preface."

29. Dunstan, "Hymnody in Christian Worship," 459. Tate and Brody adapted Psalms to metrical music for more "singable" Scripture.

One can read the New Testament focus on eternal life through the resurrection of Jesus Christ introduced into Ps 90.

Hymnody and hymnography also gained much ground through the Methodist movement. In 1780, a large collection, some 750 hymns, entitled *Collection of Hymns for the Use of the People Called Methodists* was published and contained hymns organized under headings of Christian experience; many of these hymns were by Isaac Watts. John Wesley, in the preface to this collection, writes:

> In what other collection of this kind have you so distinct and full an account of scriptural Christianity? Such a declaration of the heights and depths of religion, speculative and practical? Strong cautions against the most plausible Errors; particularly those that are now most prevalent? And so clear directions for making your calling and election sure; for perfecting holiness in the fear of God?[30]

This book was subsequently republished and greatly expanded with the nearly 4,000 hymns credited to Charles Wesley. These later editions contain the doctrines of the Christian faith as well as the seasons of the Christian year, but, as noted above, they are organized according to the Christian life experience with such headings as "The Goodness of God," "For Believers Rejoicing," and "Society Meeting." Many collections of hymns were produced after this initial example and hymnography increased exponentially. However, even in the midst of this increasing excitement surrounding hymn writing and singing, the role of hymns and their place within the service was not universally agreed upon in England. In the Church of England, hymns were used as an embellishment to the service, "as a means of edification for the people whilst other activities were in process."[31] The Roman Catholic church began to see a rise in its hymn writers, but its use of hymns at this time was outside the normal worship practice. It was primarily in the "Dissenting" traditions that hymns were used regularly as a part of worship and it was a form of meditation and reflection upon and response to the preached Word of God.

As the various religious movements and denominations moved to the New World and continued to blossom with the Great Awakening, so did their musical preferences. John Wesley was no stranger in the United States, and as the Methodist movement grew here, the popularity of the Methodist hymns spread. There is also evidence in Philadelphia of Catholic hymns as early as 1787 originating from the prayer portion of an earlier Catholic

30. Wesley, "Preface."

31. Dunstan, "Hymnody in Christian Worship," 463.

devotional. Each denomination traces its roots back to the earliest settlers which adopted its form of worship. The history of hymnody in the United States is as fascinating and variegated as the different ways in which the various states and territories grew and diversified, and it far surpasses the scope of this section to follow it. However, one particular development must be mentioned, the Negro Spiritual.

Although the Great Awakening and its many revivals gave the people music in which they could sing of their experiences and feelings, concentrating on the soul as well as Scripture, it found a unique reception in the African American slave population. As LeRoy Moore Jr. explains:

> Here was a religion which could give to the slave—no, not give to him, but evoke in him—an inner fire when all else was bleak and cold, a religion elevating him beyond the tribulations of daily existence to realms of glory, to a direct experience of God, almost a fusion of the soul in God, bypassing all intermediaries . . . In his soul, in the recesses of himself and in the company if his brother believers, he was free from his oppressors at last, free in himself and free in God.[32]

This is what the Christianity of the New Awakening (primarily Methodist and Baptist) offered the slave and, beginning a few decades before the Civil War, a large portion of the slave population embraced Christianity. But they did not adopt the music of the white church leaders. They created a musical experience of Scripture and soul that praised and glorified God or instructed each other on Biblical truths while expressing the community's experiences and hopes at the same time. The songs were as much about their current situation as they were about the glory of God and His Word. As noted in the chapter on Wisdom and the Black Church, music often was as much an instrument of wisdom as the preacher, giving the worshiper wisdom that not only taught theology but also how to maneuver in a hostile and oppressive world.[33] This was a radical new development in Christian music[34] and its impact on hymnody in America is still resounding.

To summarize, let us reexamine the roles that music has played in the church throughout this brief survey to see if we can detect a common theme. We noted that in the earliest instances, those written in Paul's correspondences, hymns were used for personal praise and devotion as well as corporate

32. Moore, "Spiritual," 661.

33. See Ernest Ledbetter's chapter in this volume.

34. I do not say hymnody just yet as it took many years before these pieces were able to be written down and the music recorded.

praise and tools to edify one another. The hymns that are present in the NT are centered around the life, death, and resurrection of Jesus Christ and use imagery language, engaging the emotions as well as the intellect. These early hymns were didactic as well, used at times of special rites such as baptism. The second century demonstrates much the same pattern: leaders exhorting their flock to express thanks to and glorify God through songs in individual times of devotion and praise.

In the third century, with the continuing struggle in defining and codifying the young church's beliefs, hymns were used to teach the true apostolic faith, thus combatting heresy among the common folk as well as some popular leaders. This didactic function of instructing the masses on true teaching continued throughout the centuries as the main role for music, while also being used for individual devotion. Not until the Reformation does one note the new role of music in involving the congregation in the service truly take root. At this time, Scripture is still the main source for hymnography. Hymnography grows exponentially over the next two centuries and grows to take on a new role with the Great Awakening and spiritual revivals accompanying this momentous movement. While still praising God and thanking Him for His many blessings, being rooted in Scriptures, the hymns of the New Awakening also include instances of the experiential, of close fellowship with Jesus and other believers, communion with God. These were songs of heart and soul and feeling. The Negro Spirituals took this music and added to it a communal experience, a grounding of the sacred song in the current context of a certain community. This was an entirely new application of hymnody and one that has shaped American Christian music ever since.

What can we glean from this brief synopsis that might help us in answering our original questions? Common throughout is the presence of praise and glorifying of God, both individually and corporately. The role of music as teacher is also a thread that runs throughout the history of the church, whether it be instruction in Scripture and biblical truths or Christian living, running parallel with music using Scripture as its sole muse. What developed in the modern era of the church was music and hymnody that reflected a more personal, more experiential nature of the life of a Christian, music that expressed and celebrated communion with God and fellowship in the body of Christ. Another musical child of the modern church was songs (later hymns) that expressed the situation and specific experiences of a particular community through its exposition of Scripture, praise, or relation of personal experience and deep emotion.

Music's Impact

Have you ever had the moving experience of listening to Handel's "Messiah" at a live performance? After years of listening to recordings of this master-piece, I finally was able to attend a live performance in Cleveland, Ohio. As dictated by tradition, the audience rose to their feet at the opening strains of the "Hallelujah Chorus." As the goosebumps rose on my skin, tears streamed down my face. I had rarely been so elevated by a musical experience. I knew every musical phrase by heart, being a student of classical music, and was able to hear the various voices and their parts. But the exhilaration was more than the knowledge of the structure of the piece. It was more than the beauty of the piece. It was also the words and intention of the piece.

> Hallelujah, hallelujah,
> For the Lord God omnipotent reigneth!
> The kingdom of this world is become the kingdom of our Lord,
> and of His Christ and he shall reign forever and ever!
> King of kings forever and ever; hallelujah hallelujah!
> And Lord of lords forever and ever; hallelujah hallelujah!
> And he shall reign forever and ever,
> King of kings forever and ever and Lord of lords.
> Hallelujah, hallelujah![35]

Such joy and triumphant celebration! But the experience was also more than the words of the piece. There is a synergy between the words and the music whose impact transcends our rational being and speaks to our spiritual selves. This is the unique power and gift that spiritual songs and music lend to the church. It is a blessing to be used to build up the body of Christ.

"The purpose of singing and music is to awake meaning and induce attitude."[36] One could say that this is nowhere more apparent than in church on Sunday mornings. The singing of hymns in corporate worship is com-munal when many diverse voices are joined as one in praise and thanks-giving, regardless of ability. According to Gelineau, this corporate singing engenders feelings of unity and belonging, touching on the essential mystery of the *koinonia* of the church. On an individual level, one study writes that, "It can be argued that sound is more intimate than sight . . . Nowhere is this impact more apparent than in the case of music."[37] Additionally, melody and song can make Scripture easier to remember for the participant, unfolding

---

35. Punctuation and condensing of wording are mine.

36. Gelineau, "Music and Singing," 441.

37. Barrados et al., "From Sound to Significance: Exploring the Mechanisms Un-derlying Emotional Reactions to Music," 281.

the message in an attractive manner and allowing time for meditation upon that message. Music appeals to the emotions. Scripture can be delivered to the congregant not only rationally but also emotionally. Even instrumental music can be a form of worship when it is used in segments of celebration or preparation or as it accompanies a sacrament. In this section we will examine how music impacts the listener or participant and determine how this information might aid us in understanding music as a tool.

When a person listens, remembers, or thinks about a certain piece of music, they are involved in one or more forms of vicarious performance: either a form of imitation or simulation.[38] This type of vicarious performance or participation is called "mimetic participation" and includes singing, humming, repeating the lyrics, or even simply thinking about the music. Mimetic participation in a piece of music creates a sense of shared achievement and belonging with everyone else involved in that piece of music. Mimetic participation is both on a conscious as well as sub-conscious level and has tremendous impact on motivations and conceptualizations. It can also limit conceptualizations, both literal and metaphoric. While this all sounds very clinical and analytical, it is also common sense. There is a reason that certain tunes and rhythms stick in our memory more readily than others ("ear worms"). We are more easily able to remember and hum (participate in) these melodies. Ads written with repetitive phrasing or alliteration are easily remembered. Those choosing the music played in grocery stores and other shopping venues attempt to identify demographics willing to spend the most money and then program music that would be popular and identifiable by this demographic in order to create a shared identity between them and the retailer and engender conceptualizations that encourage spending (the glory days, when times were simpler, what I used to eat at Grandma's, etc.). Additionally, they avoid music that would not be readily understood or recognized by the target demographic or music that might have controversial roots or associations, thus limiting negative associations to the retailer. Music is a powerful motivator both consciously and sub-consciously due to the hearer's participation in that music and the sense of belonging and achievement that participation affords.

Music, as well as vocal music, is analyzed when heard. Decisions are made initially on whether a listener "liked" a piece of music or not. Leaders in the church are painfully aware of this fact. However, what may not be as well known is that repeated exposure to the disliked piece increases

---

38. Cox, *Music and Embodied Cognition*, 11. The studies used for this piece of work were conducted on classical music, but it was stated that it would be equally relevant for other forms of music, including songs with lyrics.

the understanding and appreciation of the music.[39] Continued exposure
to a piece of music increases a listener's internal examination and analysis
of that piece, and they begin to know what comes next and can anticipate
notes and words. This increases the participant's reward, and they begin to
make sense of the music. In common vernacular, it begins to grow on them.
This also happens with well-known, well-loved music, entrenching it even
more deeply in the hearts and minds of the listener or participant. As Cox
explains, "Music is an emergent entity."[40] Its existence within a group of
people begins in the first person as performance, the one playing or singing. It then grows into a quasi-first-person entity as those who listened
then participate mimetically while listening and reacting to the music. The
music takes on second person existence through those receiving the music,
the sounds and/or words. There is also a quasi-third-person element to its
entity as those who heard now reflect on the experience they had with the
music. Just like a person, people can "get to know" music, get to know it
better, understand it more deeply, appreciate it, interact with it daily, miss it
if it is absent, and learn from it.

The musical experience as a whole has a number of components within
the participation of the listener: emotional, physical, behavioral, perceptual,
cognitive, existential, and developmental.[41] We briefly examined an aspect
of the cognitive component above. However, not all of the components will
be present at all times in all experiences of music. Listeners, or participants,
often say that emotion is the most important element in a musical experience. For the psychologist, studying the source and cause of the emotional
response to music can be challenging. Note the following definition of emotional causation to understand this difficulty: "In the paradigmatic case, an
emotion is aroused when an event is appraised as having the capacity to
influence the goals or plans of the perceiver."[42] This appraisal would be difficult to ascertain in a listener of instrumental music as it is unclear how
the composition might impact the goals for the listener's life. In contrast,
the emotion causation takes on special meaning when ascribed to music
in the church, whether sung or not, if that music deals with the goals of
the Christian. From another angle, an individual's emotional reaction to
music is affected by their level of focus on the music (are they attending a
concert or is it background music), which in turn is directly impacted by
their immediate context (at a restaurant or attending church). Obviously,

39. Cox, *Music and Embodied Cognition*, 48.

40. Cox, *Music and Embodied Cognition*, 48.

41. Barrados et al., "From Sound to Significance," 282.

42. Barrados et al., "From Sound to Significance," 282.

a church setting has the ability to focus the listener's attention not only on the music, but potentially on coordinated messages. Even though this brief glimpse into the exciting field of emotions and music does not even scratch the surface of the information available, one can begin to see the deep and potentially meaningful connection between the two.

While the above looked at only two psychological effects of music, mimetic participation and emotions, these two brief discussions begin to show how music directly impacts the message congregants receive and how emotions can reinforce that message. Those who listen to and participate in the music in church services reflect on and participate in that music and the words repeatedly after leaving church. The message conveyed by the hymn is reinforced by this repeated participation, whether it be by humming, or singing, or simply reflecting on the words. The emotional aspect, although difficult to quantify and quantitatively evaluate, is no less impactful. Emotion felt in music allows for the service to address the whole person, a being not only of rational mind but of spirit as well. While hymns can be an explicit confession of faith in Christ, they can also be heart-felt, spiritual-filled devotions.

Wisdom through Music

How does this look back at the history of music in the church and the impact music has on its listeners help us in understanding how leaders can use music to build and encourage a wisdom culture? Let us first review what wisdom is and what a culture of wisdom might look like. Then let us examine how wisdom might emerge through music and how music can be used to foster and encourage the growth of wisdom in our church families.

Tomes and treatises have been written concerning the definition and defining characteristics of wisdom. As this essay does not endeavor to add anything to that timeless treasure, a brief review of a few salient points from the opening chapter and some insights from other sources will suffice to provide a framework. As noted by Daniel Hanlon in this volume, wisdom can be defined as "skill," whether it be for craftsmen, artists, or intellectuals. A second level of wisdom which builds on this definition is the skill to live life well. The book of Proverbs demonstrates this concept of wisdom as living in a certain way; the book also explains why living life wisely would be desired. Through its personification of Wisdom as a woman, as well as Folly as a woman, Proverbs demonstrates that the choice between living wisely and living foolishly is the choice between life and death. But it is important to note that wisdom is not only the skill of living wisely, it is also the willingness to listen to and accept the teachings of wisdom. It is not only an action but also a state.

Given the desire to accept wisdom's teaching and to learn the skills of living well, on what does one base the evaluation of wise or foolish? To what does the one desiring wisdom look for guidance? Again, as succinctly summarized for us in chapter 1, fear of the Lord is the source of knowledge and wisdom. Conversely, "Fools despise wisdom and instruction" (Prov 1:7b). The glue between fear of the Lord and wisdom is a recurring concept throughout the OT. Not only is it a theme in Proverbs, but also Job, Ecclesiastes, and Deuteronomy, and is also prevalent in extra-biblical sources such as Sirach and Wisdom of Solomon. What does fear of the Lord look like in a practical sense? Again, referring to Proverbs, to fear the Lord means, "to walk in all his ways, to love him, to serve the Lord your God with all your heart and with all your soul, and to keep the commandments of the Lord your God and his decrees that I am commanding you today, for your own well-being" (Prov 10:12–13). Living wisely, or living life well, means to live according to the way God intended his creatures to live, according to his will, loving and serving him. As fallen creatures, we need instruction and guidance to keep us on the godly path, thus the commandments and decrees. So here we understand both aspects of wisdom mentioned above, living skillfully and being willing to accept wisdom's guidance, combined in describing the fear of the Lord, which is the source of wisdom. A very neat package.

Another way of summarizing the diverse definitions of wisdom, very much in line with the above, comes from Scot McKnight who offers the following definition: "wisdom is living in God's world in God's way."[43] He goes on to note that wisdom is more than simply an education as it is formed out of relationship, and not just any relationship, but a relationship with one endowed with wisdom. Further, one must be willing to receive from and emulate the wise person, not simply be in fellowship with them. Supported by wisdom's description in Prov 1, McKnight describes this as "receptive reverence,"[44] again demonstrating the willingness to listen and accept the teachings of wisdom in addition to living them out in life.

The above discussion has been built primarily from discussions of wisdom in the OT, which is fitting in that initially, knowledge of the will of God was covenantal and set out in Torah. But what does wisdom look like through the lens of the NT, specifically through the life, death, resurrection, and ascension of Jesus Christ? How does the church's life in the new covenant

43. McKnight, *Pastor Paul,* 172.

44. McKnight, *Pastor Paul,* 174, quoting William P. Brown.

affect its living in God's world in God's way? In short, it doesn't. The church is called, no less than was Israel, to walk in all God's ways, to love him, to serve the Lord God with all its heart and soul. The adjustment comes in guidance for fallen people in discerningwhich courses of action are wise, which ways lead to skillful living and to life, and what should be received and accepted in a reverent manner. Jesus has now taken the place of Torah as a guide for wisdom. Christ Jesus is the wisdom from God for God's people, for those who believe in Jesus Christ (taken from 1 Cor 1:30). The standard of wisdom is now belief in Jesus, in who he is and what he did.

One final facet of wisdom ought to be mentioned, especially in light of our pursuit of wisdom through music: that of the role of tradition in wisdom. As noted above, wisdom is learned and acquired through relationship with those who are known to be wise. If these sages are wise, then it follows that they became so also through relationship with those who were wise before them. Carrying this back through time, there must be a chain of wisdom that has been preserved and gifted from one generation to the next. This is wisdom tradition. As McKnight explains, this wisdom tradition is preserved from the past to be used in the present, but also to be passed on through learning and emulation to the future, ensuring that present actions and future directions are consistent with the wisdom from the past. This is not to say that wisdom is contrary to change. Wisdom can adapt because it *is* handed down from generation to generation and each step encounters new challenges, new environments, and new modes of transmission. In fact, wisdom benefits from some adaptation, as long as the central message of the wisdom—living in God's world in God's way—remains true to tradition.

Now, let us pull all these threads together and see how leaders can engender wisdom through music. Wisdom is living in God's world in God's way. As Paul writes to the Colossians, "we have not ceased praying for you and asking that you may be filled with the knowledge of God's will in all spiritual wisdom and understanding, so that you may lead lives worthy of the Lord, fully pleasing to him . . . " (Col 1:9b–10a). Paul goes on to explain how the church was to know what this new standard of wisdom was by using a hymn:[45]

> He (Christ) is the image of the invisible God, the firstborn of all creation; . . . He is the head of the body, the church; he is the beginning, the firstborn from the dead, so that he might come to have first place in everything. For in him all the fullness of

45. Gordley, *Christological Hymns*, 118–19. Gordley notes that the vast majority of scholars have agreed that this was a hymn, although there is disagreement as to its original form, use, and purpose.

God was pleased to dwell, and through him God was pleased to reconcile to himself all things, whether on earth or in heaven, by making his peace through the blood of his cross (Col 1:15–20).

In examining the early church's hymnody, we see this cross-centered theme constantly repeated. The hymn in Colossians, noted above, is an excellent example. While there is debate whether or not this passage was actually sung, it is not debated that it is written in a poetic or hymnic fashion and served a special purpose in early Christian worship.[46] Gordley notes that this passage was used frequently in the early church and that it was instrumental in the formation of early Christians, as well as the doctrine on Christ and his cross. The Philippian hymn (Phil 2:6–11) is another example of exhibiting wisdom as the cross in hymnic form. Quoting Gordley, "This poem promotes a set of beliefs, values, and practices, as well as memories of historical events, that support a way of being that is quite different from the social and cultural values that were prominent within ancient Greek or Roman cities."[47] Reciting or leading the congregation in these hymns was a practice in wisdom, both in teaching the way of the cross, the way to walk in the world, as well as learning and reflecting upon these ways. Additionally, the language used in these hymns was poetic and lyrical for a purpose. The wording and the rhythm evoked images and ideas in a mode that was not necessarily rational or logical; it appealed more to the imagination and the emotions.[48] We know from our previous brief survey of the impact of music through the emotions, that emotional responses can be affected by focus and environment, as well as one's perception of how one's life and goals might be impacted by the stimulus. For the early Christians, listening and likely participating in these hymns, with their poetic and lyrical language, together in an intimate and tightly knit gathering, knowing that every word held value for their lives and transformative power, reflecting and contemplating on what they are learning, the singing of hymns was central and indispensable to the transmission of wisdom.

Moving forward, while churches were still singing psalms and musically modified Scripture, hymnography took on a more creative flair in order to address the needs of the day. These hymns moved beyond the "crucifixion-death-resurrection-ascension" contents of the NT hymns and reflected specific issues raised in the church such as the effects of the redemptive work of Christ, and the current relationship between Christ and his church.[49]

46. Gordley, *Christological Hymns*, 29,30.

47. Gordley, *Christological Hymns*, 109–10.

48. Gordley, *Christological Hymns*, 30.

49. Cf. Gordley, "Clement of Alexandria's Hymn to Christ the Savior."

Hymnody continued to be a prominent tool in teaching both in what Christ did for the church and how he continues in relationship with her. We also have evidence that the theme of praise and thanksgiving, to which the church is exhorted, continued with vigor at this time. One can see that the tradition of wisdom being taught through the use of hymns had been passed down through the early generations and how it was being used to instruct Christians on living their life in Christ. The singing of Christ-centered hymns had become a tradition and a practice in wisdom itself.

There is no need to retrace the entire history of hymnody and wisdom through the ages for the pattern will be the same. Singing hymns of thanksgiving and praise to God, focusing on the cross of Christ, is a tradition handed down through millennia of the church. This music transmits wisdom through its lessons and encourages wisdom through reception of these lessons, by participation and reflection. Through mimetic participation and emotional response, music delves deeper into the listener and draws them to itself on a different level than simply the rational or logical, so that wisdom is imprinted not only on their minds but also on their hearts, reinforcing the wisdom gained on multiple levels. Music is a powerful tool in the hands of church leaders and serious, prayerful thought should be given to choosing wise music for those whom they lead. Simply because music is "unwise" does not mean that it will not have an equally long lasting and emotional response as wise music would. And, "unwise" music can do as much harm as wise music can do good.

Practical Wisdom for Music in the Church

First, look to tradition for inherited wisdom and be willing to learn from it. The hymnic tradition that has been handed down from the beginnings of the church centers on hymns of praise and thanksgiving and focuses on the death and resurrection of Jesus Christ. As the tradition changed somewhat to accommodate new questions and new understandings arising from the growth of the church, the tradition added hymns which taught about Christ's continuing work and involvement with the church. Christ, as the visible incarnation of the invisible God, is the center and focus of the traditional hymns. If one wishes to encourage and teach wisdom, beginning with the fear of God, learning to live in God's way in his world, with Christ as the standard of what that means, then hymns should have Christ as their central focus. Leaders should examine the hymns of their current traditions, those most frequently sung. What is their central focus? Is it Christ? Is it God? Even if the hymns are expressing the experience of a

group or community, as the spirituals did, it is possible to still maintain
focus on Christ, giving thanks and praise to God, as evidenced by many of
those pieces, and the psalms as well.

Next, look at the words and the actual music. You do not have to be
a choir director to do this. What words are repeated? What words does the
melody highlight or emphasize? After you sing, what remains in your mind
an hour later? Do these phrases and words reflect the centrality of Christ,
his life, death, resurrection, ascension, and continuing work? Do they give
glory or thanksgiving to God? They should. If the words which remain with
you center around "me," "my life," "my battles," "my dreams," or anything
self-centered, carefully reconsider the piece. There are many things God
has done for each of us individually and as the body of Christ, for which
we should give thanks and celebrate joyfully. There is nothing wrong with
singing praise for those bountiful gifts and blessings, but the focus and the
majority of the phrases in the praise should be on God and his Son, Jesus
from whom the gifts flow. As Paul explained to the Corinthians, "He is the
source of your life in Christ Jesus, who became for us wisdom from God,
and righteousness and sanctification and redemption . . . " (1 Cor 1:30).
Jesus has primacy in all and over all as the source of life. Without him there
would be no gifts for which to be thankful. Thus, for wisdom to prevail,
even songs of praise for blessings, individual or corporate, must be focused
on Christ. Remember that the congregation is going to participate, actively
(one hopes), mimetically, and emotionally in these hymns. The words and
the music will continue to resonate and impact them long after they leave
the sanctuary. In choosing music with wisdom at its core, where rhythms
and melody emphasize words and phrases centering on Christ, you are
helping to impart wisdom to the congregation.

As mentioned at the opening, most church leaders will, at one time or
another, be confronted with disagreements surrounding musical options
and opinions. Many churches offer two services, one traditional and one
contemporary, so as to please everyone's preferences. Other churches take
the plunge toward one style or the other and hope for the best. Choosing
music for services can lead to turbulent waters and a leader must not only
choose wisely but also educate the church on the right role and function
of music. The form the music takes is secondary (or even tertiary). The
hymns we should sing are not for our emotional well-being or personal entertainment and enjoyment. One does not go to church to watch a concert
or to be entertained. Music is for the praise and glorification of God. The
biblical and christological focus of wise hymns are also tools for edification and education in the church. Wise music is about praise, worship,
and thanksgiving. Pure and simple. And if debate surrounding the type

and sound of the music is demanding so much attention that it is causing friction in the congregation, then the focus has been removed from Christ and the music is a distraction. It is not wisdom but folly. Those who refuse to sing wisely chosen hymns because of one factor or another are acting foolishly, and a wise leader will need to teach and possibly admonish them so as to teach them wisdom.

Music reaches the spirit through emotion as well as rationale and resonates there long after the mind has moved on to other thoughts. Wisdom is found in music that guides the mind and emotions toward God through Christ. It puts the congregation in a mind of thankfulness, of praise for blessings, of glorifying God, of recalling the great things he has done, and of Jesus Christ and his life, death, resurrection, and ascension around which we center our lives. As we often receive wisdom from tradition, I will close with the final instruction from John Wesley from his "Directions for Singing":

> Above all sing spiritually. Have an eye to God in every word you sing. Aim at pleasing him more than yourself, or any other creature. In order to this attend strictly to the sense of what you sing, and see that your Heart is not carried away with the sound, but offered to God continually; so shall your singing be such as the Lord will approve of here, and reward when he cometh in the clouds of heaven.[50]

Bibliography

Baber, Charles. "Wesley's Directions for Singing." https://um-insight.net/in-the-church/local-church/wesley-s-directions-for-singing/.

Barrados, Goncalo, et al. "From Sound to Significance: Exploring the Mechanisms Underlying Emotional Reactions to Music." *American Journal of Psychology* 128 (2015) 281.

Cox, Arnie. *Music and Embodied Cognition: Listening, Moving, Feeling and Thinking.* Bloomington: Indiana University Press, 2016

Dunstan, Alan. "Hymnody in Christian Worship." In *The Study of Liturgy*, edited by Cheslyn Jones et al., 507–18. New York: Oxford University Press, 1978

Gelineau, J., SJ. "Music and Singing in the Liturgy." In *The Study of Liturgy*, edited by Cheslyn Jones et al., 493–506. New York: Oxford University Press: 1978

Gordley, Matthew. "Clement of Alexandria's Hymn to Christ the Savior." https://matthewgordley.blogspot.com/2019/12/clement-of-alexandrias-hymn-to-christ.html.

———. *New Testament Christological Hymns: Exploring Texts, Contexts and Significance.* Downers Grove, IL: InterVarsity Academic, 2018.

---

50. Baber, "Wesley's Directions for Singing."

Johnson, H. Wayne. "Practicing Theology on a Sunday Morning: Corporate Worship as Spiritual Formation." *TrinJ* 31 (2010) 5–6.

Leonhard, Clemens. "Which Hymns Were Sung in Ancient Liturgies?" In *Literature or Liturgy? Early Christian Hymns and Prayers in their Literary and Liturgical Context in Antiquity*, edited by Clemens Leonhard et al. Tübingen: Mohr Siebeck, 2014.

Leonhard, Clemens, and Hermut Lohr, eds. *Literature or Liturgy? Early Christian Hymns and Prayers in their Literary and Liturgical Context in Antiquity*. Tübingen: Mohr Siebeck, 2014.

Lohr, Hermut. "What Can We Know About the Beginnings of Christian Hymnody?" In *Literature or Liturgy? Early Christian Hymns and Prayers in their Literary and Liturgical Context in Antiquity*, edited by Clemens Leonhard et al. Tübingen: Mohr Siebeck, 2014.

Martin, R. P. "Hymns, Hymn Fragments, Songs, Spiritual Songs." In *Dictionary of Paul and His Letters*, edited by Gerald F. Hawthorne et al. Downers Grove, IL: InterVarsity, 1993.

McKnight, Scot. *Pastor Paul: Nurturing a Culture of Christoformity in the Church*. Grand Rapids: Brazos, 2019.

Moore, LeRoy, Jr. "The Spiritual: Soul of Black Religion." *American Quarterly* 23 (1971) 661.

Wesley, John. "Preface." *A Collection of Hymns for the Use of the People Called Methodists*. https://www.ccel.org/w/wesley/hymn/jw.html.

WISE CHURCH ECONOMIES

By Brandon Evans

Y ou are reading a book about wisdom, and Prov 3:13–18 is clear—if you
gain wisdom, you will become rich. But this does not mean that those
with *hokmah* ("wisdom") are promised an enviable net worth. Wisdom itself is more valuable than any currency, investment account, property, pos-
session, or financial status.[1] Those who possess it are owners of a priceless
resource. Material wealth may be acquired with wisdom. But wisdom can
never be acquired with money.[2]

There is no shortage of literature, sermons, and classes available on
concepts like money, work, possessions, stewardship, and generosity. There
is always a need for individuals to experience a "conversion of the wallet," as
Martin Luther put it.[3] This chapter, however, integrates these financial topics
and focuses on the bigger picture of nurturing wise church economies.

It might seem odd to call a local church an economy. But an economy
is simply a system of production, management, and consumption of resources. On the macroeconomic level, this includes complex national and
global systems. On the microeconomic level, this includes the behavior of
individuals and organizations—including churches. Just as the church is a
body of interconnected members, it is also an economy of interconnected

---

1. In the Wisdom Literature, there is a strong correlation between wisdom and
wealth, especially in the metaphorical sense of wisdom *being* wealth (Pss 112:3; 119:14;
Prov 3:13–18; 8:18; 13:18; 14:24; 22:1, 4; Eccl 7:12). The apocryphal wisdom books
display similar themes. Wisdom of Solomon, for example, extols wisdom in its myriad
expressions, and, like Proverbs, displays wisdom as more valuable than material riches
(7:7–9; 8:5; 8:17–18).

2. See Job 28:12–19.

3. Martin Luther is reported to have said that humans need to experience three
conversions: of heart and mind and purse. See Powell, *Giving to God*, xvi.

stewards.[4] This does not mean that churches equate to religious businesses seeking to make a profit. But churches do acquire resources (like money, property, and equipment) to steward in a way that produces value in return. Churches are also called to care for the economically disadvantaged and can influence larger economic policies and structures. These are all functions of an economic system. On top of this, each local church is a public representation of how God's new creation economy is meant to function. God is the provider of all things. And he is the one who defines the way of wisdom in all areas of life. Wise churches display God's economic wisdom.

Saying that is easy. Living it out is the hard part. Mammon is a seductive god. There is always the war between the ideals and realities of the budget, and the invisible hand of the market can squeeze and punch. If wisdom is a skill, then economic wisdom might be an *expert level* skill.[5] As pastors and leaders, we do not have the power to change the human heart or alter global economic systems. But we do have the power to nurture God's economic wisdom within our churches through our leadership.

There is a significant amount of biblical real estate devoted to economic topics.[6] And there is an undeniable canonical consistency on the subject. All the major themes in the Old Testament are reaffirmed in the New (with the notable exception of material rewards for faithfulness).[7] So I have distilled the biblical witness from Genesis to Revelation into what I would consider to be three prominent cultural characteristics of a wise church economy—1) a culture that aims for the wealth target, 2) a culture of economic empowerment, and 3) a culture of economic integrity.

---

4. DeYmaz and Li, *Coming Revolution in Church Economics*, 78, frame the local church as a microeconomy as well, saying, "Let's consider the local church . . . as its own economic system in which there is . . . an expectation that those benefiting from services rendered will pay a portion of the total costs incurred in the process."

5. I will not cover topics related to wealth management—budgeting, investing, estate planning, etc. There are many helpful resources on those subjects. Instead, I will largely focus on the role we pastors (and leaders) play in shaping our local church cultures in relation to production and distribution of financial resources.

6. Money, livestock, property, family, tithing, and taxation, among others, are intersecting concepts related to economics in the Bible. I will not speak to economic systems in general, but will primarily focus on the interplay between biblical wisdom and economic concepts such as money, possessions, financial structures, and economic context.

7. Blomberg, *Neither Poverty nor Riches*, 84.

A Culture that Aims for the Wealth Target

Wisdom in general is "life within limits," as Daniel Hanlon pointed out in the opening chapter. So wise churches operate within God's economic limits because all material provision ultimately stems from him (Deut 8:17–18; Matt 6:25–34). God has created a good world with resources for humanity to harness in a way that produces flourishing. Money is presented in the Bible, especially the Wisdom Literature, as a gift from God to be enjoyed (cf. Eccl 5:19–20). Economic wisdom, then, begins with an expressed dependence on God for all resources. Rejecting God's provision leads to an arrogant self-sufficiency, and the perpetuation of financial corruption. The wise do not fall into this trap.

But dependence on God for material provision does not limit our human responsibility to plan, labor, and manage it. Wealth is a good gift, but it is a good gift to *pursue*. In the Wisdom literature, financial stability is consistently connected to diligent work.[8] And the wise management of our finances and property is our human responsibility. Wealth is squandered through reckless living.[9] A wise church economy is characterized by individuals who see money as a tool, not a master. Jesus conveys this concept in the puzzling and amusing parable of the dishonest manager (Luke 16:1–9).[10]

He urges his followers, like the crafty lame duck manager in the story, to use the resources at their disposal, namely unrighteous wealth (*mamōna tēs adikias*), to "make friends." Wealth is "unrighteous" in the sense that it is of *this* age.[11] Jesus's point is that the resources we have at our disposal are to be used for kingdom purposes. Mammon, however, tries to convince us to relentlessly pursue financial gain because "money can buy happiness." And this is actually *true*—but only to a point. A landmark study from Princeton concluded that as income goes up, so does a positive assessment of one's life in terms of success and worth. Effectively, a higher net worth leads to a higher sense of personal accomplishment. But, the same study interestingly observed that humans have an emotional well-being tank that can only be filled so much until it overflows. With more money comes a greater sense of emotional satisfaction—but then a limit is reached.[12] After that point, money does not add any emotional boost.

8. See Prov 6:10–11; 12:27; 13:11; 28:19.

9. See Prov 29:3.

10. For a survey on the various interpretations of this parable, see Marshall, *Gospel of Luke*, 614.

11. Green, *Gospel of Luke*, 593, notes, "Jesus insinuates that mammon has no place in the age to come."

12. The "top of the cup" income from the study was around $75,000 (although the

Feasibly, a wise member of the middle class could have the same emotional state stemming from their net worth as Jeff Bezos.

So, like many aspects of wise living, there is a target to shoot for when it comes to our financial resources. In essence, wisdom guides us to work to provide enough with an appreciation for what one has been given by God. That is the target. The words of Agur in Prov 30:8–9[13] provide a summarized prayer of the wealth target—contentment with enough so as to be freely devoted to the worship of YHWH:

> Give me neither poverty nor riches,
>   but give me only my daily bread.
> Otherwise, I may have too much and disown you
>   and say, 'Who is the Lord?'
> Or I may become poor and steal,
>   and so dishonor the name of my God.

The wealth target is a thankful appreciation of enough. But the target can be missed. Undershooting the wealth target manifests in a lazy work ethic, impulsive and reckless spending habits, and a lack of financial planning. Material riches are often linked to spiritual dangers, but material poverty carries risks as well. *Desiring* to be rich can lead a person to stray from Christ (1 Tim 6:9–10). The poor are prone to envy, theft, and the worship of human leaders who promise prosperity. Poverty in the Bible is not romanticized as a virtue in and of itself. The wise pursue a sustainable and secure financial lifestyle that enables them to *benefit* others. This is why Paul warns the Thessalonian church against idleness and being a financial burden to others (2 Thess 3:6–12). An individual is to work, even with ambition to prosper, and to provide for family. The wise are called to exhibit financial responsibility, spend within their means, and pay debts. Some may fail to hit the target (and there's more to say about wisdom in response to that), but only the rare few are called to *intentionally* miss the target.

The wealth target can be overshot, too. This is expressed in a hoarding of wealth, an overprotective stinginess, or an anxiety about maintaining a complex and expensive lifestyle. Walter Brueggemann argues that the central temptation for Israel in the promised land was coveting.[14] That might be the central temptation in our land, too. But the love of money and possessions does not produce satisfaction (Eccl 2:1–11; 5:10; 6:2) and endless toil for more wealth is foolishness (Prov 23:4; Eccl 4:8). With

---

exact figure certainly varies by time and location); cf. Kahneman and Deaton, "High Income Improves Evaluation of Life but Not Emotional Well-Being," 16489–93.

13. I will use the NIV translation, unless otherwise noted.

14. Brueggemann, *Land*, 59.

increasing wealth comes the possibility of numerous abuses, misuses, and dangers. The rich are prone to being wise in their own eyes (Ps 49:6; 52:7; Prov 28:11) and the more wealth one has, the more risk there is that pride will ruthlessly puff up the soul.

An overconfidence that stems from a high net worth has been empirically verified. There's a recent study in *Journal of Personality and Social Psychology* where participants were given a flashcard memory game. Afterwards, they were asked to rate how they thought they did compared to others on a scale of 1–100. The researchers found that those with more education, higher income, and a higher perceived social class had "an exaggerated belief that they would perform better than others, compared with their lower-class counterparts."[15] The well-to-do didn't *actually* score higher on the test, but they *believed* that they did. That's the temptation that accompanies wealth—to think we're better than others because of our financial status. But this is not true in God's new creation economy. The faithful, those who embody God's wisdom, are the ones who will be rewarded in the age to come. So the rich are not to boast in their riches (Jer 9:23–24) because earthly wealth disappears with judgment (Ezek 27:27).

Wise churches consist of people who aim for the target of godliness with contentment, which is in itself a valuable state of being (1 Tim 6:6–10). We arrived into this life with nothing, and the same will be true for the next. But, as Paul says, if in the meantime we have what we need, we will be content.[16] Those, however, who relentlessly pursue wealth run into danger—temptations, traps, and harmful desires that lead to ruin. The love of money is *a* root (not the only root, but maybe the most invasive one) of all kinds of evils. An insatiable desire for more causes people to wander from the faith and bring pain upon themselves. Wisdom, however, redirects us from the relentless pursuit of more to the thankful appreciation of enough.

As church leaders, we are called to guide people towards the wealth target. We are to encourage diligent work and the pursuit of a sustainable income, as well as urge for responsible stewardship and generosity (more on this below). Each individual in our congregations is called to be financially wise. But this concept applies at the ecclesial level, too. In other words, if we zoom out and look at our local church as a unit, is *it* aiming for the wealth target? As is true at the individual level, a wise church exhibits a sustainable budget that is able to benefit others. This includes adequate staffing (and adequately paying the staff), providing hospitable facilities, and offering

---

15. Belmi et al., "Social Advantage of Miscalibrated Individuals," 254–82.

16. Paul specifically lists food and clothing, but this can be seen as a shorthand for "needs."

financial benevolence. As leaders, we must avoid undershooting the target by not inspiring enough contributions or by squandering the resources we have been given. We also must avoid overshooting the target by idolizing productivity and expansion and equating a lavishly expensive ministry with a spiritually healthy one. A wise church displays the thankful appreciation of enough both individually and corporately.

The Divestiture of Excess—Generosity

For many of us in the modern west God has provided a surplus and that is a good thing. Hitting the wealth target in our churches, then, requires a culture of generosity. Being generous is not a mere suggestion. It is the way of wisdom. In the Bible, the faithful rich *always* display generosity.[17] When more is acquired by us, more is required of us. Scot McKnight argues that Paul charged the primary leader of his churches to nurture a culture of generosity.[18] The divestiture of excess is a crucial component of economic wisdom because it keeps us from overshooting the wealth target while others in our community suffer. Generosity, rather than hoarding or lavishly spending, is an ultimate display of dependence on God's provision.

The parable of the rich fool (Luke 12:13–21) provides the paradigmatic warning for hoarding. In the story, a (already) rich man's land produces an abundance. It is noteworthy that Luke emphasizes that the *land* produces plentifully. It's not that the rich man didn't work for his field's production, but that he is not solely responsible for his income. (How many of us have likewise benefited from productive soil?) The rich fool, however, ignores the source of his provision and his chief focus is where to store *his* crops. "And he said, 'I will do this: I will tear down *my* barns and build larger ones, and there I will store all *my* grain and *my* goods. And I will say to my soul, 'Soul, you have ample goods laid up for many years; relax, eat, drink, be merry'" (Luke 12:18–19). He sees his skyrocketing wealth not as a gift to be shared, but as an entitlement to selfishly indulge. But that night, the rich man dies and his wealth goes to someone else (who didn't earn it and probably won't adequately appreciate it). So Jesus's closing point is this—this is what happens to those who lay up treasures for themselves and are not rich towards God. It's not that the rich fool is killed for his self-indulgence in a sort of retributive justice from God. It's that his abundance of wealth cannot change the fact that his life is a vapor. When he was alive, he did not use his prosperity according to God's will and thus

---

17. Blomberg, *Neither Poverty nor Riches*, 145.

18. McKnight, *Pastor Paul*, 82.

rejected God in the process. That is what makes him a fool. If he had been wise, he would have been "rich towards God," meaning he would have used his material wealth to meet needs in the world.[19] Augustine memorably sums up the rich fool's folly: "He did not realize that the bellies of the poor are much safer storerooms than his barns."[20]

Now one of the purposes of the parables, and especially the parable of the rich fool, is that Jesus wants us to imagine ourselves in the story—are we rich fools? The lie that Mammon tells is that the relentless pursuit of more is good. Bigger is better. Extravagance leads to happiness. And the ultimate lie is that what we earn is completely ours to keep. But Jesus reverses worldly values. He urges his followers to get off the hamster wheel of overconsumption and to instead be generous with our surplus. If we can give Mammon away, it doesn't own us. A grateful generosity is a characteristic of a wise church. Wise individuals and churches display the power of God over the power of Mammon.

To sum this up, let's envision an individual who practices God's economic wisdom in Jesus's preferred method—a parable. This is the "parable of the rich fool" reimagined as the "parable of the rich *sage*."

> And he told them a parable, saying, "The land of a rich man produced plentifully, and he thought to himself, 'What shall I do, for I already have all that I need?' And he said, 'I will do this: I will take a portion of God's generous gift and give to those in the fields next to me who had a lean harvest, and I'm going to use part of my surplus to invest in my church and my community, and there I will bless others with God's grain and God's goods. And I will say to my soul, "Soul, you have all that you need and this life is but a vapor; relax, eat, drink, be merry, and give thanks to God for providing an abundance of possessions."' And God said to him, "Wise one! This night your soul is required of you, but your generosity has shown that your true treasure is in heaven, where it belongs." So is the one who lays up treasure in heaven and is not rich toward themselves.

To Tithe or Not to Tithe? A Call for Consistency

Our local churches rely on the generosity of our individual members. And there are a number of organizations that specialize in fundraising strategies.

19. As John Nolland, *Luke 9:21–18:34*, 688, says, "To 'become rich with God in view' is to use one's material wealth for the relief of real needs in the world."

20. Quoted in Edwards, *Gospel According to Luke*, 372.

I can't speak to those tactics but I do think that forming cultures of generosity begins with consistency in our teaching on the subject—specifically in relation to the practice of tithing.

The word "tithe" is often used in connection with calls for generosity, so it's worth visiting the Torah's instruction on the practice. First of all, tithing was not unique to God's covenant people. It was a common practice in the ANE, and Israel was no exception.[21] The expressed purpose of the tithe was to provide for the Levites, resident aliens, orphans, and widows—in other words, those who did not own land and thus could not profit from the proceeds of their property. *Economic equity was the primary goal of the tithe.* Additionally, the collective income from the tithes was indispensable for maintaining the temple system itself.[22]

It is important to note that tithing was not an act of generosity. The tithe was an obligation, and for all intents and purposes, a tax. Paying the tithe was enforced, sometimes aggressively. Josephus writes that some high priests sent their men to the farmers' barns to seize tithes during the time of king Agrippa (*Ant.* 20.181, 206–7). A person could make a vow to give property to YHWH in addition to the obligatory tithe (see Lev 27:14–24). These vows were not required (although a person was held accountable to the promises in their vow), and can be considered voluntary acts of generosity.[23] Tithing, however, cannot be.

It's also important to note that the Torah's instruction on the content and recipient of the tithe is complicated. Leviticus, Numbers, and Deuteronomy display a divergence of details. Lev 27:30–33 calls for tithes of grain, fruit, and livestock to be set apart as "holy to the Lord." Num 18:21–32 instructs allocation of the tithes to go to the Levites. Deut 12:5–19 instructs people to take tithes of grain, wine, and oil into the sanctuary and *eat them* with the Levites. (Deut 14:22–27 reiterates this and adds a provision for those who live too far away to sell their tithes and use the proceeds to buy whatever their appetite craves for the feast.) And Deut 14:28–29 and 26:12–13 stipulate that every third year the tithes are to be stored in the towns, rather than the sanctuary, and made readily available to the economically vulnerable. (This was the first known form of social welfare.)[24] It seems that the inconsistencies in these texts are reconcilable if we hold

---

21. None of the extant laws deal with tithing though other documents show that it was a widespread practice in the Ancient Near East; cf. Baker, *Tight Fists or Open Hands?*, 239.

22. Milgrom, *Leviticus 23–27*, 2425.

23. Hartley, *Leviticus*, 486.

24. Baker, *Tight Fists or Open Hands?*, 247–48.

that there was one tithe that was adapted for contextual reasons.[25] But the history of interpretation on the tithe is understandably complex because of these incongruencies. Rabbinic interpretation saw three separate tithes, the "first tithe" from Numbers, the "second tithe" from Deuteronomy, and the third year tithe, which, when added together, would cost the worshiper 23.3 percent of their total annualized income.[26] The tithe does not simply equate to "give ten percent to the church."

Despite its complexities there is a pragmatic benefit to teaching the tithe. Randy Alcorn presents the popular sentiment that while the tithe may not be explicitly commanded in the New Testament, it is a helpful reference point for today.[27] Alcorn argues that teaching the tithe is logical and practical, clear and consistent, and can be taught to children. He adds that encouraging tithing increases a believer's commitment to God's work and facilitates spiritual growth. Many of us share Alcorn's reasoning.

If tithing is taught, then consistency is imperative. Every Christian who has income (even if it is minimal) should be required to tithe, and the total *must be* 10 percent (or, if you want to follow rabbinic interpretation and free up sanctuary space, 23.3 percent).[28] And individuals should contribute a tenth of every source of income—wages, inheritance, allowance, rebates, sunken treasure discoveries, birthday gifts—*everything*. Tithes cannot truly be called generosity. They are obligatory. Only freewill offerings above and beyond the 10 percent mark can be considered gifts. We cannot teach a form of church tax and call it "generosity." (Imagine the IRS saying "thank you for your generosity" when you submit your tax return.)[29] And if the 10 percent is still taught in principle, shouldn't all the tithe principles be taught? Shouldn't congregants give their tithes directly to church staff and benevolence seekers every third year (like Deut 14:28–29 calls for)? And shouldn't tithers get to enjoy part of their tithe in the form of a party (as Deut 12:5–19 and 14:22–27 instruct)? The complication with the tithe is that it cannot be translated simply into our modern contexts.

25. "Modern scholars . . . generally believe there was one tithe, with a development in the legislation due to changing historical circumstances" (Baker, *Tight Fists or Open Hands?*, 242).

26. Blomberg, *Neither Poverty nor Riches*, 46–47.

27. Alcorn, *Managing God's Money*, 117–18.

28. Alcorn is consistent on this. For him, 10 percent is a starting block, and, appealing to Mal 3:1, giving any less is akin to robbing God (*Managing God's Money*, 126).

29. And the question is also raised on whether or not the gleaning laws still apply. And the Sabbath. And more. The tithe does offer the pragmatic benefits that Alcorn points out. It also complicates many other issues. Approach the tithe wisely.

Many, however, hold that the tithe is not a new covenant obligation. The alternative approach is to teach a wholescale generosity of possessions with a plea for *donating to* the local church. Money is needed to support the ministry, and the generosity of the congregation is the mechanism through which funds are raised to meet the needs of the community as well as fund the ministers.[30] Jesus may have observed the tithe, but he did not instruct it for his new covenant people. It's also noteworthy that nowhere in Paul's letters is there a hint of tithing, which, as a former Pharisee, would have been something he had practiced (at least until his conversion) and something his gentile audience would certainly need to be convinced of.[31] Instead, Paul urges voluntary generosity.

As McKnight argues, Paul sees all Christians as members of a mutually supportive network of generosity, and that this is first to the household of faith.[32] Paul's fundraising efforts for the struggling Jerusalem church in 2 Cor 8–9 serves as the definitive example. He calls the contributions a "relief" (*diakonia*), a "grace" (*charis*), a "sharing" (*koinonia*), and an "abundant gift" (*eulogia*). Here, Paul is tapping into the wisdom of generosity to meet the needs of a struggling congregation.

If teaching the tithe requires teaching con*sistency*, the donation approach requires teaching con*sistently*. Generosity is not automatic, and because of this it needs to be persuasively (and frequently) encouraged. Paul may not have enforced the tithe, but he did not passively raise funds. As Craig Blomberg says, Paul employs "psychologically sophisticated rhetoric" to spur donations for the Jerusalem church.[33] He even plays to a spirit of fundraising competition.[34] Pastors and teachers must likewise find the line between guilt and avoidance when it comes to calls for our congregations to be generous. And this requires winsomeness. The advantage of teaching the tithe is an appeal to obedience that lends itself to producing more consistent church income (in exchange for certain hermeneutical inconsistencies). Those, however, who don't teach the tithe can expect to consistently fundraise to meet needs.

I'm probably not going to settle your mind on whether the tithe is still in effect or not. That requires a larger biblical theological argument that is

---

30. Paul advocates for the right of ministers to be compensated for their work, even though he himself did not exercise this right (1 Cor 9:1–27).

31. Verbrugge and Krell, *Paul and Money*, 273.

32. McKnight, *Pastor Paul*, 98–101.

33. Blomberg, *Neither Poverty nor Riches*, 193.

34. "As was often done in the ancient Hellenistic world, though not always as tactfully, the apostle appeals to a spirit of competition to enjoin virtuous behaviour" (Blomberg, *Neither Poverty nor Riches*, 192).

outside the scope of this essay. My overarching point is that consistency matters when it comes to fostering a culture of generosity. A culture of wisdom will display generosity, primarily to those in the household of faith. The generosity of our churches reflects how God's economy is meant to work.

A Culture of Economic Empowerment

While many in our modern western churches benefit from financial surpluses, there are many who don't. Economic inequality is a human reality. And as inequality perpetuates, the poor are further disadvantaged. God's vision for those who have, then, is to elevate those who don't. Empowerment of the poor is arguably the central economic concept in the Bible. It is a theme that appears in every section of Scripture. Even Proverbs, which is a common source for personal financial ethics, displays far more of a concern for social justice than it is often credited for.

Economic empowerment begins with equity. Equity does not mean equality. Equity has to do with fairness and justice. The Lord despises uneven scales (Prov 11:1; 20:23). And he will one day settle the economic score. In the Bible, poverty is not inherently linked to laziness. Nor is it linked to a certain standard of living. The poor today have access to information on their phones that far exceeds the famed library of Alexandria in antiquity. Today's poor can take hot showers, which Solomon could not even fathom. They can travel across the country, even if it is by bus, in a way that even the wealthy a century ago couldn't dream of. Poverty is more closely associated with *powerlessness*. And churches are called to empower the poor in their midst. Empowerment is more than no-strings-attached charity. It elevates the disadvantaged so that they can provide for themselves. Wise churches foster economic empowerment within their congregations.

God has called his covenant people to display a counter-cultural concern for the poor. This is a guiding ideal in the Torah in the legal system, agriculture, finance, employment, and trade.[35] The Torah is *vastly* more concerned with social equity than other Ancient Near Eastern law codes. The Torah is clear that land ownership (and with it economic power) is God's allotted gift, not a spoil of the winners (Exod 15:17; Lev 25:23; Deut 8:7–18). Because of this, property rights and profit margins are eclipsed by humanitarian concerns for the economically vulnerable. The Torah focuses on the rights of the working class, whereas its contemporaries in the ANE emphasize the rights of the employers.[36] Terms and conditions for employment were

35. Baker, *Tight Fists or Open Hands?*, 286.
36. Baker, *Tight Fists or Open Hands?*, 299.

far more favorable to the working class in the Torah than in other law collections.[37] The ideal is that people would work hard but not be overworked, be given a fair wage, and be charged fairly for goods and services.

Additionally, the very rhythm of work and rest in the Torah displays a deep concern for economic equity and empowerment. The Sabbath has been described as "perhaps . . . the greatest social revolution in the history of mankind."[38] The seventh day was not only dedicated to God—it provided refreshment for the laborers. While the wealthy can afford to recreate, the poor often do not have such a luxury. But the Sabbath ensured that they did. The sabbatical year, where the land was to be rested and its "natural" produce was to be consumed, extended this revolution. The purpose of this year is to meet the needs of the poor (since the land effectively became communal property during it). There is no ANE parallel to the sabbatical year.[39]

The Sabbath and sabbatical year (not to mention the year of Jubilee) served, in part, to curb the snowballing accumulation of wealth.[40] In non-sabbatical years, the gleaning laws, in which landowners were commanded to share part of their property, ensured that the poor had provisions at every harvest.[41] There is no ANE parallel to this practice, either.[42] What cannot be overlooked in the gleaning laws is that the poor needed to *work* for their sustenance. The landowner is instructed to merely leave the edges of his field unworked (and therefore didn't have to put forth any additional effort for the poor). The poor, then, needed to labor to supply for themselves.[43] Gleaning was a practice of charity, but an empowering form of it that balanced generosity and dignity.[44]

37. Baker, *Tight Fists or Open Hands?*, 307–12.

38. Baker, *Tight Fists or Open Hands?*, 294.

39. Baker, *Tight Fists or Open Hands?*, 224.

40. Blomberg, *Neither Poverty nor Riches*, 42–43.

41. Gleaning is prescribed in Lev 19:9–10; 23:22; Deut 24:19–22; and depicted in Ruth 2.

42. Baker, *Tight Fists or Open Hands?*, 233.

43. Paul, likewise, offers a consistent balance of care for the poor (Rom 12:13, 16; Gal 2:10; 1 Tim 5:3–16), and the responsibility of the capable to work (Eph 4:28; 1 Thess 5:14; 2 Thess 3:6–12). Generosity is not something to be exploited.

44. Another practice prescribed to provide for the poor was "scrumping" (eating the produce of a field as you pass through; Deut 23:24–25). There is no ANE parallel to this, either. While the poor were able to scrump, they were not able to take anything with them. They could only satisfy their immediate hunger, and no more. This instruction protected property owners from theft, but elevated the needs of the hungry over their land rights. Through it the entire covenant community benefited. See Baker, *Tight Fists or Open Hands?*, 248.

The Torah presents even more protection for the poor in the form of systemic debt relief (Deut 15:1–11). While this did happen periodically in Mesopotamia,[45] Israel's system was radical in comparison (and is radical by today's standards, too). Loans with interest are extremely profitable for the wealthy, and can be a means of perpetuating poverty cycles if the poor are unable to climb out of debt (1 Sam 22:2; 2 Kgs 4:1; Prov 22:7). The ANE generally favored the right of those with capital to charge not only interest, but *exorbitant* interest, with rates on money often in the range of 20–50 percent, and rates on grain loans rising as high as 100 percent![46] However, charging interest on loans in Israel's covenant community was explicitly prohibited (Exod 22:25; Lev 25:35–37; Deut 23:19–20). This meant no points could be charged on monetary loans, and no markup could be added to agricultural sales. Loans were effectively made as if to family, not as a business venture.[47]

This instruction on interest-free loans was not meant to encourage borrowers to take advantage of the system but to help the poor who are unable to repay (the wicked borrow but do not repay, as Ps 37:21 says).[48] This also didn't mean that people were free to borrow money for speculation or property advancements, but rather out of need. Loan collateral was condoned, but even it was not to hinder the poor, and creditors were prohibited from hounding their debtors (Exod 22:26–27; Deut 24:6; 24:10–13). As David Baker observes, "The creditor's 'right' to his money is of far less significance than the basic respect he owes a fellow human being."[49]

Economic equity and empowerment was intricately woven into God's instruction for his covenant people. Although the church, as the fulfillment of Israel, is not a national economy like the tribes of Jacob, the new covenant community is to share the same values. God's concern for equity and empowerment has not changed. Empowerment of the poor could even serve as an evaluative standard for whether or not a local church is embodying God's economic wisdom.

---

45. Baker, *Tight Fists or Open Hands?*, 276.

46. Baker, *Tight Fists or Open Hands?*, 253–54.

47. The poor were protected in the legal system as well. Bribery is explicitly prohibited (Exod 23:8; Deut 10:17; 16:19–20) because the rich have power to distort justice with illicit payments. And the categorical denunciation of payments to judges was unique to Israel and served to protect vulnerable classes, who otherwise couldn't afford to pay.

48. The Mishnah likewise holds employers to the obligation of settling unpaid wages, as well as purchasers settling unpaid bills for merchandise and criminals paying fines (*m. Shevi' it* 10:1–2).

49. Baker, *Tight Fists or Open Hands?*, 272.

Cleansing the Sanctuary

Economic corruption and wisdom are antithetical. As McKnight says, Jesus "set the tone for economic justice in his kingdom mission."[50] All four Gospels chronicle Jesus's cleansing of the temple (Matt 21:12–16; Mark 11:15–18; Luke 19:45–47; John 2:13–16). A harmonized picture of this event is one of merchants selling oxen and sheep and pigeons, and money-changers converting currency to Tyrian silver coins (the "official" coin of the temple tax) with a profitable markup.[51] This was likely happening in the court of the gentiles, thus making it a public spectacle of economic exploitation.[52] In John's account, Jesus says "Get these out of here! Stop turning my Father's house into a market [*emporion*]!"[53] And it was a lucrative market. Josephus claims that there were 256,500 sacrifices on one passover alone (*J.W.* 6.422–27).

In the midst of this corrupt system, Jesus overturned the tables, and, depending on whether John refers to the same cleansing or a second one, fastens a whip to drive people out. His attack was not against the temple itself, but against those who had diverted its purpose from worship to profit. This was nothing but the action of the divine prophet-king confronting a broken system in the covenant community. Jesus had exposed that the system, and its leadership, was culpable before God because the worship of God had been exchanged for the worship of Mammon.[54] Jesus, however, was not totally against the temple system. He approved of the generous contributions from individuals to support it. But he did criticize the way in which the system had been corrupted.

There is an interesting text where both the commendation of individual generosity and condemnation of systemic injustice intersect. The widow's offering (Luke 21:1–4) has traditionally been seen as an example of radical generosity from the widow (and is a passage that easily preaches in a generosity sermon). The traditional message from this passage goes something like "it's not the amount of the gift that matters, but the heart behind it."

---

50. McKnight, *Pastor Paul*, 80.

51. Fitzmyer, *Gospel According to Luke X–XXIV*, 1267; Bovon, *Luke 3*, 19.

52. Morris, *Luke*, 300; Bovon, *Luke 3*, 19.

53. In the synoptic accounts, Jesus quotes Isa 56:7 and Jer 7:11: "It is written, 'My house shall be called a house of prayer,' but you make it a den of robbers." The Jer 7 context urges the pursuit of justice and cessation of oppressing the sojourner, orphan, and widow (see Jer 7:5–6).

54. Jesus's actions severed his relationship with the Jewish leadership, specifically the Sanhedran, High Priest, and Sadducees, and triggered his execution; cf. Luke 19:45; see Bock, *Luke*.

However, there is compelling evidence for a *negative* interpretation of the widow's offering—namely, that Jesus is pointing out that the woman is a victim of a corrupt financial system that exploits the poor and wastes wealth on opulence. The message in this interpretation, then, is along the lines of "God is bringing (and will bring) judgement to corrupt systems and justice to the poor." Scholarship today seems to be divided on the interpretation.[55]

In isolation, the pericope indicates that Jesus is praising the widow's sacrificial generosity. Contemporary literary parallels exhibit similar messages of approval for a small gift from the poor in contrast with extravagant gifts from the rich.[56] And the grammatical evidence for the praise interpretation is strong. The widow is offering a gift (*dōron*) into the treasury box (*gazophulakion*), not an illicit tax into the pockets of extortionary priests.[57] She is the poorest of the poor, but she ostensibly has income. Luke describes her as "needy" (*penichros*), utilizing a term that could emphasize that she works for her provision.[58] And Luke carefully notes that she is offering the smallest of gifts, two small copper coins (*lepros*).[59] This meager sum—equating to 1/132 of a day's wage[60]—was "all her life" (*autēspanta ton bion*). Her gift stands in stark contrast with the gifts from the abundance of the rich and thereby displays a radical sacrifice on her part. And because of this, her contribution is worth more than all of theirs combined.[61]

When the widow's offering is looked at in isolation, Jesus is effectively saying, "Look at the widow! The rich gave from their surplus, but she has been wholly sacrificial. What greater picture of generosity is there than that?" But this event cannot be taken in isolation. The context of this passage is key to the lament argument, and the context strongly indicates that Jesus is *condemning* the temple system as he points out her offering.

---

55. In favor of Jesus's praise for the widow, see Nolland, Bovon, Edwards, Bock, and Morris. In favor of the lament interpretation, see Marshall et al., "Widow's Mites," 256–65.

56. Greek (Euripides, *Danae*), Jewish (*Leviticus Rabbah*), and Buddhist literature are the primary examples, see Bovon, *Luke 3*, 93.

57. "The treasury appears to have been used for safekeeping of legal documents and private wealth, along with accumulated temple wealth and valuable items, as well as for the collection of tithes and gifts" (Nolland, *Luke 9:21–18:34*, 978).

58. Bovon, *Luke 3*, 94.

59. Edwards, *Luke*, 588–89.

60. Green, *Luke*, 728.

61. The Greek ambiguously reads "more than all of them" (*pleion pantōn*). This construction, missing the possessive pronoun which would distinguish individual gifts, leads me to conclude that Jesus's assessment of her generosity is that it was of greater total than all the gifts being offered into the treasury that day.

The greater section of the pericope runs from 20:45—21:5. Immediately preceding her donation, Jesus warns against the scribes who "devour widows' houses" (Luke 20:47). This ravenous consumption of the economically vulnerable possessions is then immediately pointed out by Jesus as the widow is placing her gift in the offering box (Luke 21:1–4).

Then, in the subsequent pericope (Luke 21:5–9), Jesus pronounces judgment on the temple system. While some were marveling at how the building was adorned with beautiful stones and offerings (the widow is not exactly giving to a needy organization),[62] Jesus predicts the destruction of the temple and with it the whole system that has produced the "den of robbers." When this context of the widow's gift is considered, Jesus is effectively saying, "Look at the widow! The rich are giving an offering from their discretionary funds, but the widow is giving everything she has. Do you see the corruption? The system is exploiting her. But it's coming down."

This is a seemingly irreconcilable fork in the interpretive road. It seems to me that those who opt for the "praise" interpretation do so from a vantage point of individual responsibility. The widow is giving a proportionately extravagant gift. It is not a tax. What she is doing is commendable. She epitomizes one who is storing up treasure in heaven. This is all present in the text. On the other side, however, those who opt for the "lament" interpretation do so from a systemic vantage point. The widow, despite her good intentions, is being exploited by a system that profits from the poor. Her freewill offering is not as free as it would seem. And Jesus brought (and is bringing) justice to the situation. This, too, is present in the context.

What are we to do with this? The praise interpretation certainly inspires fundraising efforts. However, the lament interpretation certainly speaks to larger ecclesiological and societal issues and is a necessary message for the modern western church. But I think it is reasonable to hold both interpretations at the same time.[63] These are not two competing interpretations, but different perspectives and emphases on the same event. There are two interconnecting levels in the widow's offering. On one level, the individual level, the widow is in fact demonstrating sacrificial generosity. And she is an example for each of us to emulate. But on another level,

62. Luke uses *anathēma* "votive offering" here, as opposed to *dōron* "gift," which he used earlier. Together, the picture is that the money deposited into the treasury (including the widow's) is ostentatiously displayed in the temple building.

63. Craig Keener hints at this conclusion in his short comment on Luke 21:1–4: "The temple sported ostentatious wealth, and its officials would probably waste this widow's money; but this powerless woman, ignorant of that likelihood, acts in good faith and is the greatest giver in God's sight" (Keener, *IVP Bible Background Commentary*, 233).

the social level, the temple system had, in fact, been corrupted. And it was destined for destruction.

This condemnation of systemic corruption is a warning to church leaders who govern the church finances. How many marvel at the "beautiful stones" of our church buildings while the poor in our congregations are coerced into contributing out of their need? The widow's offering, like much of our human experience, is layered. In a modern parallel, Jesus might commend the convenience store clerk's generous gift of $25 to Luxury Mall Community Church while simultaneously condemning Luxury Mall Community Church (and its leadership) for extorting the poor, lavishly spending its proceeds, and elaborately adorning its facilities while the pastors grow rich.

The bottom line is that wise churches, like the Torah envisioned for Israel, are to be economically distinct from our surrounding context. Stinginess, favoritism, and corruption should not exist in our congregations.[64] Empowerment of the poor in our congregations is a vital expression of economic wisdom. This has been evident in wise churches since Pentecost, and early Christian economic practices were likely attractive to subsistence level urbanites (where the early church developed out of) because they offered relief from the quest for honor and provided a status realignment that was rare in the Roman world.[65]

Economically Empowering Church Strategies

The general consensus is that nascent Christianity displayed an unparalleled concern for the poor, just as Israel did in comparison to ANE cultures.[66] The earliest congregation of the Jesus Movement exemplified this as they sold and distributed their possessions to any who had need (Acts 2:44–45; 4:34). This was not a one-time divestiture, as if a Christian is called to renounce any property after conversion. Rather, this was periodic acts of generosity to meet immediate needs.[67] Some continued to own fields, and, as the Ananias and Sapphira account shows, Christians

---

64. James proclaims that a congregants' value should not be based on their net worth. Whereas in the Roman world civic prominence could be purchased by the rich, James forbids showing favoritism to them (Jas 2:1–13). He asks, "Has not God chosen those who are poor in the eyes of the world to be rich in faith and to inherit the kingdom he promised those who love him?" (Jas 2:5). Additionally, faith that does not provide for the real needs of the covenant community is not really faith (Jas 2:14–17).

65. Longenecker, *Remember the Poor*, 278.

66. Longenecker, *In Stone and Story*, 104.

67. Blomberg, *Neither Poverty nor Riches*, 165.

maintained the right to keep the proceeds of a sale. The generous, how-ever, sought to use their proceeds to meet the needs in the church family through the centralized authority of the apostles.

This is the essence of what our church budgets are to reflect today. And how we allocate our funds speaks loudly about God's economic values. Our budgets and goals can be strategically geared to nurture cultures of economic empowerment. I must admit that I approach this topic carefully since I am a young pastor with limited experience in this arena. I also ac-knowledge that the devil is in the logistical details. There isn't a one-size-fits-all standard, so I'll explain how my church seeks to embody the wisdom of economic empowerment.

My church, Reno Christian Fellowship, is situated in a wealthy neigh-borhood and has been blessed with years of surplus budget (on top of a valu-able property that is fully paid off). We also have a profitable preschool and a solar field behind our building that provides us with free power. We have been an economically prosperous church, both individually and corporately. Like many churches, we offer benevolence to people in our congregation and devote money to local and global ministries that serve the poor. But our main strategy for empowerment has been to support churches in our region that are economically disadvantaged. For example, during the height of the COVID-19 pandemic we provided funds to cover three months of operating costs for one of our church partners, Ministerio Palabra de Vida, because many of their members were furloughed by the Reno casinos. We have also participated in several fundraising matches with churches in less affluent areas of Reno, which has spurred generosity in their churches as they have received gifts from ours. Reno Christian Fellowship has strategi-cally empowered poorer congregations for several years. But as I studied the subject of economic empowerment, I began to dream of how we could do more. What if we made our facilities and office supplies more accessible to the poor? What if we initiated a "no interest loan" program to help people in our church network pay for college or start a business or provide a down payment for a home? God's economic wisdom has made me less comfortable with the status quo. Maybe it will for you, too.

A Culture of Economic Integrity

Up to this point, I've described the local church as an economy of intercon-nected stewards. But church economies are not isolated. They are also shaped from the top down by macroeconomic systems. As pastors, we are forming wisdom cultures in our churches that are influenced by larger economic forces that are beyond our control. But despite these pressures, our churches must maintain integrity within our imperial economic system. The vision from the Bible puts the church at odds with any global economic system. Because of this, there is a need for a prophetic witness, embracing what is good in our larger economic milieu while rejecting what is corrupt.

It's interesting that Jesus doesn't directly speak against the larger Roman economic system, despite the fact that, by the Roman period, the average Israelite was less affluent than in previous generations.[68] And the sum total of mandatory financial contributions for an Israelite is staggering by today's standards in America. Between the tithes, temple tax, freewill offerings, and tribute to Rome, the tax burden of the average person was between 30–50 percent of their income.[69] Yet Jesus does not directly confront tax rates, property rights, slave labor practices, or colonization. Jesus even quickly affirms paying taxes to Caesar since they fall within his realm of authority (Luke 20:19–26). And he did not organize a Jerusalem Tea Party or purple cloth boycott. For many of us today, we wish he did. It would make our current economic (and political) opinions a little clearer. But it seems Jesus's primary focus is transforming the human heart and the covenant communities. His kingdom would have an entirely transcendent economic system. Even though Jesus doesn't directly confront larger economic systems, his values sow the seeds for prophetic witness. As Kraybill says, "If we took the radical teachings of Jesus about wealth, power, and violence more seriously, we might feel greater tension with our own culture."[70]

Our primary concern as leaders is forming a wisdom culture within our churches, but there is also room for a denouncement of the financial corruption, just as the prophets condemned the practices of foreign nations (Ezek 26–28; Isa 14:4, 12). Rev 17–18, John's vision of the destruction of Rome (symbolized through a depiction of the goddess Roma and linked to ancient Babylon), offers this kind of larger prophetic witness in its condemnation of corrupt economic systems and those who profit from them.[71] Rome is elaborately adorned and merchants grew rich from her. But John warns of her impending judgment because of her corruptions.

The Roman economy is obviously different from ours in the modern west but there are a number of parallels between then and now that are worth noting. Material prosperity marked the early Roman empire (the standard

68. Blomberg, *Neither Poverty nor Riches*, 88. The subjugation of Israel led to economic burdens that fueled rebellion.

69. Blomberg, *Neither Poverty nor Riches*, 89.

70. Kraybill, *Imperial Cult and Commerce in John's Apocalypse*, 38.

71. Westfall, "Epistle of Enoch and Revelation 18:1–24," 147.

of living was comparable to seventeeth to eighteenth century Europe, which is extraordinary in comparison to its contemporaries). The Roman empire, centralized in the city of Rome, was a source of economic benefit to the subjugated people scattered across the known world.[72] The urban centers were growing, and with that the imperial economy and incomes. Markets were specialized and market forces drove much of the economy. Banks and loans were widespread (and with that, so was debt).

Those at the top of Rome's economic pyramid were often ruthless and seized resources upwardly in a "brazenly acquisitive fashion."[73] Wealth was concentrated in the hands of the senators and knights at the top of the socio-economic pyramid while slave and working class labor provided the labor for the economy.[74] The elite controlled resource distribution.[75] And upward mobility was not likely.[76]

The middle class was virtually non-existent in Rome. Bruce Longenecker argues that there was not a middle class in the Roman world, but "middling classes." His nuanced socio-economic sketch shows that 80 percent of the population in the Roman world hovered around subsistence level, with varying degrees of stability. In modern terms, this would include individuals who are able to pay basic bills but work in unstable industries (construction or tourism, for example) and don't have many reserves. While these individuals can survive at subsistence level for a duration of time, they are vulnerable to the effects of civil unrest, recessions, and other harsh realities.

In general, the Roman elite did not worry about the poor, were shielded from beggars by their servants, and displayed a lack of understanding of the realities of poverty and underemployment.[77] Any systemic change relied on the elite because they controlled economic structures.[78] But instead of initiating systemic change, the rich in Rome paraded their wealth through luxurious pleasures and built lavish estates for themselves. They disdained the poor, who were exploited and neglected.[79]

So John the Revelator saw the pursuit of wealth through participating in the Roman imperial economic system, which was inextricably

72. Kraybill, *Imperial Cult and Commerce*, 78–79.

73. Longenecker, *In Stone and Story*, 27.

74. See Temin, "Economy of the Early Roman Empire," 133–51.

75. "The distribution of the population within the most imbalance advanced agrarian societies was close to being inversely proportional to the distribution of resources and power." Longenecker, *Remember the Poor*, 21.

76. Longenecker, *Remember the Poor*, 25.

77. Longenecker, *Remember the Poor*, 80–81.

78. Longenecker, *Remember the Poor*, 107.

79. Beard, *SPQR*, 440–41.

linked to emperor worship and associated with violence and injustice, as a dangerous trap for Christians.[80] He prophetically urges his readers to "come out of her [Rome]" (Rev 18:4), to separate from Rome by resisting what Cynthia Long Westfall identifies as "imperial power, systemic injustice, economic collaboration, compromise with the lifestyle of luxury, and the underlying idolatry."[81] The way of wisdom requires an unswerving commitment to the values of Jesus, especially in relation to wealth and power. In the end, God vindicates the faithful (18:20) and vanquishes the unfaithful empire (18:21–24). The fall of the empire produces despair in those who profited from her (18:9–19).

But this does not mean a total separation from the larger economic system, if that were even possible. Just as Jeremiah urged exiled Israel to build houses, plant gardens, marry, have kids, and seek the welfare of their city (Jer 29:5–7), Christians under any empire are to live faithful lives within as a countercultural witness to the surrounding world.

As John the Revelator shows, a prophetic critique of larger economic systems is utterly necessary for the formation of economically wise churches. This is entirely relevant today. Civil unrest and calls for economic reform have been in the forefront of public conversation for the past decade. As of this writing, the economic climate in America has been rapidly polarizing. On one hand, the stock market has soared after a brief collapse in March 2020, while record numbers have been left unemployed (and on the verge of homelessness). The United States has long been experiencing a consolidation of capital at the top of the socio-economic pyramid while the cost of living has far outpaced minimum wage (and wages in general). This polarity has only increased during the COVID-19 pandemic. Large companies (and their investors) have seen their net worth skyrocket while millions have been laid off. Temporary unemployment benefits, which are meager by any standard, were lucrative enough for many employees to delay going back to work because they would make substantially less *at their jobs*.

As pastors, we are not expected to be experts on the economy. But suffice it to say that there are merits and problems within any economic system. A wisdom culture can discern these, so I think it is crucial that pastors (carefully) expose the inconsistencies between God's wisdom and

---

80. DeSilva, *Unholy Allegiances*, 68–69, comments, "The wealth to be enjoyed by participating in the larger global economy was, as far as John was concerned, a dangerous lure toward sharing in the violence and political injustice that undergirded such an economy, as well as sharing in the economic injustice that allowed the resources and produce of the provinces to be siphoned off to satisfy the immoderate cravings of Rome's inhabitants and worldwide elite."

81. Westfall, "Epistle of Enoch and Revelation 18:1–24," 151.

economic corruption. In our churches, our "inner-Pharisee," our innate love of money, is often spoken against. But what about our "inner-Saddu-cee"? The one that is prosperous and comfortable in the economic climate, the one who benefits from the status quo.

After encountering Jesus, Zacchaeus, the filthy rich chief tax collector who profited greatly from the corrupt tax collection system, repents by giv-ing half his wealth to the poor and paying a fourfold restitution to anyone he has defrauded (Luke 19:1–10). His encounter with Jesus resulted in finan-cial repentance. How often do we preach messages that produce a similar reaction for those who have benefited from a broken system?

Together, our churches can have influence. Conversion can trigger powerful forms of economic protest, notably seen in the Ephesian Chris-tians burning an exorbitant amount of highly valued magic books (Acts 19:19–41).[82] The bottom line is that the church is called to counter-cultural economic practices within its local communities, and is to maintain an in-tegrity amidst imperial economic systems.

In conclusion, the goal is for our churches to embody God's economic wisdom. This includes nurturing cultures that aim for the wealth target, empower the poor, and maintain economic integrity. In these ways, we can show the world its creator's wisdom.

Bibliography

Alcorn, Randy. *Managing God's Money: A Biblical Guide.* Carol Stream, IL: Tyndale, 2011.

Baker, David L. *Tight Fists or Open Hands?: Wealth and Poverty in Old Testament Law.* Grand Rapids: Eerdmans, 2009.

Beard, Mary *SPQR: A History of Ancient Rome.* London: Profile, 2016.

Belmi, Peter, et al. "The Social Advantage of Miscalibrated Individuals: The Relationship Between Social Class and Overconfidence and Its Implications for Class-Based Inequality." *Journal of Personality and Social Psychology: Interpersonal Relations and Group Processes* 118 (2020) 254–82.

Blomberg, Craig. *Neither Poverty nor Riches: A Biblical Theology of Material Possessions.* Downers Grove, IL: InterVarsity, 1999.

Bock, Darrell L. *Luke.* Downers Grove, IL: InterVarsity, 1994.

Bovon, Francois. *Luke 3: A Commentary on the Gospel of Luke 19:28–24:53.* Minneapolis: Fortress, 2012.

Brueggemann, Walter. *The Land: Place as Gift, Promise and Challenge in Biblical Faith.* Philadelphia: Fortress, 1977.

DeSilva, David A. *Unholy Allegiances: Heeding Revelation's Warning.* Peabody, MA: Hendrickson, 2013.

---

82. The value was the equivalent of 50,000 days' wages; cf. Blomberg, *Neither Pov-erty nor Riches*, 173.

DeYmaz, Mark, and Harry Li. *The Coming Revolution in Church Economics*. Grand Rapids: Baker, 2019.

Edwards, James R. *The Gospel According to Luke*. Grand Rapids: Eerdmans, 2015.

Fitzmyer, Joseph A. *The Gospel According to Luke X–XXIV: Introduction, Translation, and Notes*. New Haven, CT: Yale University Press, 2008.

Green, Joel B. *The Gospel of Luke*. Grand Rapids: Eerdmans, 1997.

Hartley, John E. *Leviticus*. Word Biblical Commentary 4. Dallas: Word, 1992.

Kahneman, Daniel, and Angus Deaton. "High Income Improves Evaluation of Life but Not Emotional Well-Being." *PNAS* 107 (2010) 16489–93.

Keener, Craig S. *The IVP Bible Background Commentary: New Testament*. Downers Grove, IL: InterVarsity, 1993.

Kraybill, Nelson. *Imperial Cult and Commerce in John's Apocalypse*. Sheffield: Sheffield Press, 1999.

Longenecker, Bruce W. *In Stone and Story: Early Christianity in the Roman World*. Grand Rapids: Baker, 2020.

———. *Remember the Poor: Paul, Poverty, and the Greco-Roman World*. Grand Rapids: Eerdmans, 2010.

Marshall, I. Howard. *The Gospel of Luke: A Commentary on the Greek Text*. Exeter: Paternoster, 1978.

McKnight, Scot. *Pastor Paul: Nurturing a Culture of Christoformity in the Church*. Grand Rapids: Brazos, 2019.

Milgrom, Jacob. *Leviticus 23–27: A New Translation with Introduction and Commentary*. New Haven, CT: Yale University Press, 2008.

Morris, Leon. *Luke: An Introduction and Commentary*. Downers Grove, IL: InterVarsity, 1988.

Nolland, John. *Luke 9:21–18:34*. Word Biblical Commentary 35B. Dallas: Word, 1993.

Powell, Mark Allen. *Giving to God: The Bible's Good News about Living a Generous Life*. Grand Rapids: Eerdmans, 2006.

Temin, Peter. "The Economy of the Early Roman Empire." *The Journal of Economic Perspectives* 20 (2006) 133–51.

Verbrugge, Verlyn D., and Keith R. Krell. *Paul and Money: A Biblical and Theological Analysis of the Apostle's Teachings and Practices*. Grand Rapids: Zondervan, 2015.

Westfall, Cynthia Long. "The Epistle of Enoch and Revelation 18:1–24: Economic Critique of Rome." In *Reading Revelation in Context: John's Apocalypse and Second Temple Judaism*, edited by Ben C. Blackwell et al., 146–52. Grand Rapids: Zondervan, 2019.

Wright, Addison G. "The Widow's Mites: Praise or Lament?—A Matter of Context." *CBQ* 44 (1982) 256–65.

WISE SPIRITUAL FORMATION

By Pete Goodman

Wisdom can arise from the most unexpected of places. For instance, one of the most insightful and meaningful nuggets of sage advice I've ever received came from the great scholar and theologian Bill Murray when warning his small groundhog captive seated behind the wheel of their speeding truck, "Don't drive angry!" It's guidance I've tried to be mindful of in all walks of life, but especially in speaking of and to the church. It's a far too simple and overtrodden path to offer a sharp and critical tongue to anything and everything that frustrates us about this beautifully complicated community of imperfect and diverse people. Nonetheless, while not anger necessarily, there is a disturbing reality present within much of our western church culture, of which, more than anything, I find myself exhausted.

It's the same phone call, the ever-recurring conversations on my office couch, the carousel of counseling sessions with the broken and hurting people who come seeking help and advice in navigating their dysfunction. Over and over again I hear the story of tragic lives teetering on the brink of divorce, bankruptcy, addiction, depression, anxiety, anger, bitterness; completely broken and shattered lives due to bad choices and decision making. Now, before you judge me as cold-hearted and advise I change careers . . . yes, I understand we live in a broken world where sin abounds in spades and being available to the hurting and broken is par for the course of professional ministry. It is what I signed up for. However, the part I find most wearing is how often these are *Christians* sharing their tragic stories of dysfunction. And while I certainly have a desire to help however possible, I can't help but question how it is that a community of people who claim to be committed to following the giver of life so often have just as screwed up lives as those who don't. Where is the disconnect?

It was this incongruence that led me to abandon the faith of my early childhood for a season. Not an issue of belief in God per se, that never wavered in my young mind. Just like it never seemed to for so many who sit on my couch and preface their stories of dysfunction with, "I'm a Christian and believe in God, but . . . ." Rather, it was the seeming irrelevance of it all. So many who spoke of a better life in Christ rarely demonstrated anything comparably better in their actual lives. Not coincidentally, what ended up leading this particular prodigal back home to faith wasn't a fear of hell, a guilty weight of my sin, or some inner conviction that I needed a savior but a constant yearning in my soul for a better life that continued to elude me just as much out in the pigsties of the world as within the Christianity of my childhood. And I am convinced I'm not alone. The desire for a life truly worth living and lived well beckons to all of us. The question, however, is to where will the world turn in their search to find it?

Wisdom in the Stars

In 1988 *The New York Times* bestseller list was chock full of the most familiar literary names of the day: Clancy, Rice, King, Ludlow, Steele . . . there was even an appearance by a young Donald Trump. But among those expected authors sharing the top of the list one name stood out for how odd and quite unexpected its inclusion was. Above most of those household novelists with lucrative movie rights attached to their works was the first release by a then relatively unknown English physicist named Stephen Hawking. A brilliant cosmologist who pioneered advances in understanding black holes, quantum mechanics, and the universe at large, Hawking penned his work, *A Brief History of Time,* as an attempt to bring normally incomprehensible scientific concepts and theories to everyday people in a way they could understand. And it worked! The book flew off the shelves and stayed atop the best seller list for the next 5 years, eventually selling over 10 million copies and quickly making him a massive, world-wide celebrity until his death in 2018.

But for many people hearing such an intriguing anecdote, the perplexing question is essentially . . . why? How does a book written by an unknown astrophysicist explaining outlandishly deep and complex mysteries of science strike such a resounding chord with everyday people to the point that travelers were choosing it in airport bookstores over and against the latest Tom Clancy thriller of the day? One clue to understanding this mystery can be found in Hawking's closing words. His final paragraph, a short summation of his ultimate goal of discovering a grand unifying theory of the universe offers a profound and resounding hope that piques the interest of the masses as much, if not more than any other work of the day. It's essentially a dream, a hope for humanity's eventual discovery of our *ultimate purpose* and to finally know *why we exist*. Or, in his own final words, to come to "know the mind of God."[1]

In reading such a dramatic and bold ambition at the end the book's appeal and popularity becomes far less mysterious. Who doesn't want to know our ultimate purpose and why we exist? In fact, Hawking himself would later remark that had he not included that closing line the sales "might have been halved."[2] For to know God's mind, to grasp the ultimate reason and purpose for our existence would be the greatest and most important, life-changing discovery in human history. The appeal of his book was never in society's hidden interest in science but in what is essentially embedded in the heart of everyone, a desire to know purpose in order to make the most out of life: to answer that most disconcerting question of whether our lives actually have a meaning. And: to know if unveiling and understanding it could potentially help us make the most of life. If only the underlying design of creation could be mapped out and explained, then perhaps we could be more confident that we are living in the best way possible, in line with the universe's intentions. In short, Hawking wasn't appealing to our inner science geek but to the idea that perhaps the stars themselves can reveal the elusive answers to the deepest question about life and how we can succeed at it.

This desire for making sense of the world in order to find purpose and success is hardly a new phenomenon. It was no mere innovation of America's decade of greed. Rather, the pursuit of the knowledge necessary to understand the universe and its secrets to making the most out of our brief stint floating through its empty space has existed long before we possessed the technology to intimately study its starry depths. Many ancient cultures were just as driven with the desire to answer the ultimate question—what is good for humans. So much so was this the case that this quest became the central aim of almost all learning in the ancient world.[3] Such was the case with the Greeks who, beginning with Socrates and his quest for *eudaimonia* or "the good life," sought to make sense of the cosmos in order to discover what is best for human flourishing or happiness. And of course, directly relevant to our study were the Jewish people who routinely sought the blessed and peaceful life God created them to experience by paying attention to his intended order.

---

1. Hawking, *Brief History of Time*, 131.

2. Paris, "Hawking to Experience Zero Gravity."

3. Crenshaw, *Education in Ancient Israel*, 72.

As we saw in the opening chapter of this book, for both Jews and pagans alike this path to success, this sought-after key to unlock the good life was known as *wisdom*. It was the skill or knowledge necessary to steer a proper and successful course through life.[4] That is, wisdom was about having enough understanding about the world and its wiring that one might rightly discern the correct course of action in order to bring about the most good in one's existence. Or as Crenshaw described it, "intuitions about mastering life for human betterment."[5] And, while often theoretical in nature, wisdom was ultimately focused towards the practical. Wisdom sought to understand the deep mysteries of the cosmos and human existence *in order* to know how best to navigate daily life and the routine decisions that most impact the goodness of life. For it is in the daily, seemingly mundane and regular choices and actions that the eventual direction of our lives is steered, for better or worse.

Our "Gospel" and Wisdom

And this all has serious implications which the church and its leadership need to consider. For, if these questions of ultimate purpose, success, and how one ought best to live are at the heart of every human, are they not also inevitably intertwined with the church's message and mission? It has been commissioned to reach a world and its people desperate for a better life and who seek answers any place they can potentially be found, even the seemingly confounding field of astrophysics. But what answers have they generally heard coming from the collective voice of Christianity? When they have peered within the four walls of the local church community, have they glimpsed a path to the life they desperately long for, a life relevant for discovering and being what God created them for? Or, have they more commonly been inundated with an oft-irrelevant sounding message concerning only their legal status before a God they don't know and an eternal destination they tend to think little of with little impact on life today?

Herein lies a tension for many church leaders between two areas of focus in ministry. On one hand, the modern evangelical movement has placed a premium on preaching a gospel centered around repentance of sin and acceptance of Christ as Savior in order to be forgiven, made right with God and receive a guarantee of heaven.[6] This is understood by many western

4. Witherington, *Jesus the Sage*, 37–49.

5. Crenshaw, *Old Testament Wisdom*, 11.

6. For a more robust treatment on what should be understood as the gospel message, see McKnight, *King Jesus Gospel*.

Christians to be the primary mission of the church, a fulfillment of the Great Commission to make disciples of all nations. However, this concentration has often relegated to the B-team of church ministry any substantial emphasis on spiritual formation, discipleship and Christian living. The question of where people are *going* takes precedent over who they are *becoming*.

Now in fairness most church leaders would say they see both these aspects of Christian ministry as important and desire to live with a healthy balance. However, which one takes priority as the dominant message and mission of the church is too often misaligned. For while it is certainly true that people need to hear the truth and be told the message of Jesus, that message must not be hollowed of what a person is saved *for* and *how* it impacts daily life. If it is, humanity's ultimate purpose will be overshadowed by, rather than discovered through, the cross of Christ. The Christian message will continue to fail to connect and resonate with the basic questions the world desires answers to if *when they seek wisdom for living the church only offers comfort in dying*.

It is necessary, therefore, for church leaders to examine seriously their primary focus through the lens of wisdom and the implications it has on their mission, message, and practice. Doing so will result in two important shifts. First, their understanding of the church's work in the world will consider God's original intention and purpose for people as *central* to the Christian message and mission and lead to a greater focus on how humans live over where they end up post-mortem. Such a wisdom-based approach to ministry will naturally prioritize the idea of *spiritual formation* as the primary end goal of ministry, not with a focus on rule following and legalism but on helping people to become and live out that which they were always created to be, seen most clearly in the person of Jesus. And secondly, in doing so, their relevance to the world will increase as their message connects directly with the God-given desire in all people to be successful and make the most out of life.

To demonstrate this, we must first understand wisdom's pursuit of human purpose and its connection to finding success in daily life. From there attention on Jewish wisdom specifically will reveal the truth of our purpose embedded in God's created design. And once that intent is clearly recognized, we shall see how the only way to fully realize it in our lives is by being transformed into the image of Jesus—the heart of spiritual formation and ultimate mission of the church in a broken and dysfunctional world.

Wisdom in Creation

Just as Hawking sought the answers to our ultimate question of purpose amidst the stars, wisdom has always been intricately tied to cosmology, to the origins and intentions behind the universe. For it was reasoned that in understanding and making sense of the world in which we live, and in turn comprehending our envisioned place within it, there alone will success be achieved. Essentially, knowing *why* we exist is the path to know *how* best to exist. Of course, underlying this is an important assumption—it presupposes intention and design. The ancient concept of wisdom required that the cosmos and all its inhabitants were more than an evolutionary accident but actually endured on purpose and for a reason. Therefore, a more appropriate way to describe this perspective would be to say that wisdom was directly tied to *creation theology*. The rationale behind the very possibility a purpose or design even exists—that the very concept of wisdom truly rests on more than mere human imagination—was based upon the work of some form of wise and intelligent creator. It assumed the universe and all that lives within it were created with wisdom and design and therefore some purpose exists.

This was most certainly true for the Jewish sages, as in the book of Proverbs which declares, "by wisdom the LORD laid the earth's foundation" (3:19) and wisdom "was there when he set the heavens in place" (8:27).[7] Or as the Psalmist sang of God's wonderful design and good intentions for all creation, he stated that "in wisdom you made them all" (104:24). That creation has intention serves as the foundation of wisdom—it tells humanity that there is order and reason to our existence. And in turn, because the cosmos has an ordered reason, a successful course through life can be navigated by discovering and living within and toward that purpose.

What's more, for the Jews specifically, not only was there an intention behind creation but that intent was *good* and for humanity's benefit, quite unlike some other wisdom creation stories of their Ancient Near East neighbors. Where other wisdom accounts like the Babylonian *Enuma Elish* described creation as the result of raging heavenly warfare or an attempt to abate preexisting chaos, with little interest in the good of creatures, the Genesis account describes a benevolent artist bringing beauty and goodness because he himself is good.[8] As Middleton describes it, "a wise designer and artificer, a good artist making a coherent, harmoniously functioning

---

7. Scripture quotations are from the NIV.

8. For a comparison of Ancient Near East creation accounts and their relationship to Genesis, see Middleton, *Liberating Image*.

cosmos, according to a well-thought-out plan" for the benefit of creatures.[9] Wisdom for the Jews was thus rooted in and around the belief that life on earth was foundationally good and that there was a moral structure to creation, creature, and the universe in general.

Consequently, because God is both wise and good those who discovered and followed His design found the good life humans were created for.[10] And it should not be glossed over that therein lies the essential goal or aim of wisdom. Studying cosmological design was not just about scientific curiosity but ultimately about success and living well. Wisdom's aim at discovering and following the intended created order, of aligning oneself with the ultimate purpose embedded in creation, was *in order* to live out the good, blessed intention of existence rather than simply gaining knowledge for knowledge's sake. The ancient Greeks, for example, pioneered an entire school of thought known as philosophy (literally, "the love of wisdom") in an effort to address this primary issue, the well-being of the individual. Its aim was to seek out wisdom in order to find the best life possible. Because in their view the good life was essentially available to all humans who can think and thus act according to our *intended* nature—or wisely.

This pursuit of the good life through wisdom was not confined to the pagans. Rather, the Jewish people also sought a very similar goal and centered much of their thought and attention around the repeated desire for their lives to "blessed" (Heb. *barak*). This term carried the implication of success in life, of having that very thing all human beings long for—to live and enjoy the life the Creator God lovingly intended.[11] Blessing was essentially human flourishing. The book of Proverbs speaks often of finding a blessed life through wisdom (3:13, 18), which Witherington suggests speaks to our common human pursuit of "a happy and prosperous, trouble-free and long life in this world."[12] Like their neighboring pagan sages believed, this blessed, happy life was to be discovered through the acceptance and acting upon a certain realm of knowledge and understanding related to the divine order. It was all based upon the premise that there is an *appropriate* way to think and behave embedded within us at creation that will lead one to the life we all seek. One only need to discover it. Or, as Hawking so eloquently put it, "to know the mind of God."

9. Middleton, *Liberating Image*, 74.

10. Witherington, *Jesus the Sage*, 112.

11. McKeown, "Blessings and Curses," 85–86.

12. Witherington, *Jesus the Sage*, 26.

Wisdom in Creation

But while the central aim of wisdom was the same across cultures, the starting point and path forward differed greatly. For how one achieves such a lofty goal as to know and live out our intended purpose varied greatly and was often based on nothing more than human intuition or feeble attempts to study and understand nature. But while so many gazed into the heavens or turned inward at the human psyche to guess at answers it was the Jewish people who offered the greatest response to the question of purpose and how one becomes wise and lives successfully. For rather than basing wisdom on seemingly blind attempts to make sense of the stars or mankind's own mental make-up, the Jewish sages centered it upon divine revelation directly from the Creator, starting with an explanation of the very act of creation itself and our purpose within it.

Like many creation stories in the ancient world the Genesis account offers affirmation that the world was in fact created with wisdom by an intelligent creator. However, quite unlike its counter parts it offers a unique and special picture of humanity's express purpose distinct from any other in the ancient world, whereby humans are described as being created in God's *image* (Heb. *selem*) and designed for an exceptional purpose (Gen 1:27). For while some creation accounts like the *Epic of Atrahasis* bleakly reduced humanity's purpose to the role of assuming "the drudgery of the gods," assigning humanity the purpose of little else than a life of servitude and hard work, Genesis paints a much different picture. It portrays God as a King presiding over the cosmos who chooses to entrust humanity with special authority as his delegated emissaries to represent his rule in the world.[13] Thus, being made in his image speaks to a great purpose or calling human beings were designed for as God's representatives and agents to the rest of creation, having been granted authorized power to share God's governance and creative development of his earth.[14] This description drips of royal, kingly imagery, demonstrating how Genesis sees humans as possessing great dignity, worth and, not least of all, responsibility to act appropriately and in line with God's intentions in order to accomplish such a purpose.

To be given such a responsibility necessarily means that how we behave, how we go about living and representing him, acting on his behalf and caring for the world he made and loves, is directly tied to our reason for being and whether or not we can ever be successful and do it well. Such an understanding of our intended purpose has little to do with our eternal destination and

---

13. Middleton, *Liberating Image*, 88.
14. Middleton, *Liberating Image*, 26.

everything to do with who we are as people and how live here and now. This
is why many early church fathers believed being in God's image was directly
related to being and becoming more like him in thought and action, with a
purpose to function like God in all ethical concerns as his designated rulers.
The concept of being God's image was, according to Gregory of Nazianzus a
"source of normativity," or the standard of what humans should be and how
they should behave in the world.[15] We are essentially embodied idols (also
Heb. *selem*) of God, which represent him and carry his divine presence, expressing his glory and will to the entire world in which we were created to
govern rightly and wisely in line with his design.[16]

Therefore, as wisdom would reason, it can only be through acting
and living out this envisioned purpose, functioning in the way he intended
his image bearers to behave that the good life he made us for can ever be
experienced. If we were indeed created with the expressed intention of
representing and reflecting God, of living in his image, then *that* is ultimately what it means to be human and success can only be found in
enacting that reality. Anything less would be contrary to our purpose. It
would be *de-humanized* behavior, misaligned with why we exist and thus
not logically leading to the results we hope for.

Indeed, this is the picture the Jewish wisdom account of creation offers for why humanity has strayed so far from living good and blessed lives.
After revealing that God created the cosmos with wise and benevolent intentions and shared the privilege of his rule with his image bearers, we are
then given a picture of the choice offered them to either continue to adhere
to his wisdom, to live in line with the Creator's intentions and allow Him
to determine what was *good* or *evil* for human existence, or to seek it on
their own. It was as N. T. Wright says, a choice to recognize wisdom "as
an attribute of the creator to be gained through worshipping and obeying
that God" or to seek a "supposed independence."[17] In this infamous story
a snake, a symbol associated with both death and wisdom in the Ancient
Near East,[18] convinces the primordial image bearers to believe they are
better off seeking wisdom and the best course for life apart from their
maker (Gen 3:4–5). But while such wisdom seems appealing and free of
the strings attached to serving God (3:6), in truth it only leads to ruin and
dehumanization of God's image bearers, and ultimately to the wreckage of
his entire creation (3:14–19; cf. Rom 1:18–32). The choice to seek wisdom

---

15. Thomas, *Image of God in the Theology of Gregory of Nazianzus*.

16. Bates, *Salvation by Allegiance Alone*, 147–51.

17. Wall et al., "Acts, Romans, 1 Corinthians," 433.

18. McKeown, "Blessings and Curses," 736.

from an earthly creature rather than the heavenly creator leads humans to become, in the words of Athanasius, "the cause of their own corruption and death."[19] For any attempt to navigate life apart from the intended design of the one who gave life is by nature un-wise and will inevitably lead to failure. In essence humans do not experience the goodness of God's creation because we have chosen to reject God's design for our lives, to seek wisdom apart from his design and thus suffer the consequences. And as James would later affirm, we still have the same choice. We can continue to seek wisdom that comes down "from above" which leads to the kind of life we were created for, or wisdom which is "of earth, natural, demonic" which leads to all kinds of de-humanized, evil behavior (Jas 3:15).

Therein lies the heart of Jewish wisdom, the connection between purpose, design, and living successfully rooted directly in the Genesis creation account. *Humanity's created purpose is to be like God in how we live and to govern and care for his world as he would. And true wisdom is choosing to live that out in our daily lives in order to experience the good life he created us for.* Thus, the author of Proverbs could confidently affirm that the beginning, the groundwork or foundation of all wisdom is the "fear of the Lord" (Prov 1:7). It is rooted in the healthy respect and understanding of one's place in regard to God, where we are creature and he is creator and his will and expectations are authoritative over our lives. Where he is firmly situated as the primary source of all wisdom, all knowledge and understanding about what is good for men. It is, in the words of James to "submit yourself to God" while resisting the lying false source of wisdom (Jas 4:7). It is a choice whether to pursue wisdom and direction from our creator and allow him to define and guide the kind of behavior that we were made for and thereby live a life of blessing and goodness (Prov 8:35). Or, to decide for our own selves and seek it in lying serpents and lifeless stars—an inevitable pathway towards less life.

Wisdom in the Torah

However, we must remind ourselves once again that wisdom doesn't just seek to know *why* we are alive, it hungers to know *how* to fully live. Thus, simply understanding the objective and ultimate source of wisdom fails to hold practical relevance for people unless we know how, in living, to actually apply it. One can certainly believe there exist *right* and *wrong* ways to live rooted in the created order without having any concrete notion as to what those ways are. This led Greek philosophers like Plato to imagine

19. St. Athanasius, *On the Incarnation*, 30.

their own lists of behaviors that supposedly marked appropriate living (virtues), countered by self-destructive behaviors (vices) which bring ill to one's existence.[20] While Aristotle taught that through education in wisdom the passions and *wrong* thinking could be brought into harmony with a *correct* view of intended human existence, whereby proper beliefs could provide the foundation for desired human flourishing. Likewise, the Stoics sought to align their thinking with the appropriate order of the cosmos and to control compulsions and desires which are counter to nature and bring disorder and in turn, unhappiness. For all of them the choice of vice or virtue was simply the result of irrational and destructive passions, that is, acting counter to how we *should* behave. This could be overcome with reason and proper philosophical education.[21] But it should not be missed that such lists of *good* versus *evil* behavior, proper or inappropriate thinking, are based solely on human perception and reason. They are all a creature's attempt to grasp after the creator's intentions, hidden in the cosmos, not to build on a foundation of having actually been told through divine revelation *why* certain behaviors or thoughts are better than others. In a biblical worldview, such is picking fruit from the tree of good and evil and hoping against hope it isn't poisonous.

So yet again we see that Israel far surpassed any other human pursuit of wisdom in the ancient world. For not only did the one true creator God reveal to them their created purpose as his image bearers, he also revealed what being an image bearer actually looked like in everyday, practical life. Far removed from those who simply imagined their own list of virtues to follow or meaning to find in the constellations, the Jews rooted their pursuit of wisdom in the revealed Word of God, his Torah.

Although often translated as *law,* the word *torah* actually means something closer to guidance or direction. While *torah* certainly contains rules to live by, it was far more than just a legal code. Rather, it was a revelation of who God is and what he desires of his people. It was as W. D. Davies described, "all that God had made known of his nature, character and purpose and of what he would have man be and do."[22] Far from just an arbitrary list of rules for control and punishment, it served to illuminate who God is and the path one walks to fully resemble him. It was, in essence, God's wisdom on display, his vision to creating the circumstances in

---

20. For a treatment on the Greek approach to wisdom and formation, see Thompson, *Moral Formation According to Paul.*

21. Witherington, *Jesus the Sage,* 12–13.

22. Davies, *Paul and Rabbinic Judaism,* 149.

which people would flourish.[23] This is why the Jewish sage Ben Sira could say, "in all wisdom there is the fulfillment of the Torah" (Sir 19:20). He understood wisdom and the Law to be intricately wed together, with the Law essentially being the manifestation of wisdom in history.[24] Similarly, the author of 4 Maccabees, who shared the Greek belief that ethics and moral decisions are concerned with the control of emotions and desires saw the Torah alone as able to clarify which passions were to be overcome (1:17; 2:8–9). The Wisdom of Solomon also consistently emphasized that unrighteous behavior originates in human reasonings apart from God's wisdom as expressed in his Torah (2:21; 3:10). And, while Philo generally accepted Plato's list of virtues and vices, it was only obedience to Torah that would ever result in their practice (*Virtues* 100).

Torah observance was thus the heart of wisdom for the Jewish people. It served as the path one must walk in order to live out what it means to be created in God's image and in turn find the blessed, happy life all people so desperately seek. And the fear of the Lord, or an acceptance of God's kingship and right to guide our lives and direct our behavior served as the starting point. The later rabbis would speak of this as either *confessing* the commandments and taking upon oneself the yoke of Torah, an indication of one's acceptance of God's reign and his right to guide one's life, or *denying* the commandments and casting off the yoke, indicating a disavowal of God's kingship and willful disobedience.[25] Wisdom was to confess Torah as God's rule and faithfully obey it in order to experience the good life he created us for.

Perhaps nowhere is this idea stated more directly and clearly than in the words of the law giver himself, Moses, a man "educated in all wisdom" (Acts 7:22). He told the people that if they would diligently obey all God's commands, they would be happy and blessed, "abounding in prosperity" in a land flowing with milk and honey—while curses and despair awaited those who would ignore and disobey (Deut 28). This is principally why they would so stringently teach their young these commands and impress obedience upon them. According to Crenshaw, all education in Judaism was for the building of character through the knowledge of God, in order to help the younger generation overcome their wrong, evil desires and be obedient to God's Law . . . in order to flourish.[26] *Following Torah was the very key to success the world seeks.* And so only through an acceptance of its yoke and instruction in its teaching would Israel become wise and make the right

23. Harris, *Big Picture*.

24. Witherington, *Jesus the Sage*, 86.

25. Sanders, *Paul and Palestinian Judaism*, 3026.

26. Crenshaw, *Education in Ancient Israel*, 3.

choices to find such success. Only, that is, until God's wisdom revealed itself in a new and better form.

Wisdom in Human Form

In announcing the inbreaking of God's redemptive, creation-restoring kingdom through the arrival of Israel's king, the Gospel of John begins with a profound statement that the Word (Gk. *logos*) of God present at creation "took on flesh" and lived among us (1:14). This is an important statement for our study when we consider the direct and close connection between the terms *logos* and wisdom (Gk. *sophia*). As Witherington points out, the two are closely linked in much Jewish wisdom literature (Wis 9:1–2, Sir 24:3), and here we now surprisingly find the idea of wisdom embodied in the person of the logos.[27] The long-awaited Messiah who would come to lead the people back to their God and reestablish the blessings promised in ages past was, shockingly, much more than a mere man but actually God's truth personified (John 14:6). In Jesus, the divine wisdom of God, originally revealed in the pages of the Torah, had now shown its true face to the world by becoming a human being.

This was, of course, a monumental shift regarding the human search for wisdom, purpose, and regaining the image of God. For the Torah, while valuable in pointing to God was ultimately only a hint, a shadowy, blurry reflection of what being his image truly looked like and what it meant to be fully human. In fact, it mostly only succeeded at serving to remind just how far we had fallen from what we were made to be (Rom 7:7). But in Jesus the world can finally see the real thing, up close and personal. For now, rather than using written words to try to convey a profound reality of intended human existence, Jesus, the image of the invisible God (Col 1:15) stands as the physical expression of all God's wisdom on display and the clearest, truest picture of what it means and looks like for us to be human. Hence the reason Christ can be called the culmination (Gk. *telos*) of the law (Rom 10:4). This word *telos* was used by the Greek philosophers to speak of the end goal or purpose of a thing or action. Christ is the law's ultimate goal, what it was always pointing to and trying to create—a human being fully alive and perfectly bearing God's image as we were created to do. He said himself that he didn't come to abolish the law, but to fulfill it (Gk. *plerōsai*), that is, to more perfectly reveal its original intention (Matt 5:17). He lived out what Torah was always pointing humans toward, a return to our original design and purpose. He showed the world first-hand exactly what a

27. Witherington, *Jesus the Sage*, 286.

human being was always created to be and how we were always intended to live by enacting and speaking the will and wisdom of God directly with every action and utterance.[28] And this wasn't completely unexpected. According to Davies, there was an expectation among the rabbis that when the Messiah came he would bring a sort of "new Torah" which would not be contrary to the Law of Moses per se, but explain it more fully and better instruct God's people how to live in the new age.[29] This was fulfilled in the person of Jesus who, through the incarnation, placed the truth and wisdom of God on display for all to see. He stands as the visible fulfillment of God's intentions for what it means to be human.

Importantly for our discussion, this embodied wisdom of God then called the world to *follow* and place their loyal faith *in him*.[30] For as the Word made flesh, he shifted the focus of our obedience away from the law and directly onto Himself. Now his teaching, life model, and Spirit have become our archetype and the referent for loyal commitment to God in place of the written law.[31] Whereas formerly one discovered God's wisdom and what it meant to live out our purpose solely through the study and adherence to Torah, one now finds it by becoming a disciple of the living Torah. The pathway towards life *to the fullest* so desperately sought after is now illuminated to those who would choose to be guided by the good shepherd (John 10:10), who is God's wisdom made man.

Wisdom in Spiritual Formation

Herein lies the heart of spiritual formation and Christian discipleship. Jesus's call to follow him and become his disciple, and in turn go and make disciples of the rest of the world (Matt 28:19–20), was an invitation for humanity to come and be transformed into his image. For to be a disciple is to learn from and thus *become like* the one being followed. It's about absorbing in and patterning one's life according to their example, to be made complete (*telos*) from their teaching and wisdom.[32] Discipleship's aim is to be formed into the likeness of another by following, learning from, and obeying their directions.

---

28. Kingsbury, *Matthew*, 45.

29. Davies, *Paul and Rabbinic Judaism*, 72.

30. For a full discussion on this point and the connection between faith and loyalty, see Bates, *Salvation by Allegiance Alone*, 155–60.

31. Dunn, *New Perspective on Paul*, 52.

32. Witherington, *Jesus the Sage*, 29.

Therefore, if our goal, our completion (*telos*), is to become full image bearers of God as wisdom suggests, then walking with, learning from, and directly imitating the full image of God seen in Christ is the only way forward. It is by loyally following and obeying him, trusting him to guide our life and decision making, actually living as his disciples that we begin to mirror him in thought and action and begin to be transformed into his image (Phil 3:8–11; Rom 6:5–11; Gal 4:19). Through faithful allegiance to Jesus and a commitment to accept his word as God's wisdom to guide our lives, to take His yoke upon us and confess him as Lord we begin to live out and reflect his character, his will, his life and light to the entire world around us just as we were always created to. And though we have continually fallen far short of reflecting God's glory (Rom 3:23), choosing to be a loyal disciple of Jesus, with the goal of becoming like him reforms us to that original purpose. As Irenaeus said, "what we had lost in Adam we have now recovered in Christ Jesus."[33]

In short, *becoming like Jesus is the end goal of a Christian disciple for it is the end goal of why a human was created.* And thus wisdom, the pursuit of our purpose, and how to best achieve it would call all those listening to find true life by following Jesus and being formed into his image. For let us not forget, though commonly overlooked, ignored or just misunderstood in our continued preaching of sin, lawbreaking, and eternal destinations is that at the heart of Jesus's message was an offer of the very prize wisdom has always sought to win. In announcing that he came so that we may have "life to the fullest" (John 10:10) he was inviting us to enjoy that which sages and teachers from all cultures have searched out, that which the human heart has longed for throughout history. As the embodiment of God's wisdom Jesus came to give humanity far more than a blissful afterlife, but a blessed daily life. Michael Gorman sees this in Paul's thought when speaking of maturity (Eph 4:13) as well as the peace (shalom) of God, the blessing and fullness of life promised by Jesus.[34] Or as Dallas Willard said, "God's redemptive act in Jesus is the offering of a new kind of life for his people today."[35] It was this on offer, following the resurrection of Jesus, that the entire Christian movement and this thing we call spiritual formation ultimately rests. It carries a relevance and impact on human life here and now whereby daily decisions and actions chosen, either in-line with Jesus or apart from him, have a direct impact on our lives. As wisdom is about seeking the ability to succeed at and make the most of life, Christ is the perfect embodiment of that goal. And so, becoming his disciple

33. *Against the Heresies*, 3.18.1.
34. Gorman, *Becoming the Gospel*, 142.
35. Willard, *Spirit of the Disciplines*, 37

and being formed into his likeness is what success in life ultimately looks like. To walk as Jesus did is the wisest choice possible.

Wisdom in the Cross

Before returning to the implications of this for the church, a short (but important) rejoinder must be included. Lest I be mistaken for just another prosperity preacher offering a light and fluffy, health and wealth message with an overly humanistic view of discipleship, it cannot be missed that the spiritual formation which brings about authentic, life giving Christo-formity by nature *requires* loyal obedience to Christ Jesus in all things. That is simply a non-negotiable. For our human wisdom—what we think in our broken and depraved minds will bring us success (Rom 1:28)—more often than not runs counter to God's wisdom, it simply doesn't add up. Just consider what must have seemed the most shocking and unreasonable statement by Jesus when his initial disciples were told that if they wanted to truly follow, they must deny themselves and "take up their cross" (Matt 16:24). Or that to become great in his kingdom they must "become a slave" (Matt 20:27). Love your enemies? Forgive those who persecute you? Lay down your life for others? His instructions often appear as a radical departure from what our brains think will bring us contentment and goodness. It's quite often a counter-intuitive path of difficulty and sacrifice that simply doesn't align with what we think will lead to our betterment. Thus, many who hear Jesus speak turn away as so often the wisdom he offers sounded like nonsense, counter to how they think to gain success (John 6:66). But again, that is because our intuition is fundamentally distorted and not in line with God's intentions for his creation.[36] This is why Paul would say "the message of the cross is foolishness to those who are perishing, but to us who are being saved it is the power of God" (1 Cor 1:19). The wisdom of God exemplified in the cross calls us to live in a way that is counter to how we naturally think our lives should best be lived, our own human wisdom.

Therefore, the only way forward is to choose the fear of the Lord—to give our loyal, obedient allegiance to King Jesus and follow his leading and commands regardless of how it might seem in our minds. Or in the wisdom of Proverbs, to "trust in the LORD with all your heart and lean not on your own understanding" in order to have your paths made straight (3:5–6). We must choose to obey even when it doesn't make sense, when

---

36. For an in-depth study of the way humans are affected in their thinking by our immersion in a fundamentally broken and sinful world, see Eastman, *Paul and the Person*.

it's overly difficult or contrary to what we think is best. The only path to the life he offers is to trust that he knows what is better and choose to follow in the power of his spirit living within us.[37] This is not an easy, self-help message, but a decision to stay along the narrow path and keep walking even when painful or contrary to what we think is best, even when the path leads us directly to the cross.

Wisdom in Ministry

Let us return then, to the question of priority in ministry. Simply put, viewed through the lens of wisdom we find that discovering what it means to be human and how one should go about living is not a secondary goal behind arriving at the pearly gates unscathed. Becoming like Jesus is not just a good idea or something to make God happy but about finding the life he intended when he first breathed life into the earth's soil. It's about choosing to live out the purpose of our existence. Therefore, how could it be relegated to any status other than primary in the church's mission and message to the world?

We see this affirmed in the words of Paul who would have clearly rejected any notion that spiritual formation was some sort of side project or optional addendum to the real goal of salvation. Rather, it was the very plan of God from the start to restore our humanity by transforming us into the image of Jesus (Rom 8:29). This is the aim, the goal of life and why Paul taught "with all wisdom" for us to become "fully mature (*teleion*) in Christ" (Col 1:28). Which, not coincidently, was the same word Jesus used when telling his followers to be perfect (*teleios*) like God (Matt 5:48). Which means, he was calling us to grow and mature to become what we were always created to be. It simply cannot be understated that this transformation is the *end goal*.[38] Becoming like Jesus is the purpose of Christian discipleship and therefore, by reason, the ultimate end goal of all Christian ministry as well.

Unfortunately, however, too often this need for transformation is reduced to the need for a transaction, an adjustment in legal status that ensures the appropriate destination following our death. In such a reduction, the glorious opportunity to experience the good life we were created for today is minimized to a type of life insurance policy promising a post-mortem paradise in God's kingdom, a blessed hope that awaits the final curtain closing on our just-passing-through journey. Countless church leaders have made it their primary work and focus to "win souls" by convincing them to

---

37. For a discussion on the vital role of the Holy Spirit in empowering us to obey and be transformed, see Keener, *Gift and Giver*.

38. DeSilva, *Transformation*, 45.

simply believe a few key propositions about Christ's work on the cross and trust everything needed is already done. This sadly disregards and pushes to the sidelines of barely attended midweek church services any discussions of discovering the magnificent life we were created for through committed, loyal obedience to Jesus and his teachings, of being transformed back into God's image and rightly and wisely caring for his world and each other as he created us. We then watch as a movement to heal the world devolves into a passive waiting to escape it. Such an approach has far too often served to keep Christianity as little more than an empty philosophical system with no real impact for many of its adherents. Obedience is optional as long as one is "saved" and headed to the right place. And the whole while, a world seeking meaning, success, and wisdom to make the most of their lives finds little of value in a Christianity concerned far more with getting souls to heaven than with helping souls find their purpose.

Now, to be clear, certainly we should never separate Jesus's offer of life from what is clearly an everlasting promise. Christ has defeated death and those who have pledged their loyalty to him and received his spirit can be assured God will give them immortality just as he promised (1 Cor 15:53–54; 2 Tim 2:10). However, we must maintain a distinction between a promise of life that *lasts* forever verses a promise of life that only *begins* after death. As the wisdom of God, Jesus offers a new life that launches the moment we choose to trust and obey him for wisdom in all our decision making.

What's more, it is also unquestionably true that in order to move forward in this life with God forgiveness is a necessary first step. It is hardly my intention to downplay the need for the cross and human repentance. However, while an important *step* in the process, it is not the *goal* and should not be the primary focus of our message; any more than apologizing to my wife when I do something inconsiderate should be seen as the goal of marriage. It is a vital aspect of maintaining a healthy relationship with her but the point, the *telos* is . . . enjoying a happy and healthy marriage with her.

Therefore, as ministry leaders viewing God's commission through the eyes of his wisdom it is paramount that spiritual formation and discipleship never been seen as a side project of the church, an optional add-on package to the "real work" of saving souls from hell. Rather, *it is the central aim of God's restoration process of all creation and the primary mission of the church and its leaders*. The great commission to go into the world and make disciples of all nations is not simply about sharing a message to elicit a particular belief but about "teaching them to obey" (Matt 28:19–20) the embodied wisdom of God in Christ in order to lead his image bearers back to their intended purpose. Why? Because complete obedience to and reliance upon Jesus and his wisdom and teaching is not just a good idea but the only pathway to ever discovering and living out what we were truly made for.

This means that God's wisdom at work in the life of his church should be about pursuing the end goal of humans becoming more like Jesus above all, concerned far more with the development of their character than just their end destination. Its leaders should be spiritual teachers and doctors rather than just insurance salesmen. And the focus of their message should be about more than how one is forgiven but how one goes about living, discovering life through wise decisions and choices that align with God's image and plan for humanity as revealed in Christ and led by his spirit working through us. For that is the heart of wisdom. It's about daily life—actions, decisions, ways of thinking that affect every part of our existence. It's not an overly mystical, head-in-the-clouds approach to following Jesus that only concerns itself with the future. Rather, it's concerned with the daily decisions that make up our lives and how we treat those around us here and now, how we live and govern God's world appropriately. It is to find our true purpose and follow Jesus in living it out in every aspect of our lives as we are transformed with ever-increasing glory back into the image of our maker.

Conclusion

Stephen Hawking and all those who rushed to read his potentially wise words were simply doing what many have and will continue to do—seek wisdom for why we are alive and how we are to succeed by looking outward toward the heavens. *But our purpose as humans is not hidden in the stars, it is revealed in the face of Jesus.* And ultimately, creatures will never find their meaning looking to creation but only to the creator. We will never know the mind of God and his true wisdom for our lives by studying his handiwork, but by conforming to his image as revealed in the life and teachings of Jesus. For in him, through his Spirit we are being given the mind of Christ (1 Cor 2:16) to know and experience what it means to be fully human and live a good and blessed life. And when we do, when we live out obedience to Jesus and his wisdom and discover true life, we fulfill what the prophet Daniel predicted, saying: "Those who are wise will shine like the brightness of the heavens, and those who lead many to righteousness, like the stars for ever and ever" (Dan 12:3).

Do you see it? When we live out God's wisdom, *we become the stars the world looks to for the answers to life's deepest questions.* We shine his glory as fully alive human beings and serve as a north star for a dying world's desperate voyage towards life, hope and meaning. But it won't happen if the church is not dedicated and focused on being Christ-formed. There will be nothing shining in the night sky for people to look up to, our message will fall on deaf ears, and even those who confess to believing the truth about Jesus will never experience the life he offers. It is up to the leaders of the church, the pastors and teachers who form the direction, plans, activities, and overall message of each community, to view their ministries through the lens of wisdom and recapture the goal of the church's mission. To wisely bring loyal, faithful commitment to King Jesus in every aspect of daily life back to the forefront of what it means to be a Christian. And to brilliantly shine to a world desperate for meaning and help in finding a truly good life that he has come to give it . . . and give it to the fullest.

Bibliography

Athanasius, St. *On the Incarnation: The Treatise De Incarnatione Verbi De.* Rev. ed. New York: St. Vladimir's Seminary Press, 1983.

Bates, Matthew W. *Salvation by Allegiance Alone: Rethinking Faith, Works, and the Gospel of Jesus the King.* Grand Rapids: Baker Academic, 2017.

Crenshaw, James L. *Education in Ancient Israel: Across the Deadening Silence.* London: Yale University Press, 1998.

———. *Old Testament Wisdom: An Introduction.* Rev. ed. Louisville: Westminster John Knox, 1998.

Davies, W. D. *Paul and Rabbinic Judaism.* Rev. ed. New York: Harper Torchbooks, 1967.

DeSilva, David A. *Transformation: The Heart of Paul's Gospel.* Bellingham: Lexham Press, 2015.

Dunn, James D. G. *The New Perspective on Paul.* Grand Rapids: Eerdmans, 2008.

Eastman, Susan Grove. *Paul and the Person: Reframing Paul's Anthropology.* Grand Rapids: Eerdmans, 2017.

Gorman, Michael J. *Becoming the Gospel: Paul, Participation, and Mission.* Grand Rapids: Eerdmans, 2015.

Harris, Brian *The Big Picture: Building Blocks of a Christian World View.* Milton Keynes: Paternoster Press, 2015.

Hawking, Stephen. *A Brief History of Time.* 10th Anniversary Edition. New York: Bantam, 1998.

Keener, Craig S. *Gift and Giver.* Grand Rapids: Baker, 2001.

Kingsbury, Jack Dean. *Matthew.* Rev. ed. Nappanee: Evangel, 1998.

McKeown, J. "Blessings and Curses." In *Dictionary of the Old Testament: Pentateuch,* edited by T. Desmond Alexander et al., 85–86. Downers Grove, IL: InterVarsity Academic, 2003.

McKnight, Scot. *The King Jesus Gospel: The Original Good News Revisited.* Rev. ed. Grand Rapids: Zondervan, 2016.

Middleton, J. Richard. *The Liberating Image: The Imago Dei in Genesis 1.* Grand Rapids: Brazos, 2005.

Paris, Natalie. "Hawking to Experience Zero Gravity." *The Daily Telegraph,* April 26, 2007. https://www.telegraph.co.uk/news/worldnews/1549770/Hawking-to-experience-zero-gravity.html.

Sanders, E. P. *Paul and Palestinian Judaism: 40th Anniversary Edition.* Philadelphia: Fortress, 2017.

Thomas, Gabrielle. *The Image of God in the Theology of Gregory of Nazianzus.* New York: Cambridge University Press, 2019.

Thompson, James W. *Moral Formation According to Paul: The Context and Coherence of Pauline Ethics.* Grand Rapids: Baker Academic, 2011.

Wall, Robert W., et al., eds. *Acts, Romans, 1 Corinthians.* The New Interpreter's Bible: A Commentary in Twelve Volumes 10. Nashville: Abingdon, 2002.

Willard, Dallas. *The Spirit of the Disciplines: Understanding How God Changes Lives.* San Francisco: HarperOne, 1999.

Witherington, Ben, III. *Jesus the Sage: The Pilgrimage of Wisdom.* Minneapolis: Fortress, 2000.

WISE RACIAL JUSTICE

Wisdom from the Sorrowful Ones

By Ernest F. Ledbetter III

I humbly admit that throughout the course of my days I have been accused of being wise beyond my years. Being a skeptic while also pursuing the title of scholar, I have longed to truly understand what this meant. Studying the rhetoric of Elihu in the book of Job further complicated this colloquial compliment. The Bible would teach me that age and wisdom do not always correlate. Understanding that the saying simply was to mean that I probably possessed more wit than the person I was encountering had expected, I became fascinated with the word that is often casually thrown around—wisdom. Wisdom as it is expressed in Prov 1:7 is the fear of the LORD. Scholars are unsure as to what this properly translates into due to the fact there are many researchers and believers alike that find it troublesome to have to be afraid of God in order to obtain wisdom.[1]

Since "Lord" in the text is capitalized, we know that the term in the Hebrew manuscript is Yahweh. It is at the moment of the revelation of the great tetragrammaton that we can consider what the is proverb is attempting to convey to its reader. In Exod 3, Moses is tending to his flock when he notices a bush that is on fire that is not being consumed. As he approaches the bush, a voice from the midst of the fire in midst of the bush begins to speak to Moses. Yahweh calls out to Moses to prohibit him from coming any closer until he has made some revisions to his own appearance that would qualify him to be nearer to the fire. Yahweh requires him to remove his shoes and declares that the ground that he is standing upon is holy. What can be inferred here is that the presence of God changes the quality of his surroundings regardless of what they were before his revelation.

---

1. See the opening chapter by Daniel Hanlon.

Yahweh introduces himself as the ancestral deity of Moses's forefathers which causes Moses to cover his face—ironically, he no longer feels worthy to observe the same fire that drew his attention in the first place. The text says that he was afraid to look at God.[2] The term that is used for afraid is *yare'* which does connect to terror. However, the etymology of the word terror connects with the idea of something awesome—in other words, something that inspires awe. As he is hiding his face, the Lord begins to reveal, prophetically, that he has been observing the oppression of Moses and his people historically and Yahweh also reveals what His plans are as it concerns their future liberation. It is the reverential behavior and humility that prepare Moses to receive the wisdom of Yahweh.

Throughout the Proverbs experience and understanding through reverential fear are revealed to lead to God's wisdom. Wisdom is provocatively likened to a feminine entity which should be pursued and attained by any means necessary. Even more provocative than the anthropomorphism of wisdom is the pain that it brings in Eccl 1:18. The text says, "For in much wisdom is much grief: and he that increaseth knowledge increaseth sorrow." Now if the fear of the Lord is the beginning of wisdom—and I am encouraged to pursue wisdom at all costs—how strange then does it seem that the writer of Ecclesiastes informs the reader that much wisdom causes sorrow? I can attest that the wisdom I have been complimented to possess was instilled within me through the lessons learned as I continue to be involved with the institution that formed me in the first place—the Black Church. I propose that this "invisible institution"[3] known as the Black Church is and has always been the Wisdom Culture for the Black man, woman, and child since its inception. To be Black in America is hard to reconcile. Furthermore, to be a Black Christian in America can be quite the epistemological paradox. The Black Church provides the wisdom that both teaches the Black community how to maneuver through all sociopolitical endeavoring and activity while trying to live and survive in America.

The Transatlantic Problem: The Reason
the Black Church was Born

As economic expansion in Europe was ensuing, Europeans had to figure out a way to justify their exploits of resources, goods, and people from nations, particularly Africa. The justification became that they were taking the gospel to the savages and thus slavery was a form of evangelism. Gomez Eanes

2. Exod 3:6. Unless otherwise indicated, Scripture quotations are from the KJV.

3. Raboteau, *Slave Religion*, 110.

de Zurara, also known as Azurara the Chronicler, once said as he found solace in the spiritualization of slavery.

> And so their lot was now quite contrary to what it had been; since before they had lived in perdition in soul and body; of their souls, in that they were, yet pagans, without the clearness of light of holy faith; and in their bodies, in that they lived like beasts without any custom of reasonable beings—for they had no assessment of bread and wine, and they were without the covering of clothing or lodgment of houses; and worst of all, they had no understanding of good, but only knew how to live in bestial sloth.[4]

This was certainly a perversion of what Jesus meant in Matt 28:19 which commands believers to "Go therefore and make disciples of all nations, baptizing them in the name of the Father and of the Son and of the Holy Spirit." What is happening in this fourteenth century, as claimed by Azurara, is that the African is a savage and completely exchanges into European culture as the culture of Christ. *Thus, the Christian crusade was to teach Africans Eurocentric hegemony under the auspices of evangelism.* His rationalization would be repeated for many centuries by Christian apologists in order to continue the justification of oppression.[5] This would be the foundation of the caste system that would constantly transform over time to keep people of darker hues oppressed in the Western world. It was an assumed superiority that suggested that subjugation and control of African peoples were implemented out of God's providence.

Alexander Tsesis writes, "this institution was one of unrequited exploitation and broken family life that provided its victims with only the bare amenities and forced them into lifelong, hereditary servility; slaveholding was the aspiration of many whites living in the South who longed for a sense of economic independence and social standing through the ownership of human capital."[6] To this day, the broken family is the bane of the Black community. The ideal of universal freedom, particularly as John Locke presented it, made its way into the Declaration of Independence, but it did not end slavery.[7] The governmental documents that would be the foundation of our nation never considered Blacks in its idea of freedom. Thus, two Americas were born as its founders never intended for the Black man to be free; this contradiction is still alive today. Studies of eugenics would further

---

4. Raboteau, *Slave Religion*, 114.
5. Raboteau, *Slave Religion*, 114.
6. Tsesis, *Thirteenth Amendment and American Freedom*, 2.
7. Tsesis, *Thirteenth Amendment and American Freedom*, 3.

perpetuate the ideology that Blacks were inferior to the white races that were in control of the documents written for this New American government to declare its independence. A moral dilemma of viewing slaves of African descent as subhuman and soulless was birthed and perpetuated to ensure a caste system unto perpetuity that would cause America's economy to boom for centuries to come.

Many scholars regardless of race thought the American system of government could never fail a people that it was never intended to cover and protect. It would seem that the Fifth Amendment, which protected the inalienable rights of all men, would have contradicted the peculiar institution of slavery. However, to deem African enslaved men, women, and children as chattel, would prove to be a far more complex situation than the framers would care to admit. So, the question becomes, Did not the North and the Civil War and its adjustment of the Thirteenth Amendment abjure the ideology and practice of the peculiar institution of slavery? The problem is further exacerbated in the knowledge that the emancipation of slaves was an economic front more than it was a moralistic decision and agreement that all men were born free. It is to be understood that the rights of property owners were protected by the Fifth Amendment as Blacks were considered chattel and not human beings. Tsesis argues, "Therein lay the need for a clear constitutional pronouncement against slavery and all its manifestations; unfortunately, in the face of Supreme Court conservatism, even the language of the Thirteenth Amendment for a time turned out to be inadequate."[8] It was economic motives that drove the amendments instead of ethical righteousness. To secure the Union the battle over slavery was fought—it was not that the North believed that the slaves should be free—the North was tired of the southern states becoming wealthy due to the institution of slavery.

It was Frederick Douglass who as an escaped slave would repudiate the innate contradiction of the enslavement and concessions of law in dealing with the ethics pertaining to America's treatment of the slave.[9] Frederick Douglass would further argue:

> If we adopt the preamble, with Liberty and Justice, we must repudiate the enacting clauses, with Kidnapping and Slaveholding. . . . Every slaveholder in the land stands perjured in the sight of Heaven, when he swears his purpose to be, the establishment of justice—the providing for the general welfare, and the preservation of liberty to the people of this country; for every such

8. Tsesis, *Thirteenth Amendment and American Freedom*, 6.
9. Tsesis, *Thirteenth Amendment and American Freedom*, 7.

slaveholder knows that his whole life gives an emphatic lie to his
solemn vow.[10]

Slaveholders were in perjury of the documents that gave America its independence. Justice was not served to the people of African descent. If God
were in fact the Father of us all then we would not be able to be enslaved as
the government desired to continue. The clause that declared that African
enslaved persons were only to be three-fifths human had a major impact on
the elections within the South.[11] Men who would escape slavery still had
to deal with the Fugitive Slave Acts that returned property to the owners.[12]
This act had no dissenting voices and slavery would continue its growth in
fifteen of the thirty colonies of the Union.

As if the enslavement of human lives were not enough, religion would
further frustrate the situation. Charles II would begin to encourage the
proselytization of slaves in the New World in 1660. There were even battles
between Catholics and Protestants as to who would convert the most savages in the New World—not because they wanted to see souls saved but
because they did not want their excursions to look like missionary failures
numerically.[13] Unfortunately the slave masters of the New World cared more
about the economic profitability of the slave than the Christianization of the
slave.[14] Morgan Godwin, a preacher of the time, received much criticism
for mentioning that the slaveholders priorities chose mammon over Christ
in 1685.[15] Albert Raboteau asserts that these slaveholders feared the implo-
sion of slavery as an institution if they allowed their slaves to be baptized.
Missionaries often complained about the refusal of being allowed to teach
the slaves about the gospel. The great commission then became the greatest
enemy to the economic well-being of the slaveocracy. Instead of building
Christ's Kingdom, the American majority was more interested in creating
its own American Empire on the backs of enslaved Africans.

This problem had to be fixed. Slave owners quickly understood that,
through the manipulation of what the Scripture taught on servanthood and
discipleship, baptizing the slave could be beneficial to the docility and un-
questioned obedience of the slave. By 1706 legislature had been passed in
the colonies that guaranteed that the baptism of the slave did not change
their status from chattel to human, thus making the government stronger

10. Tsesis, *Thirteenth Amendment and American Freedom*, 7.

11. Tsesis, *Thirteenth Amendment and American Freedom*, 7.

12. Tsesis, *Thirteenth Amendment and American Freedom*, 9.

13. Raboteau, *Slave Religion*, 115.

14. Raboteau, *Slave Religion*, 115.

15. Raboteau, *Slave Religion*, 116.

than the transformative power of Jesus. Again, the faith caused another problem for the slave owner. Instruction would take time out of the day that the slave could be working. Teaching the slaves would utterly affect production from the slave which would essential lower profits for the slave owner.[16] Raboteau argues, "The danger beneath the arguments for slave conversion which many masters feared was the egalitarianism implicit within Christianity."[17] This further conveys that the connection and claim to Christian fellowship would strain the relationship of the socioeconomic hierarchy of slave-master.[18] There was an utter fear that the baptism of slaves and the Christianization of the plantation would cause utter confusion and lead to chaos and revolt—such revolution would be in slaves seeing themselves equal in the sight of God. Ironically, this is what the Founding Fathers would write in their documents declaring independence. A trinity of sorts was born of slave owners, missionaries, and slaves. Whether or not the slave was converted depended mostly on their having to reconcile that the gospel preached liberty and justice along with their current condition.[19] Christian disciples are commanded to take the gospel to pagans and to convert them through teaching. However, in America the pagan was brought to work for the disciple and the Christian teaching was prohibited.

Ashamedly it was not only the slave masters who had an issue with the conversion of slaves but much of the resistance came from the pulpit of clergymen. Rev. Charles Martyn of South Carolina preached that once a slave was baptized, they "became lazy, and proud, entertaining too high of an opinion of themselves, and neglecting their daily labor."[20] Due to the inability to conquer the prevailing thought that slaves would not rebel once they received Christ as their Savior, slaves had to agree to the following before they were baptized:

> You therefore, in the presence of God and his Congregation, that you do not ask for the Holy baptism out of any design to free yourself from the Duty and Obedience you owe to your Master while you live, but merely for the goodness of Your Soul and to partake in the Graces and Blessings promised to the Church of Jesus Christ.[21]

16. Raboteau, *Slave Religion*, 117.
17. Raboteau, *Slave Religion*, 119.
18. Raboteau, *Slave Religion*, 119.
19. Raboteau, *Slave Religion*, 137.
20. Raboteau, *Slave Religion*, 140.
21. Raboteau, *Slave Religion*, 140.

This was a baptism reinforcing the bondage that the ordinance of baptism was to free them from. It was the equivalent of giving a prisoner the key as long as they promise never to release themselves from the cage.

It is worth noting that this process of conversion shifted the identity of the enslaved from Africans to Negroes.[22] The slave was reborn into a new identity, only to further fit firmly at the bottom of the American racial caste. This process was a psychological severing from nation and ethnicity and a changing into a color and labeled property instead of being dignified as fellow human beings. It would be the impetus of white supremacy that would keep the economic institution of slavery alive and strong. In doing so a duality of parallel worlds was created. Epistemologically, missionaries began to notice that the catechisms of the Negroes took on something different than its original delivery. An inspirational subversion of the catechisms and lessons they taught the slaves took shape. The theology and doctrine once learned and internalized became something more than just the mimicking of their white counterparts—the slaves began to combine the teachings with the culture of their African traditions past down from generation to generation.[23] The lessons that were taught did not always become the messages receive—an internal theological subversion was taking place.[24] To add to the complexity of this nuance was the combination of singing, dancing, drumming, and spirit-possession which derived from the slaves' heritage. This would be the beginning of an institution within an institution.

The Birth of the Black Church

An event that would change the landscape of American slavery would be the revivals of the Second Great Awakening during the nineteenth century. During this time Negroes were allowed to attend white churches. However, they had to either sit in the balconies, on the floor, or outside the doors and windows in order to participate. When there were too many slaves to attend the service, this inconvenience allowed for them to begin having their own separate services. These churches would sometimes be supervised by a white preacher or pastor but soon the churches would have their own autonomy while maintaining association with the mainline denomination. Even when state legislatures began to prohibit Negroes from preaching, the Baptist churches would continue to license and ordain

22. Raboteau, *Slave Religion*, 143.

23. Raboteau, *Slave Religion*, 143.

24. See Bowens, *African American Readings of Paul*.

Negro preachers.[25] They were restricted to only preaching when their masters would give them permission and they were required to do all funerals
and weddings for their enslaved peers.

In essence, these things began the nascent beginnings of what would
be called the Black Church. As aforementioned, something greater than
religious participation was being created here. It was a socioeconomic phenomenon that sprung from the bicultural synthesis that, in turn, created a
Black Christian community.[26] W. E. B. Dubois wonderfully chronicles the
importance of the Black Church in his seminal work, "The Souls of Black
Folk," written in 1903. As a sociologist he explains that there were three
important elements to the new institution: the preacher, the music, and the
frenzy.[27] He conveys that the preacher is the most unique personality developed by the Negro on American soil.[28] The preacher he remarks has to be "A
leader, a politician, an orator, a 'boss,an intriguer,' an idealist—all these he
is, and ever, too, the centre of a group of men, now twenty, now a thousand
in number."[29] The Black preacher was the giver of wisdom and the chief of
the community. Dubois argues that the preacher's importance to the group
dwells in the wittiness, skill, and sincerity of his oratory that allows him to
maintain his status as the wisdom giver.

He then explains another important element—the music of Negro
religion. Dubois believes that the simple rhythmic music that was heard in
the Black churches derives from the shores of Western Africa. He critiques
it as a caricature of its Eurocentric counterpart. He further asserts that it is
still the most beautiful offering from American soil in that it is original and
springs forth from the tragic souls, blending sorrow, despair and hope.[30]
Along with the wisdom given to the people from the Black preacher, the
music was a culture of coded wisdom that would teach not only theology
but how to socially move within the oppressive nation. Finally, Dubois
highlights what he calls the "Frenzy." This is the exuberant and ecstatic
behavior that is exhibited when the Negro would experience supernatural
joy.[31] Observing the congregation Dubois states, "It varied in expression
from the silent rapt countenance or the low murmur and moan to the mad
abandon of physical fervor,—the stamping, shrieking, and shouting, the

25. Raboteau, *Slave Religion*, 153.

26. Raboteau, *Slave Religion*, 154.

27. Dubois, *Souls of Black Folk*, 190.

28. Dubois, *Souls of Black Folk*, 190.

29. Dubois, *Souls of Black Folk*, 190.

30. Dubois, *Souls of Black Folk*, 191.

31. Dubois, *Souls of Black Folk*, 191.

rushing to and fro and wild waving of arms, the weeping and laughing, the vision and the trance."[32] These were the three foundational things that helped the Negro connect to the invisible sublime that he longed for. The experience and enjoyment of the foundational elements of the institution gives the wisdom that allows the Black believer to revere God but also keep him aware of the sorrow that is never removed in daily life.

Understanding the importance of the role that the institution of the Black Church played in the life of the Negro, Dubois noticed something deeper than just the conversion of enslaved men, women, and children. Something more cerebral: this new environment for the Negro explained his focus for "higher life" but Dubois wanted to examine some of the harder questions about the ethics and sociological implications of the invisible institution. He wanted to know how the slave reconciled slavery with his theology, what was his worldview, and what were his longings, desires, and disappointments.[33] These answers he felt could only come from the Black Church's development and the study of it. Dubois would go on to argue that it was interesting that the religious philosophy and theology of poor whites was a direct robbery from the Black Church. The ethos of the Black Church gained prominence as it spread due to the music Dubois emphasizes.

The study of the Negro Church is vital to understanding American History.[34] Its foundation still gives relevance as to why there is still the need for it today. What Dubois wrote in 1903 is still "gospel truth" today— "The Negro church of to-day is the social centre of Negro life in the United States, and the most characteristic expression of African character."[35] What is illustrated is that the Black Church was more than just a place of religious instruction but that it was a meeting place for all things that its congregants participated in. The church for the Negro was the center of existence: "the church proper, the Sunday-school, two or three insurance societies, women's societies, secret societies, and mass meetings of various kinds. Entertainments, suppers, and lectures are held beside the five or six regular weekly religious services."[36] Much of the economics of the Negro was collected there as well as employment information was disseminated there. All of the Negro's social, intellectual, and religious power were centralized here. It was the church that reinforced the morals and family structure. It was the final authority of what was considered good and right.

32. Dubois, *Souls of Black Folk*, 192.
33. Dubois, *Souls of Black Folk*, 193.
34. Dubois, *Souls of Black Folk*, 193.
35. Dubois, *Souls of Black Folk*, 193.
36. Dubois, *Souls of Black Folk*, 194.

He states that the church "reproduced in microcosm, all that great world from which the Negro is cut off by color-prejudice and social condition." The Negro in America was able to stomach the utterly inhumane oppression through the supplementary nature of the church—what the world denied the Negro the church gave to him.

Dubois excellently goes on to emphasize that the Black Church produced some of the most powerful Negroes in the world.[37] Due to its incredible impact he further writes how every Negro of the Antebellum South was a member of a Black Church. No other institution has the power and impact upon a people as the Black Church does. Dubois explains that it must be understood that the institution of the Black Church "antedates" or predates the Negro home. The heart of the Negroes' ethics was formed through this institution when the slaveocracy did not allow Negro families to thrive. They were on the plantations in shacks and many times sold off and separated for the economic purposes of the slave owners. Dubois believes that this created the sorrow of the invisible institution—a fatalism or longing for the next life due to the hopelessness of the present one.[38] The more that the Negro learned of the Scriptures, the more he began to realize the insufficiencies of the bastardized version of Christianity that he had been taught. For many the despair turned their humility and moral strength to submission as it seemed that nothing would change—but maybe it would in the next life. Ironically for many Negroes the home was crushed under the shadow of the church.[39] It was becoming increasingly impossible to reconcile their freedom in Christ with their bondage to their masters.

Dubois goes on to illustrate that there was a fifty-year span in the Antebellum South wherewith the Black Church harnessed its despair and hoped for freedom—it consumed the Black preacher and all of the music.[40] New wisdom was passed on through lyrics such as

> O Freedom, O Freedom, O Freedom over me! Before I'll be a slave
> I'll be buried in my grave and go home to my Lord And be free.

Prophetic declarations of freedom and longing for death—the longing to be with the Lord was essentially a theological concept but it was a social desire as well of finally experiencing freedom. The grave becomes the door to a new world free of oppression. The Black Church would be the asylum

---

37. Dubois, *Souls of Black Folk*, 194.
38. Dubois, *Souls of Black Folk*, 199.
39. Dubois, *Souls of Black Folk*, 201.
40. Dubois, *Souls of Black Folk*, 201.

for the Negro all the way through Emancipation.[41] The Black Church would now have to create and maintain the wisdom of the Negro in specific areas which included:

> the peculiar problems of their inner life,—of the status of women, the maintenance of Home, the training of children, the accumulation of wealth, and the prevention of crime.[42]

This is what Dubois calls "The Negro Problem." Now emancipated, the Negroes' problems in America are only exacerbated more. This changed the behavior and maneuvering of the Negro; he often becomes bitter and vindictive; and his religion, instead of a worship, is a complaint and a curse, a wail rather than a hope, a sneer rather than a faith.[43] The free Negro's internalization of religion would become more than faith but a social critique of American injustice and oppression. America was shifting into a new caste system to oppress the Negro now freed. Still only deemed three-fifths human it became increasingly difficult to enjoy freedom when legislation was constantly created to reduce the Negro in America back to the status of being a savage only worth being enslaved. Dubois conveys a new wisdom—a wisdom that I still adhere to today.

The Double-minded Black man

The Bible declares in Jas 1:18 "A double minded man is unstable in all his ways." The Black man in America is born into this doublemindedness. This concept is what Dubois is most known for and I believe it is because it is a reality for most, if not all, Black people. He states that there is something that separates him from the rest of the world—a question. The question is "How does it feel to be a problem?"[44] It pains me even as I continue to write the words of this chapter because I feel as helpless and befuddled as Dubois did in 1903. One-hundred and seventeen years later the Negro is still being asked this question. Dubois goes on to explain how in his childhood an event took place that made him fully aware of his otherness—his being a problem. There comes a time in every Black life where the wisdom will be revealed to you that you are different. I too had a revelatory moment that changed my perspective on the world. It was in the early 2000s (maybe 2006) when my father and I travelled to Detroit, Michigan—my

---

41. Dubois, *Souls of Black Folk*, 202.

42. Dubois, *Souls of Black Folk*, 203.

43. Dubois, *Souls of Black Folk*, 203.

44. Dubois, *Souls of Black Folk*, 2.

father had to preach, and I was happy to be his ride-along buddy. Upon finishing the ministerial duties my father wanted to expose me to a new world and opportunity. He explained to me that you can travel to Canada by way of an underwater tunnel from Detroit. Excited at not only the opportunity to go to another country but to do so through an underwater tunnel caused my inner child to awaken with glee. I can still smell the water as we rode through the tunnel and arriving at the border of Canada as we had to pass through customs. The officer came to the car and asked for my father's identification. We noticed that other cars were passing by us on either side rather quickly. After a few minutes, the two officers came to the car yelling, "Out of the car and put your hands against the wall." They had the guard dogs on leashes sniffing the car and us for what seemed to be drugs. Scared out of my mind I listen for my father's exclamation, "What is this about?" After they found nothing in the car and nothing incriminating on us, they ordered us to get back into the car. Apparently, a gun record from 1985 showed on the computer which alerted the officers to throw two Black men against the wall and search them with dogs—I hope that you are able to pick up on my sarcasm. We were both dressed in suit and tie and had already explained that our business in Detroit was that my father was preaching there—none of those things mattered. Traumatized by the event, I never forgot the experience—I saw life differently then—I saw myself differently. I then saw life through this veil.

It is this self-awareness and Black hermeneutic that creates what Dubois coins as double-consciousness. Because of the American Negroes' history he is born with what Dubois illustrates as a veil. It functions as the buffer between self-identification and how the world perceives you. It is a second-sight or to be considered a gift of wisdom of being able to perceive yourself through the eyes of others in America.[45] The double-consciousness is the fact that though he be one man, he possesses two souls—one is American and the other is Negro. He says, "—an American, a Negro; two souls, two thoughts, two unreconciled strivings; two warring ideals in one dark body, whose dogged strength alone keeps it from being torn asunder." As I reread this book for maybe the seventh or eighth time, tears formed in my eyes as I have never read words that more capture the Black Experience in America today. To be African American is to be a walking paradox: born in a nation that distinguishes you by a land you have little to any knowledge of and a multiplicity of languages your tongue has never and probably will never speak. The Negro does not wish to Africanize America nor does he want to bleach his soul through Americanism—he just wants

45. Dubois, *Souls of Black Folk*, 4.

to belong or at least receive the answer to the question. The reconciliation of peace that is not afforded to him even through his Christianity further frustrates him in that it seems that God has made the Black American a stranger in his own home.

The double-consciousness affects the Black life in an inexplicable way. Paradoxically attempting to satisfy two worlds that never reconcile only allows the Black mind and heart to accomplish half of the goal. The Black musician is trying to be true to his soul while simultaneously being recognized by the people who may enjoy his entertainment but not his personhood. The Black preacher has the aforementioned power and prominence in the Black community but his cultural traditions are deemed sub-intelligent by the majority culture. I have felt this temptation while in different settings within seminary. Having the double-mindedness, do I behave how I would normally do in my context or do I transform into that which is more acceptable to the majority culture? My inner urban African culture being controlled by the assumed suburban erudite seminarian expectation. This dual aim ends up missing both targets. Even during group lunches with classmates, I have felt the peering eyes from near and afar questioning my placement with my white peers. Behind the veil I have to internally validate myself and have answers ready if questioned. There is a strain of having to explain my skin through tokens of being a pastor, a doctoral student, a lover of jazz or anything other thing that may alert common ground for the separation that is caused by my politically weaponized skin. It is exhausting having to represent an entire race daily in hopes that I am not seen as what America has so long portrayed people of darker complexion.

What Does It Mean to Be American?

There are lyrics to a particularly important song in popular culture that exclaims, "I'm proud to be an American, where at least I know I'm free." It is with bitterness that I hear this song because it is not the truth for the Black American still. So the question becomes what it means to be an American. Just as there is a double-consciousness in the mind of the Black Man, there are two Americas. There is the mythos of what America is and then there is the reality of America. The mythos is grounded in American exceptionalism and illusionary patriotism. The term American carries the connotation of being white, middle class, conservative, pro life, Christian, suburban, gun owning, and Republican. I could have kept the list going but I risk having a run-on sentence. This is the façade that makes it practically impossible to determine where predominate white culture ends and where Christianity begins.[46] The focus of white American Christianity was developed through the selecting of Scriptures that fit the white world—the world that they were building.[47] Thus Jesus in the mythos of America became the reflection desired in the mirror of every white American.

How was this mythos created? It is the same fertile ground that created the Black Church. The oppression that seems to be America's motivation for sociopolitical advancement has always been a part of its story. The assumed mythos that is a part of the American story is that this was a Christian nation founded by our righteous and holy founding fathers. We have already extensively discussed the oppression of the Africans brought to the New World but what kind of ideology was prevalent in order to make such inhumane behavior systemically ingrained in the politics. And if this truly is a Christian nation, then why isn't the name of Christ anywhere in the legal documents?

To place it simply before diving in. To be conservative meant that you were in support of the white supremist culture and to be liberal meant that you support the humanity of Black peoples in America. The answer lies within the understanding of the Western world's obsession with the Enlightenment. When white scholarship felt that it had found its philosophers and physicists to challenge normative political and religious concepts, the writings of Voltaire, Francis Bacon, Isaac Newton, and John Locke became just as important as the Bible. I still remember sitting in high school and college classes questioning in my own mind why I had to constantly read the words of these rationalists that never registered with my own soul—it would later be revealed that my double-consciousness was at work and that the concepts would lead America into its oppressive downward spiral. The god of America became reason. We know this because the majority of the founding fathers were either deists or Christian deists. Thomas Paine who led the movement from Christian orthodoxy to deism, once penned:

> The opinions I have advanced . . . are the effect of the most clear and long-established conviction that the Bible and the Testament are impositions upon the world, that the fall of man, the account of Jesus Christ being the Son of God, and of his dying to appease the wrath of God, and of salvation, by that strange means, are all fabulous inventions, dishonorable to the wisdom and power of the Almighty; that the only true religion is Deism, by which I then meant, and mean now, the belief of one God, and an imitation of his moral character, or the practice of what

46. Goza, *America's Unholy Ghosts*, 31.
47. Goza, *America's Unholy Ghosts*, 32.

are called moral virtues—and that it was upon this only (so far
as religion is concerned) that I rested all my hopes of happiness
hereafter. So say I now—and so help me God.

He further claimed that deism was superior to Christianity.[48] Whereas he
was a non-Christian deist, the other founding fathers attempted to reconcile
their deism with Christianity.[49] Deists dismissed the belief in the Trinity, the
incarnation and divinity of Jesus, they did not believe in the virgin birth nor
did they believe in the resurrection.[50] They also did not believe in any of the
"irrational acts" of the Bible. For example, anything that was supernatural was
ignored. They do not believe in the atonement of Jesus nor do they believe in
sin passed down through humanity.[51] Deists believe that no personal relationship with Jesus or God was necessary and that he as the divine architect and
being nature's God (which he is called in the Declaration of Independence)
was utterly uninterested in the livelihood of humanity.[52]

This is all necessary information in contemplating how a Christian nation can enslave African people for over two hundred years. The answer is
that the reality of America was founded upon the principles that there was
no such thing as sin and if you believed that it was, then you are clearly irrational. If there is no sin and Jesus was not the incarnation or embodiment
of God and the atoning sacrifice that sets all sinners free, it mattered not if
the enslaved were baptized or not. The secular government did not believe
as the church did. If there is no focus on the miracles of Jesus which often
exposed the need to take care of the oppressed, then there is no need to
focus on the poor of the country—Negroes. Since there is no Holy Spirit to
convict and lead believers into all truth, there would be no logical forbid-
dance of enslaving people and denying rights.

This is important today because though there have been many amendments to the document originally penned by these men, it is still to be
understood that the founding fathers produced documents that created a
secular, not Christian government, that still is systemically oppressing the
same people that it has always. Thus, America seems to have two souls as
well. The mythos that is currently being perpetuated as the Land of the Free
and boasting of its exceptionalism while being the country with the most
people incarcerated. The reality is that America hides behind the conservative Christian façade and mythos. It is the very thing that is going on in the

48. Holmes, *Faiths of the Founding Fathers*, 39.
49. Holmes, *Faiths of the Founding Fathers*, 44.
50. Holmes, *Faiths of the Founding Fathers*, 47.
51. Holmes, *Faiths of the Founding Fathers*, 47.
52. Holmes, *Faiths of the Founding Fathers*, 48.

political situation as we prepare for the presidential election (of 2020). To critique or to oppose anything connected to the mythos of America you are seen as unpatriotic. You are further seen as a radical liberal if you attempt to alleviate the oppression of Black people.

The Wisdom of the Black Church

The beauty of the Black Church is dependent upon the ugliness which created it. They are inseparable. The sorrow of being oppressed crushed the Black soul and left it with a culture of creative wisdom. The power of song in struggle for Black survival—that is what the spirituals and blues are about.[53] It was the music that would stir the peoples' hearts. It was often the music that caused people to feel the presence of God which gave them the courage and the strength to endure the hardships of their oppression.[54] It would be the church music and the wisdom taken from it that would prove to be the prime cultural expression of the Black community.[55] The thematic of the blues and the spirituals was to acknowledge the despair and to make it through the storm—as aforementioned each song hinted at the continuance through the struggle. A song such as Wade in the Water is as follows:

> Wade in the water, Wade in the water, Children wade, in the water, God's gonna trouble the water, Who's that, young girl dressed in red Wade in the water, Must be the children that Moses led God's gonna trouble the water.

At first glance it simply looks like lyrics to a Negro spiritual. However, being a part of the culture known as the Black Church I know differently. The first thing to know is that the very song is a protest of sorts. It is a reflective song, but it parallels the releasing of the Hebrew slaves during the Exodus. If you know the story of the children of Israel, you know that God parted the Red Sea so that they would not be wading in water and thus drown. So the song has a hidden code of wisdom. The enslaved were preserving instruction through song. If a runaway slave would wade in water it was practically impossible for the blood hound to pick up the scent of the slave. In order to preserve the subversive art, the original biblical text had to be intelligently understood. James Cone argues that Black music must be lived before it can be understood.[56] Cone would further argue that it is not

53. Cone, *Spirituals and the Blues*, 10.
54. Cone, *Spirituals and the Blues*, 11.
55. Cone, *Spirituals and the Blues*, 11.
56. Cone, *Spirituals and the Blues*, 13.

enough for the student of Black music to use the academic tools to research this culture but that one has to actually come in contact with the faith in the experience that it affirms[57] Black music of the Antebellum, be it religious or secular, invites you to the sources of Black life and survival. It would seem that the God of the spirituals is not the same God of the white songs. The words are spelled the same but are pronounced differently and evoke a different energy.[58] I've been to white churches and I am an extension of the Black Church. In both institutions you can hear "My Lord's getting us ready for that great day." In the Black Church context Lord will be heard almost always as "Lawd." The Black Church still honors the linguistic protest of the language they learned as slaves—they were intelligent to say yes sir and yes ma'am. However, to have their own autonomy they subverted the language with "yessuh" and "yes'm." Here in song Lord is converted to Lawd and allows for a rendering that harmonizes sorrow and joy.[59] It is the music that aims directly for the consciousness of the community.[60]

The sorrows of the Black soul also work to establish the center of Black culture's wisdom—the preaching. Whereas the Black Church is an invisible institution and encompasses all denominations, the most common ingredient is the emphasis placed on the sermon. Yes, the music connects and stirs the spirit within, but it is the Word of God being broken down that either makes or breaks the preacher and or church. Black congregants want to know what God is saying to them through specified texts. They do not want to hear opinion, speculation, or theological suppositions—tell us what thus sayeth the Lord.[61] Regardless of how creative of a storyteller the preacher is, expository preaching is expected. Though uneducated while living in the antebellum South, the learning and memorization of texts filled in the void of their former West African oral cultures.[62] It is through preaching that the anxiety of the sorrowful double-consciousness can be soothed.

As Cone purports, the God of spirituals in the Black Church and the God of the white worship songs of the white or evangelical church are two different Gods. So then are the Christs that are the savior of them. America has attempted to make Jesus a European with blue eyes and blond hair. However, it would be through the preaching of the Black preacher that would inform the listener that the text says that Jesus had hair like lamb's wool and his

57. Cone, *Spirituals and the Blues*, 14.
58. Cone, *Spirituals and the Blues*, 15.
59. Cone, *Spirituals and the Blues*, 15.
60. Cone, *Spirituals and the Blues*, 16.
61. Mitchell, *Black Preaching*, 47.
62. Mitchell, *Black Preaching*, 48.

hands and feet looked like brass burned in the fire. The artistic wittiness and the creative spirituality would lead Black souls to a cultural understanding that Jesus looked more like them, than their oppressors—this also helped to internalize the story of Jesus as a Black man under white Roman oppression. Around Christmas time sermons about the Messiah being born and Herod attempting to kill the babies would force Joseph to have to take baby Jesus to Egypt. The Black preacher would express the inability to hide a white baby in a Black neighborhood. This sort of affirmation is also seen in preachers as well as poets explaining the ethnic implications of Simone of Cyrene carrying Jesus's cross. The white supremacist of that day, the Romans, compelled or forced him to help Jesus. The creative preacher would note that he was an oppressed African forced to help another man of color with his burdens. This has been the wisdom that has helped Black believers survive through conservative silence and abuse—that the Black man has been invited nearest to Jesus to suffer with him underneath the pressure of his cross. The cross for the Negro is American oppression.

Many believed that due to the election of an African American president that we were in a post racial society and that the wounds of our nation's original sin were washed away through his election. But with the current political climate it is apparent that the wounds are still fresh. Protests all over the country and world. New cases weekly of more police brutality. More coded racial politics thrown from behind the façade of conservative politics and their disdain for liberals who help the oppressed—our sorrows continue to add up. People are looting and rioting, marching, and strategizing—why? It seems that nothing has changed since the founding fathers established this supposed Christian nation. Whereas the sorrows of the oppressed are multiplied, it gives me hope in that more beauty will be birthed out of the Black Church. It is apparent that its music, its preaching, and its Spirit are still needed now more than ever. Black Church culture is misunderstood by the outsiders looking in as well as the insiders looking out thinking that other styles are more sophisticated.

But as for me, I can never turn my back on the place that gave me a culture of wisdom—no, not even when it stems from my sorrow. I take my shoes off upon its holy ground and draw nearer to the fire and listen to the message prepared for me. Completing this chapter and preparing its contents have made me sorrowful, but the wisdom gives me hope as it gave my ancestors. David wrote in Ps 119:71, "It is good for me that I have been afflicted; that I might learn thy statutes." The Black Church cannot exist nor can it disseminate any wisdom if it were not for the affliction of American oppression—it has and continues to provide the instruction of how to manage the stress of being Black in America religiously and socially it continues to provide the wisdom that affords the Negro the ability operate within the nation that does not seem to care about repenting.

Bibliography

Bowens, Lisa M. *African American Readings of Paul: Reception, Resistance, and Transformation*. Grand Rapids: Eerdmans, 2020.

Cone, James H. *The Cross and the Lynching Tree*. Maryknoll, NY: Orbis, 2011.

———. *The Spirituals and the Blues*. Maryknoll, NY: Orbis, 1991.

DuBois, William Edward Burghardt. *The Souls of Black Folk: Essays and Sketches*. Chicago: A. C. McClurg, 1903.

Goza, Joel Edward. *America's Unholy Ghosts: The Racist Roots of Our Faith and Politics*. Eugene, OR: Wipf & Stock, 2019.

Holmes, David L. *The Faiths of the Founding Fathers*. Oxford: Oxford University Press, 2006.

Mitchell, Henry. *Black Preaching:The Recovery of A Powerful Art*. Nashville: Abingdon, 1990.

Raboteau, Albert J. *Slave Religion: The "Invisible Institution" in the Antebellum South*. Oxford: Oxford University Press, 2004.

Tsesis, Alexander. *The Thirteenth Amendment and American Freedom: A Legal History*. New York: New York University Press, 2004.

WISE MARRIAGES

By Joshua Little

"At the touch of love everyone becomes a poet."[1] Plato's words on love and affection resonate with so many of us. When you are struck by Cupid's arrow, what previously seemed dull and colorless now bursts forth with light, love, and excitement. And you experience a combination of thrill, fear, and vulnerability all at once. This common experience called "love" we share as human beings is why we can still resonate with stories written hundreds of years ago like Shakespeare's *Romeo and Juliet,* Charles Dickens's *Great Expectations,* and Jane Austen's *Pride and Prejudice.*

Along the journey of courtship many couples decide to take the plunge and get married. But once all the festivities of the wedding have passed and the honeymoon is but a memory, couples are forced to forge forward into a new reality together. And at this point, the truth comes out: **Marriage is hard**. Over time, married couples face waning appreciation, financial stresses, religious differences, declining sexual intimacy, lack of communication, parental challenges, addiction, loss, dysfunctional family dynamics, work-life struggles, infertility, infidelity, and situations alike. Honestly, I think you'd be hard-pressed to find a couple who had been together for a while who hadn't experienced struggle in their marriage a season or two.

In the United States today, nearly 50 percent of marriages end in divorce.[2] If there was ever a place where wisdom was desperately needed today it's within our marriages. God desires all of the couples within our churches, neighborhoods, and communities to be healthy, vibrant, and a reflection of God's love for humanity. But that won't come about by luck or accident. It will only come to fruition when we, as pastors and leaders,

---

1. Plato, *Symposium,* 196, E. (Lamb, LCL).

2. https://www.wf-lawyers.com/divorce-statistics-and-facts/?fbclid=IwAR3TltwwP -A2yWY2NLJd6JZGO4y2AzsRAdLozmVMNF2EDWK1aqLplkJu4eg.

intentionally, consistently, and thoughtfully disciple our couples in how to do marriage well.

While there is a plethora of Scriptures that give guidance to doing marriage well, one passage that stands out is Eph 5:21–33. Undoubtedly, Paul's words here are controversial to the modern reader. In this passage, it appears as though Paul advocates for a gender hierarchy in marriage—warranting husbands authority and power over their wives. And thus, this text can be seen as a "foe" to women. For instance, in 2010, *The Daily Telegraph* reported a story about a vicar in England who:

> told his congregation . . . that the behavior of modern women was to blame for Britain's high divorce rate. He said: 'We know marriage is not working. We only need to look at the figures— one in four children have divorced parents. Wives, submit to your own husbands.'[3]

In response to the vicar's statement numerous women in the congregation critiqued his sentiments and use of the biblical text. And even some women stopped their giving to their local parish. Certainly, this passage comes with its fair share of critics and cheerleaders. As such it would be easy to avoid or gloss over Paul's words here in Eph 5. But in this chapter I want to propose that weaved throughout Eph 5:21–33 is wisdom that is essential for every marriage within our churches. Maybe it is possible that we are misunderstanding Paul's teaching here—and a result, we're missing an opportunity to help husbands and wives hear the call of Christ on their lives and their marriages.

Now, maybe you're reading this chapter, and you're not married. Perhaps you're unmarried, divorced, or widowed. Maybe you're a high school or college-aged student, and you're thinking, "I'll just skip this chapter." But before you move on I'd ask you to pause and consider journeying through the ensuing pages. Certainly you'll have friends or family members who are married at some point in your life. And possibly God will allow you to share the wisdom found here with them. Maybe what you read in Eph 5:21–33 is helpful later in life because your circumstances change. But I'd also mention that Paul's wisdom to the Ephesians in 5:21–33 goes far beyond the confines of marriage. It has the potential to transform your relationships with family members, friends, neighbors, and coworkers. So I hope you'll continue to read along.

---

3. Bunyan, "Vicar Tells Women to 'Submit to Husbands.'"

Wise Marriages according to Ephesians 5

One thing that must be recognized in studying Eph 5:21–33 is that it is considered a "household code" (Eph 5:21—6:9; Col 3:12—4:6; 1 Pet 2:11—3:22). According to Pheme Perkins "most scholars agree that the household code came to New Testament writers from Hellenistic Jewish sources."[4] Thus, other household codes existed before the New Testament was written. In the introductory chapter to this book Daniel Hanlon pointed out that the household code in Ephesians is situated in Paul's argument for ethical wisdom in the church. The household code offers wisdom for marriages.

Throughout the Greco-Roman corpus management of the household was critical because it was understood as a microcosm of the much larger society. In other words, if harmony was to exist in the city-state, it must exist in the family. According to Plato unity within a family would only be achieved if slaves, children, and wives submitted to the male authority or *pater familia* (*Republic* II.369B, D; III.414D). Although the *pater familia* did not necessarily use his power in an abusive way, under Roman law his authority was unconditional. In Aristotle's *Politics*, he echoes Plato's sentiments, emphasizing that the role of men is to "rule" over women as a part of their nature. He notes:

> A husband and father, we saw, rules over wife and children, both free, but the rule differs, the rule over his children being a royal, over his wife a constitutional rule. For although there may be exceptions to the order of nature, the male is by nature fitter for command than the female, just as the elder and full-grown is superior to the younger and more immature.[5]

For Plato, Aristotle, and other Greco-Roman philosophers, while the father was acknowledged as the unconditional authority, it was virtuous for him to oversee slaves with mercy, children with fondness and his wife as a free member of the *polis*.[6] Slaves, children, and wives were understood as servants for the benefit of the household.[7]

According to David Balch, Aristotle's household code in his *Politics* is "the most important parallel to the N.T. codes. It demonstrates that the pattern of submissiveness . . . was based on an earlier Aristotelian *topos* 'concerning household management'; the discussion of these three

4. Perkins, *Ephesians*, 126.

5. Aristotle, *Politics* Book 1, XII.

6. Plato, *Republic* II.369.B, D; III.414D; 415A-D; Aristotle, *Politics* 1254a 8–24; 1259b 25–35; Aristotle, *Ethics* I.8: V.5–V10.

7. Plutarch, *Crassus* 2:6–7.

relationships in a household was not a Jewish or Christian innovation."[8] With this in mind, we will compare and contrast Aristotle's words on the household with Paul's words in Eph 5:21—6:9 with the aim of gleaning wisdom on marriage and relationships.

As we dive into the text, it is important to understand the context of Paul's teaching. Paul has encouraged followers of Jesus to walk wisely by making the most of the time (5:15–16). To do this, one must understand God's will by being filled with the Spirit (5:17–18). As a result of being filled with the Holy Spirit, believers will submit to one another out of reverence for Christ (5:21). Here, Paul's encouragement to mutually submit to one another serves as a hinge between 5:15-20 and 5:22—6:9. Having said that, let us turn our attention to our passage:

> Be subject to one another out of reverence for Christ. Wives, be subject to your husband as you are to the Lord. For the husband is the head of the wife just as Christ is the head of the church, the body of which he is the Savior. Just as the church is subject to Christ, so also wives out to be, in everything, to their husbands. (5:21–24)[9]

In verse 21 Paul writes, "Be subject to one another out of reverence for Christ." The Greek term *hypotassomenoi*, the present middle or passive participle used in 5:21, means "to be subject." As a masculine participle, Paul's encouragement is aimed at all followers of Christ. Ben Witherington points out that throughout Greek literature the root verb *hypotassō* refers to "arranging or placing someone under something else and in the middle, as is here, to order or arrange oneself under something or someone."[10] Usually, this verb in the passive is traditionally proceeded by a dative "to persons worthy of respect."[11] But here, it is proceeded by *allēlois*, the dative reciprocal pronoun meaning "one another."

All throughout Paul's letter to the Ephesians he emphasizes the vital role the Holy Spirit plays in the lives of believers. Followers of Christ are sealed with the Spirit once they hear the gospel message and believe (1:13). Believers have access in Christ to God through the Holy Spirit (2:18). God's Spirit dwells within Christ's body, the church (2:22). Apostles and prophets have experienced revelation by the Spirit (3:5). The Spirit strengthens believers by giving power (3:16). Paul warns followers of Christ not to

---

8. Balch, *Let Wives Be Submissive*, 34.

9. Unless otherwise indicated, Scripture quotations are from the NRSV.

10. Witherington, *Letters to Philemon, Colossians and Ephesians*, 316.

11. BDAG 848; cf. also 1042.

grieve the Spirit (4:30). Believers are encouraged to be filled with the Holy Spirit (5:18), use the sword of the Spirit (6:17) and pray in the Spirit at all times (6:18). Needless to say, walking with the Spirit is a constant theme throughout Paul's words in Ephesians.

For Paul, when followers of Christ are filled with the Holy Spirit, it leads to mutual submission. While mutual submission is not natural behavior for human beings, it is possible as individuals and couples overflow with God's Spirit and are guided by God. Harold Hoehner writes:

> Unbelievers tend to take great pride in individualism and in-dependence, which leads to selfishness. However, believers are to act differently. Jesus instructed the disciples that the world would know that they are his disciples if they love one another (John 13:34–35). Also, in other contexts Paul instructs believers to love one another with brotherly love and to prefer one an-other by showing honor (Rom 12:10) and in humility to count the other better than themselves (Phil 2:3).[12]

The mutual submission that Paul encourages among believers is not some-thing to brush aside. Rather, it should be done *enphobō Christou*, "out of reverence for Christ." In Homer's use of the verb *phobeō*, it usually suggests "flight" as a result of being frightened.[13] Afterwards the notion of "fear" or "panic" became the prevalent understanding for the term. It is challenging to determine the proper translation in this passage. For some scholars, "rev-erence" or "respect" capture Paul's sentiments. Other scholars, like Wilhelm Mundle, recommend "fear, awe or reverence."[14] Whichever translation is chosen, it is clear that Paul seeks to give weight to the importance of mutual submission in reverence/awe/fear for Christ.

Next, Paul directs his teaching to wives: "Wives, be subject to your husband as you are to the Lord" (5:22). While the phrase *haigynaikes* can generally refer to women, within this context it makes the most sense to translate it as "wives." Thus, Paul is not broadly prescribing that all women be submissive to all men. Rather, Paul is encouraging wives to submit to their own husbands.

At this point, it is vital to remember how easy it is for us to project our Western cultural values and assumptions upon Paul and his first century, Greco-Roman world. In just the past 100 years or so we've seen women pre-sented new opportunities to enjoy and flourish including equal opportunities for education, the right to vote, and the right to serve in nearly every way

---

12. Hoehner, *Ephesians*, 717.

13. Hoehner, *Ephesians*, 717.

14. Mundle, "Fear, Awe [φόβος]," 623.

in society. This can lead us to look at Paul's teaching and think, "Are you a friend of women? Where is the wisdom in your words? Why didn't you seek to abolish the marital hierarchies that existed in your time?" Questions like these will inevitably surface. It is undeniable that Paul was enmeshed in a first-century, Greco-Roman culture that viewed women as inferior to men. And here, he does not seek to overturn those structures. But I believe, as we continue on in this passage, we'll see Paul introduce counter-cultural ideas for the transformed relationship God envisions for husbands and wives.

The reasoning Paul offers in encouraging wives to submit to their husbands is found in verse 23: "for the husband is the head of the wife just as Christ is the head of the church, the body of which he is the Savior. Just as the church is subject to Christ, so also wives ought to be, in everything, to their husbands" (5:23). Here, Paul gives an analogy between the relationship of husband and wife and the relationship of Christ and the church. This metaphor of Paul's rises and falls on the word translated "head." The Greek term here, *kephalē*, has been the source of much scholarly debate over the past few decades. The widely-held understanding of it up through the 1970s was that it carried connotations of leadership and authority.[15] This translation has led some scholars to believe Paul's teaching here advocates for a hierarchical order within the family that God established from the beginning of time. J. H. Yoder writes that there is no "difference in worth [between husband and wife], but in the family, for its order and unity, there must be leadership, and the responsibility of leadership is that of the husband and father."[16] Francis Foulkes repeats this sentiment, noting that "the man's place in the family is one of leadership, to be qualified by the highest demand for love in the verses that follow."[17] However, a handful of scholars push back against this translation, claiming that the word does not denote authority. Instead, they contend that "head" was a symbol that regularly expressed the idea of "source." It seems as though Stephen Bedale was the first scholar to put forth this translation.[18] And other interpreters have expounded on Bedale's work. Philip Payne, in his book *Man and Woman: One in Christ*, argues that "head" is better understood as "source" rather than "authority." He writes:

> Through its mouth the head provides nourishment to keep it warm and water to cleanse the body, washing out items that corrupt. Through its eyes, ears, nose and tongue, it alerts the body

15. Arnold, *Ephesians*, 381.
16. Yoder, *Politics of Jesus*, 185.
17. Foulkes, *Ephesians*, 162.
18. Bedale, "Meaning of *Kephale* in the Pauline Epistles," 211–15.

to danger and protects it. Through its lips, it expresses words of love and exhortation that purifies. The head is the source of all these things for the body.[19]

Gretchen Gaebelein Hull agrees with Payne's conclusion as better understood as "source"—referencing its use in 1 Cor 11:3: "But I want you to understand that Christ is the **head** of every man, and the husband is the **head** of his wife, and God is the **head** of Christ" (1 Cor 11:3). From Hull's perspective, if Paul is utilizing "head" to refer to "authority" or hierarchy of some kind, it creates Trinitarian doctrinal challenges in the text.[20]

The translation as "source" does not come without its share of challenges and critics. In Eph 1:22, Paul writes, "And he has put all things under his feet and has made him the **head** over all things for the church, which is his body, the fullness of him who fills all in all" (1:22). Here, the term seems to be used to proclaim that all things are under Christ's authority. We see similar usage of *kephalē* in Col 2: "For in him the whole fullness of deity dwells bodily, and you have come to fullness in him, who is the head of every ruler and authority" (Col 2:9–10). This leads Klyne Snodgrass to note: "Paul is not arguing that Christ is the source of principalities and powers, but that he has authority over them."[21]

Regarding the use of the term in Eph 5:23 it is clear from the context that Paul is not advocating for abusive use of power of husbands against their wives. In fact, headship for Paul is dovetailed with the idea of Christ as "savior of the Body." Christ loved and gave himself up for the church (5:25), made her holy, cleansed without blemish and blameless (5:26–27), and fed and cared for her (5:29). But the question remains: How does one exercise headship? Does this mean when married couples are at a stalemate in decision-making, the husband has the authority to make the final choice?

Markus Barth describes headship in his commentary on Ephesians, concluding in 5:25 that headship means that a husband should "go ahead" or take the initiative in self-sacrificial service and love as Jesus has done in his relationship with the church.[22] Consequently, "head" means head servant or servant leader. This sentiment reminds me of Jesus's teaching in Luke 22. A quarrel breaks out among the disciples as to who is considered the "greatest." Jesus turns to the disciples and tells them:

19. Payne, *Man and Woman*, 288.

20. Hull, *Equal to Serve*, 195.

21. Snodgrass, *Ephesians*, 295.

22. Barth, *Ephesians 4–6*, 618–19.

The kings of the Gentiles lord it over them; and those in authority over them are called benefactors. But not so with you; rather
the greatest among you must become like the youngest, and the
leader like the one who serves. For who is greater, the one who is
at the table or the one who serves? Is it not the one at the table?
But I am among you as one who serves. (Luke 22:25–27)

For Paul, Jesus is the model of true headship for husbands. This leads him
to write:

Husbands, love your wives, just as Christ loved the church and
gave himself up for her, in order to make her holy by cleansing her with the washing of water by the word, so as to present
the church to himself in splendor, without a spot or wrinkle or
anything of the kind—yes, so that she may be holy and without
blemish. (5:25–27)

Just as Christ poured himself out as a sacrifice for the church, husbands
are called to follow in his footsteps. Rather than engage in the ways of the
gentiles, who lord their authority over others, husbands are called to sacrifice
for their wives as Jesus has sacrificed for the church. The present imperative
"love" emphasizes the notion that a husband's love for his wife is an ongoing
process. This kind of love seeks the highest good for a loved one. Similar to
Paul's previous appeal to wives, his exhortation for husbands to love their
wives is not dependent on the wife's response. As Clinton Arnold remarks, "It
makes no provision for the wife to earn her husband's favor. The command
entails the husband's responsibility regardless of his wife's behavior, health
condition, appearance, or any other deterrent."[23]

Here Paul sets a high bar for the kind of love husbands should have for
their wives—by comparing the relationship between husband and wife with
the relationship of Christ and the church. Christ's love for the church is demonstrated by giving his life for her (5:25). This does not mean it is obligatory
that husbands die for their wives. Rather a husband must deny himself to
express his love for his wife. At this point in his teaching Paul demonstrates a
departure from the Greco-Roman and Second Temple literature regarding a
husband's relationship with his wife. Within the household codes of his time,
exhortation for husbands to love their wives is not a mainstay. Men's freedom
and superiority is paramount in Aristotle, Plato, Philo, and Josephus's writings. While it's true that Paul doesn't eradicate the hierarchy embedded in
the patriarchal household codes of the first century, what he does do is invite
husbands and wives to imitate the mindset and posture of Christ. And as a

23. Arnold, *Ephesians*, 383.

result of their obedience and faithfulness to Christ and their mutual submission to one another, couples begin to tear down, rather than support, the patriarchal and hierarchal confines between husband and wife. As we see later in Eph 6, this invitation to carry the mindset of Christ and participate in the overturning of hierarchal norms is also extended to the relationships between parents and adults and masters and slaves.

In verse 26, Paul expounds on the christological metaphor by explaining how Christ set apart the church and purified her through the washing of water by the word. Centuries before Paul penned these words, the prophet Ezekiel anticipated the day in which this would happen: "I will sprinkle clean water upon you, and you shall be clean from all your uncleanness, and from all your idols I will cleanse you" (Ezek 36:25). It is important to note here that Paul is not utilizing water language to refer to baptism of individual Christians in verse 26. The Greek noun *loutron*, which denotes a "bath," "bathing place," or "water for bathing," only occurs three times in the Septuagint (Sir 34:25; Cant 4:2, 6:6). And each time it carries with it a notion of "washing." It is more likely that Paul is referring to the Jewish custom known as the bridal bath.[24] In Ezek 16:8–14 Yahweh is described as bathing Israel, his bride, with water, washing the blood from her and putting ointment on her (Ezek 16:8). Thus here Paul is recognizing that Christ is doing a sanctifying work within the church by the proclamation and application of the Word through the power of the Holy Spirit. As Witherington notes: "The goal is nothing less than the church becoming holy and without fault, going on to perfection."[25] And Christ's love is that which makes the bride (the church) without fault. Paul continues:

> In the same way, husbands should love their wives as they do their own bodies. He who loves his wife loves himself. For no one ever hates his own body, but he nourishes and tenderly cares for it, just as Christ does for the church, because we are members of his body. (5:28–30)

Paul starts v. 28 with a comparative phrase: "in the same manner." Clearly, Paul is bringing us back to the example of Christ's relationship with the church. J. Sampley, in his book, *And The Two Shall Become One Flesh*, highlights that verses 28 and 29 should be understood with the backdrop of Gen 2:24: "Therefore a man leaves his father and mother and clings to his wife, and they become one flesh" (2:24).[26] In the process of

---

24. Bock, *Interpreting the New Testament Text*, 404.

25. Witherington, *Letters*, 330.

26. Sampley, *And Two Shall Become One Flesh*, 139–45.

forging a new path forward together, husband and wife become "one flesh." Witherington explains, "It does not say that the two simply become one, or one person, but rather 'one flesh.' In other words they become different parts of a third entity—a couple."[27] Here Paul is highlighting the reality that as couples are filled with the Holy Spirit and live as "one flesh" they practice a close and intimate relationship that encompasses every aspect of life: emotional, physical, and spiritual.[28] A husband is encouraged to throw aside self-preservation and self-interest to care for his wife because they are no longer two separate entities, but a new creation: one new flesh. Just as Christ nourishes and cares for the church, husbands are called to tenderly care for their wives. In short, the love demanded from husbands is christologically defined. This is what proper headship looks like. This is what it means to embrace and live into the transformed relationship that comes about through the power of God's Spirit. Next, Paul explicitly links his previous exhortation towards husbands to Gen 2:24:

> 'For this reason a man will leave his father and mother and be joined to his wife, and the two will become one flesh.' This is a great mystery, and I am applying it to Christ and the church. Each of you, however, should love his wife as himself, and a wife should respect her husband. (5:31–33)

Interestingly, Paul makes a change to the Septuagint's rendering of Gen 2:24. Rather than begin his sentence *heneken toutou*, "on account of this," he chooses to alter it to *anti toutou*, "on account of this." While this does not modify the meaning, it could be a strategic rhetorical tool Paul is utilizing. Frank Thielman explains: "he viewed the phrase as a fitting way of connecting the substance of the quotation with his previous argument. In other words, we should think of *anti toutou* as having true argumentative force: 'on account of' something Paul has just said, 'a man will leave his father and mother.'"[29] So what is it that Paul is trying to emphasize here? Is Paul underscoring the truth that Christ and the church are one body? Is Paul stressing here that the husband and wife are one body? I tend to believe that while both themes are important, Paul is accentuating the unity in relationship between Christ and the church. This is seen most clearly from Paul's own words: "This is a great mystery, and I am applying it to Christ and the church" (5:32). Paul's concluding statements here on the relationships between husband and wife and Christ and the church

27. Witherington, *Letters*, 331.

28. Arnold, *Ephesians*, 393.

29. Thielman, *Ephesians*, 389.

underscore that transformed relationships in the Spirit consist of sacrifice and humility. As Barth puts it:

> The special form of *agape* between husband and wife flourishes within the framework of the general love for neighbors and enemies, is the school and test case of the latter, and publicizes its reality in power. The wife is the husband's primary and exemplary neighbor.[30]

Having walked through Paul's words in Eph 5:21–33, the question remains: What wisdom can be gleaned from this passage regarding marriage today? One important feature of wisdom is the ability to do something well. So, from Paul's words, how can we practice transformative marital relationships well and lead others to do the same?

Now What?

From Eph 5:21–33 the most critical wisdom gleaning on transformative relationships between husbands and wives is the need for couples to be **open to the Spirit** (Eph 5:18). For Paul, transformed relationships are not a by-product of willpower or intellect. Rather, transformed relationships only manifest as husbands and wives are open to and filled with God's Spirit. As Paul explains in Gal 5: "The fruit of the Spirit is love, joy, peace, patience, kindness, generosity, faithfulness, gentleness and self-control" (5:22). As a believer walks with the Spirit, this fruit is birthed in every relationship and aspect of his or her life.

I didn't grow up in the church. It wasn't until I turned 17 years old that I started attending a church on the west side of Indianapolis. In full transparency, the only reason I visited the church was because a girl I liked attended there as well. God works in mysterious ways. While there I learned a lot. I learned about God and his son Jesus. I learned about the importance of reading the Bible. I learned about my sin and need of a savior. But along the way, it felt like something or someone was missing. And that someone was God's Spirit. As Scot McKnight puts it: "Our theology was one of the Father and the Son, and the Spirit was ignored, neglected or minimized. At best the Spirit got 'third place' in the God-contest for supremacy."[31] It wasn't until I started attending college and immersing myself in community with believers of different denominational traditions that I felt comfortable talking about the Spirit and opening myself up to him.

---

30. Barth, *Ephesians*, 719.
31. McKnight, *Open to the Spirit*, 6.

Here's the truth: **Every single one of us is made by God to be open and receptive to his Spirit.** Dorothy Sayers put it this way: "The spiritual [element in each of us] is so utterly a part of our nature that we cannot cast [that element] out; if we deprive ourselves of the eternal Absolute, we shall inevitably make an absolute of some temporal thing or another."[32] During the last moments before Jesus's betrayal, arrest, and crucifixion, he told the disciples huddled around the table:

> If you love me, you will keep my commandments. And I will ask the Father, and he will give you another Advocate, to be with you forever. This is the Spirit of truth, whom the world cannot receive, because it neither sees him nor knows him. You know him, because he abides with you, and he will be in you. (John 14:15–17)

In Eugene Peterson's contemporary rendering of the Bible, *The Message*, he translated the Greek word *Paraklēton* ("Advocate" in the NRSV) as "Friend." Thus, Jesus makes a promise to the worried disciples: in my coming absence, my Father will send a true Friend to you. As Frederick Bruner explains, this Friend is an "abiding personal promise of presence, intended, as we will learn, to bring the disciples the deepest possible lifetime comfort, encouragement and friendship."[33] The Spirit is a Truth-Teller who teaches us all things and reminds us of everything Jesus said (John 14:26). The Holy Spirit puts to death the deeds of our old selves, that we might live anew (Rom 8:13). God's Spirit gives wisdom and revelation that we might know Christ more intimately (Eph 1:17). Without the Spirit, our attempts to pursue holiness fall short (Heb 12:14). But in the power of the Spirit, we are able to experience sanctification (2 Thess 2:13). **Every single one of us is made by God to be open and receptive to his Spirit.**

But too often we close ourselves off to the Advocate, the Friend—God's Spirit. Sometimes we're locked down from the Holy Spirit because of fear: fear of the unknown, fear of the loss of some sense of control, fear of awkwardness, or discomfort. And sometimes we're closed off to the Spirit because we don't know how to open ourselves to the Advocate, the Friend. So let me ask you a question: As a pastor or leader within the church, are you intentionally and faithfully empowering and equipping your people, and more specifically your couples, to be open and responsive to the Holy Spirit? Are you creating environments, practices, and cultures in which individuals and couples are encouraged to lean upon

32. Sayers, *Mind of the Maker*, 87.
33. Bruner, *Gospel of John*, 835.

the Holy Spirit in every facet of their lives (marriage, parenting, work-life, finances, neighboring, addictions, etc.)?

To expect the marriages in our churches to be healthy and vibrant apart from the Holy Spirit is like expecting an unplugged lamp to miraculously turn on. Without its source of power the lamp just casually sits there. But once power is reconnected the lamp can do what it was designed to do: shine light in the darkness. We cannot and should not settle for marriages within the Body that are simply moralistic in nature. We must strive to foster marriages within the church that are transformative relationships because of the power of the Holy Spirit.

Another wisdom gleaning from Eph 5:22–33 we receive regarding marriage is the importance of **mutual submission**. Marriage is not some sort of business or corporation in which one person is determined the leader while the other person is required to follow. A fixed hierarchy of husband over wives is not God's design for transformative marital relationships in Christ. Rather, Christian marriage is such that husband and wife, as their union is filled with the Spirit, honor, respect and submit to one another as they navigate through life.

In addition to Eph 5:22–33, we see this in Paul's discourse to husbands and wives in 1 Cor 7. Seemingly in response to a previous letter from the Corinthian Christians, Paul pens these words to challenge an inaccurate perspective on marriage, spirituality, and the end of time:

> Now concerning the matters about which you wrote: "It is well for a man not to touch a woman."But because of cases of sexual immorality, each man should have his own wife and each woman her own husband. The husband should give to his wife her conjugal rights, and likewise the wife to her husband. For the wife does not have authority over her own body, but the husband does; likewise the husband does not have authority over his own body, but the wife does. Do not deprive one another except perhaps by agreement for a set time, to devote yourselves to prayer, and then come together again, so that Satan may not tempt you because of your lack of self-control. (1 Cor 7:1–5)

With his warning against sexual immorality, Paul gives direct teaching to husbands and wives. They are encouraged not to deprive one another of regular and voluntary sexual intimacy. Instead, they are to generously give to one another. Furthermore, husbands and wives are directed to yield authority over their bodies to one another. For Paul, this is the servanthood that was modeled by Jesus in his ministry and crucifixion (Phil 2:5–8). And as his followers, we are called to follow in his footsteps by not clinging to authority, but yielding it—particularly when it comes to our spouse. Craig Blomberg describes how Paul's words would have been received by his first century audience: "Against the highly patriarchal societies of antiquity, this mutuality stands out in sharp relief. Most non-Christian husbands would have been horrified at the notion that their bodies belonged to their wives."[34] But this is exactly how Paul is urging Christian husbands and wives in Corinth to live: mutual submission.

One fundamental aspect of mutual submission is the recognition of the necessity of **difference**. In the beginning, when God created the cosmos, He did so by a series of divisions: the land from the sea, fowl from the fish, livestock from wild animals, and male and female. In Rom 12:6, Paul writes that followers of Jesus, "Have different gifts that differ according to the grace given to us." Each believer is gifted by the Holy Spirit with different gifts for "equipping the saints for the work of ministry, for the edifying of the body of Christ" (Eph 4:12). Thus, when opportunities or challenges surface, we rely upon one another and the Spirit's different gifting within us. Difference is good thing. Difference is a God thing. In mutual submission, we recognize the necessity of different perspectives and different giftings. Within the context of marriage, as husbands and wives face opportunities and challenges, they must be cognizant of the ways the Holy Spirit has gifted each of them and must be willing to submit to one another in areas or circumstances of weakness. For example, if a wife is gifted in administration or finance and the husband is not, the husband should yield to his wife when consensus is not reached on financial decisions. Or if a husband is gifted in mercy and the wife is not, the wife should yield to her husband and his thoughts on caring for their downhearted teenager.

Another facet of mutual submission is a shift from a me-centric posture to an **others-focused perspective**. In mutual submission in marriage, we equally give to one another and consider each other's interests more important than our own. As the apostle Paul writes: "Do nothing from selfish ambition or conceit, but in humility regard others as better than yourselves. Let each of you look not to your own interests, but to the interests of others" (Phil 2:3–4). This is easier said than done. In my own marriage, from time-to-time, my wife Becky and I come to impasses regarding certain decisions. And I wish I could say I handle those moments perfectly, but I don't. Too often I allow self-interest to get in the way of decision-making. But Jesus calls me down a different path, a path of yielding my own interests to the interests of my wife. And this is the path that leads to the transformed relationship I deeply long for.

34. Blomberg, *1 Corinthians*, 137.

If we're going to equip the couples within our churches to mutually submit to one another, it is essential that couples in our churches are part of mentoring relationships. In Rom 12:15 Paul writes, "Rejoice with those who rejoice, weep with those who weep." Undoubtedly, there will be moments of celebration in marriage. But there will also be moments of frustration, miscommunication, and pain. Wherever a couple finds themselves in this season, they will always benefit from a mentoring couple investing in their life and demonstrating what it looks like to mutually submit.

Mentors step up and pray for couples as they journey through life together. A mentor serves as a safe place to process marriage dynamics and an encouragement for spouses to have the mindset of Christ. They are wells of wisdom, truth tellers and a demonstration of what marriage could look like. In the same way that Jethro mentored Moses, and Moses mentored Joshua, Eli mentored Samuel and Samuel mentored Saul and David, every single of us can benefit from a mentor in our lives. So what would it look like for you, in your current context, to establish a mentoring culture for couples? How would couples in your church be better equipped if they had another couple intentionally investing in their lives and marriage?

It is important to note that mutual submission is not a practice exclusively for marriage alone. Every believer should practice mutual submission as a part of the alternative community Jesus has birthed: the church. Rather than cling to authority or power, we recognize that God is in charge of his church. We learn to celebrate the gifting of others (coworkers, neighbors, family members, friends) and collectively discern God's will. When hard choices have to be made and consensus can't be reached, we yield to one another as the Spirit has gifted us. By practicing mutual submission in everyday life, we experience the transformed relationships Jesus has in store for each of us.

Third, alongside the application of mutual submission, it is important we don't overlook or neglect the **reframing of headship** in Eph 5:22–33. Rather than reinforce a headship associated with domination and control like his first centuries Greco-Roman peers, Paul reimagines headship in light of Christ as sacrifice, service and provision. In John 13, Jesus displays what true headship looks like. As the disciples share the last supper with Jesus before his betrayal, he stoops down and begins to wash their feet. For the disciples, this was unimaginable. Colin Kruse explains:

> A wife might wash her husband's feet, children might wash their father's feet, and disciples might wash their master's feet, but in every case it would be an act of extreme devotion. Foot washing

was normally carried out by a servant, not by those participating in the meal, and certainly not by the one presiding at the meal.[35]

In fact, later rabbinic teachings stated it was not acceptable for Jewish slaves to wash other people's feet. This chore was only reserved for gentile slaves. Needless to say, I'm sure the disciples were uncomfortable and perplexed as their rabbi, Jesus, washed their feet. After some back-and-forth conversation with Peter, Jesus finishes up and has a few words for the disciples:

> 'Do you know what I have done to you? You call me Teacher and Lord—and you are right, for that is what I am. So if I, your Lord and Teacher, have washed your feet, you also ought to wash one another's feet. For I have set you an example, that you should do as I have done to you. Very truly, I tell you, servants are not greater than their master, nor are messengers greater than the one who sent them. If you know these things, you are blessed if you do them. (John 13:12–16)

Washing dirty feet wasn't below the dignity of their Lord and Rabbi Jesus. With that being the case, Jesus argues that as his disciples, washing feet shouldn't be below their dignity either. In the kingdom that Jesus is ushering in, the "greatest" are those who offer meek service to the "least."

Henri Nouwen, in his journal *The Road to Daybreak*, describes a foot washing ceremony he attended at a L'Arche community in France. After the community leader had read the John 13 passage, one-by-one he began to wash the feet of community members. Then, the community as a whole partook of the Eucharist together. As Nouwen took in the scenes and sounds of that morning, he wrote:

> Sitting in the basement room in Paris surrounded by forty poor people, I was struck again by the way Jesus concluded his active life. Just before entering on the road of his passion, he washed the feet of his disciples and offered them his body and blood as food and drink.[36]

Nouwen concluded his thoughts by writing that as the community leader washed feet and gave his friends bread and wine, "it seemed as if—for the moment—I saw a glimpse of the new kingdom Jesus came to bring."[37] I believe this is what Paul envisioned as he discussed headship in Eph 5:22–33. Husbands are encouraged to serve their wives with the same humility, sacrifice,

35. Kruse, *John*, 325–26.
36. Nouwen, *Road to Daybreak*, 158.
37. Nouwen, *Road to Daybreak*, 158.

and generosity that Christ demonstrated for the church. They should not lord authority, power or hierarchy over their wives (Luke 22:25–27), but instead should abundantly love and care for their wives.

As leaders and pastors within the church, we must intentionally raise our boys and young men to see headship and women through this lens. Every ten minutes, somewhere in the world, an adolescent girl dies as a result of violence. Nearly one-in-five girls is sexually abused at least once in her lifetime. Here in the United States, 18 percent of girls report that they have become victims of sexual assault. Women are prevalently sexually objectified within our American culture. **And this is not OK.** God grieves at the ways in which we harm each other and don't live into this new kingdom he has established.

If our churches are to be filled with healthy individuals, healthy couples and healthy marriages, we must begin to disciple our young men to understand what it looks like to lead and love well. We must demonstrate proper headship—and invite them to become co-laborers in the new kingdom Jesus is ushering in.

Conclusion

Undoubtedly, attempting to interpret Eph 5:22–33 has its fair share of challenges. For some, this passage seems to promote patriarchal, hierarchal ideas in marriages and relationships today. For others, Paul's words here are dismissed as irrelevant to the world we live in or irredeemably confusing. But throughout this chapter I've put forth the notion that embedded within Paul's writings is wisdom that marriages and couples within our churches today desperately need. Eph 5:22–33 is a part of the canon of Scripture. And as such, it should be viewed as having theological value.It is prevalently used in the context of worship services and weddings. So it would be negligent to avoid or ignore this passage outright.

Within Paul's words in Eph 5, it is clear that in order for couples to foster healthy kingdom marriages, husbands and wives must be open and receptive to the Holy Spirit. Without God's Spirit, it is impossible to experience the transformation, sanctification, and unity that God intends for husbands and wives. As couples rely upon the Spirit, husbands and wives are invited to mutually submit to one another out of reverence for Christ. Patriarchy, hierarchy, and control are not found in marriages that are shaped by Christoformity. Rather, Christ-formed marriages are such that husbands and wives give to one another and consider each other's interests more important than our own. Within the marital relationship husbands are encouraged to practice headship. Like Christ has done for the church, the husband is called to exercise headship by humbly and sacrificially loving and caring for his wife. He is called, by God, to take the initiative and pour his life out for his bride.

Bibliography

Arnold, Clinton. *Ephesians: Exegetical Commentary on the New Testament.*Grand Rapids: Zondervan, 2010.

Balch, David. *Let Wives Be Submissive: The Domestic Code in 1 Peter.* Chico, CA: Scholars, 1981.

Barth, Markus. *Ephesians 4–6.* New Haven, CT: Yale University Press, 1998.

Bedale, Stephen. "The Meaning of *Kephale* in the Pauline Epistles." *JTS* 5 (1954) 211–15.

Blomberg, Craig. *1 Corinthians: The NIV Application Commentary.* Grand Rapids: Zondervan, 1994.

Bock, Darrell. *Interpreting the New Testament Text.* Wheaton: Crossway, 2006.

Bruner, Frederick. *The Gospel of John.* Grand Rapids: Eerdmans, 2012.

Bunyan, Nigel. "Vicar Tells Women to 'Submit to Husbands.'" *The Telegraph,* February 12, 2010. http://www.telegraph.co.uk/news/religion/7221802/Vicar-tells-women-to-submit-to-husbands.html.

Foulkes, Francis. *Ephesians.* Downers Grove, IL: InterVarsity Academic, 2008.

Hoehner, Harold. *Ephesians: An Exegetical Commentary.* Grand Rapids: Baker Academic, 2002.

Hull, Gretchen Gaebelein. *Equal to Serve: Women and Men in the Church and Home.* London: Scripture Union, 1987.

Kruse, Colin. *John.* Downers Grove, IL: InterVarsity, 2017.

McKnight, Scot. *Open to the Spirit.* Colorado Springs: WaterBrook, 2018.

Mundle, Wilhem. "Fear, Awe [φόβος]." *NIDNTT* 1 (1975) 623.

Nouwen, Henri. *The Road to Daybreak: A Spiritual Journey.* New York: Doubleday, 1988.

Payne, Philip. *Man and Woman: One in Christ.* Grand Rapids: Zondervan, 2009.

Perkins, Pheme. *Ephesians.* Nashville: Abingdon, 1997.

Sampley, J. *And Two Shall Become One Flesh.* Eugene, OR: Wipf and Stock, 2002.

Sayers, Dorothy. *The Mind of the Maker.* San Francisco: HarperCollins, 1987.

Snodgrass, Klyne. *Ephesians: The NIV Application Commentary.* Grand Rapids: Zondervan, 1996.

Thielman, Frank. *Ephesians.* Grand Rapids: Baker Academic, 2010.

Witherington, Ben, III. *The Letters to Philemon, Colossians and Ephesians.* Grand Rapids: Eerdmans, 2007.

Yoder, J. H. *The Politics of Jesus.* Grand Rapids: Eerdmans, 1972.

WISE TEACHING

By David S. Johnston

I magine a teacher who has poured her heart and soul into investing in her students. She thoughtfully prepared her lessons and wisely and purposefully presented each concept so that they might more fully understand. At the conclusion of the semester she reviews the feedback anxious to see what their takeaways were, what stood out to each of them and above all what they learned. To her shock she reads words like: vague, impenetrable, incomprehensible, ambiguous, cryptic, hidden, mysterious, hyperbole, exaggeration, and shock. The teacher is crushed. By most accounts she is a failure—her message was not received. However, these were the very tools Jesus employs frequently in his teaching. Yet no one, not even His greatest critics would label Jesus as a failure as a teacher. His teachings are memorable. His teachings turned the accepted norms on their head. He turned to world right-side up. He challenged people and they continued to hunger for more.

Jesus was a teacher like no other. Early in the Gospel of Mark, "the people were amazed at his teaching, because he taught them as one who had authority, not as the teachers of the law" (Mark 1:22).[1] Jesus teaches with such authority he left the religious leaders bumfuzzled, bewildered, incensed, and most of all enraged. Upon a quick review of the first few chapters of Mark's Gospel, we see two crowds. One crowd is pressing against Jesus so much he has to escape on a boat in order to teach them. The other crowd (those in power) is pressing Jesus in their plot to kill him. They would be okay if he just drowns in the lake. This tension between those on the "inside" and those on the "outside" is never resolved.[2] This tension also helps us understand the seriousness in what may be going on behind the text.

1. Unless otherwise noted, all biblical references employ the NIV.

2. At least not until after Jesus's death and resurrection when those who gathered with him truly had to decide to follow him or not.

And yet throughout the Gospels Jesus drew huge crowds. Whether you wanted to absorb his every word and learn all you could from him or you wanted to help plot his death, you could not help but follow him. People wanted to know what he was doing and why he was doing. There was an irresistible enigma to him. They could not get enough of Jesus and this mission he was on. He is the ultimate charismatic teacher and leader.

Jesus was on a mission to preach about the expected kingdom, but he ushered in the kingdom by preaching the kingdom and he did this while walking from village to village. He did not stay in one place and try to attract a group it was more natural. Jesus was walking along and would stop to teach (on a mountain, by the sea, etc.).

What is it about Jesus's teaching and his style of teaching that was so attractive? Can we recapture this today? This chapter seeks to focus on Jesus the teacher and how his teaching requires discernment. As we spend time in these discernment drenched episodes of Jesus's teachings, a wisdom culture emerges. Jesus operated out of a wisdom culture and created a wisdom culture. Jesus must and should absolutely impact how we teach and preach today. We need to hear and learn from him. In mimicking his unique and effective manner of teaching we create a wisdom culture in our churches today. As we teach like Jesus as followers of Jesus, we will create a stirring in our world, in our midst drawing others into the kingdom of God, just as he did. They cannot resist the irresistible draw of who Jesus is, his message, and a desire to be part of what he is doing even today.

In order to gain an understanding of how to teach like Jesus, exploring Jesus the rabbi in his first-century context is critical.[3] Following this exploration and the role of discernment, the centrality of the parable of the sower is presented as a key to understanding Jesus, and with some essential interpretive aids, a platform for us to teach as Jesus taught.

Jesus Taught Counter-culturally

Take the passage in Mark 10:34–45 when James and John are quibbling over having the two best seats, those closest to Jesus. "Then James and John, the sons of Zebedee, came to him. 'Teacher,' they said, 'we want you to do for us whatever we ask'" (Mark 10:35). James and John deserve to be honored for their service with Jesus. This did not sit well (no pun intended) with the rest of the disciples and they became indignant. "Jesus called

3. Also see Daniel Hanlon's chapter in this volume (pp. 1–24) for a Christ-centered understanding of wisdom, especially that "wisdom is identified with the person of Christ."

them together and said, 'You know that those who are regarded as rulers of the Gentiles lord it over them, and their high officials exercise authority over them'" (Mark 10:42). This idea of "rulers of the Gentiles," "lording over them" and "exercising authority over" is not a positive picture, but it was how the ancient world operated. Jesus then has a way of turning the world's understanding of honor and importance on its head.

> Not so with you. Instead, whoever wants to become great among you must be your servant, and whoever wants to be first must be slave of all. For even the Son of Man did not come to be served, but to serve, and to give his life as a ransom for many. (Mark 10:43–45)

Here Jesus is not shaming James and John as much as he is challenging them (and all the disciples) to choose shame. The same shame he chose when he gave "his life as a ransom." "Whoever wants to become great among you must be your servant, and whoever wants to be first must be slave of all" (Mark 10:43–44). By asking them to act like a slave to each other or choose a lower social class Jesus is advocating the opposite of what James and John were asking and the opposite direction that most people during that time desired. Jesus has taken this deeply ingrained cultural accolade that is desired by all and challenges them to set it aside. This is radical, counter-cultural. Teachings like this were not well received by those in authoritative positions.

Those who are in authority to teach—the scribes, Pharisees, and teachers of the law—know they did not give Jesus the authority to teach. Initially we think they are perplexed when they ask him in Mark 11, "by what authority are you doing these things?" Jesus asks them a few questions and after they refuse to answer Jesus responds, "I'm not going to tell you." What an interesting approach. Those in authority are not confused—they are challenged. This carpenter from Nazareth is not supposed to be teaching.

But he does and uses a variety of teaching approaches, strategies, and techniques. Even modern literary and narrative approaches see a variety of different types of teachings from Jesus. To name a few: Jesus told stories, used object lessons, made short memorable statements, used repetition, used repetition (gotcha), and answers a question with a question. He was silent at the right times. He reads Scripture, quotes Scripture, tweaks Scripture.[4] We also have examples of Jesus using cryptic language. He knows he is not going to be understood. The Son of Man will be rejected. Mark ends

---

4. A fascinating exercise is to read one of the Gospels and note how much variety Jesus utilizes as he teaches. For a more academic approach see Byrskog, *Jesus the Only Teacher.*

his Gospel with us deciding if we are on Jesus's side or if we find it safer perhaps wise to abandon him.

Scholarship has asked what type of teacher was Jesus? A sage, or prophet, or apocalyptic, or just an average Jewish rabbi? These debates fall under historical Jesus studies which eventually become a catch-all for anything controversial you want to say about Jesus.[5] What kind of teacher was Jesus and what does this mean for the church today as we seek to preach wise teachings? Every category that attempts to sum up what king of teacher Jesus was falls short. He was more. Jesus was more than a prophet, more than a wise sage, and more than a typical Jewish rabbi. These categories, however, can be helpful as we process the vast teachings of Jesus that may fall into a specific genre. It is worth noting that Jesus's teachings do have overlap. For example, Jesus often presents wise teachings in prophetic ways.

Jesus Taught about the Kingdom of God

Jesus's favorite topic or image is of the Kingdom of God. For us it is a summary of his teachings for Jesus it was natural and never forced nor was it confusing.[6] He was always talking and teaching about the Kingdom. The Kingdom of God concept can be confusing for us primarily because we are not sure if the refers to now or future. The Kingdom of God is a thought-provoking symbol that is both *de jure* and *de facto* rule of God. It also marks the end of resistance to God's rule in that God is and always has been king.[7] When you spend much time in Jesus's teachings you really want what he is ushering in. The kingdom life that Jesus promises is appealing and challenging and demanding. When he was alone with his disciples Jesus said to them, "the secret of the kingdom of God has been given to you" (Mark 4:11).

Jesus Taught about the World to Come

Another popular topic that is related to the Kingdom is that Jesus spent time teaching about the world that is yet to come. We have large sections of Jesus's teachings that pertain what we refer to as the end of the world or the beginning of the new world. These apocalyptic sections are God's ways

---

5. See Allison, *Constructing Jesus*, esp. ch. 2: "More Than a Sage" and ch. 3: "More Than a Prophet."

6. Keck, *Who Is Jesus*, 68.

7. Keck, *Who is Jesus*, 80.

of completing or bringing to the world back in line with his purposes.[8] God will repair the broken creation and restore scattered Israel. This will happen after a time of "woe"[9] and tribulation and ultimately God will rule, forever.[10] In the parable of the sower, the good soil produces a large crop at harvest. "Harvest" was a buzz word for eschatology.

The essence of who Jesus is, and generalizations about his teaching—Kingdom of God and the world to come—are important conversations, but for us as preachers and teachers we need a simpler approach. Dallas Willard says concerning discipleship, "following Jesus is doing what Jesus would do if he were you."[11] As preachers and teachers we need to ask a similar question—"how do we teach like Jesus?" We have short sayings of Jesus filled with wisdom and longer narratives like the Sermon on the Mount and Olivet Discourse. We cannot just simply repeat these and assume those listening "get it." We have to speak to people today in terms that are relative and relatable to today.

We need to be comfortable with a "double reading" or "double listening" approach.[12] We have to meet people where they are and provide them a way out, a way up, a way unlike anything they have seen or been offered previously. Take the parables as an example.

Jesus Taught in Parables

The greatest example of Jesus's teachings are Jesus's parables.[13] The parables are the *crème de la crème* of Jesus's teaching.[14] Parables are fun to read and full of color, yet difficult for us to study and even a greater challenge to preach. Scholars have spent much ink trying to classify Jesus's parables. For the purposes of this chapter we need to determine if parables are part of wisdom literature. They certainly have wisdom-like characteristics, but they sound

8. Keck, *Who is Jesus*, 70.

9. See Mark 13.

10. Allison, *Constructing Jesus*, 32.

11. This paraphrase is found in several of Dallas Willard's writings. See his *Great Omission* (2006) and *The Divine Conspiracy* (1998). For a more scholarly approach follow Morna Hooker's idea of "interchange" in that as those "in Christ" participate with Christ what is true of him becomes true of us. See Hooker, *From Adam to Christ*.

12. See John Stott, *Contemporary Christian* (InterVarsity, 1995), summed up well in McGrath, *Mere Discipleship*.

13. Anyone who preaches the parables needs to consult Snodgrass, *Stories with Intent*. I have also benefitted from Blomberg, *Interpreting the Parables*; Blomberg, *Preaching the Parables*; Scott, *Hear Then the Parable*.

14. Keck, *Who Is Jesus*, 63.

different, and probably because Jesus uses apocalyptic and prophetic language in parable form. In parables Jesus is speaking the language of the prophets, yet we can approach them as wisdom literature. David Buttrick affirms this approach by summarizing, "parables are a type of wisdom literature used in prophetic ways."[15] Parables are able to deconstruct our assumptions and at the same time give us a glimpse into the Kingdom of God.

Parables of seeds, crops, harvest, and farming use the most common metaphors to describe life with its hardship and its prosperity, instruction, and judgment and blessing of God. Agricultural images are common in the Old Testament, New Testament, and throughout the literature from the Greco-Roman world.[16] "Parables are the most distinctive feature of Jesus' teaching and the method he utilized most to explain the kingdom of God, to illustrate the character of God, and to demonstrate God's expectations for his people."[17] The power of the parables seems due in part to their ability to conceal and reveal.[18] Snodgrass takes an approach that "nothing is in parables except to reveal" and that Jesus does not want to "prevent understanding although many parables are enigmatic."[19] However, Mark 4:12 (NRSV) says, "in order that 'they may indeed look, but not perceive, and may indeed listen, but not understand.'" There seems to be some lack of understanding, mystery, or hiddenness in Jesus's parables. "But to those on the outside everything is said in parables" (Mark 4:11b). Here, Jesus is using difficult and harsh language to the degree he does not want everyone to know. Parables have a sense of concealment. By concealing, the ability to understand is hidden or prevented.[20]

Eventually, the parable's concealment leads to an openness.[21] We see this in the parable of the lamp on a stand (Mark 4:21–25). In metaphor and mystery parables he uses images of lamps, light, and seed to stimulate thinking. Jesus is trying to initially hide or prevent understanding until his hearers

---

15. Buttrick, *Speaking Parables*, 7.

16. According to Burton Mack, "The image of agricultural endeavor, especially that of sowing seed, was the standard analogy for paideia (i.e., teaching and culture) during this time." See Mack, "Teaching in Parables," 143.

17. Strauss, *Mark*, 179.

18. Contrast Mark 4:1–13 and Luke 7:36–50.

19. Snodgrass, *Stories with Intent*, 133. Tolbert, *Perspectives on the Parables*, 42–43, makes the case that the original hearers did not have an existential crisis each time they heard a parable. While I tend to want to recreate the shock of the parables, I too need to be careful to read too much of the interpreter into the text. Cf. Dowd, *Reading Mark*, 38.

20. 4 Ezra 14:26, 45–48 has a hiddenness when Ezra is instructed, "some you shall deliver in secret to the wise."

21. Dowd, *Reading Mark*, 43.

discern. Jesus's parables require discernment. Jesus uses common images and stories but the way he uses them require more than merely listening. Many of these simple parabolic images are in fact riddles, metaphors, and some have some elements of allegory. They hide in order to reveal.[22] This hiddenness requires a time of discernment. This parable creates space for a response. It's during this time of wrestling with what he is actually saying that we move from hidden to revealed. Snodgrass acknowledges this movement saying, "nothing is in parables except to reveal."[23] Parables hide and reveal but discernment is key to moving from just hearing to understanding.

Parables Require Discernment

Before we discuss the parable of the sower let's review with a quick summary of reasons why we need discernment when it comes to parables. There is very little consensus and a variety of views with how to approach the parables and disagreement then comes with each parable. Parables borrow from both wisdom and apocalyptic literature. Parables contain an element of mystery and hiddenness. Mark 4:12 says parables prevent understanding. Parables use vivid imagery to stimulate thinking. For these reasons, parables require discernment.Let's look at one of the most popular of Jesus's parables the parable of the sower as found in Mark 4.

The Parable of the Sower

The parable of the sower (Mark 4:3–20; Matt 13:3–23; and Luke 8:5–15) on the surface appears to be the easiest and simplest parable to grasp. All three Gospel writers give it a place of significance in their Gospel accounts. Perhaps that has something to do with the fact that it is one of the few parables that Jesus explains to his disciples. This parable is important for understanding Jesus and can lend insight into how to teach like him.

We have a few problems to address. First, scholars have yet to agree as to what this parable means. Despite Jesus's explanation provided in the gospel accounts there is still mystery and questions surrounding the parable. Second, we tend to focus too much on the seeds and soil of this parable. As if those hearing have to determine which seed or soil type they are, but that common approach misses the thrust of the parable and is virtually devoid of discernment. Too many teachers have been distracted by the details and

22. Snodgrass, *Stories with Intent*, 143.
23. Snodgrass, *Stories with Intent*, 133.

not focused on the message, the point. Here are a few common charts that are often created when preaching/teaching this parable:

The Four Types of Seeds

Seeds on the Path	Seeds on the Rocks	Seeds on the Thorns	Seeds on the Good Soil

Or if we want to be creative, we focus on the different soil types:

Hard Packed Soil	Rocky Soil	Crowded Soil	Fertile Soil

Then the four meanings become:

Satan Snatches	Give up During Hard Times	Distracted by the world	Hear and Obey

Third, it is also worth noting that we as preachers tend to see ourselves as a sower. After all, just as the Sower sows the Word of God, we are preaching the Word of God. Those hearing are one of the different types of soil hearing the Word of God and need to decide which type of soil they are.

Our sermons, we may need to remind ourselves, have polyvalence— they mean different things to different people. Mark Allen Powell in his book *What Do They Hear* shares that pastors empathize with Jesus whereas our listeners empathize with the disciples.[24] Often we as preachers assume when we preach a sermon about Jesus that our listeners leave wanting to be more like Christ. However; according to Powell, our hearers do not automatically

24. Powell, *What Do They Hear?*, 51–52.

think, "how can I be like Christ?"[25] Instead our listeners are already asking, "how do I live this out?"[26] We have to acknowledge that our listeners may not resonate with the characters we resonate find as central to the stories we share.[27] By the time we process the four seeds or four soils and the four explanations, we have a simple chart which becomes our simple outline to teach or preach. The parable of the sower no longer becomes about the sower and the challenge or take-away is, "which type of soil are you?" There is nothing wrong with this reading of the parable of the sower, but I think we can do better than this charted individualistic approach.

Jesus's most widely read and vastly preached parable is the key to understanding all of Jesus's parables. When N. T. Wright talks about the sower, he even summarizes the core of all of his books namely this is a summary of the story of Israel, the end of exile, and the renewal of all things. Once you read Wright's take on this parable you could in turn say this parable is the key to understanding N. T. Wright.[28] Mary Tolbert in *Sowing the Gospel* astutely sees this parable in Mark 4 as a summary of the first half of Jesus's life and ministry found in Mark 1–8.[29] The parable of the sower is not just one of Jesus's parables it is the parable of parables. If we can accurately teach this parable then our listeners will gain insight into all of Jesus's parables. However, if we focus too narrowly on seeds and soil, we miss the thrust of this parable and our listeners may leave with a distorted or at least a small view of the gospel. We need better interpretive keys to understand this teaching of Jesus. Snodgrass surveys the interpretive options for this parable in *Stories of Intent* and lands on three overlapping interpretive options: the narrative context (i.e., the story of Israel), the Isa 6 quote, and the theme of "hearing." Let's look at each of these three interpretive keys. Each of these three keys should help us understand Jesus, his message, and the appropriate response to him. And the end result of this approach will be our ultimate aim, a wisdom culture.

25. Powell, *What Do They Hear?*, 56.

26. Powell says laity has a propensity toward application. See Powell, *What Do They Hear?*, 92.

27. He also makes the case that we need to avoid answering questions that our congregation is not asking. Powell, *What Do They Hear?*, 106.

28. I have been a fan of N. T. Wright's work for some time now, but any help we can get to understand his narrative is always appreciated. For his take on this parable see: Wright, *Jesus and the Victory of God*, 230–39.

29. Tolbert, *Sowing the Gospel*, 87–230. She also believes the parable of the vineyard summaries the last half of Jesus's life.

The first interpretive key to understanding the parable of the sower is to maintain a connection to the story of Israel.[30] Following Wright and others, the "seed" is understood as representing the remnant of Israel. God sowing true Israel in her own land marks the end of exile. Jesus shows up and begins to preach the Kingdom of God is near and those following Jesus are a part of true Israel.[31] Jesus is the fulfillment of the promise of Abraham and all nations will be blessed through him. Every approach to the parable of the sower must consider the role Israel plays in the story of Jesus and the Kingdom of God. Understanding this narrative context is important for understanding this parable and the gospel. Wright makes a connection between Isa 6 when it explicitly refers to the remnant with the image of the "holy seed." Which is interesting because Jesus is quoting from Isa 6 which brings us to our second interpretive key to understanding the parable of the sower.

> He told them, "The secret of the kingdom of God has been given to you. But to those on the outside everything is said in parables so that,
>
> "'they may be ever seeing but never perceiving, and ever hearing but never understanding; otherwise they might turn and be forgiven!'"
>
> Then Jesus said to them, "Don't you understand this parable? How then will you understand any parable? (Mark 4:11–13)

The parable seems then to be framed with Isaiah 6 in mind, which means the parable, the interpretation, and the quotation can be unified. Isaiah 6:9–10 is the starting point and reference point for the organization of this section of Mark.[32] This connection between the calling of Isaiah in Isa 6 and the beginning of Jesus's ministry are rarely mentioned. It's important to deal with the complexity of Jesus's teaching resulting in his rejection. Just like Isaiah. Therefore, this is a retelling of Israel's rejected prophets.[33]

The "so that" at the beginning of verse 12 deserves further attention. This *hina* clause makes this passage one of the most difficult in the NT since Jesus appears to be saying that he teaches in parables in order to blind the eyes of his listeners (taking the clause in its most common sense

---

30. For Wright this parable is a retelling of Israel's controlling narrative. See Wright, *Jesus and the Victory of God*, 230–39.

31. One of the marks of the "true remnant" is having ears to hear, see Wright, *Jesus and the Victory of God*, 230–39.

32. Snodgrass, *Stories with Intent*, 157–61.

33. See Wright, *Jesus and the Victory of God*, 230–39.

of purpose).[34] Jesus's teaching does not always result in understanding.[35] We have to wrestle with this a bit because this view does not sit well with most of our understandings of Jesus and his teaching strategy. We want Jesus's message to be clear. However, Jesus may not be heard, just like Isaiah will not be heard. This is forceful language used to drive home the point that we need to listen to Jesus, discern his message, and live for him. What, one may wonder, if Jesus is using hyperbole and irony here and that he means the opposite of what he is saying? This is challenging for us and should drive us to ask, "what is the point of Jesus's teachings?"

Sharyn Dowd thinks the Gospel writers are wrestling with God's hardening of Pharaoh's heart when God rescued his people out of Egypt as found in Exodus.[36] Here Mark is trying to resolve that tension with Jesus's teaching. God accomplished his purpose of exodus by hardening Pharaoh's heart and God accomplishes his purpose of salvation not just despite Jesus's listeners rejection, but because of it. This is difficult for us to process, but God provides salvation because and through Jesus's rejection. Why else would God tell Isaiah that he is going to be misunderstood. Isaiah still shared his message, and many did not understand and he by all accounts was rejected. But redemption is coming soon. Michael Bird recently tweeted, "Mark is repeating Isaiah's gospel: the Kingdom of God is near, judgment and salvation are coming with him."[37]

The only valid "hearing" is hearing that produces fruit. Anything else falls under Isa 6:9–10: "'they may be ever seeing but never perceiving, and ever hearing but never understanding; otherwise they might turn and be forgiven!'" Which leads to our third interpretive key to the parable of the sower, the theme of hearing.

34. After surveying a few options Strauss, *Mark*, 185, concludes saying, "the most natural sense is to take *hina* as a purpose clause, in which case Jesus would be saying that his purpose for teaching in parables is to blind the eyes and make deaf the ears of those who are 'outside.' Yet this negative function of the parable must be understood within the narrative contexts of both Isaiah and Mark." Young and Strickland, *Rhetoric of Jesus in the Gospel of Mark*, 151n74, conclude "There is no real evidence that Mark's intended readers would have heard anything other than the full force of *hina* as 'in order that.'"

35. *2 Bar* 51:1–6 has a contrast between those planted with the root of wisdom in their hearts along with those who despise the law thereby inhibiting their ability to hear wisdom. See also 2 Bar 54:4–16 and 1 En 48:7; 82:2–3; 104:12.

36. Dowd, *Reading Mark*, 46–47. Hardening is a theme of Mark in 3:5; 6:52; and 8:17–21.

37. Michael Bird, Twitter, posted 2/24/20, https://twitter.com/mbird12/status/1231708961222668288. Bird could have Joel Marcus or Rikki Watts in mind since both believe Mark's Gospel could be called the Gospel According to Isaiah, see Marcus, *Mark: 1–8*; Watts, *Isaiah's New Exodus in Mark*.

This parable focuses on the responsibility of hearing, understanding, and responding to Jesus's message. Hearing is the main theme of the parable of the sower.[38] "Hearing" or "listen" is used 13 times in Mark 4 and frames the entire parable.[39] This is the only parable in Mark with the imperative "Listen!" According to Strauss, this imperative is a "a continual spiritual attentiveness."[40] It is worth noting that "hearing" is not just receiving information, but it is more of absorbing the message and then doing something with it. The phrase "whoever has ears" is repeated in key positions in each of the Synoptic Gospels. This phrase is also key according to Tom Thatcher for when a riddling session is underway. And is "always used in the Gospels to highlight ambiguous statements that 'you have to puzzle over.'" When Jesus says, "whoever has ears" it is more than an attention getter, he expects a response that will clarify what he is talking about. Tom Thatcher agrees saying all riddles must be answered. By closing this parable with "'Whoever has ears,' Jesus leaves its hearers with the responsibility of discerning and applying its meaning."[41] Indeed the challenge of "hearing" is given several times in Mark 4:

> "Listen! A sower went out to sow . . . (v. 3)

> And he said, "Whoever has ears to hear had better listen!" (v. 9)

> so that although they look they may look but not see, and although they hear they may hear but not understand, so they may not repent and be forgiven. (v. 12)

> Whenever they hear, immediately Satan comes and snatches the word that was sown in them. As soon as they hear the word . . . (v. 15–16)

> Others are the ones sown among thorns: They are those who hear the word . . . (v. 18)

> But these are the ones sown on good soil: They hear the word and receive it and bear fruit . . . (v. 20)

---

38. Snodgrass, *Stories with Intent*, 128, describes "hearing" as the "dominate idea."

39. Mark 4:3, 9 [twice], 12 [twice], 15,16, 18,20,23 [twice], 24,33 (emphasis mine). Mark uses these frames or inclusio throughout his Gospel as a key rhetorical tool. This repetition or "dwelling" used rhetorically is common in other literature too. See *Rhetorica ad Herennium* (4.42.54; 4.45.58), Cicero, *De Oratore* 3.53.202, Quintilian, *Institutes* 9.1.28.

40. Strauss, *Mark*, 181.

41. Thatcher, *Jesus the Riddler*, 37.

If anyone has ears to <u>hear</u>, he had better <u>listen</u>!" 24 And he said to them, "Take care about what you <u>hear</u> . . . (v. 23)

So with many parables like these, he spoke the word to them, as they were able to <u>hear</u>. (v. 33)

"Hearing" is repeated throughout the Old Testament too and has huge ramifications in the story of Israel, in Isaiah, and in the life of God's people. When Jesus repeats "hearing" he is echoing the Shema of Deut 6:

Hear, O Israel: The LORD our God, the LORD is one. Love the LORD your God with all your heart and with all your soul and with all your strength. These commandments that I give you today are to be on your hearts. Impress them on your children. Talk about them when you sit at home and when you walk along the road, when you lie down and when you get up. Tie them as symbols on your hands and bind them on your foreheads. Write them on the doorframes of your houses and on your gates.

The Shema becomes a central pillar and prayer for God's people. The core of the Shema is Yahweh's specific wisdom teaching to his student Israel—to love. A central theme resonated by Jesus who builds on Deut 6 by adding, "love your neighbor as yourself." Mark shares an interesting interaction in chapter 12 Jesus has with a "teacher of the law" who asks Jesus which is the most important of all the commandments.

"The most important one," answered Jesus, "is this: 'Hear, O Israel: The Lord our God, the Lord is one. Love the Lord your God with all your heart and with all your soul and with all your mind and with all your strength.' The second is this: 'Love your neighbor as yourself.' There is no commandment greater than these. The teacher of the law responds, "Well said, teacher . . . ". Jesus likes this teacher's receptivity and tells him "you are not far from the kingdom of God" (Mark 12:29–31).

"Hearing" is also covenant language. Isa 55:3 says, "give ear and come to me; listen, so that you can live. I will make an everlasting covenant with you." We see similar language in the Psalms. "Listen, my people, and I will speak; I will testify against you, Israel. I am God, Your God" (Ps 50:7). And "Hear me my people, and I will warn you if you would only listen to me, Israel" (Ps 81:8). We have "hearing" in early Jewish writings, "Hear me, O Israel . . . For I will sow my law in you, and it shall bring forth fruit in you, and you shall be glorified through it forever"(4 Ezra 9:30).Jesus is standing on a familiar platform of hearing from God when he preaches this parable. This theme of hearing seems to connect the story of Israel and the quote from Isa 6.

After examining these interpretive keys (story of Israel, Isa 6, and theme of "hearing") we are now ready to ask what is the point of the parable and arguably what is the message of the gospel? The parable of the sower is not asking, "what type of soil are you?" Instead the parable is asking, "Are you hearing Jesus like those of the fourth soil who hear and obey?" Hearing is the main point of this parable and is key for creating a wisdom culture in our churches today. We have four soil types, but really the only option is the fourth Good Soil that produces fruit. The good fertile soil represents a receptive hearing that results in doing:

Scholars discuss the differences and ordering of the indicative and imperative, the being or who you are and the doing or what you do. Hearing involves both of these. We need God's word and we need his living word to speak into our lives today as we live out his word. Hearing includes listening and obeying. When we spend so much time explaining the four types of soil, we lose the main thrust of this parable which is found in true hearing.

From the parable of the sower and parables in general we can explore three components of creating a wisdom culture:

Hearing Jesus—Engaging Discernment—Following Jesus

We hear Jesus and his message, discern that message in community, and commit to live for him by following him. First, we have to hear from Jesus. Jesus and his message are central to cultivating a wisdom culture in churches today. Again, it's not what type of dirt are we, but are we listening to Jesus. Second, we have to engage in a time of discernment. When we create the time and space for congregations to discern, people are able to move from hearing Jesus to (third) obeying Jesus. It is during this time we internalize his words and put them into practice. Discernment is the time between hearing the word and the action. This is a discerning space—a time to decide if you really want to hear Jesus. The purpose of Jesus's metaphors is never to confuse, it might be to put off temporarily or to provoke thought but never to intentionally cause them to misunderstand the message.[42] I think Jesus wants to be understood just like we want to be understood when we teach. We need to be

42. Young and Strickland, *Rhetoric of Jesus*, 147.

comfortable enough to allow our people time to discern. Discernment helps maintain the connection between word and deed. All three components are needed to create a wisdom culture today.

You would think once the disciples process what he was saying they would just have written down their final assessment, yet it seems they maintained a level of ambiguity as if that is what creates an openness to what Jesus was saying. When Mark is "gospeling" he is teaching us about Jesus and his message—the Kingdom of God. This parable teaches us Jesus is worth listening to, obeying, and following. Jesus is imagining a world where God's people can hear from him, obey him, and live as his people in his kingdom—just as it was originally supposed to be lived.

What Jesus teaches is vitally important for our present and our future. Jesus teaches and the disciples are not immediately open to understanding. Jesus has to explain the parable of the sower to the disciples later. On one hand this seems odd, Jesus does not do this often. On this other hand it makes sense when you look at the entire parable. The disciples are not hearing Jesus. They may be represented by one of the first three soils, but the point is they are not a part of the fourth soil. They are not hearing Jesus. This is confirmed with the rest of Mark's Gospel. By Mark 8 the disciples are oblivious to who Jesus is and what it means to follow him.[43] All the more reason for us to take some time to ponder. Jesus the radical teacher, often misunderstood, is usurping our current way of operating. Such disruptions to our status quo and our current way of thinking require reflection and discernment. When it comes to wisdom you have to wait, it takes time. Just like the time between Jesus teaching the parable and Jesus explaining the parable and the time between when Mark uses it to tell us the gospel the story of Jesus. We need these moments to process the ramifications of what Jesus is saying. We cannot assume those who heard Jesus knew exactly what they were supposed to do with what he was saying. Even when Jesus explains it to them.

Wise Preaching Today

Lisa Piccirillo in July 2020 started a tenure-track position as an assistant professor of mathematics at MIT teaching undergrads. At 27 she was able to solve the Conway knot problem, a problem that has vexed many mathematicians for over 50 years. Her brilliance was in her ability to see the art and beauty in math. In a recent *Boston Globe* article that chronicles her story she gives advice to people entering the field:

43. We would not expect the disciples to have hearts that are hardened.

When universities organize math conferences, she says, they should avoid inviting speakers who "give talks where they go really fast and they try to show you how smart they are and how hard their research is. That's not good for anyone, but it's especially not good for young people or people who are feeling maybe like they don't belong here." What those people in the audience don't know, she says, is that nobody else really understands it either.[44]

Many church crowds are similar to these math conferences filled with listeners who have no idea what we are talking about. Often pastors are responding to issues that most of the listeners are oblivious too. So how do we know if people actually understand what we preach or teach? Could you imagine being able to preach like Jesus? If Jesus were preaching the parable of the sower today, how would he preach it? What would he do to draw his listeners in, so his listeners can hear him? Maybe we can learn from Jesus's parable of the sower how to preach like Jesus and how our teaching can create a wisdom culture in our church or ministry.

The gospel is a counter-narrative to our narrative. There is a tension between what is on the surface and what needs to be heard and discerned on a deeper level. We miss this when we focus instead on clarity and simplicity. For example, we do this when we distill the gospel down to a few key points in order to provoke more "decisions." What our listeners think of as gospel is not the gospel as found in the Gospels. We do the same with the parable of the sower by making it about a soil chart. Both miss the point of the gospel and are not sharing the gospel in the way Jesus "gospeled." We need a more robust understanding of Jesus, the gospel, and his Kingdom and our preaching needs to reflect that. In order to create a wisdom culture, we have to preach the same gospel Jesus preached.

The second way our teaching can create a wisdom culture is by avoiding overexplaining. When we as preachers explain everything in the text we lose the amazement and awe of what Jesus is saying. Remember Mark 1:22, "the people there were amazed by his teaching because he taught them like one who had authority."[45] When we preach we think the people are going to be amazed by how much we know. So we dump all the information we can for anyone who will listen. Instead, we need to maintain an amazement similar to that which is characteristic of Jesus's teaching by opening space for people to spend time discerning.

44. Wolfson, "Math Problem Stumped Experts for 50 Years."

45. Chris Keith has such insight into a carpenter from Nazareth who was not educated like the scribes and teachers of the law yet shows up and teaches with authority. See Keith, *Jesus against the Scribal Elite*.

According to Keck, the Kingdom of God functions "best when polyvalence is allowed to evoke multiple associations to invite future thought and
appeal to our emotions."[46] We have to do more than just say, "listen to this,
look at how cool this is." The parable of the sower is a great example of a text
where we overexplain the explanation. Often times to such a degree that we
are missing the point of the story.

There is a time for imperatives and "urging" like Paul in Eph 4:1, but
like the Gospel writers, we need to "let those who have ears—hear." Preaching is announcing the kingdom of God, it is proclaiming the gospel. This
is a privilege. Do those listening to our sermons leave wanting to explore
and hear more? This kind of "hearing" leads to discernment and is how we
create a wisdom culture.

The third way our teaching creates a wisdom culture is to acknowledge
we are not the sower. We must maintain a close intimate relationship with Jesus. And yes, we as followers need to be like Christ. And yes, we ought to teach
like him. But often when we place ourselves in prominent positions even in
biblical stories our egos get in the way. For example, do you as a preacher
teacher resonate more with Jesus instead of the disciples? Like Yahweh instead
of the people of Israel? We preachers often do just this. When this happens we
end up thinking too much of ourselves and are frustrated by a lack of response
to our teaching. Instead we need to approach the text with humility, and we
need to preach with humility. If you are the sower in the parable of the sower,
you have missed the point. We are one of the soils.

When we explain and overexplain, the text or story loses its bite or
authority and is detrimental to letting the text be the text. We have made
it about something that it is not intended to be. We do not want those
listening to us to walk away with a skewed understanding of the message
because we are so creative. We can show off by our deep biblical knowledge
and we can show off with our creative understanding of the text. Look at
how smart I am, clearly, I have studied this passage and know what it is
saying. Look at how many books and how learned I am. I have all this
knowledge and insight. Everyone tells me I preached a great sermon, and
yet maybe I have missed the point.

The next way our teaching can create a wisdom culture is by giving
the Holy Spirit space to work. We have to give people time to discern.
Such openness and dependence upon the Holy Spirit is crucial. "The Holy
Spirit is needed for wise living in the church."[47] When we overexplain the

46. Keck, *Who Is Jesus?*, 70.

47. See the introductory chapter, "What is Wisdom?" in this volume by Daniel
Hanlon.

text highlighting all the details we can interfere with the Holy Spirit's role in our preparation and our delivery. When we tell our listeners what they should or ought to be doing we are taking the place of the Holy Spirit in their lives. We are solving the puzzle for them. We have to trust the discernment process. Does our preaching allow the Holy Spirit to convict and lead them to making the necessary changes in their lives? Over application eliminates the need to discern and does not create wisdom cultures. You have to trust the Spirit during your preparation, delivery, and after. Instead, we can give our people some breathing room to make space for the Holy Spirit to speak to our people.

One final way our teaching can create a wisdom culture is to allow those listening to your sermons to engage the discernment process in community. When your sermon is over if you haven't revealed all your cards, and if you have maintained humility and given the Spirit space to work then those hearing should want to discuss the implications with other believers. This is crucial to creating a wisdom culture. This is where God's people find ways to obey Jesus. We don't want our people to work for it. We want it to be easy. We as a preacher think that once the sermon is over then we are done. Instead the sermon should be the starting point that is part of a larger process that allows dialogue and questions. The preaching event is important, but to create a wisdom culture we have to give people time to process.

Conclusion

This parable and all parables are not supposed to be made into a chart. Parables are made to be heard and ingrained in "hearing" is obeying. Parables are not supposed to be charted, instead they need to be chartered. For the parables to be heard today our people need to spend some time in them. They need to discern how to live out the parables in the context of a community that shares this desire. Eugene Peterson's "long obedience" is applicable here. To be a "disciple (*mathetes*) means we are people who spend our lives apprenticed to our master, Jesus Christ. We are in a growing-learning relationship, always."[48] Our preaching and teaching play a part in helping people in the lifelong pursuit—to hear and obey Jesus with every aspect of their lives. Following Jesus involves our entire lives and our entire lifestyle for the rest of our lives. It is a complete dependance and allegiance toward Christ alone.

While we really do not know what the disciples talked about after Jesus explained the parable to them, I do not think they had a conversation

48. Peterson, *Long Obedience in the Same Direction*, loc. 123–24.

around what type of soil they were. Clearly, Peter you are rocky soil, James and John you have been plucked out the soil by birds. No, instead they were probably asking each other, "Did you just hear that?" "Hey so do you think you are the good soil?" "Can you believe Jesus?" We need to ask the same questions.

Ultimately there are only two types of people—those who follow Christ and those who don't. For Mark it is those on the "inside" or those on the "outside." Those who take up their cross and follow or those who are unwilling to give everything they have to follow him. Tolstoy posited a similar analogy in his novel *Anna Karenina,* "happy families are all alike; every unhappy family is unhappy in its own way." While we might be unique in our failure to follow Christ however, regardless of how we fail, we still ultimately fail.[49]

As a result of our teaching, do people hear from Jesus? Do our sermons, lessons, and devotional thoughts result in people hearing from Jesus? Do they have time to discern his message? When this happens, we are creating a wisdom culture in our church. Our preaching and teaching can create a wisdom culture. This is not accomplished when we focus on charted soil types. To emulate Jesus's teaching, we need to teach in a way that results in our hearers "hearing."

Bibliography

Allison, Dale C. *Constructing Jesus: Memory, Imagination, and History.* Grand Rapids: Baker Academic, 2013.

Blomberg, Craig L. *Interpreting the Parables.* Downers Grove, IL: InterVarsity Academic, 2012.

———. *Preaching the Parables: From Responsible Interpretation to Powerful Proclamation.* Grand Rapids: Baker Academic, 2004.

Buttrick, David. *Speaking Parables.* Louisville: Westminster John Knox, 2000.

Byrskog, Samuel. *Jesus the Only Teacher: Didactic Authority and Transmission in Ancient Israel, Ancient Judaism and the Matthean Community.* Coniectanea Biblica: New Testament Series 24. Stockholm: Almqvist & Wiksell International, 1994.

Dowd, Sharyn. *Reading Mark: A Literary and Theological Commentary on the Second Gospel.* Macon, GA: Smyth & Helwys, 2000.

Hooker, Morna D. *From Adam to Christ: Essays on Paul.* Eugene, OR: Wipf & Stock, 2008.

Keck, Leander E. *Who Is Jesus?: History in Perfect Tense.* Columbia: University of South Carolina Press, 2004.

Keith, Chris. *Jesus against the Scribal Elite: The Origins of the Conflict.* Grand Rapids: Baker Academic, 2014.

49. This could be why we have three soil types that fail and are challenged to hear and be receptive to God's Word.

Mack, Burton L. "Teaching in Parables: Elaboration in Mark 4.1–34." In *Patterns of Persuasion in the Gospels*, edited by Burton L. Mack et al., 143–60. Sonoma: Polebridge.

Marcus, Joel. *Mark: 1–8*. Anchor Bible. New Haven, CT: Yale University Press, 2010.

McGrath, Alister E. *Mere Discipleship: Growing in Wisdom and Hope*. Grand Rapids: Baker, 2019.

Peterson, Eugene H. *A Long Obedience in the Same Direction: Discipleship in an Instant Society*. Downers Grove, IL: InterVarsity, 2000.

Powell, Mark Allan. *What Do They Hear?: Bridging the Gap between Pulpit and Pew*. Nashville: Abingdon, 2007.

Scott, Bernard Brandon. *Hear Then the Parable: A Commentary on the Parables of Jesus*. Minneapolis: Fortress, 1989.

Snodgrass, Klyne R. *Stories with Intent: A Comprehensive Guide to the Parables of Jesus*. 2nd ed. Grand Rapids: Eerdmans, 2018.

Stein, R. H. *The Method and Message of Jesus' Teachings*. Rev. ed. Louisville: Westminster John Knox, 1994.

Strauss, Mark L. *Mark*. Zondervan Exegetical Commentary of the New Testament. Grand Rapids: Zondervan, 2014.

Thatcher, Tom. *Jesus the Riddler: The Power of Ambiguity in the Gospels*. Louisville: Westminster John Knox, 2006.

Tolbert, Mary Ann. *Perspectives on the Parables: An Approach to Multiple Interpretations*. Philadelphia: Fortress, 1979.

———. *Sowing the Gospel: Mark's Work in Literary-Historical Perspective*. Minneapolis: Fortress, 1996.

Young, David M., and Michael Strickland. *The Rhetoric of Jesus in the Gospel of Mark*. Minneapolis: Fortress, 2017.

Watts, Rikki E. *Isaiah's New Exodus in Mark*. Grand Rapids: Baker Academic, 2000.

Wolfson, John. "A Math Problem Stumped Experts for 50 Years. This Grad Student from Maine Solved It in Days." *Boston Globe*, August 20, 2020. https://www.bostonglobe.com/2020/08/20/magazine/math-problem-stumped-experts-50-years-this-grad-student-maine-solved-it-days/.

Wright, N. T. *Jesus and the Victory of God*. Minneapolis: Fortress, 1999.

WISE GOSPELING

By John Phelps

At some point in life we all need to consult with an expert. I'm not a DIY kind of a guy. I can barely use a screwdriver and often break things that I try to fix. So if I have a problem with a car or an appliance, I am quick to call an expert mechanic or repairman. I am also a passionate golfer. My wife, baby luv, might say I am obsessed with golf. So when I had the opportunity to sit within feet of Tiger Woods as he hit golf balls warming up to play in a professional golf tournament, I was riveted. When Tiger's club hit the ball, it sounded like the loud snap of a bull whip. The ball jumped off the clubface and made a sizzling sound as it soared toward the target. Tiger Woods might be the greatest golfer to ever strike a golf ball, and if he offered me advice on how to play golf, I would sit in rapt attention hanging on every word.

Tiger Woods is an expert in golf, and Peter and Paul are experts in what the gospel is and how it should be presented. In the introductory chapter Daniel Hanlon discussed how wisdom is a way of knowing, and that knowledge is available through observation. When we observe experts we gain wisdom. As pastors and leaders we would be wise to listen to and learn from the apostolic experts' example of gospeling. Luke in the book of Acts, under the inspiration of the Holy Spirit, gives us written snippets and snapshots of the earliest gospel sermons ever preached. In this chapter I will exegete in some detail, and then compare and contrast the gospel presentations of Peter in Acts 2:14–41 and Paul in Acts 13:16–41 in search of gospeling wisdom for today. Strangely, these sermons are often overlooked when it comes to presenting the gospel today. Scot McKnight notes that the sermons in the book of Acts are the elephant in the pulpit, saying:

> We want to know what the first gospel was really like. We want to know how that first generation of apostles evangelized and we want to know how that early gospeling compares to what we

call evangelism and the gospel today. Time and time again, and I can't explain this, our discussion of gospeling simply ignores those gospeling sermons in the book of Acts . . . Could there be any better source for evangelism than a half dozen or so gospel sermon summaries from the first generation of apostles.[1]

There is no better source for gospel theology and evangelistic preaching than the sermons in Acts.

One of the biggest obstacles to mining the wisdom of Peter's and Paul's gospeling is that fact that we do not have a word for word recording of their actual sermons. Michael Bird asks a very necessary but somewhat shocking question that most never consider asking when studying these sermons saying, "Are the sermons by the apostles in Acts a reliable account of their preaching, or did he (Luke) just make them up?"[2] Thor Strandenaes answers Michael Bird's question resoundingly, "No, Luke did not make them up." He says, "The pattern which is reflected in each of the speeches is not likely to have been merely a Lukan creation. Luke based his transmission of the missionary speeches on the oral and written sources which were at his disposal, as well as his own memory (Luke 1:1–4; Acts 1:1)."[3] So Luke is using sources as well as his own memory to piece together the sermons. The reason these sermons are relatively short is because they are summaries and not complete speeches. Christoph Stenschke contends that the reason for their shortness is because Luke's audience would have been familiar with the life of Jesus from his Gospel so much of Jesus's biographical information would have been omitted from these sermons.[4]

In some ways the entire premise of this chapter hangs on the work of C. H. Dodd, who explains why we should prioritize the book of Acts in our understanding of gospeling over the epistles. He says, "The epistles are, of course, not of the nature of kerygma. They are addressed to readers already Christian, and they deal with theological and ethical problems arising out of the attempt to follow the Christian way of life and thought in a non-Christian world. They have the character of what the early church called 'teaching' or 'exhortation.' They presuppose the preaching. They expound and defend the implications of the gospel rather than proclaim it."[5] Dodd is arguing that

1. McKnight, *King Jesus Gospel*, 114.

2. Wright and Bird, *New Testament in Its World*, 607.

3. Strandenaes, "Missionary Speeches in the Acts of the Apostles and Their Missiological Implications," 344.

4. Stenschke, "Presentation of Jesus in the Missionary Speeches of Acts and the Mission of the Church," 1–18.

5. Dodd, *Apostolic Preaching and Its Developments*, 4–5.

we get Peter and Paul's presentation of the gospel in its rawest and realest form when they are preaching in Acts to unbelievers. In the epistles Peter and Paul are teaching and exhorting in a church context, not a purely evangelistic context like Acts. In their epistles Peter and Paul are exploring and expanding church dogmatics in the context of solving pastoral problems, not presenting the gospel to unbelievers.

As we enter into a study of the sermons in Acts it is helpful to think of the book of Acts as a two-story literary house. The first floor of the house is the actual historical events, the sermons of Peter and Paul. Peter and Paul are preaching the gospel in their historical context after the resurrection and ascension of Jesus to give birth to the early church. The second floor of the house is Luke's historical, literary, and theological purposes in recording the events as many as thirty or more years after they occurred. To properly interpret the facts and details of the gospel in Acts, they must be placed in their proper setting. Like a puzzle that needs a box top picture, so the verses in Acts require a box top framing story for the book of Acts. The box top of Acts is the gospel going to the ends of the earth. It is the map of the gospel movement told through the stories of Peter in Acts 1–12 and Paul in Acts 13–28. What we are going to find as we study the sermons of Peter and Paul is that they frame the gospel within the larger story of Israel. The gospel is not a Roman's road as much as it is a Jewish journey.

It is important to establish the larger framing story from the outset, and I'll tell you why it is so crucial in a moment, but first let Peter frame the story for us. If Peter is talking to a Jewish audience, then one would expect him to frame the story in a Jewish way using Old Testament Scriptures, which he does. In his Acts 2 sermon, which takes place during the Jewish feast of Pentecost in Jerusalem, Peter quotes Old Testament texts like Joel 2:28–31; Ps 16:8–11; and Ps 110:1. But what is most interesting and unexpected is that when Peter preaches to gentiles in Acts 10, he doesn't adapt or reframe the story. While he doesn't quote Old Testament texts to gentiles, he does start the story in the same place as Acts 2 with Israel. He says to his gentile audience, "You know the message God sent to the people of Israel telling the good news . . . " (Acts 10:36). Paul follows the same gospel game plan. When presenting the gospel to Jews, he uses the Old Testament to tell the story, and while he doesn't quote Old Testament texts to gentiles in Acts 17, he starts the story by going back to the Old Testament story of Adam and creation.

The framing story of Israel functions as the box top for the gospel pieces. Without Israel's story as the framing story, the gospel turns inward and becomes individualistic instead of focusing upward on God and to

God's Messiah.[6] If we tell the gospel within the larger story of the Bible, then the gospel is the resolution of a story problem, instead of an individual sin problem. McKnight aptly describes the gospel as, "Israel's story in search of a Messiah solution."[7] With this framing story in place it's time to gain some gospel wisdom from our experts.

There is a close connection between wisdom and the gospel. In the book of Proverbs, we are told, "The beginning of wisdom is the fear of the Lord."[8] It is my contention that the beginning of the fear of the Lord is responding to the gospel. So, learning from our experts in gospel preaching, Peter and Paul, just seems like the smart place to start in gaining gospel wisdom. Think of these Acts sermons as the first sermon series in the early church.[9]

Wise Gospeling in Acts 2:14–41

To understand what Peter is doing in this sermon, think of him as a defense attorney. He is defending Jesus. The crowd has already convicted Jesus and had him crucified. Peter is calling three witnesses to speak on Jesus's behalf. The first witness is fulfilled Scripture. Peter is going to call to the stand Joel 2:28–32; Ps 16:8–11; and Ps 110:1. The second witness is the apostolic witness. Peter says, "God has raised this Jesus to life, and we are all witnesses of the fact" (2:32). The last witness Peter calls to the stand is the Holy Spirit. Peter points out that the Spirit has been poured out saying, "Exalted to the right hand of God, he (Jesus) has received from the Father the promised Holy Spirit and has poured out what you now see and hear" (2:33). As Peter builds his case in defense of Jesus, everything crescendos to his closing argument. He closes his case by declaring, "Therefore let all Israel be assured of this: God has made this Jesus, whom you crucified both Lord and Christ" (2:36). The twin claims of Davidic rulership and deity define who Jesus is. In a Jewish context for Peter to call Jesus the Christ or Messiah, the long-awaited Davidic ruler, was a courageous claim, but then to add that he was divine by calling him *Lord* was more than audacious. It was a jaw-dropping, pin-dropping, mic-dropping moment!

In some ways first-century preaching works just like twenty-first century preaching. It is highly likely that Peter begins his sermon with some humor. He swats away some hecklers attempts to harass and mock him.

6. McKnight, *King Jesus Gospel*, 62.

7. McKnight, *King Jesus Gospel*, 37.

8. Prov 9:10. Unless otherwise noted, all biblical passages referenced are from the NIV.

9. White, "Apostolic Preaching of the Lord Jesus," 34.

They were teasing and testing Peter saying, "This isn't a miracle! It's just a matter of too much wine!" So, Peter pushes back with a little sarcasm, "It's a little too early to start drinking, don't ya think? It's 9:00 a.m. in the morning. We haven't even eaten breakfast yet! No one starts drinking at this time of day!" In the back and forth, Peter puts the hecklers in their place and begins his sermon without most people even knowing it. He gains the trust of the audience with his witty response.

Peter begins his evangelistic sermon with some eschatology. It's not hellfire and brim stone eschatology, but it is about the Day of the Lord. He calls his first witness of fulfilled Scripture to the witness stand and starts with Joel 2:28–32, which is about a locust plague and the coming Day of the Lord. Bock comments on Peter's eschatological emphasis at the start of his sermon, "It is laid out in a this-is-that (*touto estin*) form that is similar to what one sees in pesher style interpretation found at Qumran . . . ."[10] Peter makes a slight alteration in the Joel quotation, which opens up a can of hermeneutical worms that are beyond the scope of this chapter.[11]

Ancient writers felt much more freedom than we do in our day to modify or adapt a quotation to help make a point, to make a text more relevant. Keener writes, "Peter adds to Joel's text at various points to bring out the implications, especially that this is the eschatological gift of prophecy and hence that the eschatological time of fulfillment of the promises has come (cf. similarly Jesus's explanation about Isa 61:1–2 in Luke 4:21). Jewish interpreters reworded textual allusions where it suited them or where they regarded their interpretations as a reasonable inference."[12] Peter adds the phrase "last days" and in so doing is saying Pentecost's pouring out of the Holy Spirit is the inauguration of the Day of the Lord. Bock notes, "Later Jewish interpretation connected the Joel citation to the other OT texts that explained the Spirit's coming in the eschaton, a link that was conceptual in nature."[13] By pairing Pentecost with the Day of the Lord, Peter is preaching both eschatological blessing and coming judgment.

Although Peter begins his gospel sermon by referencing Joel 2:28–32 to explain the tongues of fire and people speaking in tongues, it would be all too easy to miss the gospel significance of the Joel quote. Peter begins his gospel presentation not only with eschatology but with sociology. Peter had

10. Bock, *Acts*, 111.

11. There are many hermeneutical methods used to address New Testament authors use of the Old Testament. Whether you use a pure predictive approach, sensusplenior approach, typological approach, or a christological reading backwards approach, it doesn't significantly change the application of these sermons for gospel wisdom.

12. Keener, *Acts*, 875.

13. Bock, *Acts*, 112.

no idea how far reaching the sociological impact of the last days reference was relationally and missionally for the community of Christ followers. Acts 2:17 refers to the outpouring of the Spirit on "all people" (*sarx*, flesh). The emphasis is easy to miss—ALL.[14] At this point in the story Peter was purely focused on only his Jewish family's access to the good news of Jesus, but Luke writing thirty or more years later can see what Peter didn't see. Luke sees gentile access to the good news of Jesus. There is universality in the gospel that Peter is preaching, unbeknownst to him. John Stott wisely points out, "All people (*pasa sarx*, 'all flesh,' 17a) means not everybody irrespective of their inward readiness to receive the gift but everybody irrespective of their outward status. There are still spiritual conditions for receiving the Spirit, but there are no social distinctions."[15]

Peter uses the close of the Joel quote in Acts 2:21, "everyone who calls on the name of the Lord will be saved," as a springboard to Jesus. Acts 2:21 is the jumping off point where Peter spends a large part of his sermon arguing, "that the Lord's name on which his hearers must call in this salvific era is Jesus (2:21, 34, 38)."[16] Later on in his sermon, Peter is going to come back to this "calling on the Lord to be saved" language. Peter's Jewish audience upon hearing the Joel quote would have assumed that Peter was talking about Yahweh and deliverance from the judgment of the Day of the Lord. It is only through Yahweh that one can delivered from the judgment of the Day of the Lord. However the connection between Yahweh and Jesus becomes quite significant later in the sermon in Acts 2:36 and Acts 2:40. Keener concludes, "Whether or not Peter recognizes it at this point (cf. 10:28) his own Spirit-inspired preaching already foreshadows for Luke (in the context of the whole story of Acts) the ultimate inclusion of the gentiles (2:21; 39; perhaps also first in 3:26)."[17]

Verse 22 signals a shift in the sermon. After unpacking the Joel quote, Peter seeks to refocus his audience and grab their attention saying, "Men of Israel, listen to this." Peter is preparing to call his next major witness of fulfilled Scripture from Ps 16:8–11 and is ramping up for his resurrection rhetoric in vv. 22–33. But before he launches into a lecture on

---

14. We see this universal and horizontal emphasis furthered in Peter's gospel presentation in Acts 10. Peter's message of peace in Acts 10:36 had radical ramifications for social realignment. Peter's preaching to gentiles implies the horizontal, human to human reconciliation of the gospel is as significant as the vertical dimensions of reconciliation with God. The reason for vertical reconciliation with God is so that horizontal reconciliation can happen between ethnic groups to form the new family of God.

15. Stott, *Message of Acts*, 74.

16. Keener, *Acts*, 920.

17. Keener, *Acts*, 920.

resurrection, he addresses the life of Jesus. Stenschke notes, "When Jesus entered Jerusalem, he was no stranger."[18] The audience would have been familiar with Jesus. While there is only one verse on Jesus's ministry, the life of Jesus is as much a part of the gospel as his death and resurrection. Peter uses a trifecta of terms to authenticate Jesus: *miracles, signs and wonders* (2:22). Keener observes, "Because Luke is here expounding the Joel quotation, he views these signs as proofs that the eschatological, messianic era has arrived in part."[19]

Often at the center of gospel debates there are heated discussions regarding the divine and human roles in salvation. Peter puts this tension on full display in Acts 2:23. First, Peter says Jesus's crucifixion was a part of God's purpose and foreknowledge, but then he adds an emphatic you put him to death. We see the sovereign plan of God unfolding in the death of Jesus without diminishing human responsibility. In the latter half of v. 23, with two plural Greek verbal forms (*prospēxantes, aneilate*), Peter indicts both Roman and Jewish leaders as well as the whole nation of Israel for killing Jesus. It is as if Peter points his finger out into the audience and accuses everyone there, "You all did this!" There is both sovereignty and human accountability side-by-side in this gospel presentation.

It is in this section of the sermon that we have the only mention of the cross (2:23), but it is not used in a theological or soteriological sense. The cross is used just as a term for how Jesus was put to death.[20] Peter doesn't make any connection between the cross and forgiveness of sins in this sermon. In fact, he quickly moves past the cross to concentrate on one of the main theological themes of his talk, resurrection in vv. 24–33. Luke doesn't seem to have a strong emphasis on the cross and the doctrine of propitiatory atonement. However, his silence about atonement cannot be construed as rejection. Luke's emphasis is on the victory won, on resurrection, not on the cross and death. Luke's audience would have required little explanation of the cross. Peter's gospel presentation isn't about death and suffering for sin. It is about a victory won! It is a celebration sermon. Death couldn't hold Jesus. Peter paints a powerful picture of how death wasn't strong enough to defeat Jesus in Acts 2:24. Bertram captures the essence of Acts 2:24 well

18. Stenschke, "Presentation of Jesus in the Missionary Speeches of Acts and the Mission of the Church," 2.

19. Keener, *Acts*, 924–25.

20. There is no atonement theology developed in Peter's Acts 10 sermon, but there is an allusion to Deut 21:22 and the shameful death of crucifixion. There is considerably more focus on the resurrection of Jesus and the witnesses to the resurrection than on the cross.

with this analogy, "The abyss cannot hold Christ any more than the womb can hold the child."[21]

In vv. 25–33 Peter calls his second witness to the stand of fulfilled Scripture, Ps 16:8–11. In vv. 25–28 Peter quotes the LXX version of Ps 16:8–11 with minor adaptations. Then Peter interprets the Psalm in vv. 29–31, and in vv. 32–33 he shows how the psalm relates to recent events.[22] Peter's treatment of Ps 16 forces us to deal with how New Testament authors use Old Testament texts. If we follow a traditional, literal, historical, grammatical approach to Ps 16, then this Psalm is about David, and God's promise of protection from premature death. Allen Ross gives us an example of how a literal interpretation would look saying, "This psalm is a celebration of the joy of fellowship that David realized comes from faith in the Lord. The psalm may have been written when he faced great danger in the wilderness or opposition in his reign. Whatever its occasion, David was convinced that because he had come to know and trust the Lord as his Portion in life, he could trust Him in the face of death."[23] Yet Peter says in Acts 2:31 that Ps 16 is about Jesus, "Seeing what was ahead, he spoke of the resurrection of Christ, that he was not abandoned to the grave, nor did his body see decay."

Peter does something radically different from a literal, historical, grammatical approach to the Old Testament. Bock states, "Peter's reading presses all the language here in a very literal direction. The text is not about premature death but about not being left in hades."[24] Peter is saying that this text is literally about Jesus, not David. Peter is reading Ps 16 backwards looking through the cataclysmic, apocalyptic events of the cross and reimagining the true meaning of the text.

The heart and soul of the Psalm 16 passage is Ps 16:10, "you will not abandon me to the grave, nor will you let your Holy One see decay." Peter is using this text to teach the bodily nature of Jesus's resurrection. The body did not see decay. Our defense attorney is saying, "If you can't produce a body, then you must admit that Jesus is the Davidic king of Psalm 16." His audience would know that David was buried in Jerusalem. Keener says, "David's tomb was near Jerusalem (1 Kgs 2:10; 2 Chr 32:33) and its traditional site, apparently still known after the exile (Neh 3:16), continued to be so in the first century . . . .The site of David's tomb is lost to us today."[25] Peter's logic is pretty

---

21. Kittel et al., *Theological Dictionary of the New Testament*, 1354.

22. Bock, *Acts*, 126.

23. Ross in Walvoord and Zuck, *Bible Knowledge Commentary*, 803.

24. Bock, *Acts*, 126.

25. Keener, *Acts*, 951–52.

simple. If David's body is in the grave, then Ps 16 can't be about David. His literalistic interpretation of Ps 16 leaves no room for a body in a grave. Since David's body is in the grave, Ps 16 is about Jesus because Jesus is not in the grave. At the very core of Peter's gospel presentation is the bodily resurrection of Jesus. Nine verses (2:24–32) out of a twenty-eight verse summary of Peter's Pentecost sermon are devoted to resurrection. It could be argued that resurrection is the center of Peter's gospel. Luke gives us more information about resurrection than any other theme in the sermon.

Within Peter's resurrection reframing of Israel's story[26] David's kingship is interwoven. There is a thick thread of Davidic messianic fulfillment in Peter's gospel presentation. David plays a starring role in Peter's sermon, which tips us off to kingdom theology in Peter's gospel presentation. David looms large in Peter's prophetic interpretation of Ps 16. In Acts 2:30 Peter draws upon Ps 132:11 as he reminds his Jewish audience of the promises given to David to have a descendant on the throne, and resurrection is the reason Jesus has a right to the Davidic throne.

The resurrection fulfillment of Psalm 16 is a powerful witness in Peter's defense of Jesus. As Ps 16 steps down off the witness stand, Peter calls his next witness. In Acts 2:32 Peter calls himself and the rest of the apostles to the witness stand. He says, "God has raised this Jesus to life, and we are all witnesses of the fact." The "we" in Acts 2:32 is a reference to the eyewitness testimony of the apostles to Jesus's resurrection. Peter and the apostles who abandoned Jesus at the cross are now courageously defending him and proclaiming him because they saw a resurrected Jesus with their own eyes. They ate with him and talked with him and touched him.

In Acts 2:33–35 Peter calls Ps 110:1 to the witness stand. Because we are so familiar with resurrection we may miss one of Peter's main gospel points. If Peter were here today and we could talk with him about his sermon, he might get a little miffed if we missed one of his most powerful arguments in his gospel defense of Jesus. The gospel isn't just about resurrection. In Acts 2:33 Peter introduces the exaltation of Christ. Fernando comments, "While we often speak of the ascension of Christ the scriptural term exaltation may be a more appropriate word since it implies the significance of the event. In the New Testament the resurrection and exaltation of Christ are held in close association with each other almost as if they

---

26. Peter with Luke's assistance is careful to place the gospel within the larger framing story of Israel's story. What is so striking about Peter's sermon to gentiles in Acts 10 is its strong Jewish flavor. He specifically says that this gospel of peace was "sent to the people of Israel." In Acts 10:37, 39 he locates the gospel physically in Judea, Galilee, the land of the Jews, and Jerusalem.

constitute a single event."[27] Bock adds, "As important as the resurrection is to show that Jesus is alive and vindicated, it is even more significant an indication of where Jesus went (to God's right hand, to God's presence) and what he does from there (giving the gift of the Spirit)."[28]

The exaltation of Christ means that Christ is at the right hand of the Father. The phrase "right hand of God" in Acts 2:33 is significant. Being at "the right hand of God" is a metaphor for a place of honor.[29] Being in this position of honor has kingdom implications. Keener states, "Jesus being at the Father's right hand to reign indicates that the Kingdom has been inaugurated in some sense (Acts 1:3), though in some sense not yet (1:6; 3:19–21)."[30]

Peter needs a witness to support his contention that Jesus is reigning from heaven in God's presence. Ps 110:1 is his witness, but he makes it clear that Ps 110:1 is not about David. Tremper Longman gives a helpful overview of the meaning of Ps 110 saying:

> Psalm 110 is a royal hymn that centres on two divine oracles (vv. 1, 4) directed to the king. While the title names David as the composer, the first verse in its original context can only be understood as an oracle from God ("the LORD") to the king ("my lord"). In other words, the psalm is addressed to the king, not given by the king, although the title will allow the New Testament authors to apply the psalm in a different direction (see *Meaning*). Recent research comparing Psalm 110 with Assyrian royal prophecies suggests that 'Psalm 110 was delivered at the temple by a prophet, possibly a temple functionary, as part of Israel's cultus and pertains to the newly minted king.'"[31]

However, Peter does not follow the literal, historical, grammatical interpretation but uses a christological interpretation to apply it to Jesus. Again, Peter's logic is fairly straightforward. David didn't ascend into heaven, so Ps 110 isn't about David. In the LXX translation of Ps 110, the Greek term for Lord both times it is used is *kyrios*. However, in the Hebrew text the first word for "Lord" is *Yahweh* but the second word for "Lord" is different, *Adonai*. By quoting Ps 110:1 Peter is strongly hinting at Jesus's divinity and will outright declare it in Acts 2:36. Fernando says, "Peter sees this as God speaking to Jesus, who is David's Lord."[32]

27. Fernando, *Acts*, 104.

28. Bock, *Acts*, 133.

29. Keener, *Acts*, 946–48.

30. Keener, *Acts*, 956.

31. Longman, *Psalms*, 381.

32. Fernando, *Acts*, 104.

There is one last feature of Jesus's exaltation. In Acts 2:33 Peter declares that Jesus is the mediator of the pouring out of the Spirit at Pentecost. In the Old Testament, Yahweh was the one who poured out the Spirit (Isa 44:3; Ezek 11;19; 36:26–27; 37:14; 39:29). According to Acts 1:4 the Father is the one who promised the Spirit. Keener writes, "Luke thus portrays Jesus as the 'Lord of the Spirit,' who gives God's Spirit in Acts 2:33; such a role necessarily involves a 'high,' even divine Christology (Luke 3:16)."[33] The divinity of Jesus is being declared in subtle and not so subtle ways. And by virtue of the audience seeing and hearing the outpouring of the Spirit, they have become witnesses to the Lordship of Jesus.

Having created an airtight defense of Jesus, our attorney Peter makes his closing argument in Acts 2:36. He declares the divinity and Davidic rulership of Jesus when he says Jesus is both "Lord and Christ." Christ is an undisputed messianic title, and Lord it has been shown can be a divine title. LORD is a divine title in the LXX.[34] G. E. Ladd concludes from Peter's use of *Lord*, "It is amazing to find the term used of both Jesus and God. Not only is Jesus, like God, *kyrios*; the term is used both of God and the exalted Jesus in practically interchangeable contexts."[35]

After Peter's rests his case with his closing argument in verse 36, he calls for the audience to render their verdict on Jesus. In verses 37 to 40, the jury at Jerusalem comes in with their ruling. In Acts 2:37 we read, "they were cut to the heart." It is as if the crowd confesses to the crime of killing Jesus. They throw themselves on the mercy of the apostle and ask, "What shall we do?" We get Peter's altar call instructions in Acts 2:38–41. What is stunningly absent from this first gospel altar call is the invitation to believe or have faith in Jesus.

The gospel is not just a message. It is an appeal to action. The gospel asks us to "repent and be baptized" (2:38). The action is accompanied by forgiveness of sins and the Holy Spirit (2:38). To repent means at its most basic level to change one's mind. The Greek term *metanoeō* means, "to change one's *nous*," i.e., opinion, feelings, or purpose. If it is perceived that the former *nous* was wrong, it then takes on the sense "to regret," "to rue," in various constructions, and often with an ethical nuance.[36] Peter is asking his Jewish audience to change their mind regarding Jesus as Messiah and God in the flesh. One can think of repentance as a faith term. Think of repentance as a person that believes one thing to be true but has a change of mind

33. Keener, *Acts*, 958.

34. Keener, *Acts*, 922.

35. Ladd, *Theology of the New Testament*, 371.

36. Kittel et al., *Theological Dictionary of the New Testament*, 639.

and believes something different now. Interestingly Marshall commenting on Acts 2:38 states, "Repentance and faith are the two sides of the same coin."[37] Peter doesn't use the Greek word for faith (*pistis*) in this sermon, but is it possible that repentance is a synonym for faith?

Closely coupled with repentance is water baptism, the expression of repentance. For the hearer of the gospel, there is a change of mind that Jesus is Messiah, and that new belief is demonstrated through the behavior of water baptism. Keener concludes, "Since Pentecost, water baptism became 'the effective representation' of the Pentecost experience 'for every succeeding person and generation' (Acts 2:39)."[38] Also linked to repentance is the forgiveness of sins (Acts 3:19, 5:31, 11:18; Luke 24:47).[39] The close connection of baptism and forgiveness of sins in Acts 2:38 has led some to conclude baptism is necessary for regeneration. Acts 2:38 is a battle ground for complex grammatical arguments for and against baptismal regeneration. Keener maintains, "Grammar alone will not easily decide the theological point here."[40] It takes more than one isolated passage to sustain such a doctrine. If baptism were a requirement for regeneration, one would expect to find baptism associated with the offer of forgiveness everywhere forgiveness is proffered in the New Testament. In Acts 3:19, we see repentance and forgiveness without the requirement of baptism. F. F. Bruce beautifully describes the significance of baptism saying, "Baptism in water continued to be the visible sign by which those who believed the gospel, repented of their sins, and acknowledged Jesus as Lord were publicly incorporated into the Spirit-baptized fellowship of the new people of God."[41]

The second benefit of the gospel is the gift of the Holy Spirit. Bruce defines this gift saying, "The gift of the Spirit is to be distinguished from the gifts of the Spirit. The gift of the Spirit is the Spirit himself, bestowed by the exalted Lord under the Father's authority."[42] Peter points out that the Spirit had been promised (Acts 2:39) and is most likely a reference to the new covenant (Isa 44:3; Ezek 36:26–27; 37:14). This promise of the Spirit is for the Jewish audience in Jerusalem, and Peter adds "for all who are far off," which could easily have just meant Diaspora Jews but Luke has far

37. Marshall, *Acts of the Apostles*, 81.

38. Keener, *Acts*, 976.

39. Peter concludes his gentile gospel message with the offer of forgiveness of sins through Jesus name for everyone who believes (10:43). The interesting twist to this offer is that prophets testified about this gospel offer. Again, even in a gentile context, Peter is linking this gospel message to the Old Testament.

40. Keener, *Acts*, 975.

41. Bruce, *Book of Acts*, 70.

42. Bruce, *Book of Acts*, 71.

more in mind. Acts 2:39 is a portent of the inclusivity of the gospel extend-ing to gentiles. The pouring out of the Spirit at Pentecost is the occasion for the first post resurrection gospel presentation, and according to Acts 2:33, the pouring out of the Spirit is evidence of the exaltation of Jesus. Bock uses interesting language when he comments on the gospel benefit of the Spirit, "At the core of the gospel is the offer of the gift of the Spirit and what the Spirit provides to the one who believes . . . . It reflects core Christian orthodox teaching about the content of the gospel. All four references to a gift in Acts are to the giving of the Holy Spirit to those who respond to the preaching of the church (2:38; 8:20; 10:45; 11:17)."[43] Keener adds, "Con-version and the gift of the Spirit are inseparably connected theologically."[44] It can be inferred the gift of the Spirit is not just a benefit of the gospel but a component of the gospel itself.

Peter concludes his sermon in Acts 2:40 with echoes from Israel's past. The words "perverse generation" would have stirred painful wilderness mem-ories. It is a stern warning and threat of judgment. Marshall states, "'Perverse Generation' is an Old Testament phrase for the people of Israel who rebelled against God in the wilderness (Deut 32:5) and is applied in the New Testa-ment to those who reject Jesus(Phil 2:15; cf. Luke 9:41; 11:29; Heb 3:10)."[45] This is no feel good finish with a happy story that inspires the audience. Pe-ter's final words are, "Save yourselves or judgment awaits!"[46]

Wise Gospeling in Acts 13:16–41

Peter exits the stage in Acts 12, Luke gives us clues regarding the progress of the gospel to the ends of the earth as he names the cities Paul is visiting on his first missionary journey. The gospel has moved beyond Judea and Samaria into Asia Minor on its way to Athens and Rome. Paul is traveling through the Roman empire, and he preaches his Acts 13 sermon in Psidian Antioch, the capital of southern Galatia and the chief of a series of military colonies founded by Augustus.

The apostle Paul takes over from Peter as the main actor from Acts 13 to the end of Luke's second work, and this sermon helps propel Luke's Acts 1:8 narrative forward to the end of the book. A new era of gentile gospel focus is dawning as Peter, the apostle to the Jews, fades off the scene. Contrary

43. Bock, *Acts*, 144.

44. Keener, *Acts*, 985.

45. Marshall, *Acts*, 82.

46. We see the same emphasis upon judgment in Peter's gospeling in Acts 10:42. Jesus is described as the judge of the living and the dead in Acts 10:42.

to what one might expect from a gentile missionary, Paul often begins his gospel mission in the uniquely Jewish setting of a synagogue. Paul went first to the synagogue in almost every city in which he preached the gospel (Iconium, 14:1; Thessalonica, 17:1–3; Berea, 17:10–12; Athens, 17:17; Corinth, 18:4; Ephesus, 18:19 and 19:8). F. F. Bruce explains, "Paul, by his own account was called distinctively to be Christ's apostle to the Gentile world. Yet Luke portrays him as going to the synagogue first in one place after another. Paul knew that the gospel which he was commissioned to proclaim was directed to all and sundry, 'to the Jew first and also the Greek' (Rom 1:16); he knew moreover that in synagogues of Greek and Roman cities he was likely to find some Gentile sympathizers attending the sabbath services, and if they could be won to faith in Christ they might form a nucleus of believers in each city that he visited."[47] We see in the Acts 13:16 and 26 synagogue setting, Paul is speaking not just to Jews but also to God-fearing gentiles. He is forming the nucleus of his gentile mission with God-fearing gentiles

This sermon falls into two parts with the message of salvation in Acts 13:26 serving as the center. The first part of the sermon, 13:16–25, is about the provision and promises made to Israel. The second part of the sermon, 13:27–37, is about the fulfillment of the promises made to Israel through Jesus the Davidic Messiah. Acts 13:38–41 is the evangelistic call to respond.[48]

Paul opens his sermon with a history lesson, modeling for us the importance of a framing story.[49] The gospel story only makes sense in a larger context, and the larger context is the history of Israel. In Acts 13:16–25 Paul walks us back in time and preaches through the story of Israel from God's election of the patriarchs all the way to the promise given to David of a king and a kingdom to come from his descendants. Paul traces Israel's history through Egypt, into the wilderness for 40 years, into the promise land with the conquest of Canaan. Then he takes us into the period of Judges, and into the monarchy beginning with Saul. Paul's history lesson crescendos with king David and the Davidic covenant. Keener points out how the story is one of God's benefaction to Israel giving them land (13:19), judges (13:20), a king (13:21) and finally a Savior (13:23).[50] Verse 23 is significant in that it

47. Bruce, "Significance of the Speeches for Interpreting Acts," 22.

48. Keener, *Acts*, 2053–55. Keener provides several very interesting outlines of the Acts 13 sermon.

49. In Paul's evangelistic sermon in Acts 17, he follows a very familiar pattern. He sets the gospel within the larger framing story of Israel, but he does so without referring to specific Old Testament texts. He alludes to Old Testament themes and theological concepts such as creation and Adam.

50. Keener, *Acts*, 2058.

connects Jesus to David and alludes to 2 Sam 7 and the Davidic Covenant. Jesus is the climax of God's saving story for Israel.

In Acts 13:24–37 the story makes a huge historical leap in time from David and fast-forwards directly to John the Baptist and Jesus. Acts 13:26 is the hinge that opens the door to Jesus and sets the stage for Paul's presentation that the promises of the past have been fulfilled now in the presence of this audience in the person of Jesus. This message is one of salvation. Salvation is a theme that runs through both Peter and Paul's sermons (Acts 2:40; 13:26; 13:47). Salvation refers to the promise of a Savior to Israel in Acts 13:23, and it is the good news promised to patriarchs in Acts 13:32–33. More specifically this promise to the patriarchs is a reference to the promise made to Abraham of land, descendants and a son (Gen 12:1–3; 17:5–8, 21; 21:1; Gal 3:29).

Gromacki summarizes Acts 13:27–37 well, saying:

> Paul proclaimed that Jesus is the fulfillment of the promised Messiah through David and that God raised him up after he was killed in fulfillment of the OT Scriptures (Acts 13:27–37) . . . . Paul supported the fulfillment of this promise by quoting three OT Messianic passages: Psalm 2:7 (v.33), Isaiah 55:3 (v.34) and Psalm 16:10 (v.35). These OT texts all found fulfillment in the resurrection of Jesus from the dead.[51]

Paul, just like Peter, uses two literal, kingly, Davidic Psalms, Psalms 2 and 16, to refer to Jesus. Both Paul and Peter boldly assert that these Psalms are not about David. Whatever your hermeneutic, you must find a way to get from the literal Old Testament interpretation of these Psalms referring to David to Paul and Peter's hermeneutic that make these Psalms about Jesus. It is this author's contention that it takes a christological, backwards reading hermeneutic of the Old Testament to reimagine and reinterpret these Psalms to be about Jesus, not David. Paul tees up the message of salvation in Acts 13:26 and then proceeds to focus almost exclusively in Acts 13:27–37 on the death, burial, and resurrection of Jesus as fulfillment of Old Testament promises. He spends the most amount of his time on resurrection in Acts 13:30–37 as opposed to just a few verses on Jesus's death in Acts 13:28–29.[52] This resurrection has witnesses according to Acts 13:31. The term *witness* is an important one in the book of Acts. In Acts 1:8 the apostles

---

51. Gromacki, "Preaching the Gospel in Acts and Today," 35.

52. It is safe to say that there is no full-fledged gospel presentation without a reference to resurrection. It is Paul's reference to resurrection in his gospel sermon in Acts 17:31–32 which was so controversial that it caused an abrupt interruption and end to his sermon.

are commissioned to be witnesses, and Luke uses these sermons from the eyewitnesses to show the Acts 1:8 mission being accomplished.

Paul's sermon ends in Acts 13:38–41 in some ways like a typical sermon today with application. Paul is asking for action. Think of this as his altar call. He starts this response section with "therefore," connecting the response to resurrection. It is as if Paul is saying, "Because Jesus rose from the dead, you must respond." It is because Jesus is raised that the forgiveness of sins is available. A connection is made with the content of the gospel, resurrection, and forgiveness of sins. The question must be asked, "Is forgiveness a result of the gospel or is it a core component of the gospel? Is forgiveness of sins something you must believe in or is forgiveness of sins a benefit that accrues because of your belief in the death, burial and resurrection of Jesus?" The close association of forgiveness of sins with resurrection lends credence to forgiveness of sins as a core component of the gospel. Paul's creedal, traditional confession of the gospel in 1 Cor 15:3–5 supports this contention as well.

The response necessary to receive the gospel is developed in v. 39. The Pauline response required is belief or faith. John M. Duncan suggests that the reason Paul's sermon does not call for repentance is, "because the Antiochene Jews had not taken part in the rejection and crucifixion of Jesus."[53] In Paul's sermon, forgiveness of sins and belief are connected, which is not his usual expression of soteriology. Larssen astutely points out:

> Paul is here speaking in a true Lukan fashion. 'Forgiveness of sins' is for Luke the usual phrase for expressing the central content of salvation, which can be seen throughout Acts (2.38; 3.18 f.; 5.31; 10.43 ff.). In the uncontested letters of Paul this expression is missing (except a quotation in Rom 4 7, cf. Eph 1.7; Col 1.14). The succeeding clause reveals on the other hand, a clear attempt to render Pauline thoughts and style: 'It is through him that everyone who has faith is acquitted of (justified from) everything for which there was no acquittal under the Law of Moses.'[54]

One must always keep in mind the two storied nature of the book when reading Acts. Luke is summarizing Paul's sermons, which requires some Lukan interpretation. Luke does introduce typical Pauline language of justification rather awkwardly in v. 39, which raises the question of where justification fits within the gospel. Gerhard Schneider as quoted by Bock argues that justification is the Pauline call to repent.[55] Keener addresses

53. Duncan, "Peter, Paul and the Progymnasmata," 349–65.
54. Larssen, "Paul," 426.
55. Bock, *Acts*, 458.

the issue saying, "The language of 'forgiveness of sins' is more Lukan than Pauline (though Paul certainly would not have objected to it), as is the specific phrase 'law of Moses,' but the language of justification by faith rather than works is distinctively Pauline (though Luke's inclusion of the language shows that he would not object to it)."[56] Justification appears to be the Pauline equivalent to Peter's "forgiveness of sins" and was used by Paul specifically in gentile contexts to explain Israel's God.

In verse 40 Paul uses the imperative "look" to grab his audience's attention. Paul is begging his audience to open their eyes to the coming judgment before it is too late.[57] He quotes the painful lesson of Babylonian judgment from Hab 1:5 to warn his audience not to wait to receive Jesus! While Paul doesn't use images of lakes of fire, he nonetheless concludes with a harsh prophetic tone of eschatological judgment if one does not put their faith in Jesus. Noticeably absent from Paul's presentation of the gospel is an emphasis on baptism and the Holy Spirit.

It is time now for us to begin pondering what wise gospeling can look like as we learn from the experts and move into our world, and we begin by comparing and contrasting the two apostolic gospel sermons.

Gospeling Comparisons

After closely examining the gospel sermons of Peter and Paul, it is plain to see that they have far more in common than not. In fact, Peter's Acts 2 sermon and Paul's Acts 13 sermon to Jewish audiences are almost identical. They both spend a large part of their presentation framing the gospel within the larger story of Israel (2:16–21; 13:16–23). Each of them draws heavily upon the Old Testament and both of them quote from Ps 16 (2:25–28; 13:35). A strong kingdom connection is made by both Peter and Paul drawing upon Davidic promises (2:34–36; 13:23). Jesus is presented as the fulfillment of Old Testament prophecies (2:29–32; 13:22–23; 13:32–35). In both sermons the gospel story is firmly rooted in the Old Testament Scriptures. For both Peter and Paul, the resurrection is the center of the gospel (2:24; 2:31–35; Acts 13:30–37). Neither focuses much attention on the cross, Jesus's death, or atonement theology. This may be explained by the fact that Luke has already covered this in great detail in volume 1 of his Gospel. Forgiveness of sin is a key feature of the gospel in both preacher's gospel sermons (2:38; 13:38). A prominent feature in both apostle's presentation of the gospel is warnings of

56. Keener, *Acts*, 2075.

57. In Paul's gospel presentation in Acts 17:31 he alludes to Jesus without specifically naming him and warns of coming judgment.

judgment (2:40; 13:40–41). However, there are some significant differences between Peter and Paul's gospeling, which raise some substantial questions regarding the exact content of the gospel.

Gospeling Contrasts

Some of the differences in their sermons may be accounted for by Luke's literary selectivity as he uses their sermons to move his plot forward. Luke, writing as many as thirty or more years after the preaching of Peter and Paul, has his own literary agenda. In other words, we must be careful how far we push the differences because we don't have full, verbatim manuscripts of their messages. With this in mind, it is important to point out some major differences in the apostles gospeling.

Paul is contextualizing the gospel to his gentile audience as he develops new ways of explaining the framing story to an audience not familiar with the Old Testament. He introduces the concept of justification into his gospeling whereas Peter focuses on repentance and belief. While baptism and the Spirit are prominent in Paul's letters, they are absent from his gospeling in Acts 13 and Acts 17. There seems to be little emphasis on the life and ministry of Jesus in Paul's gospeling. Regarding Paul's gospeling, McKnight points out some glaring differences from Peter's gospel, "In the two major gospelings of Paul in Acts (13:16–41; 17:22–31), we do not hear tones of the exaltation of Christ to the right hand of God and we hear nothing of the gift of the Holy Spirit."[58] When there is not uniformity in presentation of the gospel, this raises questions around the exact content of the gospel.

Applications for Wise Gospeling

It is wise to listen to experts. A wise approach to gospeling would be to learn from the first gospelers, the apostle Peter and Paul. It will be instructive to notice what is not a part of their gospeling. Next we would be wise to examine what they included in their gospel.

Stunningly absent from the apostle's gospeling is any mention of God's love. Their preaching does not begin with, "God loves you and offers a wonderful plan for your life." In fact, there is very little individual focus in the apostolic gospel other than at the end of their sermons calling for repentance, faith, and baptism. The modern focus on a better life and the portrayal of God as a doting parent showering his children with love

58. McKnight, "Gospeling the Gospel in Acts," 30–44, esp. 38.

and affirmation is completely absent from their gospel. In fact, there is a strong tone of warning and the promise of coming judgment. Over and over again I was shockingly surprised by what is not found in Peter and Paul's gospel presentations. While the cross is mentioned in each of their sermons, it is purely a reference to his death and is far from the central focus of their presentation. Often just a passing verse or at most two are devoted to the cross. McKnight comments on Paul's Acts 17 sermon saying, "It is noteworthy for a gospeling passage that Paul does not mention the crucifixion, and there's not a trace of an atonement theory at work in his gospeling in Athens."[59] Maybe a way of putting the cross in its proper perspective in the gospeling in the book of Acts is to think of Acts as Billy Graham evangelistic crusades and the epistles as seminary classrooms where atonement theology is developed and discussed.

In almost every modern-day gospel presentation there is a promise of eternal life in heaven. The apostles did not make this promise in any of their Acts sermons. Heaven is not viewed as the final goal of the believer. However, there are strong eschatological aspects to their sermons such as the warning of future judgment. While there is judgment language in the apostolic gospel, there are no specific mentions of hell and the wrath of God.

Now we need to take a closer look at what is included in the apostle's gospel. Again, there are some surprising discoveries. The story of Israel plays a prominent role in framing the gospel story. The kingdom concept of a Davidic ruler with references to Ps 16 and 110 runs through their gospel sermons. The identity and divinity of Jesus is a key element in apostolic gospeling. There is a disproportionate emphasis on resurrection and exaltation in their sermons suggesting that the victory won is more significant than the penalty paid. These were not feeling good and live better, more prosperous lives sermons. There is a strong tone of warning and judgment in their gospeling. Each of their gospel sermons concludes with some combination of repentance, faith, baptism, and the gift of the Holy Spirit.

As we think about our gospeling in light of apostolic gospeling, we should think about the tone of our gospel. Does our gospel have a dark, morose, tone to it, or does it have a triumphant tone? I suggest that our gospel should have a brighter, bolder, better tone to it. The gospel should have a sound of celebration. Bock rather humorously points out this tone of the gospel problem saying, "Sometimes we are guilty of what I call Jimmy Cagney theology. Remember Cagney from the old black and white gangster movies? 'You're the dirty rat that killed my brother.' Sometimes when I hear people in the church share the gospel, the emphasis I hear is, 'You dirty rat!

---

59. McKnight, "Gospeling the Gospel in Acts," 39.

You shouldn't be doing that? We spend more time being sure people are convicted of sin than pointing them to the good news that overcomes it."[60] Let's keep the good in the good news by focusing more on the resurrection of Jesus and exaltation of Christ as King. Jesus is at the right hand of God reigning today and that is good news! The best part of the gospel is an empty tomb. Jesus took the sting out of death. Up from the grave he arose. He won the cage match with sin, death, and the devil. The backdrop of the best part of the gospel is indeed death, but Jesus's resurrection, ascension, and enthronement are the best parts of the gospel, and they should not get lost in the theological weeds of atonement theories.

We can be wiser in the way we present the gospel if we are open to the learn from the apostles. I had a profound learning experience in seminary that marked me for life in a very good way as a teacher of God's Word. Believe it or not, it happened in a Greek class. This particular Greek class was a rite of passage at the seminary I attended, not because of the exegetical papers, but because you presented your work in front of the professor and your classmates, and they interrogated you. Interrogated may be too strong of word, but it was an intimidating and frightening experience. I was a good Greek student but I was terrified to defend my paper in front of a world-renowned Greek scholar. My worst fears came true. In my defense of my passage in 1 Cor 2 my professor asked me why I interpreted a particular Greek construction a certain way. My answer started out, "Because John Stott said . . . ," to which my professor interrupted, saying, "I don't care what John Stott said. I want to know why you said what you said, Mr. Phelps. I can stack commentaries up from scholars on both sides of this issue." Now, his questions may not have been quite as harsh as I just described them, but that's my story, and I am sticking to it! I learned an important lesson as a teacher of God's Word that day to take full responsibility for my own exegetical choices. Now almost every time I teach God's Word I have a mental picture of my seminary professor sitting in the back of the room, and at the end of my sermon, he is going to ask me why I interpreted the passage the way that I did. Don't get me wrong, I'm not terrified when I teach God's word but I do take it very seriously. I hope to leave a mental picture with you that will stick for a lifetime of gospeling. Every time you present the gospel from this point forward I pray that you will have a mental picture of the apostle Peter and Paul sitting in the back of the room, and at the end of your gospel presentation, they are going to ask you questions about your faithfulness to the gospel.

60. Bock, *Recovering the Real Lost Gospel*, 36.

Bibliography

Bock, Darrell L. *Acts*. Grand Rapids: Baker, 2007.

———. *Recovering the Real Lost Gospel*. Nashville: B & H Academic, 2010.

Bruce, F. F. *The Book of Acts*. Grand Rapids: Eerdmans, 1988.

———. "The Significance of the Speeches for Interpreting Acts." *Southwestern Journal of Theology* 33 (1990) 22.

Dodd, C. H. *The Apostolic Preaching and Its Developments*. Chicago: Willett, Clark & Co, 1937.

Duncan, John M. "Peter, Paul and the Progymnasmata: Traces of the Preliminary Exercises in the Missions Speeches of Acts." *Perspectives in Religious Studies* 41 (2014) 349–65.

Fernando, Ajith. *Acts: NIV Application Commentary*. Grand Rapids: Zondervan Academic, 1998.

Gromacki, Gary. "Preaching the Gospel in Acts and Today." *The Journal of Ministry and Theology* 20 (2016) 35.

Keener, Craig S. *Acts: An Exegetical Commentary*. 3 vols. Grand Rapids: Baker Academic, 2012–2014.

Kittel, Gerhard, et al., eds. *Theological Dictionary of the New Testament*. Grand Rapids: Eerdmans, 1985.

Ladd, George Eldon. *A Theology of the New Testament*. Grand Rapids: Eerdmans, 1974.

Larssen, Edvin. "Paul: Law and Salvation," *NTS* 31 (1985) 426.

Longman, Tremper, III. *Psalms: An Introduction and Commentary*. Downers Grove, IL: InterVarsity, 2014.

Marshall, I. Howard. *The Acts of the Apostles: An Introduction and Commentary*. Grand Rapids: Eerdmans, 1980.

McKnight, Scot. "Gospeling the Gospel in Acts." *Scriptura* 103 (2010) 30–44.

———. *The King Jesus Gospel: The Original Good News Revisited*. Grand Rapids: Zondervan, 2016.

Stenschke, Christoph W. "The Presentation of Jesus in the Missionary Speeches of Acts and the Mission of the Church." *Verbum et Ecclesia* 35 (2014) 1–18.

Stott, John R. W. *The Message of Acts*. The Bible Speaks Today. Downers Grove, IL: InterVarsity, 1990.

Strandenaes, Thor. "The Missionary Speeches in the Acts of the Apostles and Their Missiological Implications." *Svensk Missionstidskrift* 3 (2011) 341–54.

Walvoord, J. F., and R. B. Zuck, eds. *The Bible Knowledge Commentary: An Exposition of the Scriptures, Volume 1*. Wheaton: Victor, 1985.

White, Aaron W. "The Apostolic Preaching of the Lord Jesus: Seeing the Speeches in Acts as a Coherent Series of Sermons." *Presbyterion* 44 (2018) 33–51.

Wright, N. T., and Michael F. Bird. *The New Testament in Its World: An Introduction to the History, Literature, and Theology of the First Christians*. Grand Rapids: Zondervan Academic, 2019.

WISE POLITICS

By Ivan Ramirez

W ikipedia provides a good definition of subversion: "a process by which the values and principles of a system in place are contradicted or reversed, in an attempt to transform the established social order and its structures of power, authority, hierarchy, and social norms."[1] Subversion rises up out of a sense of injustice, the feeling that things are not right.

2020 has given us many examples of this. Let me highlight two. When COVID-19 began to spread in the US in March and April, people were asked to implement measures to help "curve" the spread of the virus. Non-essential businesses were closed and people who were able to work from home did. Folks stopped visiting with loved ones, restaurants transitioned to takeout, and Amazon made billions. Churches stopped meeting in person and pastors learned how to use Facebook Live or Zoom.

As shepherds we had to make a decision for our people. "Do we defy the state mandates and continue to meet in person, or do we comply?" We complied. Our doors were closed. Some for the first time in a hundred years. As time went on our willingness to submit to the governing authorities was tested. After four months or so people were concerned that the government's restrictions were infringing on our right to worship and that the virus was being used for political gain so they reopened their buildings for public worship. This is subversive. It was a decision to contradict the social order out of a sense of justice.

The second example I want to mention briefly because I don't want to demean the George Floyd family or revisit the heartache, but something should be said about that moment. When the video of the murder of George Floyd came to light, it was a tipping point. People were enraged because another Black man lost his life to police brutality. Enough was enough.

---

1. "Subversion": https://en.wikipedia.org/wiki/Subversion.

Throughout America the streets were flooded with people who were angry. Feeling like a cornered animal, they lashed out.

What I find interesting in both these examples is how the church responded. I cannot speak for every believer in our country. The view of the church's response comes from my personal eye test of what I saw and heard and is not intended to speak for anyone other than myself.

Those who claim the name of Jesus had strong reactions to both the cases of subversion. In the former, some felt that it was unwise and dangerous to open up churches too soon, while others were hailing those who defied the government's mandates as heroes who were standing up for religious freedom. In the latter, many people were moved by the injustice they saw. I think there was almost universal condemnation of his murder. But not so much when it came to understanding why people were angry and how racism is perpetuated by those empowered. People I consider friends were on social media being all kinds of ignit[2] about people of color.[3] One pastor, who serves in a homogenous community, was on Facebook saying things like "If people would just submit to authority they wouldn't have any problems" and "I don't have any problems with police." Having been falsely accused of a crime myself, one that would have resulted in my spending the rest of my life in prison, this rubbed me wrong.

Another commonality among the two cases is their intersect with politics. Jackson W. in speaking of honor-shame in Romans, rightly defines politics as "public influence."[4] Whether it is church or an election, people are continuously trying to influence others how to think and act. How many times has someone new walked into your church because they were tired of the "politics" at their church (what they don't tell you is that they are usually part of the problem).

Politics influences more of our day-to-day lives than we may realize. The question facing us is not "Are we political?" but "How can we be wise in our politics?" This question is extremely important for us pastors to get right. As leaders in our churches we influence those whom God has entrusted to our temporary care. If we do not provide them with the proper guidance on these issues then they will look to the world for help. And if our conversations and sermons about politics do not reflect the character of God and the content of his Word, then we are in danger of imprinting on them something that might look right but in reality is cloaked in

2. Ignit is a term used by us coloreds to describe people who think they know what they're talking about but in reality, they don't have a clue.

3. Personally, I feel that terms like "people of color" or "minority" are unhelpful and perpetuate classism. This will be the only time I use it in this chapter.

4. Jackson, *Reading Romans Through Eastern Eyes*, 172.

the wisdom of the world. The subversive wisdom of God provides us with answers to these issues and more.

The Subversive Wisdom of God

Who is Subverting Whom?

When speaking of the subversive wisdom of God I want to begin by explaining why God's wisdom is subversive. God created all things through wisdom, "The Lord by wisdom founded the earth; by understanding he established the heavens; by his knowledge the deeps broke open, and the clouds drop down the dew."[5] In his wisdom God made all things "good."[6] Some take this to mean that God created suitable conditions for humanity.[7] While I do not deny there is an element of this present in some usages of the word, it does not account for all its forms. A fuller definition can be obtained when we see this word through wisdom. It is out of this that "the good" becomes synonymous with life.

In Genesis 1 we read how God creates light out of darkness and brings order out of chaos. Each day God is busy ordering and growing what is necessary for life. After everything is put in its place God creates his image-bearers. When God finishes his work, he looks at it and calls it good. To conclude "good" as "suitable conditions for humanity" seems a bit redundant since humans are inhabiting space created. In addition to this, when we read about the tree of knowledge of good and evil, are we to conclude that it is the tree of knowledge of suitability and evil? Understanding "good" as life has more explanatory capacity.

Unfortunately, the good world God created did not stay that way for long. Genesis recounts the hostile takeover of our progenitors in chapter 3. They had one job: do not eat from the tree in the middle of the garden. But that is exactly what they do. Gen 3:6 is our downfall as subversion. First, Eve looks at the tree as "good for food." God has already provided an assortment of trees and plants and crops that were good for food. What was so special about this tree? The difference was God said no. Second, the tree "was a delight to the eye." Since we do not have any way of knowing exactly how the garden looked, we have no definitive way of know what

5. Prov 3:19–20. All translations from the NRSV unless otherwise indicated.

6. Gen 1:4,10,12,18,25,31.

7. Walton, *Genesis 1 as Ancient Cosmology*, 170.

the scenery was like. What are the odds it was unappealing? The word translated as "delight" implies an object of desire. She wanted that tree bad. Third, Eve looked to the tree "to make one wise." The tragic element about Eve's longing for wisdom is that it was already attainable through God. The type of wisdom the tree of knowledge of good and evil offered was worldly wisdom. A wisdom from below. Adam and Eve *subvert God's authority* and reject his wisdom for a wisdom of their own.

Consequently, when we talk about the subversive wisdom of God, it is not subversive in the sense that it is rebellious. On the contrary, it is subversive in that it goes against the grain of our worldly wisdom—wisdom that subverts God's original order. Subversion works both ways. But God's wisdom *is a bottom up view in which God subverts the wisdom of this world and the power structures that have been created as a result of our subversion to God's order.* God desired a world teaming with life, guided by his wise rule and authority through his image-bearers who were to execute his governance. What he got was usurpers who establish their own rule, authority, and power structures in accordance to their own wisdom. For God to re-establish his vision for the world, God must first subvert our wisdom. He does this by starting over with Abraham.

Subversive Wisdom and Abraham

The known world and its systems are all united in Gen 11. Things are good. Everyone is getting along, they have one system of governance, people are working together. Things are good. Or are they? Tragically, this unity is at its core a subversive defiance against God. This defiance is seen in the words of the people, "Come, let us build ourselves a city, and a tower with its top in the heavens, and let us make a name for ourselves; otherwise we shall be scattered abroad upon the face of the whole earth."[8] The language of the people is reminiscent of Gen 1:26 where God says "let us make humankind in our image . . . "[9] The similarities between the words of God and the words of the people create a link between the two actions but from different perspectives. When God says "let us" it is a selfless act of creating. When the nations say "let us" it describes a selfish act of retention. God responds by scattering the people and starting anew.

God reveals himself to one who dwells among the usurpers, Abram. Wisdom of Solomon tells us, "when the peoples of the world were thrown into confusion by the combined force of their wickedness, Wisdom found one

8. Gen 11:4.
9. Gen 1:26.

who did what was right . . . "[10] God by his wisdom subverts the established orders and implements his Edenic plan through Abraham and Sarah. Abraham becomes a new Adam in which God will create a new humanity (innumerable descendants)[11] and Sarah becomes a new Eve whose seed will establish a new kingdom; a new system of governance that is in line with God.[12]

Subversive Wisdom and King David

Israel wanted a king like the nations.[13] Samuel was advanced in years and his sons were not fit to lead. The people came to him and demand a king to rule over them. A king like the other nations. God was not opposed to kings. We read above how God promised Sarah that nations and kings will come from her. The offense was not that they wanted a king *perse*, rather the offense was in wanting a king like the nations, they were rejecting God's kingship "comply with the people's request—everything they ask of you—because they haven't rejected you. No, They've rejected me as king over them."[14] Samuel complies with the request of the people, at the behest of Yahweh, but not without informing the people what kind of king they will get—one just like the nations:

> These will be the ways of the king who will reign over you: he will take your sons and appoint them to his chariots and to be his horsemen, and to run before his chariots; and he will appoint for himself commanders of thousands and commanders of fifties, and some to plow his ground and to reap his harvest, and to make his implements of war and the equipment of his chariots. He will take your daughters to be perfumers and cooks and bakers. He will take the best of your fields and vineyards and olive orchards and give them to his courtiers. He will take one-tenth of your grain and of your vineyards and give it to his officers and his courtiers. He will take your male and female slaves, and the best of your cattle and donkeys, and put them to his work. He will take one-tenth of your flocks, and you shall be his slaves.[15]

10. Wis 10:5 (Common English Bible, CEB).

11. Gen 12:1–3.

12. Gen 17:15–16 God changes Sarai's name to Sarah and promises to bless her and give Abraham a son from her. Nations and kings of people will from her.

13. 1 Sam 8:1–9.

14. 1 Sam 8:7 (CEB).

15. 1 Sam 8:11–17.

Saul is chosen as king. He has everything the people are looking for in a king: he comes from a powerful tribe, rich family, he's very handsome, and tall, popular with the ladies. What more could the people ask for? There was one thing Saul was lacking . . . wisdom. Saul's reign can be summed up as folly. He is wise in his own eyes. His rejection of wisdom is seen in the way he continuously rejects God's commands. This comes to a head in 1 Sam 13. 1 Sam 10:8 sets up the situation.

Samuel gives Saul explicit instructions to wait for him one week and not to offer any sacrifices until Samuel arrives in one week. He had one job. Rather than waiting Saul, seeing that the people were beginning to leave him for fear of their enemies, he decided to do the one thing he wasn't supposed to do. He offers up sacrifices.[16] When Samuel arrives on the seen and sees what Saul has done, and says, "you have done foolishly . . . "[17] This act, which was one in a series of foolish choices, revealed the heart of Saul, he was a fool who did what was right in his own eyes.[18]

God rejects the people's choice for king and *subverts their wisdom* by choosing a new king: David. David is different. He's a small-town shepherd. He was not stately or tall. In fact, when Samuel had Jesse's sons before him, Samuel thought maybe the Lord was choosing David's brother Eliab because of his appearance. But God's subversive wisdom does not look at the external.[19] Jesse did not even bother to bring David before Samuel. Yet, the very one who was overlooked was the one who was to be king. David didn't have all the qualities that Saul had, but he had the one that mattered most . . . wisdom. 1 Sam 13 God rejects Saul and says, "the LORD has sought out a man after his own heart . . . "[20] That is, the Lord is going to establish a new king who fears him. Prov 1:7 says, "The fear of the LORD is the beginning of knowledge; fools despise wisdom and instruction." The wisdom of king David can be perceived through his writing:

> The law of the LORD is perfect, reviving the soul; the decrees of the LORD are sure, making wise the simple; the precepts of the LORD are right, rejoicing the heart; the commandment of the LORD is clear, enlightening the eyes; the fear of the LORD is pure, enduring forever; the ordinances of the LORD are true and righteous altogether. More to be desired are they than gold,

---

16. 1 Sam 10:8.
17. 1 Sam 13:13.
18. Prov 3:7.
19. 1 Sam 16:6–7.
20. 1 Sam 13:14.

even much fine gold; sweeter also than honey, and drippings of the honeycomb.[21]

Suffice to say, the choice of David over Saul was dictated by wisdom.

Subversive Wisdom and Jesus

Up to this point, we have looked at a few key examples of the subversive wisdom of God. There are several other examples to use, but I wanted to highlight some key movements in God's plan to demonstrate how his wisdom goes against the grain of the wisdom of this world. We're almost ready to begin to speak to the topic at hand "Wise Politics" but our picture will not be clear without looking at the greatest example of subversive wisdom: Jesus.

Jesus: Wisdom of God

The battle between the wisdom of the world and the subversive wisdom of God receives its clearest articulation in 1 Cor 1:17–24. Oh-Young Kwon insightfully lays out the difference between the two:

> Paul draws distinctive contrasts between the wisdom of God and that of the world in 1 Corinthians 1–4 (e.g., 1:18–25; 2:6–7), wherein he appears to highlight intrinsic distinctions of quality between the two sorts of wisdom. Paul seems to refer to the wisdom of the world as a human-thought-based and cultural-conventions-oriented wisdom that dominated the thinking of some in the Corinthian Christian community…Contrasting with this cultural-conventions-oriented wisdom, Paul presents the wisdom of God as the "foolish" yet powerful wisdom of Christ crucified. This sort of wisdom has a power that saves and transforms people who believe in Jesus Christ (1:21, 24;2 :7).[22]

Worldly wisdom created segregation (1:12), elitism (1:20), a celebrity culture of leadership (2:1–4; 3:5, 21), spiritual fighting and jealousy (3:3), bragging about things they should be ashamed of (5:2), and lawsuits (6:1) and the like.

The fire that was fueling such activities came from the elite in Corinth. The Corinthian wisdom of the wealthy and powerful pride in their social status. Again, Oh-Young states:

21. Ps 19:7–10.
22. Kwon, *1 Corinthians 1–4*, 190.

The wealth and high social status that wealthier Corinthian Christians possessed supports the argument that some of the Corinthian Christians had frequent contacts with Corinthians who had full Roman citizenship and power, and control of the social political positions in the Corinthian civic society. They were therefore heavily influenced by the social and cultural value systems characterized by patronal networks and rhetorical conventions (1 Cor. 2:1—5:9).[23]

The elite's pursuit of status and honor would require them to support the big dinners of the rich and powerful where they would participate in drunkenness and orgies (6:12–20). They ate at temples dedicated to the emperor where they would have venerated him as a god and affirmed him as "lord, savior, and god, and implicitly worshipping his as the universal patron."[24]

The wisdom of the world sets its gaze on things like honor, status, and power. God's subversive wisdom is found in weakness, shame, and dishonor. It's found in Jesus,"... the power of God and the wisdom of God."[25] In other words, the message of the cross.

Paul's focus on the cross is not designed to introduce a theory of atonement. Far too long we have been conditioned to see red every time we read references to the cross. But this is not the meaning here. Rather, Paul points the Corinthians to the subversive wisdom of God found in a dirty, heavy cross. When Paul calls Christ "the wisdom of God" (1 Cor 1:24) he is referring to the way in which God overturns the en-cultured wisdom of honor and status with a wisdom of shame. And through the wisdom of shame and dishonor achieves his greatest victories. This wisdom is embodied in Jesus.

Wisdom Walking

Jesus is wisdom in motion. The places he goes the people he sees and things he does flow from wisdom. Naturally, if we are to develop wise politics we must look to Jesus's life, especially his interactions with power and authority as a model for developing our own. I would like to briefly look at three things: the Gospel of John's portrait of Jesus as wisdom in his opening chapter, Jesus's subversive kingdom ethic in the Sermon on the Mount, and his interactions with authorities. This will help to establish a framework for understanding how the authors of the NT theologized Jesus's life into their own contexts.

23. Kwon, *1 Corinthians 1–4*, 193.
24. Kwon, *1 Corinthians 1–4*, 191.
25. 1 Cor 1:24.

Like an epoch tale the Gospel of John opens with a view from above that captures the imagination and stirs our hearts, "In the beginning was the Word, and the Word was with God, and the Word was God. He was in the beginning with God. All things came into being through him, and without him not one thing came into being. What has come into being in him was life, and the life was the light of all people. The light shines in the darkness, and the darkness did not overcome it."[26] The opening of the Gospel of John is not only great writing (what an opener) but allows us to get a behind the scenes look at Jesus. A look that shapes our understanding of who he is in the Fourth Gospel.[27] In John what sets one person apart from another was their ability to understand Jesus as the *logos*, the one who came down from above. Understanding Jesus as the *logos* is life. Rejecting this knowledge is death. I'm going to argue that one of the main takeaways from the first chapter of John, in addition to the ones we are more familiar with, like Jesus's equality with the Father, is how Jesus is the embodiment of wisdom. We will highlight a few aspects of the christological opening of John's Gospel to bring the connection between Jesus and Wisdom to the fore.

Reading John's[28] opening words "In the beginning . . ." conjures up images of Genesis one, "In the beginning God created the heavens, and earth." The echo seems clear enough. What is not as clear to us is the connection between Gen 1 and Prov 8. In Proverbs, Wisdom is active in creating along side of God. Prov 8:22–36 describes Lady[29] Wisdom and her role in creation and ability to impart life. Wisdom says:

> When he established the heavens, I was there, when he drew a circle on the face of the deep, when he made firm the skies above,when he established the fountains of the deep, when he assigned to the sea its limit,so that the waters might not transgress his command, when he marked out the foundations of the earth, then I was beside him, like a master worker;and I was dailyhis delight, rejoicing before him always . . . "[30]

Wisdom is both a spectator and a participant. Wisdom joyfully looks on as the Master Builder creates, establishing limits for the sea, marking our the

26. John 1:1–5.

27. Witherington, *Jesus the Sage*, 287.

28. Johannine authorship does require John to be the sole author. It would be far to assume that a group of John's disciples played a big part in shaping the final form of the Gospel (see John 21:24). I will continue to use John as a shorthand.

29. Proverbs speaks of Lady Wisdom. This personification of wisdom is not ontological but more metaphorical.

30. Prov 8:27–30.

foundations of the earth. Wisdom is also an active participant. She works alongside Yahweh like a master worker.

The retelling of the creation account in Proverbs 8 informs us that God had a co-creator who was both spectator and participant named Wisdom. This is exactly what John tells us: that God had a co-creator named the Word. It would be fair then to see echoes of Prov 8:27—30 in John 1:1 where the Word is likewise present and participating in creation. This does not deify Wisdom but gives us a different angle by which the early church viewed Jesus as the embodiment of wisdom.

The relationship between Jesus and Wisdom is strengthened in 1:2, " . . . in him was life, and the life was the light of all people."[31] Prov 8:35 calls to "sons" and offers blessing to those who will listen. 8:35 says, "For whoever finds me finds life and obtains favor from the LORD . . . "[32] Ben Witherington III, in commenting on the connection between Proverbs and John, says, "There one learns that personified Wisdom was present at creation, but also that she called God's people back to the right paths and offered them life and favor from God (cf. 8:35). These are the very things being said of the Word as well in this hymn."[33]

John continues to use wisdom motifs in 1:10–12: " . . . the world came into being through him; yet the world did not know him. He came to what was his own, and his own people did not accept him. But to all who received him, who believed in his name, he gave power to become children of God . . . "[34] Proverbs 8:35–36 highlight the blessing of life for those who receive her but to those who reject her, death awaits.

The last verse I want to call attention to in chapter one that connects Jesus with Wisdom is 1:14. In 1:14 John says, "And the Word became enfleshed and pitched his tent among us . . . "[35] This passage is reminiscent of Sir 24:8–12:

> Then the Creator of all things gave me a command, and my Creator chose the place for my tent. He said, 'Make your dwelling in Jacob, and in Israel receive your inheritance.' Before the ages, in the beginning, he created me, and for all the ages I shall not cease to be. In the holy tent I ministered before him, and so I was established in Zion. Thus in the beloved city he gave me a

---

31. John 1:4.

32. Prov 8:35.

33. Witherington, *Jesus the Sage*, 284.

34. John 1:10–12.

35. Author's own translation.

resting place, and in Jerusalem was my domain. I took root in an honored people, in the portion of the Lord, his heritage.

Before commenting on the similarity between John and Sirach, let me say a quick word about the value of Second Temple Literature.

On my desk there are several Bibles and other books. The other books, whether commentaries, theologies, and more are my conversation partners. They challenge my thinking about the inspired text but we are not always in agreement. These authors inform my thinking about the Bible but they are never elevated to the same status as the Word. This is a helpful way of thinking about books like the Apocrypha. They where conversation partners with Judeans and the early church but they did not define nor supersede inspired texts. The authors of the NT lived in a world where these books existed and influenced the thinking of the NT authors when their writings were consistent with Scripture. Let's return to the matter at hand.

The word for "tent" *skene*[36] in Sir 24:8 is the same Greek word use by John in 1:14. It can be use to describe persons dwelling (Heb 11:9) but more often this word is used to describe a kind of temple that can apply to false gods (see Acts 7:43) or the dwelling place of God (see Acts 7:44; Heb 8:2; Rev 21:3).

Sirach describes Wisdom descending from God and tenting among his people. Wisdom is sent to Zion to dwell among Jacob. John's portrait of the decent of the Word, while having some key differences, is thematically the same. So much so that we can safely conclude that the Word enfleshed is the embodiment of Wisdom.

A key difference between John and Sirach in their pictures of the tenting of the Word and Wisdom is the personal nature of the Word and the rejection he encounters from his own. This rejection, the subversion by humans of God's own wisdom, results in a world-wide opportunity for anyone to receive him and by receiving him become children of God. God subverts the rejection of the Word enflesh by working through this rejection to create an opening for the world to come to him.

Another area of difference is the identity of Wisdom. Sirach's wisdom is nameless and faceless. John's Wisdom has a face and a name. The same Word who is equal with the Father is enfleshed in Jesus. Thus what Proverbs and Sirach personify as a second power present with God, John identifies as the second person of the Godhead, who came down to dwell with us. Wisdom walks.

---

36. John uses the verb for this word.

Wisdom Talks

Not only does wisdom walk, wisdom talks. In Jesus, who is the embodiment of wisdom, we see how wisdom speaks to power and authority. Spoiler alert: it is *subversive*. To say that the empowered in Jesus's day were annoyed by him would be a monumental understatement. From their perspective the whole world was beginning to follow him, which was not good for their business. Jesus walked a fine line where he spoke truth/wisdom to power while never crossing over into insurrection.

Jesus at the end of his Sermon from the Mount[37] tells the people, "Everyone then who hears these words of mine and acts on them will be liken to a wise man . . . And everyone who hears these word of mine and does not act on them will be like a foolish man . . . "[38] Jesus's teaching are wisdom. Those who become his disciples, who act on his words become wise. Rejection is folly and destruction. Who are the ones who reject him? The empowered. Jesus, even at this early stage in his ministry, speaks truth to power. This can seen through Jesus's use of "hypocrites" in the Gospel of Matthew. Have you ever been around someone who you felt was talking about you but they were not addressing you directly? I think this is what's going on here with Jesus and the empowered. He is indirectly addressing their conduct, later he will address them directly. In 7:1 Jesus says, "Do not judge, so that you may not be judged." While this can apply to all he seems to have specific people in mind. We are given some insight who he has in mind when he calls them "hypocrites" in 7:5.

Throughout the Gospel of Matthew the hypocrites are the empowered. In 6:2 Jesus tells those in the crowds "when you give alms, do not sound a trumpet before you, as the hypocrites do in the *synagogues* and streets, so that they may be praised by others."[39] In 6:5 they are not to pray like the hypocrites, "for they love to stand and pray in the *synagogues* and at the street corners, so that they may be seen by others."[40] Same goes for fasting. The crowds listening are given a template for preforming "religious" activities that is contradictory to the way the empowered have been modeling. We can already see how Jesus's teaching about judging has an eye towards the empowered.

Jesus continues to call out the empowered's hypocrisy throughout the Gospel. Jesus points out the hypocrisy of the scribes and Pharisees who

---

37. See McKnight et al., *Sermon on the Mount*, 2015.

38. Matt 7:24, 26.

39. Italics added for emphasis.

40. Italics added for emphasis.

break the commandments of God for the sake of tradition. Jesus calls them hypocrites whom Isaiah prophesied about, "'This people honors me with their lips, but their hearts are far from me; in vain do they worship me, teaching human precepts as doctrines.'"[41]

The conflict between Jesus and the empowered comes to a boiling point in chapters 22 to 26. Jesus is challenged several times by the empowered at Jerusalem. Over and over again he calls them "hypocrites" who are more concerned about their power and authority than the kingdom of God (22:18; 23:13,15,23,25,27,29). The last occurrence of "hypocrite" appears in Jesus's parable of wise and unwise slaves. The wise slave is found to be doing the masters will, while the wicked slave sees the masters delay as an opportunity to empower himself. Earlier we used Jackson's short but clear definition of politics: influencing people. The "hypocrites," those empowered, used their influence to grow their power base, increase the divide between them and the disempowered, and suppress opposition. Tragically, their primary weapon was the Word of God. They used the people's ignorance of its content, since most were illiterate, to gain and grow in power (unfortunately, this also happens in our churches).

Jesus does not hold back one bit in speaking truth/wisdom to power. Yet, he does so within their own rules. He never crosses over the line into insurrection. To be sure, the empowered accused him of this crime, but no charge against him would stick. Mark tells us, "Now the chief priests and the whole council were looking for testimony against Jesus to put him to death; but they found none."[42] The subversive words that Jesus spoke were words of truth/wisdom and as such they were above reproach. But this do not mean they were without consequences.

Wisdom Dies

When we speak truth, particularly to those empowered, we can have a mindset that things people will hear our wisdom and respond appropriately . . . . Wrong! I learned early on in ministry that people generally resist wisdom and truth. This is true now and it was true then. Speaking truth to power got Jesus murdered.

The wisdom of the world is on full display by the empowered at the trial of Jesus, and she's a "full tilt diva."[43] Since they could not best him in debates, and were bleeding power, they decided to kill him. They violate everything

41. Isa 29:13 LXX quoted in Matt 15:8–9.
42. Mark 14:55.
43. Tony Stark in Whedon, Joss, dir., *Avengers;* Walt Disney Studios, 2012.

they were supposed to stand for and show how true Jesus's spoke about them. And they seem fine with it. The most important thing to the empowered is power. When this is threatened power goes nuclear to protect itself.

The empowered use the one thing the know they can trap Jesus with . . . the truth. When Jesus is pressed under oath (they clearly did not hear his teaching on this matter) if he is the Messiah, the Son of God, Jesus replies "You have said it . . . But I tell you, in the future you will see the Son of Man seated at the right hand of Power and coming on the clouds of heaven."[44] Rather than rejoicing over this news the empowered use it to have Jesus crucified by Rome. The high king of heaven and earth, the one will receive all power over every system is crucified by his own kinsmen. Wisdom dies a shameful death. Yet hope remains.

Wisdom Wins

The subversive wisdom of God gains its greatest expression in the death of the Messiah. For it was in dying that Jesus won. Jesus overturns the power of the empowered through his death and resurrection. He ascends to the seat of power from where he holds all power and authority. He subverts the wisdom of the world through his death and by dying defeats all his enemies. This subversive wisdom is what Paul and other authors in the NT call Jesus followers to emulate in their life and politics.

Subversive Wisdom and Paul

In Rom 13:1–7 Paul instructs the church at Rome how they are to conduct themselves in the State. He uses the *subversive wisdom of God* as a guide for their conduct. Paul views the story of God from Adam to Abraham to David to Jesus as a grand display of wisdom. In Rom 11:33–36 Paul takes a moment to look back at the way God has worked in the world and breaks out in a medley of Scripture quotations in high praise to God for his wisdom, "O the depth of the riches and wisdom and knowledge of God! How unsearchable are his judgments and how inscrutable his ways! 'For who has known the mind of the Lord? Or who has been his counselor?' 'Or who has given a gift to him, to receive a gift in return?' For from him and through him and to him are all things. To him be the glory forever. Amen."

This passage functions like a door hinge moving his argument from the wisdom of God in the gospel to the outworking of this wisdom within

44. Matt 26:24.

the church. On one side of the door is the subversive wisdom of God in the degrading death and power filled resurrection that won life for all who align themselves under King Jesus. The other side of the door is the subversive wisdom of God lived out in the church.

12:1 is grammatically hyperlinked to 11:33–36 (and chapters 1 to 11 for that matter). His call to be living sacrifices flows out of the story of God and present an example of what this looks like:

> For while we were still weak, at the right time Christ died for the ungodly. Indeed, rarely will anyone die for a righteous person— though perhaps for a good person someone might actually dare to die. But God proves his love for us in that while we still were sinners Christ died for us. Much more surely then, now that we have been justified by his blood, will we be saved through him from the wrath of God. For if while we were enemies, we were reconciled to God through the death of his Son, much more surely, having been reconciled, will we be saved by his life. But more than that, we even boast in God through our Lord Jesus Christ, through whom we have now received reconciliation.[45]

A living sacrifice suffers humiliation and degradation for its enemies. It does not impose its power on the weak, on the contrary it gives its best for the weak and helpless. By this the "living sacrifices" experience the power of God. That power that is able to overcome the world.

A few verses later Paul focuses on their thought patterns in a way that is reminiscent of 1 Cor 1:18–24: "Do not be conformed to this world, but be transformed by the renewing of your minds, so that you may discern what is the will of God—what is good and acceptable and perfect."[46] Conformity to this world looks like the pseudo-wisdom that is in fact foolish since it resist God and chases after whatever feels good. Conformity is seen in chapter 2 through the hypocrisy of those who think they are in the covenant because they have the badges of the old but in reality are storing up for themselves wrath. Conformity submits to fear and all his buddies. This worldly wisdom will never bring about the power of God. Paul's opening statement in chapter 12 sets out what it means to live out the non-conformist the wisdom of God.

In 12:21 Paul instructs the church, "do not be overcome by evil, but overcome evil with good." This sets up what he will say about government power. Unfortunately this connection often goes overlooked resulting in the lost of Paul's connection with subversion. Paul's instruction to submit to

45. Rom 5:6–11.

46. Rom 12:2.

governing authorities is not requiring unchecked allegiance to those who are in power. As we saw from Jesus, this is not at all the case. But it does call us to take a posture of submission even in the mist of challenging the powers. In 13:2 says that whoever resists authority, resists God. Not all resistance is the same. There is a type of resistance that honors God even if it is confrontational to the powers while not crossing over reproachable actions centered in folly. At some point in Paul's life he "resisted" authority resulting in his martyrdom. But this resistance would have been a refusal to conform to the world and the demand of worldly powers. While we don't have a written record of his death, we can say with high certainty that he died at the hands of Rome, the superpower of his day. His death most likely came about because of his refusal to compromise the gospel.

The resistance Paul is pointing to is centered in folly and pride. It stirs up controversies and disconnection from others in the church by even talking about not paying taxes or dishonoring Rome. Which would be bad for the church. This wrongdoer resists the authority of God by not conforming to a gospel ethic centered in love, walking in the wisdom of God. Wise politics flows out of a gospel ethic of overcoming evil with good.

Subversive Wisdom and Peter

In 1 Peter we read:

> For the Lord's sake accept the authority of every human institution, whether of the emperor as supreme, or of governors, as sent by him to punish those who do wrong and to praise those who do right. For it is God's will that by doing right you should silence the ignorance of the foolish. As servants of God, live as free people, yet do not use your freedom as a pretext for evil. Honor everyone. Love the family of believers. Fear God. Honor the emperor.[47]

Peter seems to take a hard-line approach when it comes to obeying governing authorities. Especially when one considers how these authorities are partly responsible for the various trials the family of God is experiencing. But, if we read on to chapter 3, it may provide more context that may shed some light on this passage.

There are three ideas present in chapter 3 that can help us understand Peter's guidance for interacting with the state. Peter uses similar language as Paul in 3:9: "Do not repay evil for evil or abuse for abuse; but on the contrary, repay with a blessing." Though the situations are different between the church

---

47. 1 Pet 2:13–17.

at Rome and those to whom Peter is writing, the framework behind their writings are both centered in a gospel ethic that flows from wisdom.

Peter's connection to wisdom in 3:9–12 is more direct. He quotes Ps 34, a wisdom psalm, to ground his gospel ethic in wisdom: "Which of you desires life, and covets many days to enjoy good? Keep your tongue from evil, and your lips from speaking deceit. Depart from evil, and do good; seek peace, and pursue it. The eyes of the Lord are on the righteous, and his ears are open to their cry. The face of the Lord is against evildoers, to cut off the remembrance of them from the earth."[48] This psalm is categorized as a wisdom psalm. It contains key themes found in wisdom literature. Themes like the fear of the Lord (34:9,11), the blessings that flow out of the fear of God (34:10) the destructive end of the wicked (34:21), and the protection of the righteous (34:22).

Peter also grounds his words in a gospel ethic, "For it is better to suffer for doing good, if suffering should be God's will, than to suffer for doing evil. For Christ also suffered for sins once for all, the righteous for the unrighteous, in order to bring you to God. He was put to death in the flesh, but made alive in the spirit . . . "[49] The same principles we saw in Paul are all present here. Thus, when we read his instructions to the church about their conduct with the state, it is important to remember that, just like Paul, Peter's guidance flows out of a subversive wisdom that gains its greatest victory through a subversive wisdom of weakness. It can be observed that church tradition knows Peter died the death of a martyr precisely for his subversive wisdom.

Wise Politics

In order to develop wise politics *we first need to develop a gospel ethic.* I want to take a second to explain what I mean by gospel. As you have read in John Phelps's chapter the way in which the church speaks about the gospel today does not reflect the gospel.[50] A typical gospel presentation will focus on four truths: 1. Humans are sinners; 2. sin separates us from God; 3. Jesus died for your sins; 4. pray to receive Christ and you'll spend eternity with God in heaven when you die. Again, these things are all true but they are not the gospel. At best they are a theology of anthropology with some atonement theory. I'm not saying God hasn't used these truths to draw people to him. I myself prayed the sinner's prayer when I began

48. Ps 34:12–16.

49. 1 Pet 3:17–18.

50. Pp. 208–228.

my walk with him. But I wish someone would have shared with me then what I will share with you now. I want to briefly give you some key details found in 1 Cor 15 that define the gospel.[51]

1. The gospel Paul proclaimed is the gospel (15:1–2).

2. The gospel is inseparable from the story of God and the story of Israel continued on through King Jesus (15:3,4).

3. The gospel is about life of King Jesus; the Messiah (15:3).

4. The gospel is about the death of King Jesus for sins (15:3).

5. The gospel is about the resurrection of King Jesus (15:4–28).

6. The gospel is about the victory of King Jesus over death both now and at the end (15:24).

7. The gospel is about the reign of King Jesus (15:25).

There is more that can be said and other nuances that can be added but this gives us a better foundation for describing the gospel. Why does this matter? *Because a gospel ethic that comes from the plan of salvation is insufficient to hold the weight of subversive wisdom.*

A gospel ethic that can hold the weight of wise politics *needs to be robust and full.* Politics are a dirty business and a gospel that just focuses on my need to have my sins forgiven so I can go to heaven does not have the power to transform the politics of the people. All you have to do is go on any social media platform and read the comments of the people in your church. Too many are devoid of a gospel ethic that calls to be living sacrifices. Rather, they reflect the same hate and arrogance promoted by the wisdom of the world. This is directly link to a lack of understanding of the gospel and its power to transform our culture-based thinking.

Wise politics are *incarnational.* World-based-politics are inherently divisive and create an us-against-them mentality. The very idea of a political party breeds separation. A gospel ethic goes to those whom they disagree and sacrifices for their well being. Jesus models for us what it looks like to go to those who are different.

Wise politics *honors authority figures as an extension of their honor for God.* This is something the Lord has been convicting me about. I have often spoke of authority figures in a way that was not honoring them. I realized that I was also dishonoring God. I repented of this horrible sin and I'm getting better at handing over control of my tongue to the Spirit. Perhaps you need to do the same?

51. The following comes out of McKnight, *King Jesus Gospel*, 45–62.

Wise politics *speaks truth to power.* Injustices exist. Racism exists. Inequality exists. Sex trafficking exists. Most of us feel powerless to do anything of real significance about these issues and more. But there are those in positions of authority who can enact some measure of change. It is our responsibility as followers of Christ to speak truth to these issues.

Wise politics is *able to discern between the wisdom of the world and wisdom from God.* This one is tricky because culture-based-wisdom is really good at hiding. A quick gauge you can use is this, "Am I pushing people away with my political rhetoric?" This is a good gauge because worldly wisdom divide, the wisdom of God is life. God's word instructs us to strive for peace when it is in your power to do so. If my politics are causing my brother to stumble then they might be worldly.

Wise politics *wins by losing.* I'm not referring to the election results. What I'm referring to is our constant need to be right and our inability to let go of an issue until I have beaten my opponent into submission. This is not the way of Christ. He models for us a system that wins by dying. This is the subversive wisdom of God that forms wise politics.

Wise politics are not only possible *they are available* to all who answer the call of wisdom. The call that tells us to lose our lives to gain them. The call to turn the other cheek and go two miles when force to go one. This call comes from the incarnate Son who embodies and models how subversive wisdom is the means by which we can change the world. That is wise politics.

Bibliography

Jackson, W. *Reading Romans Through Eastern Eyes.* Downers Grove, IL: InterVarsity, 2019.

Kwon, Oh-Young. *1 Corinthians 1–4: Reconstructing Its Social and Rhetorical Situation and Re-Reading It Cross-Culturally for Korean-Confucian Christians Today.* Eugene, OR: Wipf & Stock, 2010.

McKnight, Scot. *The King Jesus Gospel: The Original Good News Revisited.* Grand Rapids: Zondervan, 2011.

McKnight, Scot, et al. *Sermon on the Mount.* Grand Rapids: Zondervan, 2016.

Walton, John H. *Genesis 1 as Ancient Cosmology.* Winona Lake, IN: Eisenbrauns, 2011.

Witherington, Ben, III. *Jesus the Sage: the Pilgrimage of Wisdom.* Minneapolis: Fortress, 2000.

Wu, Jackson, and E. Randolph Richards. *Reading Romans with Eastern Eyes: Honor and Shame in Paul's Message and Mission.* Downers Grove, IL: InterVarsity, 2019.

WISE SOCIAL MEDIA

By Scot McKnight

Bird-watchers over time learn to detect the distinguishing marks of birds, those features—height, bill, color, shape, posture, voice—that distinguish one bird from another. Say, a northern cardinal from a cedar waxwing. Walking around our village's small lake recently I spotted a female northern shoveler by the length of its bill and how it kept its bill down as it swam low in the water. Those are distinguishing marks, and bird-watchers know the marks.

The singular distinguishing mark of a pastor is a pastoral care for people. Pastors don't just "pastor" their own people. No, they have a character formed in Christ that is pastoral to the core, which means they treat all people with pastoral care. Perhaps the best place to check a person's pastoral care is on the person's social media. Truth be told, wise churches and search committees begin with social media, though some candidates are shrewd enough to create anonymous or pseudonymous shadow Twitter names so that they are harder to find. Good pastors don't create shadow personalities and don't have secret social media pages. If I were on a search committee and discovered a candidate had one, I'd scratch them off the list. Why are they hiding behind a false identity? What else are they hiding?

Some think pastoral care is a kind of paternalism, but paternalism for those under one's care and under one's authority and within the affirmation of a pastor are not the same as pastoring. More could be said about this but what follows expounds on that very difference.

Aimee Byrd wrote a book that called into questions some features of the so-called "biblical manhood and womanhood" movements.[1] She's a contributing person in a conservative, traditional branch of the Reformed faith. Pastors are male, theologians are male, power pervades. Some didn't

1. Byrd, *Recovering from Biblical Manhood and Womanhood.*

like her book because it exposed male power where power was not meant to be. Some of her critics, pastors mind you, went "public" on a site called Geneva Commons, a supposedly private Facebook page, and the comments became known. So much for privacy on a private Facebook page.

The comments were vile, and profoundly un-Christian and lacking Christian character. The comments ought not to have come from anyone considered a pastor as they did not have the mark of pastoral care. Sad to say, they didn't have the slightest idea of how to treat people, let alone women, let alone people under their (supposed) pastoral care. Here are some of the exchanges:

> Shane Anderson, a pastor, asks "Where is her husband?" He's insinuating that she's not acting under the authority of a male.
>
> Thomas Roof: "More housewife, less theologian pls" (she wrote a book about that)
>
> Shane again: refers to here "whining and fussing" (a gender stereotype)
>
> Joseph Spurgeon, referring to a picture of Aimee: "she is looking butch. Her femininity is withdrawn and she looks hardened."
>
> Thomas Booher: "SNL haggard look."
>
> Shane Anderson: "She has fostered the 'kick ass' look."
>
> Shane Anderson, responding to Joseph Spurgeon: "the vocal fry, the lack of logical reasoning, and eisegesis are feminine."

Other comments, unworthy of print in this context, are even more vile.

The distinguishing mark of a pastor is pastoral care. These comments lack the distinguishing mark. Words, Jesus said, come from our heart, and these words are from the heart of those who claim to be pastors. The heart they reveal, but the heart is not that of a pastor.

Words reveal. Words on social media reveal. How does a pastor use social media in a church that is fractured into tribes and in an America that is ripping apart at the old seams of what we thought was some kind of peaceable unity? How does someone with the distinguishing marks of a pastor converse on social media? I want to address in this chapter the social media presence of pastors, and to do that I will direct our attention to the wisdom of speech as found in the letter of James and then through James's wisdom explore the impact of social media, some of it quite unknown to most, and finally offer some wisdom about the pastor and social media.[2]

2. In what follows I will assume, adopt, and adapt what has already been said in my

Richard Bauckham, though commenting only briefly on speech ethics in
James, anticipated at the end of the twentieth century already the impact of
social media and the potency of James speaking into that context. In a book
published in 1999, Bauckham wrote:

> The best instance in which a contemporary concern approaches
> James' moral interest in the tongue is that of the mass media,
> whose power to distort the truth and do considerable harm to
> private (and royal) persons, as well as exerting considerable
> influence on political events, for good or ill, has become more
> and more evident, and recurrently a matter of serious public
> concern, in the recent past.[3]

I have students and acquaintances who have lost their pastoral positions or been demoted in those positions for how they have presented
themselves on social media. I know a pastor who wrote a book—his name
is Greg Boyd—about politics claiming Jesus is king and that such a confession dethrones political powers and this book led to an exodus from his
congregation.[4] I know a pastor who announced he had voted for Barack
Obama and within a month was gone; I know a pastor who was demoted
for talking about his marriage on social media in collapsing terms; I know a
Christian professor publicly denounced by friends for speaking up for social
justice concerns on social media. And I know another gifted professor who,
when young, was not promoted as he thought he should be, declared it all
on social media, and is now doing something else. I know plenty of pastors
and students whose Facebook and Twitter and Instagram accounts will be
scoured by future search committees and before the application gets to the
second interview they will be eliminated from consideration. *For you who
are pastors and wanting to be pastors*: Wise search committees will examine
(your) social media accounts as the best indicator of how you want people
to think of you. After all, your social media are as much self-presentation,
even preening, as it is simple conversation. What they will find is if you are
pastoral in your social media presence or not, and if not, they'll move to the
next candidate. They will think they can see the distinguishing marks by
how you present yourself on social media.

I, too, use social media though I ignored both Facebook and Twitter
for a long time, and I get on Instagram only a few times a year. Yet, as a
blogger of more than fifteen years I have learned some of the lessons of

---

commentary on James without citation of page numbers: McKnight, *Letter of James*.

3. Bauckham, *James*, 204.

4. Boyd, *Myth of a Christian Nation*. My thanks to Ryan Burge for comments and
reminding me of Boyd. A couple of his suggestions will appear in this chapter.

the dangerous impact of social media and the internet world. I confess that as one who has little respect for Joel Osteen's (Twitter-friendly) theology, sermons, and books, that I read a story once about him and his wife's behavior on an airplane, I thought I'd say something snarky on my blog, which I did when I referred to them as "The Blinker and his wife," and I got crowd pounded but good within minutes. I took the post down immediately and learned my lesson as speaking of another in a degrading, ridiculing manner. (I would instead now tell that story about myself and ironically call them that again!)

It is time then to examine the wisdom of pastor participation in social media. Wisdom, to reduce it to a simple definition, is living in God's world in God's way, and that way is most clearly revealed in the way of Christ.[5] Daniel Hanlon, in the opening chapter to *Wise Church* points to three dimensions of wisdom. Citing the work of Richard Clifford, wisdom is "sapiential (a way of knowing reality), ethical (a way of conducting oneself), and religious (a way of relating to the divinely designed order or to God)."[6] This kind of wisdom finds its way into life itself and one dimension of the life of a wise person is the wise use of words, and there is no greater challenge to that kind of wisdom today than social media.

Speech in James

The two primary texts about how a wise person is to speak and use the tongue are Proverbs, along with its variations outside the Old Testament canon, and I'm thinking here of Sirach,[7] and the second text is the letter of James. I will focus on James because I know it best. I begin with the observation that there are 32 imperatives in James and as many as 29 of them are about speech ethics![8] At the heart of James's speech ethics is Jas 3:1–12,[9] a text that is shaped for those who want to be teachers (3:1–2) and their tongue is the measure of their Christian completion or maturity (1:26;

---

5. I have a discussion of wisdom in McKnight, *Pastor Paul*, 169–90.

6. See Hanlon, "What is Wisdom?" Quotation of Clifford on p. 6.

7. For a full display of the contextual evidence, see esp. Baker, *Personal Speech-Ethics in the Epistle of James.*

8. Baker, *Sticks and Stones.*

9. For a sampling of the history of interpretation, see Allison, *Critical and Exegetical Commentary on the Epistle of James*, 509–13.

3:2).[10] In fact, the central passage in James, from 3:1—4:12,[11] is designed for teachers in church communities and there is more than enough in this long passage to give us all we need in pondering wisdom for the wise use of social media. One might contend the entire passage is less focused on teachers, in which case I would shift to another lane and contend that the substance of the passages provide the details needed for the pastors and their use of speech on social media. I make the following seven observations about speech from that passage, and all of the speech ethic of James emerges from the wisdom tradition and finds its primary locus in James at 3:13–18, on which passage we will make brief comments below.

First, James is aware that one of the primary temptations of pastors[12] is the tongue and James responds by saying *speech is the criterion that measures a pastor's maturity.* "Anyone," he observes at 3:2, "who makes no mistakes [or "doesn't trip"] in speaking [or "in word"] is perfect, able to keep the whole body in check with a bridle," a verse that was anticipated in 1:26.[13] In the same verse, James observes that the person who does trip in speech has a "religion" that "is worthless" or "useless." The importance of speech for measuring wisdom is a commonplace in Judaism. Sirach, for instance, asks, "Who has not sinned with his tongue?" (Sir 19:16), and a line in the Dead Sea Scrolls connects a "clean heart" with "does not slander with his tongue" (4Q525 f2ii + 3:1). James heard it perhaps first from his older brother Jesus: speech, he would have heard, is what defiles a person (Mark 7:20) and he would have perhaps heard too that anger fomenting into words leads to the fires of destruction (Matt 5:21–22).

The operative term, however, is "perfect." This is one of James's favorite terms, using it (1) for the completed, mature disciple of Jesus who has grown through trials, tests, and endurance into a fullness (1:3), (2) for God's completely adequate gifts (1:17), and (3) for the completeness of the "law of liberty," or the fullness of an ethic that is shaped by loving God and loving others (cf. 1:25 with 2:8–13). Thus, the wise pastor who is complete and mature is one who uses speech in patterns that emerge from love of

10. One of the truly great commentaries ever written is Allison's, mentioned in the previous note, but I demur from his de-Christianizing of the letter of James.

11. While not certain, a good case can be made for the entire passage as one shaped for teachers: 3:1 is overt and that extends through 3:12, 3:13's "wise and understanding" evokes language for such teachers, which means 3:13–18; 4:1–10 is not as clear but it does continue the themes of division that have been at work in 3:1–18 while 4:11–12 returns yet again to the problem of speech that divides.

12. I will use "pastor" and "teacher" as synonyms in this chapter.

13. All citations are from the NRSV unless otherwise noted.

God and love of others. Anything contrary to that kind of speech, James declares, is useless religion.

Second, *speech has an impact that far exceeds its size.* As a bridle's bit can be used to lead a horse, as a small rudder is capable of steering a large boat, so the tongue can be used in measurable excesses.[14] James's says "the tongue is a small member, yet it boasts of great exploits" (3:5, the final word in 3:3–5). Boasting here is a surprising clarification because it seems absent until mentioned but it does illuminate much of what was happening in the speech patterns of those to whom James writes this letter. One might find a hint of boasting in the need for 1:19–21's to speak of "meekness," in the bridling of the tongue in 1:26 and 3:2, in the apparent desire for too many to be teachers in 3:1 and, because of the capturing of speech as boasting in 3:5, one must think that the horse's bit and the boat's rudder at least suggest boasting. That his next passage, and our next theme, is about speech as a world of fire and poison, one might suggest again that boasting is one element of speech behind 3:5–12. The themes of 3:13–18—wisdom and gentleness countering boasting, while envy and selfish ambition fuel boasting, and the final list of goodnesses in 3:17–18's emphasis on peace and gentleness also counter boasting. It is not surprising then that at 3:14 James speaks directly of being "boastful." One could read the suggestion of boasting in all of 4:1–12 without much difficulty. I'm not overcooking the evidence so much as suggesting that the sudden use of boasting in 3:5a as it was tied to small-with-great themes in 3:3–4 seems to have been a significant concern for James. The theme comes directly at 4:16 among the traveling businessmen. Here's why: boasting was the way of Rome, the way of Rome's economic exploitations, and the way of the one on the path of glory, called the *cursus honorum.*[15] Boasting was expected of the social climber in the empire, and James knew that it was all too easy to become a friend with the world (4:4).

The point for James is little-to-big, a small item that has an enormous reach, a small tweet ("Farewell Rob Bell") that goes viral. What we say has a ripple effect upon those who hear or read what we say. A pastor who is vituperative and bombastic nurtures and is nurtured by retainers who are vituperative and bombastic, and the congregants before long begin to think such speech is holy and good and faithful and so they, too, become vituperative and bombastic and before long the church has a reputation.

14. One could argue that control of the tongue is present in the statement of 3:2 and then illustrated in 3:3–4's use of the horse's bit and the ship's rudder with the change toward the lack of control only in "yet" in 3:5. On this, see Allison, *James*, 517.

15. McKnight, *Pastor Paul*, 153–56.

The small tongue of the pastor has a far-reaching impact.[16] I have given this second observation more attention because of what I will say below about social media.

Third, *speech is like fire and poison, it destroys and kills.* Beginning again with the small-to-great theme in Jas 3:6 ("How great a forest is set ablaze by a small fire!), James opens the furnaces door to the impact of speech: It is "a world of iniquity," it "stains the whole body," it sets on fire "the cycle of nature" and does so as something straight out of hell (3:6). Further, it is a "restless evil, full of deadly poison" (3:8). It's forked: we speak blessing of God and cursings of fellow humans (3:9–10). Pick your image, it's just plain wrong (3:11–12).

Fourth, *speech seems to be uncontrollable.* This theme found in a sudden burst of exasperation in Jas 3:7–8, is stated in comprehensive terms: "no one can tame the tongue" even though we can tame the animal kingdom. Yet, it is the person who can control speech that gets the glory for James (1:26; 3:2). One can take this pessimistic observation by James flat-footedly as contradictory to what he says in 3:1 or one can take this, as it should be, as rhetoric: James wants his teachers to know that speech is the far frontier they have now entered, it is the tallest mountain to climb, and the toughest contestant in the struggle for sanctification and loving relationships. 1 Enoch's short forty-second chapter offers an explanation of the uncontrollable nature of the tongue: "Wisdom could not find a place in which she could dwell" among humans, the author tells us, so she "settled permanently among the angels," while "Iniquity" did: "she dwelt with them like rain in a desert, like dew on a thirsty land" (42:1–3).

Fifth, *the wise person speaks from a different kind of character, the character of wisdom.* One of the great passages in James is 3:13–18.[17] The complete

---

16. McKnight, *Pastor Paul*; McKnight and Barringer, *Church Called Tov.*

17. Compare it to 1QS 4:2–8:

2Upon earth their operations are these: one enlightens a man's mind, making straight before him the paths of true righteousness and causing his heart to fear the laws 3 of God. This spirit engenders humility, patience, abundant compassion, perpetual goodness, insight, understanding, and powerful wisdom resonating to each 4 of God's deeds, sustained by His constant faithfulness. It engenders a spirit knowledgeable in every plan of action, zealous for the laws of righteousness, holy 5 in its thoughts, and steadfast in purpose. This spirit encourages plenteous compassion upon all who hold fast to truth, and glorious purity combined with visceral hatred of impurity in its every guise. It results in humble deportment 6 allied with a general discernment, concealing the truth, that is, the mysteries of knowledge. To these ends is the earthly counsel of the

or mature teacher is one who does good works "with gentleness born of wisdom," avoids the angers of selfish ambition and boasting and lying, has escaped the grip of "devilish" practices forming a person's character, and so is "peaceable, gentle, willing to yield, full of mercy and good fruits, without a trace of partiality or hypocrisy." James wants those teachers in his circle of influence to be peace-makers (3:18). Harsh speech, speech designed to degrade and diminish others, does not emerge from the wise teacher or the teacher intent on peace-making. Noticeably, James calls this a "wisdom from above," a way of deconstructing the wisdom of the world (cf. 4:4) and setting loose an imagination for the way things are with God and for all God's people. Frederick Douglass has been described recently as a "darkness reader," one who knows the worldliness of the world, its darkness, and its impact on him and the need for this wisdom from above to counter the ways of systemic injustice against the black skin worn as a uniform for slaves.[18] A wise character recognizes such darknesses in our culture, as our colleague Ernest Ledbetter III has done in this volume.[19]

Sixth, *speech creates pleasure-based, worldliness-inspired, and pride-shaped "conflicts and disputes."* The speech patterns at work in 4:1-10 are negatives: "conflicts and disputes" [or "wars and battles" in 4:1,2]. They come from a pleasure-soaked life (4:1,3) and from "friendship with the world" (4:4) and from pride (4:5-10).

Hence, the life contrary to pleasures, worldliness and pride is one rooted in humility, and this is a core value for James at this point, spending six verses on that very topic. Perhaps God wants us, or does God want what God has implanted in us, the Spirit/spirit (4:5), or, as I have sought to explain, the spirit is in us longing to use us for envy-shaped self-promotion. Instead of being teachers glorifying God, these teachers were—remember the boasting—glorifying themselves. In direct contrast, 4:6 says "But he [God] gives all the more grace," and that grace opposes the proud ones and gives new life to the humble (or poor, impoverished ones; cf. 2:1-7).

The implications are spelled out in 4:7-10, and they can be summarized as surrendering to God in a way that runs from the devil, avoids the complexities of being "double-minded," that laments and weeps over

---

spirit to those whose nature yearns for truth. Through a gracious visitation all who walk in this spirit will know healing, 7 bountiful peace, long life, and multiple progeny, followed by eternal blessings and perpetual joy through life everlasting. They will receive a crown of glory 8 with a robe of honor, resplendent forever and ever.

18. Aymer, *First Pure, Then Peaceable.* I got the expression of black skin as the slave's uniform from Pastor Marshall Hatch.

19. "Wise Racial Justice," pp. 151-69.

sins and worldliness, and that results ultimately in God's glory by exalting us as his models of grace and peace and wisdom—and there can be no doubt that good speech is at the heart of what humility means. Politics today requires this kind world-resistance, and Ivan Ramirez has offered his thoughts on this very topic.[20]

Finally, *bad speech habits become judgmental of others.* Notice James's language in 4:11–12: "do not speak evil against one another" and "Whoever speaks evil against another" and then, in the ultimate form of contrarian language, "and judges another." Judging one another, James famously clarifies, makes a person God or makes the person act like he or she is God. The most narcissistic are the most judgmental, and behind the most judgmental is the narcissist. The judge judges, or exercises the judgmental function of, the law, and there is but one Judge and that is the Lawgiver, and that is God, so the one using the law to judge others makes himself (or herself) God!

Here it is then: a unit aimed at teachers and the focus is on speech ethics, and the big ideas then are sevenfold, and each of then speaks into how a pastor is to use social media:

1. *speech is the criterion that measures a pastor's maturity,*
2. *speech has an impact that far exceeds its size,*
3. *speech is like fire and poison, it destroys and kills,*
4. *speech seems to be uncontrollable,*
5. *the wise person speaks from a different kind of character, the character of wisdom,*
6. *speech creates pleasure-based, worldliness-inspired, and pride-shaped "conflicts and disputes,"*
7. *bad speech habits become judgmental of others.*

This is enough for a conversation about social media and I will use this template for my discussion about the pastor and social media. Before we turn to that, however, we need to discuss four recent studies of social media.

Four Pastoral Problems in Using Social Media

There are any number of books about this topic. If one were to ignore technical articles one could write a lengthy book sketching books *about*

20. "Wise Politics," pp. 229–47.

the impact of social media on a person and on society. I have chosen four recent studies that came my way.

Diminished Capacity for Conversation

I begin with Sherry Turkle, a professor of social studies of science and technology at the Massachusetts Institute for Technology and the author of two books pertaining to our topic, *Alone Together* and *Reclaiming Conversation*. The second is the focus here.[21] Her concern in research is what social media and device addictions do to us and therefore to our society, and she turns to the diminishment of conversations when conversations are what is needed to become a mature human. There is much to glean from Turkle so I will have to be brief and even terse in summary.

Turkle's contribution is the result of interviews of social media users and addicts and their impact on the capacity for conversation and the impact of their lack of conversation on character and ability to interact with other humans in conversations. "Conversation," she observes, "is on the path toward the experience of intimacy, community, and communion."[22] It can heal and it can cure. Conversations matter for each of us because it is in conversation that we learn to ask questions, that we discover the narratives that tell our own story, and in conversation we form relationships with others. The fundamental problem is that we are growing away from an ability to have meaningful conversations today, and hence studies show that in the past two decades there is a 40 percent decline in college students developing indicators of empathy. The ones who use social media the most are the ones most challenged "at reading human emotions."[23] She tells how office complexes reveal more and more who enter into their cubby hole with their computer, their devices, their headphones and they turn those offices into sealed-off cockpits, incapable of hearing others and also not capable then of forming conversations and developing relationships. Dinners often find family members or friends at table but with devices displayed on the table. The interruptions made visible on those devices, she states, are not interruptions for such persons but more connections.[24]

One of her more interesting points, almost made in passing, is that our mobile devices mean we will always be heard, that we can choose what we

---

21. Turkle, *Alone Together*; Turkle, *Reclaiming Conversation*. What follows is based on the second book, now expressed at times in my own words.

22. Turkle, *Reclaiming Conversation*, 7.

23. Turkle, *Reclaiming Conversation*, 25.

24. Turkle, *Reclaiming Conversation*, 35–38.

want to hear (so that our social media become echo chambers) and see and read, and that we don't ever have to be alone. The irony is that being alone with our device "with others" is not conversation so we end up often being alone together. The fear of missing out (FOMO) fuels the constant checking of our devices, and thus blocks out opportunities for conversations.

Her study explores the three chairs of Henry David Thoreau—the chair of solitude, the chair of friendship, and the chair of society. That is, in the chair of solitude we find self-reflection—as when we take a walk and, instead of sticking music in our ears, we walk listening to the sounds of nature and find ourselves musing and praying and self-reflecting. The second chair is pulled up next to us for those in our inner circles where our self-reflection turns to other-reflection, and that other-reflection makes us more self-reflective as well as empathetic with others. That second-chair conversation is the only means toward developing empathy in conversation with the third chair, our world. Because, Turkle observes, we are afraid to sit alone with ourselves, we are unable to pay attention to ourselves and hence unable to enter into meaningful conversation in society. (Can I get a witness about the truth of this on social media?) She adds a fourth chair: we now communicate more than through technology but *to* the machines themselves! Machines have no capacity for the randomness of human engagement through conversation. Machines at their highest levels are pre-programmed. Four chairs in the room and the art of conversation is required for this to be meaningful.

Instead of being formed in conversation we are being formed by social media connections, but conversation is more than connection. Connections are controlled and robotic. How many of us will admit that we prefer texting or emailing or Facebook because we can determine when to read them and when to respond and do so when convenient? (I do.) How many of us "overshare" on social media? How many of us have asked ourselves *why* we think everything we do needs to be publicized to our friends? Are such persons engaging connections as *faux* conversations? Are they lonely and looking for attention? Do the algorithms (see next section) drive them into their oversharing for an addiction to social media's affirmations? Our obsession with connections via social media that reveal our inner life, contrary to what many think, makes us lonely, make us unempathetic and thus unable to participate in a civil manner in society. She turns this all around by saying "Without conversation, studies show that we are less empathetic, less connected, less creative and fulfilled."[25] Connections are disembodied, contextual-less words. "In person," she says, "we have access to the messages carried in the face, the voice, and the body. Online, we

25. Turkle, *Reclaiming Conversation*, 13.

settle for simpler fare: We get our efficiency and our chance to edit, but we learn to ask questions that a return email can answer."[26]

One might be tempted to think that social media are entirely superficial and shallow while embodied conversations are intimate and empathy-forming, but simplicities don't measure realities. Some email changes, some direct messages, some Facebook exchanges can reach the depths. In this volume, the study of Jeremy Berg about letter-writing as a refreshed form of pastoral care reveals that the mediated word of a personal, private letter—stamped envelope or email—can effect interpersonal relational vulnerability and intimacy and thus can be the first and second chair Turkle proposes.[27]

Turkle is calling us all to sacred spaces away from devices and connections, to the first and second and third chairs. Speaking and listening are skills in need of development through the art of listening and paying close attention to self and others. She is not so pessimistic to call us all away from our devices or social media, but to using social media in the context of a life filled with uninterrupted conversations to form intimacy, empathy, and love. Someone who does call us away from social media is next.

Algorithms and Formation

A specialist philosopher in technology itself is the rambunctious thinker Jaron Lanier, whose experience in Silicon Valley has been with all the major social media and computer organizations. His book unmasks every secret of the book: *Ten Arguments for Deleting Your Social Media Accounts Right Now!*[28] I'm not *au courant* with all the literature on social media so take this for what it is—my opinion. This book should be read by every pastor for one simple reason: it will explain what is happening to you at the hands of the dark places in Facebook and Twitter. He calls this "a new kind of sinister shadow cosmos."[29] What you see in your Facebook feed as updates from "friends" is what they want you to see and what you feel is probably what they want you to feel. And it's the algorithms[30] and it's all from the bots, not actual people manipulating your feelings into the motions they want from you so you will stay addicted to their sites and buy

---

26. Turkle, *Reclaiming Conversation*, 23.

27. "Wise Letter Writing," 25–46.

28. Lanier, *Ten Arguments*.

29. Lanier, *Ten Arguments*, 35.

30. A widely-read study of how African American women are presented in the algorithms is Noble, *Algorithms of Oppression*. My thanks to Ryan Burge for recommending this study.

things through the tailored advertisements. What matters most is that bots embed a moral worldview, and we are shaped by that moral view by what we choose to read from the bots choices.

Everything you see on your personal social media—at the end of every click, every pause, every entry into a box—is filtered in the hiding places and then turned into the kind of site you are and what you will be interested in, what you will feel, and what you will buy. What the bots know, too, is that anger and fear draw more clicks than joy and kindness, so the entire algorithm of you on Facebook or Twitter is tilted significantly toward negative—let's say it, unchristian—emotions and feelings and sensations. It's all shaped by dopamine and the amygdala's energy. The freshly baptized term is "outrage." Studies show that more than 50 percent of the current outrage flows from the furnace of social media agitations. I have no evidence for that number, and I know of no study with that conclusion, but I reason it is better to be right than to get accurate numbers. (Insert your own emoji.)

Your outrage is then connected to others with similar profiles, which means who gets riled up about what you get riled up about. Your behavior then is shaped to fit in with the group, what he calls "paranoia peer groups."[31] The aim of the bots is behavior modification—your behavior modified by the bot that tells the marketers what you like. You have been sold as an ad, and you alone see your ads and no one else sees yours because they see theirs. He calls this bot word "BUMMER," which means "Behaviors of Users Modified, and Made into an Empire for Rent."[32] Originally the ad spaces were for advertisers but it attracted instead people who are manipulators of people's behaviors. The creepier the better. "The unplanned nature of the transformation from advertising to direct behavior modification caused an explosive amplification of negativity in human affairs."[33]

Not holding back at what is going on—after all he's intent on getting you and me to delete our accounts until they can be controlled by a more just economic system—he reduces BUMMER to some letters in the alphabet:

A is for attention acquisition leading to asshole supremacy.

B is for butting into everyone's lives [It's free because they spy on us].

C is for cramming content down people's throats.

D is for directing people's behaviors in the sneakiest way possible.

31. Lanier, *Ten Arguments*, 65.

32. Lanier, *Ten Arguments*, 30.

33. Lanier, *Ten Arguments*, 21.

MCKNIGHT—WISE SOCIAL MEDIA

E is for earning money from letting the worst assholes secretly screw with everyone else.

F is for fake mobs and faker society.

That's the inside character and intent of BUMMER which is the inside game of Facebook and Twitter. He knows because he was involved in creating the system.

Because everyone asks, what are his ten arguments?

1. You are losing your free will.

2. Quitting social media is the most finely targeted way to resist the insanity of our times.

3. Social media is making you into an asshole.

4. Social media is undermining truth.

5. Social media is making what you say meaningless.

6. Social media is destroying your capacity for empathy [Notice the tie to Turkle above].

7. Social media is making you unhappy.

8. Social media doesn't want you to have economic dignity.

9. Social media is making politics impossible.

10. Social media hates your soul.

Lanier's big picture is clear enough: social media is free because advertisers want the information stored and released by bots, and the bots are shaped to magnify negative social relations because everyone loves a good fight. It works off your likes and what you watch and what you click and what remains on the screen. We love our "Likes" and are depressed by the lack of "Likes." Addiction to the social media means that the social media are forming us at the deepest level of our characters. Transparent conversations will prompt dear folks to admit social media depresses by comparison and angers by inspiration. You don't control what you see, though you can learn to un-use your Facebook presenting page and go one level deeper to control what you see in updates from friends by clocking on "Most Recent." Facebook's presenting page, your page, is controlled by the bots and the bots prefer to rile you up. Days and months and years of being riled up has a way of making people angry and hateful and cynical and nasty. Lanier is right: you have lost your free will. Bots are ruling the internet, and therefore much of society. Social media are formational, and I point us back to the chapter in this book by Peter Goodman about wise spiritual formation.[34]

Grandstanding is Self-Promotion

Choose your media—Facebook, Twitter, Instagram—and you will find an opportunity to show off, to display your stuff, to promote your work, and to tell your story in ways you want your story told. From the very beginning social critics, not always accurately, called this Generation Me.[35] At no time in history has the world had a platform on which we could each march out all day long and say, "Look at me!" Social media provide each person a working knowledge of public relations through the experiences of social media.[36] I have a theological friend who thinks each of these media is inherently selfish and ought to be avoided by anyone serious about self-denial. Not all agree, so I turn to another recent study that the pastor needs to ponder.

In light of the nature of these social media, the third study that fascinates me for the pastor's use of social media is by Justin Tosi and Brandon Warmke and is called *Grandstanding*. Their sociological study concentrates on how we present ourselves as moral agents on Facebook and Twitter. Social media, with its "Like" button and its comment box where your buddies can publicly affirm you in spades, is the world's greatest temptation to grandstanding. But what is grandstanding? It is moral preening or moral peacocking so that others can see how morally virtuous you are. Their definition is broken into two parts:

1. Grandstanders want to impress others with their moral qualities. We call this the **Recognition Desire**.

2. Grandstanders try to satisfy that desire by saying something in public moral discourse. We call this public display the **Grandstanding Expression**.

   You can therefore think of grandstanding in terms of a simple formula:

Grandstanding = Recognition Desire + Grandstanding Expression

Grandstanders try to get others to think of themselves as morally respectable and they seek to be connected to others they consider morally respectable.

---

34. "Wise Spiritual Formation," pp. 130–50.

35. Twenge, *Generation Me—Revised and Updated*.

36. Thanks to Ryan Burge for this observation.

Sometimes they want to be thought of as one of the gang. Other times, they want to be thought of as morally exceptional. Either way, they usually want to be seen as morally better than others. It's about a desire for recognition and an expression that seeks affirmation of that desire, and it's all connected in other terms to boasting and pride. As in, "I'm for social justice and I can't believe how people treat these kids at the borders of our country." It's not quite "Look at me, I'm virtuous" but the implication is just that. The Likes affirm the Update and puff up the chest of the updater.

It is nearly impossible to exist in a social world without at some point either making a moral statement or liking one, and the moment one clicks "Like" one is tempted to be a grandstander. Which leads to this question: How do we detect grandstanding? Can we? I'd say—they'd say—sometimes, but not always. I take one example of a series of moral claims in public from people I know from a Facebook exchange, but it began with a tweet that said:

> What is manhood? Manhood is doing hard things for God's glory and the good of others [and the illustrations are] fixing things, hiking, gardening, shooting a gun.

A friend's Facebook update is a kind of alternative response:

> We need a vision of Christian manhood shaped around humility, service, compassion, love, gentleness and kindness—because these qualities are at the heart of discipleship, for all disciples.

In what Tosi and Warmke will call "ramping up" (see below), a response in a series of what could be seen as piling on is this:

> Even the harshest complementarians can agree with that.

These are moral claims. They are by folks I know. It is hard to assess if these are grandstanding (do they say these things for recognition?) because without tone and texture and conversation we can't determine, and this is the essential problem with calling out someone for grandstanding. What one sees is more likely what one uses as a lens.

Tosi and Warmke provide a "field guide" to grandstanding by looking at five types, but the expression of each moral statement is not a necessary indicator of grandstanding. Here are five types of grandstanding. First, *piling on*. Vice President Pence spoke at the Republican National Convention and in quoting Scripture clearly substituted Old Glory for something that pertains to Christ, which is at best sacrilegious and Christian nationalism and at worse blasphemous. What happened was piling on or what I have on my blog for years called "crowdpounding." I saw hundreds of Facebook updates that piled on. The act of piling on is not so much a personal moral statement as it is a statement of saying "I'm on a different team." The Republicans who piled on were saying, "I'm not that kind of Republican." The oddity for me is that American presidents and English prime ministers have done this forever and amen. Did those who decry Pence say a word about Abraham Lincoln's use of the blood of Abel in 1848? Speaking of Lincoln, when Jacob Blake's mother, Julia Jackson, said "a house divided against one another" about her son's shooting in Kenosha, did anyone decry that she was swiping words from Lincoln, or did anyone notice that Lincoln swiped those words from Jesus? Was that OK for Lincoln to re-use Jesus's words? I'm with Jacob Blake's mother, but the point is this: the piling on was tribalism more than it was moral and theological discernment. Which means many of the ones piling were grandstanding.

Second, Tosi and Warmke speak of *ramping up* and (unfortunately, but not a little prophetically and thirdly), of *trumping up*. Both of these describe moral claims that take the original moral claim on social media and take it to the extreme. In ramping up a social media contest is established in which if you say someone is morally deficient, someone else says they are morally degraded, and then the person is connected to Hitler or Stalin. Trumping up actually invents moral problems where there are none. This one, again ironically, makes something up about morality as when Republicans called President Obama a Muslim or a socialist or when Democrats call President Trump a fascist or a dictator. One of the more insidious instances of trumping up concerns the term "evangelical." Unless one is with one's own and one's own are evangelicals, this term has been cashed in as a loss. How so? Because media of all sorts has an obsession with calling everything religiously corrupt in America "evangelical." Christians of all sorts on social media join in and can't wait to find the next instance of corruption, and the instances are often enough taken out of context, mistaken, and the charge is therefore trumped up.

Finally, the authors turn to public displays of strong emotion, like outrage or overwhelming joy. This connects with Lanier's work on creeps who spend their time on what can rile up their marketed audience and hope to elicit from them strong emotions in favor of something but far more often against something. It is a good thing that our Facebook does not have a moral outrage button because it would eventually crash unless Facebook invented 15 levels of outrage, ending with "Apoplectic!"

Grandstanding, which is all about speech patterns and like the fire and poison of James, leads (the authors show) to polarization of society (the third chair of Turkle), to cynicism about the value of public claims to morality, and to outrage that ruins morality in a culture in need of morality. Furthermore, grandstanding trades in the intentional and overt disrespecting of other people in a number of ways, and they look at three kinds of disrespect: (1) showcasing one person over another, (2) deceives others, and (3) free-riding on the good moral talk of others. In other words, grandstanding only works by using other people. John Piper in saying "Farewell Rob Bell" used Bell to assert his own theological orthodoxy and riled up his massive base into retweeting what was deemed sanctified theological critique. It could have been done otherwise, like writing personally to Rob Bell. James again said by our speech we both bless God and curse others made in God's image.

Tosi and Warmke have a solid chapter asking if a virtuous person would grandstand. In other words, does a person of *tov* character grandstand? Their argument is that the selfishness and self-promotion nature of grandstanding fails every indicator of virtue so, No, a virtuous person does not grandstand. Politicians, they are argue round and round in the final chapter, both must and should not be grandstanders because it ruins public discourse and makes the electorate cynical about the truth-telling nature of a politician. One might be tempted to conclude that no politician can be virtuous. I'll move on.

The Digital World is Disembodied

A digital native who had curated digital worship and digital church, Jay Kim, came to the conclusion that, while digital church was altogether relevant as something connected to the normal reality of other digital natives, what this generation most craves is not a Sunday service or a church that is altogether relevant on the digital front but instead what they crave is analog. His book is called *Analog Church*, with subtitle defining what "analogy" means: *Why We Need Real People, Places, and Things in the Digital Age.*[37] Jay Kim's *leitmotif* is that the current generation isn't interested in relevance when it comes to church, but instead is interested in transcendence. What those with ears to the ground know is that discipleship transformation takes place most consistently and deeply in relationship with others, with mentors and peers, and not in online communications. Kim's study connects us with the work of Sherry Turkle and Jaron Lanier especially in that we are being formed into non-relational, non-intimate, individualized Christians for whom the church as an embodied reality becomes less and less vital. A generation of church streaming would kill the church.

The digital has replaced the analog in technology, and a technological church is digital and that means the digital church is for some replacing the old-fashioned sit with, pray for, and worship with one another analog

---

37. Kim, *Analog Church*. What follows is developed from this book.

church. Every moment spent in digital church replaces and can diminish analog church, and thus the experience of church as streaming into our homes could (negatively) affect church as an embodied reality permanently. It's simple mathematics. Or is it? In the most recent Pew study about online church during the COVID-19 pandemic, the impact of online virtual church services seems to have virtually no impact:

> While the outbreak is not over, the survey suggests that the pandemic will not produce widespread, lasting changes in patterns of attendance at religious services. More than nine-in-ten people who were regular religious attenders before the outbreak (92%) say they intend to resume their previous level of religious attendance or plan to attend religious services even more often once the outbreak is over. And within this group, most say they will watch virtual services either at the same rate or less often than they did before the outbreak.

> Meanwhile, just 2% of regular religious attenders indicate that they may substitute online or televised religious services for in-person attendance (by saying both that they intend to go to in-person religious services less often than they did before the pandemic and that they plan to watch virtual services *more* often).[38]

Perhaps, then, the hand wringing as well as the predictions of the demise of analog church can be tossed into the dustbin of anxiety.

But the incarnation reveals to us that God did not reveal a message but a person, a real Jewish guy, living a community life in Nazareth and Capernaum of Galilee, who ate and drank and prayed and taught people with names who had faces staring at him and longing for the juices he served. We are not digital creations, we are analog kind of creations. If the digital age focuses on choices and preferences, an analog church focuses on persons present to one another. If digital is about connection, analog is about communion and communication. Analog church takes time and patience while digital church is instant-on and instant-off. The digital church can only provide information while the analog's church mindset is formation through relationship. "At their worst," Kim states, "social media and digital spaces create a false sense of connection and a façade of community."[39]

In the middle of the analog church is a table set for a meal with those present. In the middle of the digital church is computer screen or a tablet or

---

38. https://www.pewforum.org/2020/08/07/americans-oppose-religious-exemptions-from-coronavirus-related-restrictions/ (#2).

39. Kim, *Analog Church*, 20.

a phone. The digital church is for devices and the analog church is for disciples. In the oddities and spontaneities of humans present to other humans one sees the face, catches the timbre of the voice's sounds, and holds the hands of the other, and nothing digital can do that. Digital forms away from analog, while analog longs for us to come back to reality.

This sketch of four studies opens for a door onto digital realities: the blocking of conversation that alone develops empathy and the capacity for intimate relations, the formational impact of social media through its bots that are designed to bring out the worst in us, the temptation to use social media to bolster our own reputation by moral preening, and the fundamental disembodied life of an increasing number of communications. So, now the question: What is the pastor to do about social media?

Wisdom: The Pastor and Social Media

The question "Where to go?" after pondering these four studies becomes "Where not to go?" I have not spoken of the goods of social media, and there are plenty, including it being fast and efficient and convenient communication, but there is a line crossed for many who think social media gets the job done. It doesn't. It gets the pastor and the congregant on the front porch of a very busy, noisy street. The big picture then is that social media is not personal presence, and pastoring requires embodied presence. So I urge pastors to spend more time in the first and second chairs, adding the third as the church gathered, than on social media. Count up your phone calls and your coffee time with others and your lunches and dinners with others—when devices are turned off or stowed away—and see if they match your social media time.

We need to begin with what matters most: social media are deeply influential on us and in us and they are shaping social and ecclesial and personal cultures.

Social Media are Formational

Pastors will need both to become more aware of the formative potency of social media, the direction of that formation toward outrage, and resist it by avoiding social media or actively resisting it in how they communicate on social media. Social media addicts are riled up because the bots at work on your Facebook and Twitter want you riled up. A life of riled up is not a life of sanctification (or conversation).

The operative theme of FB and Twitter is political speech or speech about politicians, and it both nurtures and rides the wave of the politicization of the church. In the last twelve years, if one knows how to find the numbers, the percentage of political Facebook updates and likes and comments has grown exponentially. I have a habit of deleting "friends" who decide to make most of their updates about politicians. Most of it is uninformed piling on or trumping up, and it nurtures a tribal culture that assumes a Facebook update actually changes the world. Poverty, racism, and military might get attention on social media but my reading of the last twelve years of social media piling on has not made the poor pockets of our large cities any less poor, has not stopped racism, and has not turned the military machinery into garden tools. The bots get people riled up, expressions of outrage stimulate the amygdala, and then people feel good for their preening and moral statements, but that steam evaporates into thin air before the concrete actions of creating jobs, sustaining families, and forming our inner city youth through responsible education are accomplished. I'll say it because I believe it: white people love to feel good about feeling bad about poverty and racism, but white guilt-motivated Facebook updates of outrage do not affect poverty or racism.

Outrage, then, is not social activism and outrage promotes more outrage, and pastors need to watch what is happening and learn from it. They need to chart a new path. Just listen to the words of Jas 3:13–18 and the virtues emerging from what James wants his teachers to comprehend about their teaching and pastoring:

> Who is wise and understanding among you? Show by your good life that your works are done with gentleness born of wisdom. But if you have bitter envy and selfish ambition in your hearts, do not be boastful and false to the truth. Such wisdom does not come down from above, but is earthly, unspiritual, devilish. For where there is envy and selfish ambition, there will also be disorder and wickedness of every kind. But the wisdom from above is first pure, then peaceable, gentle, willing to yield, full of mercy and good fruits, without a trace of partiality or hypocrisy. And a harvest of righteousness is sown in peace for those who make peace.

If you devote a day or a week to wisdom and understanding and gentleness, while avoiding envy and selfish ambition and boasting and falsehoods, and instead pursue what is pure and peaceable and gentle and yieldedness and mercy, while avoiding the fakery of presenting a desire persona on social media, one will be so countercultural that one may not find any reason to participate. Which might explain some lurking, but lurking is not innocent because what we choose to observe forms us.

We need to dig a bit deeper. There were seven ideas culled from Jas 3:1—4:12 about speech patterns these categories ought also to control what we talk about and how we talk on social media. As someone inching toward 70 years old, I can tell you that by and large my generation does not want to hear about your parties, your marriage problems, or the rebellion of your children. You and your friends may like this so I suggest keep it with them. In conversations over coffee at the coffee shop.

1. *speech is the criterion that measures a pastor's maturity,*

2. *speech has an impact that far exceeds its size,*

3. *speech is like fire and poison, it destroys and kills,*

4. *speech seems to be uncontrollable,*

5. *the wise person speaks from a different kind of character, the character of wisdom,*

6. *speech creates pleasure-based, worldliness-inspired, and pride-shaped "conflicts and disputes,"*

7. *bad speech habits become judgmental of others.*

Instead of piling on the outrage, pastors use of social media can be subjected to the James's measure of maturity: control of the tongue, or the speech patterns of social media. Most of us have failed here at times, but we can get a better grip on our social media and turn things in a new direction. Since I believe in the values of social media—I would never have found my old track and field teammate, the ultra speedy Mike Cole, an African American pastor in Dixon Illinois had it not been for Facebook—it is wiser to learn the art of conversation and the measure of the tongue than it is to delete all accounts. Some may need to delete, but not all.

If we ponder the impact and ripple effects of what is said on Facebook we will be more than careful about expressing outrage and criticism and piling on and trumping up. The tongue, James informed us, is a fire and a poison: what we say can set the internet on fire with poison, if I can combine the images. In our words, something goes viral. Rarely does something good go viral and there is a much greater chance of something going viral if it is ugly, mean and damning. Yes, James speaks directly to the pastor when he says the tongue seems uncontrollable. Many now experience the irresistibility of checking Facebook and Twitter and Instagram, and then know the irresistibility of dropping a comment, which sometimes is a little bit of peacocking our moral virtue. When there are divisions and battles on our Facebook page we might check to see if they are emerging from a character in us that is pleasure-based or worldliness-inspired or pride-shaped, and we may need the reminder than such thing are diabolical and at war ultimately with God. This sense of pride touches upon the work of Tosi and Warmke mentioned above: I have not counted because we can't tell for sure, but one has to ask if a majority of social media comments are not moral preening for others to "Like" us so we can be affirmed in our morality. Grandstanding was for Jesus the way of the Pharisees as excoriated in Matt 23.

Outrage more than any other form of social media speech is most often judgment of others. Judging the other means we are playing the part of God and God has no desire to share the judgment seat with you or me. Put into one framework, then, pastors need to salt everything said on social media with wisdom and have all our words shaped by the pursuit of wisdom.

Develop the Art of Conversation

Because so many young pastors today are digitally-formed and not so much conversationally-formed, I urge pastors to work at developing the art of conversation. Sherry Turkle has observed often that many digital natives are afraid of conversations and are all but clueless for how they work. A constant interruption of cell phone "connections" erases genuine conversation, though many don't think of them as interruptions at all. (They are.) So, what are the marks of a good conversation?[40] First, a good conversation (and therefore a good conversationalist) requires *a safe environment*. By this I mean space—somewhere to feel comfortable; and I mean at least two people with listening skills; and I mean the ability to disagree if necessary but not denounce, condemn, or berate. Because safety is hard to find many turn themselves into "Anonymous" or some *faux* name when they comment on social media. That decision not to be our genuine self is a cry for safety though it also means one can say what they want with impunity. A safe environment is one in which we listen and others are heard and we are heard and others listen. Jas 1:19's "be quick to listen" is the foundation of a good conversation.[41]

Second, a good conversation requires a *good topic or a good question*. This one is clear: what is a good topic for some is not for others. It is also

40. The following is rooted in the wonderful book by Benedetta Craveri, *Age of Conversation*.

41. For an excellent discussion of listening in the context of speech patterns, see Baker, *Sticks and Stones*, 88–100.

clear that some topics are better than others. Some topics are off-limits for one person and on-limits for another. There is a social skill involved here: some people perceive immediately what is on-limits or off-limits; others don't. Good conversations are not random give-and-takes that go nowhere and finish nowhere, but are mutual interactions about something that matters to both. Conversations may well include catching up with one another but that is only the front door on the front porch. Until we learn how to engage in good conversations we will never own the skill of conversations about some of the most important of topics: religion and politics.

Third, a good conversation operates on the basis of frequently-unexpressed *shared assumptions*. Many of us operate with a set of assumptions—and it would be fun to bring to expression what these really are—but we don't talk about them. When someone violates them, we raise our eyebrows or start to wiggle our fingers and maybe even break into a sweat. Perhaps it begins with the legitimacy or appropriateness of the question we ask. The fundamental shared assumptions of good conversations include honesty, transparency, mutuality, and the pursuit of what is good, right, and true.

Fourth, a good conversation requires the *spirit of exploration and experimentation*. If I ask my good friend who happens to be a philosopher and therefore practiced in the art of conversation and one who finds it delightful to turn over each stone somehow, a question, he tells me what he is thinking on the subject and he explores his mind and then he asks me what I think and then I ask him back and it goes on and on. We learn from one another. A frequent problem here is when someone gets too dogmatic or dominant. Some people have to give their opinion or make a comment about what everyone else is saying, and my experience is that those who do so are not aware they do this. If in conversing we want to explore something together, we can't have someone say "here's the answer, buffo, and there's no other possiblities."

Fifth, a good conversation *probes into wisdom*. A good conversation with a good topic or question leads to mutual exploration so each of us can learn and grow in wisdom. As a Christian, we want the conversation to lead us into the wisdom of the way of Jesus. We may only touch on that level of wisdom, we may brush against a few times, but that is the North Star of all good conversations.

Finally, a good conversation *stays within the parameter of the topic*. One of the routine challenges of conversation is wandering. We begin with a good question—Did Jesus do miracles by the power of the Spirit or in his own power? Can libertarian economics exist in a world like ours? How do we rid our society of racism? What are the marks of good pastoral preaching?—that begins on the right track but then someone begins to talk, and wander around to another topic (a previous event in life) and then we're talking about that event, which leads to another topic and we realize we are no longer on topic. This element of conversation requires either a conversation partner who keeps us in line or, better yet, conversationalists who know what is happening and put an end to it.

Why all these points? Because social media cannot abide conversations, and the more time we spend on social media and the less time we spend in conversations, the less we will probe together for wisdom in relationship with one another. Those who develop the art of conversation will find themselves diminishing their time on social media. It is wiser to ask people to develop the art of conversation than to tell them to drop social media because the former will drop the latter on its own.

What then are we to do? I suggest this: Spend at least one hour going through all of your own Facebook updates and tweets and examine them over against these seven points of James and the four studies of social media and see where you stand. Are the marks of a pastor present? Then take a stand to walk in the way of wisdom.

Bibliography

Allison, Dale C., Jr. *A Critical and Exegetical Commentary on the Epistle of James.* International Critical Commentary. New York: Bloomsbury, 2013.

Aymer, Margaret P. *First Pure, Then Peaceable: Frederick Douglass Reads James.* LNTS 379. London: T. & T. Clark, 2007.

Baker, William R. *Personal Speech-Ethics in the Epistle of James.* WUNT 2 68. Tübingen: Mohr (Paul Siebeck), 1995.

———. *Sticks and Stones: The Discipleship of Our Speech.* Downers Grove, IL: InterVarsity, 1996.

Bauckham, Richard. *James: Wisdom of James, Disciple of Jesus the Sage.* New Testament Readings. London; New York: Routledge, 1999.

Boyd, Gregory A. *The Myth of a Christian Nation: How the Quest for Political Power Is Destroying the Church.* Grand Rapids: Zondervan, 2007.

Byrd, Aimee. *Recovering from Biblical Manhood and Womanhood.* Grand Rapids: Zondervan, 2019.

Craveri, Benedetta. *The Age of Conversation.* Translated by Teresa Waugh. New York: NYRB, 2005.

Kim, Jay Y. *Analog Church: Why We Need Real People, Places, and Things in the Digital Age.* Downers Grove, IL: InterVarsity, 2020).

Lanier, Jaron *Ten Arguments for Deleting Your Social Media Accounts Right Now.* New York: Picador, 2019.

McKnight, Scot. *The Letter of James.* New International Commentary on the New Testament. Grand Rapids: Eerdmans, 2011.

———. *Pastor Paul: Nurturing a Culture of Christoformity in the Church.* Theological Explorations for the Church Catholic. Grand Rapids: Brazos, 2019.

McKnight, Scot, and Laura Barringer. *A Church Called Tov: Forming a Goodness Culture That Resists Abuses of Power and Promotes Healing.* Carol Stream, IL: Tyndale Momentum, 2020.

Noble, Safiya Umoja. *Algorithms of Oppression: How Search Engines Reinforce Racism* New York: New York University Press, 2018.

Turkle, Sherry. *Alone Together: Why We Expect More from Technology and Less from Each Other.* 3rd ed. New York: Basic, 2017.

———. *Reclaiming Conversation: The Power of Talk in a Digital Age.* New York: Penguin, 2015.

Twenge, Jean M. *Generation Me—Revised and Updated: Why Today's Young Americans Are More Confident, Assertive, Entitled—and More Miserable Than Ever Before.* Rev. ed. New York: Atria, 2014.